Statements on education, training and young people

1998-2001

Cataloguing data can be found at the end of this edition.

A great deal of additional information on the European Union is available on the Internet. It can be accessed through the Europa server (http://europa.eu.int).

Luxembourg: Office for Official Publications of the European Communities, 2002

ISBN 92-824-2143-0

© European Communities, 2002

Reproduction is authorised, except for commercial purposes , provided the source is acknowledged.

Printed in Belgium

CONTENTS

Decision No 1686/98/EC of the European Parliament and the Council of 20 July 1998 establishing the Community action programme "European Voluntary Service for Young People" 7

Council Recommendation of 24 September 1998 on European cooperation in quality assurance in higher education..21

Council Decision of 21 December 1998 on the promotion of European pathways in work-linked training, including apprenticeship..27

Resolution of the Council and the Ministers for Youth meeting within the Council of 8 February 1999 on youth participation...35

Council Decision of 26 April 1999 establishing the second phase of the Community vocational training action programme "Leonardo da Vinci"...39

Council Decision No 1999/311/EEC of 29 April 1999 adopting the third phase of the trans-European cooperation scheme for higher education (Tempus III) (2000-2006)................57

Decision No 68/2000/EC of the European Parliament and of the Council of 13 December 1999 amending the basic Decision relating to the Socrates programme so as to include Turkey among the beneficiary countries...67

Resolution of the Council and of the Ministers for Youth meeting within the Council of 17 December 1999 on the non-formal education dimension of sporting activities in the European Community youth programmes..71

Council Resolution of 17 December 1999 on "Into the new millennium": developing new working procedures for European cooperation in the field of education and training................75

Council Conclusions of 21 December 1999 on the implementation of measures to combat child sex tourism...79

Decision No 253/2000/EC of the European Parliament and of the Council of 24 January 2000 establishing the second phase of the Community action programme in the field of education "Socrates"..83

Decision No 293/2000/EC of the European Parliament and of the Council of 24 January 2000 adopting a programme of Community action (the Daphne programme) (2000 to 2003) on preventive measures to fight violence against children, young persons and women................101

Decision No 1031/2000/EC of the European Parliament and of the Council of 13 April 2000 establishing the "Youth" Community action programme..109

Council Decision of 17 July 2000 amending Decision 1999/311/EC adopting the third phase of the trans-European cooperation scheme for higher education (Tempus III) (2000 to 2006)..121

Decision No 1934/2000/EC of the European Parliament and of the Council of 17 July 2000 on the European Year of Languages 2001...125

Council Decision of 28 September 2000 concerning the conclusion of an Agreement between the European Community and Malta adopting the terms and conditions for the participation of Malta in Community programmes in the fields of training, education and youth....................133

Resolution of the Council and of the Representatives of the Governments of the Member States, meeting within the Council, of 14 December 2000 concerning an action plan for mobility........137

Resolution of the Council and of the Representatives of the Governments of the Member States, meeting within the Council, of 14 December 2000 on the social inclusion of young people..147

Council Decision of 22 December 2000 concerning the conclusion of an Agreement between the European Community and the Republic of Cyprus adopting the terms and conditions for the participation of the Republic of Cyprus in Community programmes in the fields of training, education and youth...153

Recommendation of the European Parliament and of the Council of 12 February 2001 on European cooperation in quality evaluation in school education..163

Council Decision of 26 February 2001 concerning the conclusion of an Agreement between the European Community and the United States of America renewing a programme of cooperation in higher education and vocational education and training................................169

Council Decision of 26 February 2001 concerning the conclusion of an Agreement between the European Community and the Government of Canada renewing a cooperation programme in higher education and training..179

Declaration by the Council and the Representatives of the Governments of the Member States, meeting within the Council, of 28 June 2001 on combating racism and xenophobia on the Internet by intensifying work with young people...189

Resolution of the Council and of the Representatives of the Governments of the Member States meeting within the Council, of 28 June 2001 on promoting young people's initiative, enterprise and creativity: from exclusion to empowerment...............................193

Recommendation of the European Parliament and of the Council of 10 July 2001 on mobility within the Community for students, persons undergoing training, volunteers, teachers and trainers..199

Council Resolution of 13 July 2001 on the role of education and training in employment related policies...........209

Council Resolution of 13 July 2001 on e-Learning...........213

Council Conclusions of 13 July 2001 on the follow-up of the report on concrete future objectives of education and training systems...........219

Council opinion of 14 February 2002 concerning education and training issues in the proposal for a Council Decision on guidelines for Member States' employment policies for 2002...........223

Council Resolution of 14 February 2002 on the promotion of linguistic diversity and language learning in the framework of the implementation of the objectives of the European Year of Languages 2001...........227

Resolution of the Council and of the Representatives of the Governments of the Member States, meeting within the Council, of 14 February 2002 on the added value of voluntary activity for young people in the context of the development of Community action on youth...........231

Council Conclusions of 14 February 2002 on the follow-up to the Report on the concrete future objectives of education and training systems in view of the preparation of a joint Council/Commission report to be presented to the Spring 2002 European Council...........237

ANNEXES

Decision No 182/1999/EC of the European Parliament and of the Council of 22 December 1998 concerning the fifth framework programme of the European Community for research, technological development and demonstration activities (1998 to 2002)...........253

Council Resolution of 22 February 1999 on the 1999 Employment Guidelines...........287

Directive 1999/42/EC of the European Parliament and of the Council of 7 June 1999 establishing a mechanism for the recognition of qualifications in respect of the professional activities covered by the Directives on liberalisation and transitional measures and supplementing the general systems for the recognition of qualifications...........279

Council Resolution of 21 June 1999 concerning a handbook for international police Cooperation and measures to prevent and control violence and disturbances in connection with international football matches...........317

Council Decision of 13 March 2000 on guidelines for Member States' employment policies for the year 2000...........331

Conclusions of the Council and the Representatives of the Governments of the Member States, meeting within the Council, of 4 December 2000 on combating doping...........339

Council Decision of 19 January 2001 on Guidelines for Member States' employment policies for the year 2001...........343

Council Recommendation of 19 January 2001 on the implementation of Member States' employment policies......355

Council Recommendation of 18 February 2002 on the implementation of Member States' employment policies......369

Council Decision of 18 February 2002 on guidelines for Member States' employment policies for the year 2002......383

**Decision No 1686/98/EC of the European Parliament and the Council
of 20 July 1998
establishing the Community action programme
"European Voluntary Service for Young People"**

(OJ L 214, 31.7.1998)

I

(Acts whose publication is obligatory)

DECISION No 1686/98/EC OF THE EUROPEAN PARLIAMENT AND THE COUNCIL

of 20 July 1998

establishing the Community action programme 'European Voluntary Service for Young People'

THE EUROPEAN PARLIAMENT AND THE COUNCIL OF THE EUROPEAN UNION,

Having regard to the Treaty establishing the European Community, and in particular Article 126 thereof,

Having regard to the proposal from the Commission ([1]),

Having regard to the opinion of the Economic and Social Committee ([2]),

Having regard to the opinion of the Committee of the Regions ([3]),

Acting in accordance with the procedure laid down in Article 189b of the Treaty ([4]), in the light of the joint text approved by the Conciliation Committee on 30 June 1998,

(1) Whereas the Essen European Council (9 and 10 December 1994), the Cannes European Council (26 and 27 June 1995), the Madrid European Council (15 and 16 December 1995) and the Dublin European Council (13 and 14 December 1996) stressed the need to undertake new measures to promote the social and occupational integration of young people in Europe;

(2) Whereas the conclusions of the Florence European Council (21 and 22 June 1996) stressed the importance of helping young people to become integrated into active life and, in this respect, noted with interest the idea of European voluntary service;

(3) Whereas the Amsterdam European Council (16 and 17 June 1997) expressed its attachment to voluntary service activities;

(4) Whereas the Council requested the Commission to propose practical measures to promote transnational cooperation in the field of voluntary service;

(5) Whereas, in its Resolution of 5 October 1995 on cooperation with third countries in the youth field ([5]), the Council stressed the need to step up cooperation, particularly with regard to voluntary service, with third countries with which the Community has concluded association or cooperation agreements;

(6) Whereas the European Council of 25 and 26 June 1984 asked Member States to take the necessary measures to encourage young people to take part in projects organised by the Community outside its frontiers, and recommended Member States to acknowledge as one of the objectives of their social policies the incorporation of social protection for development volunteers or the correction of shortcomings in this field;

(7) Whereas the Parliament has also expressed its support, on many occasions, for the development of voluntary service at Community level, in particular in its Resolution of 22 September 1995 on the establishment of European civilian service ([6]);

(8) Whereas, insofar as it fosters informal education, the policy of cooperation in the youth field is complementary to the education policy enshrined in the Treaty, and whereas that policy is in need of development;

(9) Whereas voluntary service activities also exist in a variety of forms in several Member States and a number of non-governmental organisations are working in this field;

(10) Whereas only limited experience has been acquired thereby and whereas transnational voluntary service activities should be developed in qualitative and quantitative terms;

([1]) OJ C 302, 3. 10. 1997, p. 6.
 and OJ C 320, 21. 10. 1997, p. 7.
([2]) OJ C 158, 26. 5. 1997, p. 12.
([3]) OJ C 244, 11. 8. 1997, p. 47.
([4]) Opinion of the European Parliament of 12 June 1997 (OJ C 200, 30. 6. 1997, p. 183), Council Common Position of 16 December 1997, (OJ C 43, 9. 2. 1998, p. 35) and Decision of the European Parliament of 12 March 1998 (OJ C 104, 6. 4. 1998, p. 206). Decision of the European Parliament of 15 July 1998. Decision of the Council of 20 July 1998.

([5]) OJ C 296, 10. 11. 1995, p. 11.
([6]) OJ C 269, 16. 10. 1995, p. 232.

(11) Whereas it is necessary to create new opportunities for the transfer and application of experience and good practice and to promote new partnerships;

(12) Whereas an independent ex-ante evaluation of a multi-annual programme of voluntary service has been carried out in accordance with the principles put in place by the Commission for the second phase of its SEM 2000 ('sound and efficient management') programme;

(13) Whereas this Decision establishes a Community framework designed to contribute to the development of transnational voluntary service activities; whereas appropriate, coordinated measures designed to eliminate the legal and administrative obstacles should be adopted by the Member States in order to improve further the access of young people to the programme and facilitate recognition of the specific nature of the situation of young volunteers;

(14) Whereas participation by young people in voluntary service activities constitutes a form of informal education, the quality of which will to a large extent be based on appropriate preparation activities including those of a linguistic and cultural nature, contributes to their future development and to broadening their horizons, promotes the development of their social skills, active citizenship and their balanced integration into society from an economic, social and cultural point of view and makes it possible to promote awareness of genuine European citizenship;

(15) Whereas the establishment of European voluntary service should be carried out in conjunction with other Community schemes to benefit young people developed in particular under the 'Youth for Europe' programme [1], and it is therefore important to make sure that they are complementary;

(16) Whereas it is necessary to reinforce the links between the measures carried out under this programme, combating the various forms of exclusion, including racism and xenophobia, cooperation with third countries and the projects pursued within the framework of social policy, particularly action assisted by the European Social Fund on training and access to employment (both mainstream and the 'Employment-Youthstart' Community Initiative);

(17) Whereas, in order to facilitate the transition to working life, complementary links need to be established between European voluntary service and, in particular, local employment initiatives;

(18) Whereas voluntary service may help to meet new societal needs and also to identify new sources of activities and professions;

(19) Whereas participation in the voluntary service activities covered by this Decision should be purely voluntary; whereas such activities should be non-profit-making and the host project should constitute a vehicle for informal educational activity on the part of young volunteers and whereas that activity can therefore in no case be equated with employment;

(20) Whereas young volunteers taking part in this programme should have adequate means of subsistence;

(21) Whereas European voluntary service activities are not a substitute for military service, for the alternative service formulae provided in particular for conscientious objectors or for the compulsory civilian service existing in several Member States, and should not restrict or be a substitute for potential or existing paid employment;

(22) Whereas the Commission and the Member States should endeavour to ensure complementarity between European voluntary service activities and similar national activities of various kinds;

(23) Whereas all young people legally resident in a Member State should be eligible to apply to take part in European voluntary service, without discrimination;

(24) Whereas the grant of residence permits and any visas required falls within the competence of the authorities in the Member States, and whereas the concept of legal resident is defined by national law;

(25) Whereas implementation of this programme should be based on decentralised structures designated by Member States in close cooperation with the national authorities responsible for youth questions, with a view to guaranteeing that Community action supports and complements national activities whilst respecting the principle of subsidiarity, as defined in Article 3b of the Treaty;

(26) Whereas European voluntary service activities are of direct concern to local and regional authorities having regard to their potential role in providing direct support for projects but also in developing local information and in following-up young people at the end of their service;

(27) Whereas the social partners should play an important role in the development of European voluntary

---

[1] Decision No 818/95/EC of the European Parliament and of the Council of 14 March 1995 adopting the third phase of the 'Youth for Europe' programme (OJ L 87, 20. 4. 1995, p. 1).

service, not only to avoid any activity that is a substitute for potential or existing paid employment, but also as part of following up the experience acquired so as to assist with the active integration of young people into society;

(28) Whereas the voluntary sector should also play an important role in enabling all young people, particularly those with the greatest difficulties, to participate in these programmes;

(29) Whereas there should be ongoing monitoring to take account in particular of the opinions of the social partners and the voluntary sector;

(30) Whereas the Commission and the Member States are to ensure that they foster cooperation with non-governmental organisations active in the youth and social fields, as well as in the areas of the environment, culture and combating the various forms of exclusion;

(31) Whereas the Agreement on the European Economic Area provides for greater cooperation in the field of education, training and youth between the European Community and its Member States, on the one hand, and the States of the European Free Trade Area (EFTA) participating in the European Economic Area, on the other; whereas Article 4 of Protocol 31 provides that the EFTA States participating in the European Economic Area shall, from 1 January 1995, participate in all Community programmes in the field of education, training and youth then in force or adopted;

(32) Whereas the 'European Voluntary Service for Young People' programme is open to the participation of the associated countries of Central and Eastern Europe (CCEE), in accordance with the conditions set out in the Europe Agreements or in the Additional Protocols, already concluded or to be concluded, on the participation of those countries in Community programmes; whereas this programme is open to the participation of Cyprus and Malta on the basis of additional appropriations under the same rules as apply to the EFTA States participating in the European Economic Area, in accordance with procedures to be agreed with those countries, without prejudice to the procedures to be completed for Malta's participation;

(33) Whereas the promotion of active citizenship and the acquisition of informal education experience, on the one hand, and the contribution of young people to cooperation between the Community and third countries, on the other, are important objectives of the 'European Voluntary Service for Young People' programme;

(34) Whereas a number of association and cooperation agreements provide for exchanges of young people;

(35) Whereas this Decision lays down, for the entire duration of the programme, a financial framework constituting the principal point of reference, within the meaning of point 1 of the Joint Declaration by the European Parliament, the Council and the Commission of 6 March 1995 ([1]), for the budgetary authority during the annual budgetary procedure;

(36) Whereas the Community's financial perspective is valid until 1999 and will have to be revised for the period beyond that date;

(37) Whereas, in the light of the conclusion of the third phase of the 'Youth for Europe' programme on 31 December 1999, the Commission will present to the European Parliament and to the Council, before 31 December 1997, a report setting out its ideas on the 'priorities of the policy of cooperation in the youth field looking forward to the year 2000';

(38) Whereas an agreement was reached on 20 December 1994 on a *modus vivendi* between the European Parliament, the Council and the Commission concerning the implementing measures for acts adopted pursuant to the procedure referred to in Article 189b of the Treaty ([2]),

HAVE DECIDED AS FOLLOWS:

Article 1

Establishment of the programme

1. This Decision establishes the Community action programme 'European Voluntary Service for Young People', hereinafter referred to as the 'programme', concerning European voluntary service activities within the Community and in third countries for young people legally resident in a Member State.

The programme is adopted for the period from 1 January 1998 to 31 December 1999.

([1]) OJ C 102, 4. 4. 1996, p. 4.
([2]) OJ C 102, 4. 4. 1996, p. 1.

2. This programme comes within the context of the general objectives of a cooperation policy in the youth field as set out in the programme 'Youth for Europe' (Article 1(2)). It is intended, while respecting equal opportunities for men and women, to encourage mobility and solidarity among young people as part of active citizenship, to promote, and give them the chance of acquiring, informal educational experience in a variety of sectors of activity, which may be one of the foundations of their future development, and to promote, through their participation in transnational activities of benefit to the community, an active contribution on their part to the ideals of democracy, tolerance and solidarity in the context of European integration and to cooperation between the European Community and third countries.

Article 2

Framework, objectives and resources

1. This programme, based on intensified cooperation between the Member States, offers young people aged in principle between 18 and 25 an attested informal educational experience, at transnational level, involving both the acquisition of skills and abilities and the demonstration of responsible citizenship in order to help them to become actively integrated into society. Young people participating in the activities of this programme are hereinafter also referred to as 'young volunteers'.

2. In accordance with the general objectives set out in Article 1, the specific objectives of this programme shall be as follows:

(a) to encourage a spirit of initiative, creativity and solidarity among young people so as to enable them to become actively integrated into society and to contribute to the attainment of the objectives of the programme;

(b) to step up participation by young people legally resident in a Member State in long-term or short-term transnational activities of benefit to the community, within the Community or in third countries, in particular those with which the Community has concluded cooperation agreements. Those activities must not restrict or be a substitute for potential or existing paid employment;

(c) to promote recognition of the value of informal educational experience acquired in a European context;

(d) to facilitate access to the programme for all young people.

3. For this purpose, and in accordance with the general objectives set out in Article 1 and the specific objectives described in paragraph 2 of this Article, the main features of this programme, which are set out in detail in the Annex, shall be as follows:

(a) to support long-term or short-term transnational activities of benefit to the community, within the Community and in third countries;

(b) to support activities intended to foster partnerships based on European voluntary service and innovative network activities;

(c) to support measures and projects intended to further the follow-up of young volunteers, to build on the experience acquired by the latter in the context of European voluntary service and thus to promote their active integration into society;

(d) to develop and support appropriate preparation, particularly linguistic and intercultural, and the integration of young volunteers, 'mentors' and European project leaders so that young volunteers can benefit from high-quality projects connected with the objectives of the programme;

(e) to support the quality of all the programme's activities and the development of their European dimension and to contribute to cooperation in the youth field by supporting, wherever possible, Member States' endeavours to improve services and measures related to European voluntary service, particularly through measures to provide young people with information on the objectives of the programme and through studies and continuing evaluation through which, where appropriate, the detailed implementing rules and the approaches of the programme may be brought into line with any needs which might emerge.

Article 3

Financial provisions

1. The financial framework for the implementation of this programme for the period 1998-1999 is hereby set at ECU 47,5 million, in keeping with the current financial perspective.

2. The annual appropriations shall be authorised by the budgetary authority within the limits of the financial perspective.

Article 4

Access to the programme — positive action

1. Special attention shall be paid to ensuring that all young people can have access, without discrimination, to the programme's activities.

2. The Commission and the Member States shall ensure that special efforts are made for young people who experience the most difficulties in being included in existing action programmes at both Community and national, regional and local levels, owing to cultural, social, physical, economic or geographical reasons. To this end, they shall take into consideration the problems encountered by this target group.

Article 5

Participation by associated countries

This programme shall be open to the participation of the associated countries of Central and Eastern Europe (CCEE) in accordance with the Europe Agreements or the Additional Protocols, which have been, or are to be, concluded on the participation of those countries in Community programmes. This programme shall be open to the participation of Cyprus and Malta on the basis of additional appropriations under the same rules as apply to the EFTA countries participating in the European Economic Area, in accordance with the procedures to be agreed with those countries, without prejudice to the procedures to be completed for Malta's participation.

Article 6

Implementation, links with other measures and international cooperation

1. The Commission shall ensure the implementation of this programme.

2. The Commission and the Member States shall ensure that there is consistency and complementarity between measures to be implemented under this programme and other relevant Community programmes and initiatives, in particular 'Youth for Europe' and programmes offering the possibility of financing volunteer projects aimed at young volunteers from third countries, as well as measures undertaken by the Member States in this field.

3. The Commission and the Member States shall foster cooperation relating to this programme so as to allow complementarity of action with that of the competent international organisations, in particular the Council of Europe.

Article 7

Cooperation with Member States

1. The Commission and the Member States shall take such measures as they deem appropriate to develop the structures set up at Community and national level for achieving the objectives of the programme, for making the programme more accessible to young people and other partners at local level, for evaluating and monitoring the measures provided for in the programme and for applying consultation and selection mechanisms. In that context, the Commission and the Member States shall take steps to ensure that appropriate information is provided and volunteers are made aware of their rights and obligations at European, national and local level, and shall endeavour to make an active contribution to ensuring complementarity between European voluntary service activities and similar national activities of various kinds.

2. Each Member State shall endeavour, as far as possible, to adopt such measures as it deems necessary and desirable to ensure the proper functioning of the programme, in particular regarding the legal and administrative obstacles to the access of young people to the programme, obstacles to the transnational mobility of young volunteers and recognition of the specific nature of the situation of young volunteers.

Article 8

Attestation

A document, drawn up by the Commission in accordance with the procedure laid down in Article 9(2) and (3), shall attest to the participation of young volunteers in European Voluntary Service and to the experience and skills that they have acquired during the relevant period.

Article 9

Committee

1. In the implementation of this programme, the Commission shall be assisted by a committee composed of representatives of the Member States and chaired by the representative of the Commission.

2. The representative of the Commission shall submit to the committee a draft of the measures to be taken in respect of:

— the committee's rules of procedure,

— the implementing provisions,

— the annual plan of work for the implementation of the measures in the programme,

— the general balance between the various sections of the programme,

— the criteria for determining the indicative allocation of funds among the Member States,

— the document attesting to participation in European voluntary service,

— the procedures for monitoring and evaluating the programme.

The committee shall deliver its opinion on the draft within a time-limit which the chairman may lay down according to the urgency of the matter. The opinion shall be delivered by the majority laid down in Article 148(2) of the Treaty in the case of decisions which the Council is required to adopt on a proposal from the Commission. The votes of the representatives of the Member States within the committee shall be weighted in the manner set out in that Article. The chairman shall not vote.

The Commission shall adopt measures which apply immediately. However, if these measures are not in accordance with the opinion of the committee, they shall be communicated by the Commission to the Council forthwith. In that event:

— the Commission may defer application of the measures which it has decided for a period of two months from the date of such communication,

— the Council, acting by a qualified majority, may take a different decision within the time-limit referred to in the previous indent.

3. The Commission may consult the Committee on any other matters relating to the implementation of this programme.

In that case, the representative of the Commission shall submit to the Committee a draft of the measures to be taken. The Committee shall deliver its opinion on the draft within a time-limit which the Chairman may lay down according to the urgency of the matter, if necessary by taking a vote.

The opinion shall be recorded in the minutes; in addition, each Member State shall have the right to ask to have its position recorded in the minutes.

The Commission shall take the utmost account of the opinion delivered by the Committee. It shall inform the Committee of the manner in which its opinion has been taken into account.

Article 10

Monitoring and evaluation

1. On implementation of this Decision, the Commission shall take the necessary measures to ensure that the programme is monitored and continuously evaluated, taking account of the general and specific objectives referred to in Articles 1 and 2, the specific objectives defined in the Annex, the provisions laid down in Article 4 and any input provided by the Committee set up under Article 9.

2. The Commission shall submit in sufficient time to the European Parliament and to the Council a report taking account in particular of the results of Community youth-related measures and accompanied, if necessary, by appropriate proposals, particularly with a view to a consistent approach to youth-related measures looking forward to the year 2000.

Article 11

This Decision shall enter into force on the date of its publication in the *Official Journal of the European Communities*.

Done at Brussels, 20 July 1998

For the European Parliament
The President
J. M. GIL-ROBLES

For the Council
The President
W. MOLTERER

ANNEX

In order to encourage mobility among young people as part of active citizenship, their practical participation in the creation of European solidarity and their active integration into society and to promote, and give young people the chance of acquiring, an informal educational experience in a variety of sectors of activity, which may be one of the foundations of their future development, the Community intends to support European voluntary service activities within the Community and in third countries, measures to follow up those activities and European cooperation measures designed to develop the quality and the European dimension of those activities.

The implementation of this programme should correspond to the needs of the target group.

By way of information, 'young volunteer' under this programme means any person aged between 18 and 25, legally resident in a Member State of the European Community. Such a young person commits himself/herself voluntarily to the fulfilment of an experience of active citizenship and informal education with a view to acquiring social, intercultural and personal abilities and skills, thus laying the foundations for his/her future development while contributing to the well-being of the community. To this end, the young volunteer participates, in a Member State other than the one in which he/she resides or in a third country, in a non-profit-making, unpaid activity of importance to the community and of a limited duration (12 months maximum) in the context of a project recognised by the Member State concerned and the Community. Full board and lodging and supervision by a tutor are provided. The voluntary service project ensures that the person concerned is covered by health insurance as well as other appropriate insurance schemes. The young volunteer receives an allowance/pocket money.

The basic principles on which the Community action is founded are as follows:

— active participation of young volunteers in both the preparation and the implementation of projects,

— local partnerships between the various public and private partners involved in the active integration of young people into society,

— transnational partnerships between host projects and projects sending out young volunteers,

— approval by the Commission subject to a positive opinion from the relevant authorities of the Member States of all host projects,

— guarantees from the point of view of the preparation, the supervision and — as far as possible — the mobility of young volunteers,

— the inclusion, within host projects, of tutors having an important role to play in the supervision of young volunteers and in the recognition of the added value of achievements, and in the preparation of measures following up the experience,

— recognition of the value of an informal educational experience acquired in a European context,

— follow-up for young volunteers and turning their achievements to account.

To this end, the Community is organizing this programme, which has four sections. The four sections are interlinked and sufficiently flexible to meet the needs of the young people concerned in the most appropriate way. The activities carried out under this programme will be complementary to those conducted in the youth field, notably under the 'Youth for Europe' programme.

SECTION 1 — **INTRA-COMMUNITY**

1. The Community will support long-term (in principle six months to one year) and short-term (in principle three weeks to three months) transnational projects which will enable young people — normally aged between 18 and 25, although exceptionally, in certain duly justified cases, applications from young people outside those age limits may be taken into consideration — legally resident in a Member State to play, individually or in groups, an active part in activities which help to meet the needs of society in a wide range of fields (social, socio-cultural, environmental, cultural, etc.) and which are likely to have a direct impact on the well-being of the populations of the host communities. The aim of these projects will be to provide young people from the Union with an informal educational experience and to bring them into contact with other cultures and languages and to experience new ideas and projects in an intercultural civil society context.

2. The assistance awarded under this section should not exceed 50 % of the total expenditure incurred linked to European voluntary service activity, subject to point 3.

3. In accordance with Article 4(2) of the Decision, efforts must be made to help young people facing cultural, social, economic, physical, mental or geographical difficulties. These efforts must be proportional to the difficulties that participation in existing action programmes raises for this target group. In this context, financial assistance greater than the 50 % provided for in point 2 may be awarded, or support given, where appropriate, for other activities likely to facilitate participation by this target group, including preparation and follow-up activities. Procedures for awarding assistance in excess of 50 % will be defined by the Committee provided for in Article 9 of the Decision.

4. Assistance will be awarded for:

long-term activities

5. Long-term activities will emphasise qualifying experience, acquired as part of European voluntary service projects, and the follow-up to young volunteers' activities.

6. A document, drawn up by the Commission in accordance with Articles 8 and 9 of the Decision, will attest to the participation of young volunteers in European voluntary service and the experience and skills that they have acquired during this period.

preparation and supervision

7. Measures intended (particularly at the linguistic and intercultural levels) to reinforce the European dimension of activities, to prepare young long-term volunteers prior to departure and to promote their integration during these activities and at the end of European voluntary service.

short-term activities

8. The Community will support short-term transnational projects intended to make young people specifically aware of the potential of measures inspired by the principle of active citizenship and the impact that such activities may have on their lives, and to familiarise all the partners with the concept of active citizenship.

9. These projects will principally involve groups. Support for individual participation in a host project may be envisaged depending on the duration of the project, its nature or the profile of the young volunteer.

SECTION 2 — THIRD COUNTRIES

1. The Community will support long-term (in principle six months to one year) and short-term (in principle three weeks to three months) transnational projects which will enable young people — normally aged between 18 and 25, although exceptionally, in certain duly justified cases, applications from young people outside those age limits may be taken into consideration — legally resident in a Member State to play, individually or in groups, an active part in third countries in activities which meet the needs of society in a wide range of fields (social, socio-cultural, environmental, cultural, etc.) and which are likely to have a direct impact on the well-being of the populations of the host communities. The aim of these projects will be to provide young people with informal educational experience and to bring them into contact with other cultures and languages and to experience new ideas and projects in an intercultural civil society context.

2. The appropriations awarded under this Section will in principle cover the costs connected with the activities of young people residing in Member States.

3. Assistance will be awarded for:

long-term activities

4. Long-term activities will emphasise qualifying experience, acquired as part of European voluntary service projects, and the follow-up to young volunteers' activities.

5. A document, drawn up by the Commission in accordance with Articles 8 and 9 of the Decision, will attest to the participation of young volunteers in European voluntary service and the experience and skills that they have acquired during this period.

preparation and supervision

6. Measures making it possible to lay or consolidate the foundations needed for the development of transnational European voluntary service projects in third countries, more specifically long-term activities.

7. Measures intended (particularly at the linguistic and intercultural levels) to reinforce the European dimension of activities, to prepare young long-term volunteers prior to departure and to promote their integration during those activities and at the end of European voluntary service.

short-term activities

8. The Community will support short-term transnational projects intended to make young people genuinely aware of the impact that such activities may have on their lives and to familiarize all the partners with the concept of active citizenship.

9. These projects will principally involve groups. Support for individual participation in a host project may be envisaged depending on the duration of the project, its nature or the profile of the young volunteer.

SECTION 3 — FOLLOW-UP, SPIRIT OF INITIATIVE AND CREATIVITY

1. The Community will support the development of follow-up projects by young volunteers, intended to help them turn to account and exploit the experience acquired during their voluntary service and to promote their active integration into society.

2. Assistance may be awarded for initiatives taken by young people at the end of their European voluntary service by helping them to launch and promote social, cultural, socio-cultural and economic activities and/or to participate in complementary educational activities. The aim of such assistance will be to enable young volunteers to develop their spirit of initiative and creativity and to foster the development of various forms of European cooperation. Priority in the allocation of assistance will be given to those young people in greatest need.

3. Special attention will be paid to the promotion of (public or private) partnerships and to cooperation with (public or private) initiatives in particular at local level in order to support, help and sponsor young people's strategies for active integration into society.

SECTION 4 — COMPLEMENTARY MEASURES

4.1. Mentors and European project leaders

1. *Award of assistance*

    In addition to voluntary service activities proper, assistance will also be awarded for measures intended to underpin the quality of the work of mentors and European project leaders. These measures will concern activities supported at intra-Community level as well as in third countries. They are intended, on the one hand, to ensure that the content of the informal educational experience is of a high quality and, on the other hand, to help to develop certification methods.

2. *Mentors*

    The term 'mentors' means people involved as tutors for young volunteers during European voluntary service activities within host projects and those who act as contact points for young volunteers and projects within relay structures situated at the national, regional or local level.

3. *Activities supported*

    Activities supported will be those intended to:
    — prepare and support mentors from the point of view of their tasks of tutoring and supervising young volunteers during transnational voluntary service activities, with special attention being paid to projects involving young people with little or no experience of transnational activities,
    — develop the ability of European project leaders effectively to carry out their administrative tasks in a European context (organization, financial aid and administrative management and follow-up of European projects, legal aspects, etc.).

4.2. Partnerships

Establishment of partnerships

1. The Community will support activities to promote partnerships at local/regional/national level — between public- and private-sector partners — geared towards European voluntary service and offering the prospect of transnational and European partnerships.

2. Assistance will be awarded for activities to facilitate and promote the establishment of transnational partnerships between local/regional/national partnerships wishing to work together within the framework of this programme either within the Community or with third countries.

3. Special attention will be paid to projects/initiatives undertaken at the local level by persons or entities which have little or no experience of or opportunity for contacts at European level.

Innovative network activities

4. Assistance will be awarded for innovative measures launched by networks, particularly in the social, socio-cultural, environmental and cultural fields and in connection with the fight against the various forms of exclusion.

5. This assistance may cover innovative activities which create networks between initiatives within the Community, in which third countries may participate where appropriate.

6. Support for these activities is intended to encourage, on the one hand, the development by these networks of innovative practical European voluntary service activities and, on the other hand, the integration within these networks of a European voluntary service dimension.

4.3. Information, research and evaluation

1. Support for activities to launch awareness, information and advisory systems at local, regional, national and Community level to promote and support the objectives of the programme.

2. In the particular area of research and evaluation connected with the objectives of the programme, the Community will concentrate its efforts on the analysis and dissemination of data, the content and pedagogical value of the informal education and the promotion of Community cooperation in this field. The Commission will, in cooperation with the Member States, monitor and evaluate this programme in an ongoing way in order, when necessary, to bring the detailed rules of its implementation into line with any needs which may arise.

Statements by the Commission

(on the elimination of obstacles to mobility)

The Commission attaches great importance to eliminating all the legal and administrative obstacles hampering access to the Community action programme 'European voluntary service for young people' and the transnational mobility of European youth volunteers.

The Commission will carefully monitor implementation of the programme, including the elimination of these obstacles, and, where necessary, will take the appropriate initiatives.

(on the Programme Committee)

The Commission will inform the European Parliament once a year about the implementing measures taken pursuant to this Decision.

**Council Recommendation
of 24 September 1998
on European cooperation in quality assurance in higher education**

(OJ L 270, 7.10.1998)

COUNCIL RECOMMENDATION
of 24 September 1998
on European cooperation in quality assurance in higher education

(98/561/EC)

THE COUNCIL OF THE EUROPEAN UNION,

Having regard to the Treaty establishing the European Community, and in particular Articles 126 and 127 thereof,

Having regard to the proposal from the Commission,

Having regard to the opinion of the Economic and Social Committee [1],

Having regard to the opinion of the Committee of the Regions [2],

Acting in accordance with the procedure laid down in Article 189c of the Treaty [3],

(1) Whereas a high quality of education and training is an objective for all Member States; whereas the Community is called on to contribute to their ongoing efforts by promoting cooperation between Member States and, if necessary, by supporting and supplementing their action while fully respecting their responsibility for the content of teaching and the organisation of education and training systems and their cultural and linguistic diversity;

(2) Whereas in its conclusions of 25 November 1991 [4] the Council stated that improving the quality of higher education was a concern shared by each Member State and by every institution of higher education within the European Community; whereas, in view of the diversity of methods used at national level, national experience could be complemented by European experience acquired, in particular, through pilot projects aimed at establishing cooperation in this area or at strengthening existing cooperation;

(3) Whereas the replies to the Commission memorandum on higher education stress *inter alia* that quality should be guaranteed at all levels and in all sectors, with differences between institutions only in terms of objectives, methods and educational demand; whereas there is general support for the introduction of efficient and acceptable methods of quality assurance which take into account European and international experience and the possibility of cooperation;

(4) Whereas a Commission study on the state of quality assurance in the Member States revealed that the new quality assurance systems had certain points in common; whereas the two pilot projects conducted subsequently were based on these core elements of existing national systems; whereas they tested a common method successfully and showed that the players in the field are all eager to pursue exchanges of experience which demonstrate the diversity of national evaluation cultures as well as the importance of quality assurance in general;

(5) Whereas, in view of the great diversity of education systems in the Community, the definition of the term 'higher education institution' to which the recommendation refers includes all the types of institutions which confer qualifications or degrees at this level irrespective of how they are described in the Member States; whereas this definition is used in the decision establishing the Socrates programme;

(6) Whereas higher education institutions have to meet the new educational and social requirements of a world-wide 'knowledge society' and the resulting developments; whereas they will, therefore, endeavour to improve the required attributes of the services they provide by developing, where appropriate, new initiatives (individually or on a collaborative basis within higher education associations), aimed at increasing the quality of teaching and learning;

(7) Whereas the technological and economic changes and their consequences for the labour market pose new challenges for higher education institutions and whereas, in view of the challenges of global competition as well as the ever increasing influx of students into higher education institutions, Member States face the task of organising their higher education systems and their relationships *vis-à-vis* State and society in ways which

---

[1] OJ C 19, 21. 1. 1998, p. 39.
[2] OJ C 64, 27. 2. 1998, p. 63.
[3] Opinion of the European Parliament of 18 November 1997 (OJ C 371, 8. 12. 1997, p. 33), Council common position of 26 February 1998 (not yet published in the Official Journal) and Decision of the European Parliament of 28 May 1998 (not yet published in the Official Journal).
[4] OJ C 321, 12. 12. 1991, p. 2.

respect existing academic standards, training objectives, quality standards, the autonomy and/or the independence — in terms of the relevant structures in each Member State — of higher education institutions, and the need to be accountable to and inform the public;

(8) Whereas discussion of the Commission communication of 13 February 1994 has demonstrated that quality assurance systems could contribute towards mutual recognition of academic or professional qualifications at Community level;

(9) Whereas the Commission White Paper on 'Growth, Competitiveness and Employment', the White Paper on 'Teaching and Learning: towards the Learning Society' and the Green Paper on 'Education — Training — Research. The obstacles to transnational mobility' indicate how important high-quality education is for employment and growth within the Community and for its competitiveness at world level; whereas these documents highlight the link that exists between the social and cultural functions of education and training, on the one hand, and their economic functions, on the other hand, and therefore the many aspects of the concept of quality; whereas it is clear that transparent educational systems are required for transnational mobility;

(10) Whereas encouraging mobility is one of the aims of Community cooperation in the fields of education and training; whereas the Commission Green Paper on 'Education — Training — Research. The obstacles to transnational mobility' examines the principal legal, administrative and practical obstacles encountered by students wishing to study in another Member State, proposes measures to improve mobility and stresses that this type of mobility is beneficial to an education of high quality which can enable individuals to compete internationally and to take advantage of freedom of movement within the Community;

(11) Whereas the size, structure and funding of higher education systems differ from Member State to Member State and the objectives of these systems will continue to evolve; whereas in certain Member States the higher education system includes universities and other higher education institutions, often pursuing vocational aims; whereas the concept, scope and methods of quality assurance will be defined by each Member State and will remain flexible and adaptable to changing circumstances and/or structures;

(12) In view of Member States' exclusive responsibilities for the organisation and structure of their higher education systems and of their budgetary constraints, and in view of the autonomy and/or independence of higher education institutions, in terms of the relevant structures in each Member State,

I. HEREBY RECOMMENDS that Member States:

A. support and, where necessary, establish transparent quality assurance systems with the following aims:

— to safeguard the quality of higher education within the specific economic, social and cultural context of their countries while taking due account of the European dimension and of a rapidly changing world,

— to encourage and help higher education institutions to use appropriate measures, particularly quality assurance, as a means of improving the quality of teaching and learning and also training for research, another important part of their task,

— to stimulate mutual exchanges of information on quality and quality assurance at Community and world level and to encourage cooperation between higher education institutions in this area;

B. base systems of quality assurance on the following features, as explained in the Annex:

— autonomy and/or independence in terms of the relevant structures in each Member State for the bodies responsible for quality assurance in their choice of procedures and methods,

— adaptation of quality assurance procedures and methods to the profile and aims of higher education institutions, while respecting their autonomy and/or independence in terms of the relevant structures in each Member State,

— targeted utilisation of internal and/or external aspects of quality assurance adapted to the procedures and methods used,

— involvement of the different parties concerned according to the purpose of the quality assurance,

— publication of quality assurance results in a form which is appropriate to each Member State;

C. where necessary, encourage higher education institutions, in cooperation with the competent structures of the Member States, to take appropriate follow-up measures;

D. call upon the competent authorities and higher education institutions to attach special importance to the exchange of experience and cooperation regarding quality assurance with other Member States, as well as with international organisations and associations active in the field of higher education;

E. promote cooperation between the authorities responsible for quality assessment or quality assurance in higher education and promote networking.

This cooperation could cover some or all of the following areas:

(a) encouraging and developing the exchange of information and experience, in particular on methodological developments and examples of good practice;

(b) fulfilling the requests for expertise and advice from the authorities concerned in the Member States;

(c) supporting higher education institutions which wish to cooperate in the field of quality assurance on a transnational basis;

(d) promoting contacts with international experts.

In pursuing these objectives the developing links between quality assurance and other existing Community activities in particular in the framework of the Socrates and Leonardo da Vinci programmes should be taken into account, as should the 'acquis communautaire' in the field of recognition of qualifications for professional purposes.

II. HEREBY RECOMMENDS:

that the Commission, in close cooperation with the Member States and on the basis of existing programmes and subject to their objectives and normal open and transparent procedures, encourage the cooperation referred to in point I.E between the authorities responsible for quality assessment and quality assurance in higher education, also involving organisations and associations of higher education institutions with a European remit and the necessary experience in quality assessment and quality assurance.

III. HEREBY REQUESTS:

the Commission to present triennial reports to the European Parliament, the Council, the Economic and Social Committee and the Committee of the Regions on progress in the development of quality assurance systems in the various Member States and on cooperation activities at European level including the progress achieved with respect to the objectives referred to above.

Done at Brussels, 24 September 1998.

For the Council
The President
J. FARNLEITNER

ANNEX

Indicative features of quality assurance

The features referred to below are common to existing European quality assurance systems. The European pilot projects assessing the quality of higher education have demonstrated that all parties involved in this area can benefit from observing these features.

The autonomy and/or independence, in terms of the relevant structures in each Member State, of the body responsible for quality assurance (as regards procedures and methods) is likely to contribute to the effectiveness of quality assurance procedures and the acceptance of their results.

Quality assurance criteria are closely linked to the aims assigned to each institution in relation to the needs of society and of the labour market; the different quality assurance procedures must therefore include allowance for the specific nature of the institution. Knowledge of the institution's objectives, be it at the level of the whole institution, at the level of a department or at the level of a single unit, is essential in this respect.

Quality assurance procedures should generally consist of an internal, self-examination component and an external component based on appraisal by external experts.

The internal element of self-examination should aim to involve all the relevant players, especially teaching staff and, where appropriate, administrators in charge of academic and professional guidance, as well as students. The external element should be a process of cooperation, consultation and advice between independent experts from outside and players from within the institution.

In the light of the objectives and criteria used in the quality assurance procedure and with reference to the structures of higher education in the Member States, professional associations, social partners and alumni could be included in the expert groups.

The participation of foreign experts in the procedures would be desirable in order to encourage exchange of experience acquired in other countries.

Reports on quality assurance procedures and their outcome should be published in a form appropriate to each Member State and should provide a source of good reference material for partners and for the general public.

**Council Decision
of 21 December 1998
on the promotion of European pathways in work-linked training,
including apprenticeship**

(OJ L 17, 22.1.1999)

II

(Acts whose publication is not obligatory)

COUNCIL

COUNCIL DECISION

of 21 December 1998

on the promotion of European pathways in work-linked training, including apprenticeship

(1999/51/EC)

THE COUNCIL OF THE EUROPEAN UNION,

Having regard to the Treaty establishing the European Community, and in particular Article 127 thereof,

Having regard to the proposal from the Commission [1],

Having regard to the opinion of the Economic and Social Committee [2],

Acting in accordance with the procedure laid down in Article 189c of the Treaty [3],

(1) Whereas the Treaty gives the Community the task of implementing a vocational training policy which supports and supplements the action of Member States while fully respecting their responsibility, in particular by promoting the mobility of persons in training, but excluding any harmonisation of the laws and regulations of the Member States;

(2) Whereas the Council, in its Decision 63/266/EEC [4], adopted the general principles and set a number of fundamental objectives for implementing a common vocational training policy; whereas by Decision 94/819/EC [5] it adopted the Leonardo da Vinci programme for the implementation of a vocational training policy of the European Community;

(3) Whereas the Florence European Council asked the Commission to make a study of the role of apprenticeship in the creation of jobs; whereas the Commission stressed the importance of apprenticeship in its communication 'Promoting apprenticeship training in Europe';

(4) Whereas the Council resolution of 18 December 1979 on linked work and training for young persons [6] advocates that the Member States should encourage the development of effective links between training and work experience;

(5) Whereas the Council resolution of 15 July 1996 [7] calls on the Member States to promote the transparency of vocational training certificates;

(6) Whereas the conclusions adopted by the Council on 6 May 1996 on the Commission's White Paper 'Teaching and learning: towards the learning society' [8] stress the need for cooperation between schools and the business sector; whereas the 1998 employment guidelines [9], and the 1999 employment guidelines, ask Member States to improve the employment prospects for young people by equipping them with skills relevant to market requirements; whereas in that context the Council invited the Member States to set up or develop apprenticeship training where appropriate;

---

[1] OJ C 67, 3. 3. 1998, p. 7.
[2] Opinion delivered on 29 April 1998 (OJ C 214, 10. 7. 1998, p. 63).
[3] Opinion of the European Parliament of 30 April 1998 (OJ C 152, 18. 5. 1998, p. 48), Council Common Position of 29 June 1998 (OJ C 262, 19. 8. 1998, p. 41) and Decision of the European Parliament of 5 November 1998 (OJ C 359, 23. 11. 1998).
[4] OJ 63, 20. 4. 1963, p. 1338/63.
[5] OJ L 340, 29. 12. 1994, p. 8.

[6] OJ C 1, 3. 1. 1980, p. 1.
[7] OJ C 224, 1. 8. 1996, p. 7.
[8] OJ C 195, 6. 7. 1996, p. 1.
[9] OJ C 30, 28. 1. 1998, p. 1.

(7) Whereas training establishments on the one hand and the business sector on the other can be complementary fora for the acquisition of general, technical, social and personal knowledge and skills; whereas in this connection, work-linked training, including apprenticeship, makes a significant contribution to a more effective social and occupational integration into working life and the labour market; whereas it can benefit various target groups and various levels of teaching and training, including higher education;

(8) Whereas the Council resolution of 5 December 1994 (¹) on the quality and attractiveness of vocational eduction and training stresses the importance of work-linked training and the need to encourage periods of vocational training in other Member States and to integrate those periods into national vocational training programmes;

(9) Whereas, in order to promote this mobility, it is desirable to establish a document known as the 'EUROPASS Training' document to record at Community level the period or periods of training in another Member State;

(10) Whereas it is important to ensure the quality of such periods of transnational mobility; whereas Member States have a particular responsibility in this area; whereas the Commission, in close cooperation with the Member States, should establish a procedure for exchanging information and coordinating the activities and arrangements developed by Member States to implement this Decision;

(11) Whereas the Extraordinary European Council on Employment held in Luxembourg acknowledged the decisive role played by small and medium-sized enterprises (SMEs) as regards the creation of sustainable jobs;

(12) Whereas work-linked training, including apprenticeship, in micro-enterprises, SMEs and the crafts sector is an important aid to employability; whereas their specific requirements in that area should be taken into account;

(13) Whereas trainees should be properly informed as to the relevant provisions in force in the host Member State;

(14) Whereas the Community Charter of the Fundamental Social Rights of Workers acknowledges the importance of combating all forms of discrimination, especially those based on sex, colour, race, opinions and beliefs;

(15) Whereas the Council, in its recommendation of 30 June 1993 on access to continuing vocational training (²), encourages access for, and effective participation by, women in continuing vocational training; whereas it is therefore important to make sure that due account is taken of equal opportunities in participation in European pathways and appropriate measures must be taken to that end;

(16) Wheres the Commission is required in cooperation with the Member States, to ensure overall consistency between the implementation of this Decision and Community programmes and initiatives in the fields of education, vocational training and youth;

(17) Whereas it is necessary to ensure continuous monitoring of the implementation of this Decision; whereas the Commission is therefore invited to submit a report to the European Parliament, the Council and the Economic and Social Committee thereon and to put forward any necessary proposals for the future;

(18) Whereas three years after this Decision is adopted an assessment should be made of its impact and of the experience gained, so that any corrective measures needed can be adopted;

(19) Whereas a financial reference amount within the meaning of point 2 of the Declaration of the European Parliament, the Council and the Commission of 6 March 1995 is included in this Decision with a view to facilitating the introduction of the EUROPASS measure without prejudice to the powers of the budget authority as defined by the Treaty; whereas Community financial support is limited to an introductory stage between 1 January 2000 and 31 December 2004;

(20) Whereas in accordance with the principles of subsidiarity and proportionality as set out in Article 3b of the Treaty, the objectives of the action envisaged for the establishment of the 'EUROPASS Training' document require coordinated action at Community level, by reason of the diversity of training systems and structures in the Member States; whereas this Decision does not go beyond what is necessary to achieve those objectives,

(¹) OJ C 374, 30. 12. 1994, p. 1.

(²) OJ L 181, 23. 7. 1993, p. 37.

HAS ADOPTED THIS DECISION:

Article 1

Objectives

1. This Decision established a document known as the 'EUROPASS Training' on the basis of the common principles defined in Article 3. It is intended as a record at Community level of the period or periods of training which a person undergoing work-linked training, including apprenticeship, has followed in a Member State other than that in which his/her training is based (known as 'European pathway(s)').

2. The use of this record and participation in a 'European pathway' is voluntary and does not impose any obligations or confer any rights other than those defined below.

Article 2

Definitions

For the purposes of the Decision, and taking account of the differences in the systems and arrangements for work-linked training, including apprenticeship, in the Member States, the following definitions shall apply:

1. 'European pathway' means, where it has been agreed to use the EUROPASS Training, any period of vocational training, which is completed by a person in a Member State (host Member State) other than the one (Member State of provenance) where his or her work-linked training is based, which forms part of that work-linked training;

2. 'person in work-linked training' means any person, of whatever age, in vocational training, at any level including higher education. This training, recognised or certified by the competent authorities in the Member State of provenance according to its own legislation, procedures or practices, involves structured periods of training in an undertaking and, where appropriate, in a training establishment or centre, whatever the person's status (contract of employment, apprenticeship contract, pupil or student);

3. 'mentor' means any person with a private or public employer or a training establishment or centre in the host Member State who has the task of assisting, informing, guiding and monitoring trainees during their 'European pathway';

4. 'EUROPASS Training' means a document establishing that the holder has completed one or more periods of work-linked training, including apprenticeship, in another Member State under the conditions defined in this Decision;

5. 'host partner' means any body in the host Member State (*inter alia* private or public employer, training establishment or centre) with which a partnership with the body responsible for organising the training in the Member State of provenance has been established, for the completion of a European pathway.

Article 3

Content and common principles

The following conditions shall apply to the EUROPASS Training:

1. each European pathway shall form part of the training followed in the Member State of provenance, according to its own legislation, procedures or practices;

2. the body responsible for organising the training in the Member State of provenance and the host partner shall agree within the context of the partnership on the content, objectives, duration and the practicalities of the European pathway;

3. the European pathways shall be monitored and supervised by a mentor.

Article 4

EUROPASS Training

1. A Community information document known as the 'EUROPASS Training', the contents and presentation of which are described in the Annex, shall be issued by the body responsible for organising the training in the Member State of provenance to all persons completing a European pathway.

2. The EUROPASS Training document shall:

(a) specify the vocational training followed in the course of which the European pathway was completed and the qualification, diploma, title or other certificate to which the training leads;

(b) specify that the European pathway forms part of the training followed in the Member State of provenance, according to its own legislation, procedures or practices;

(c) identify the content of the European pathway, providing relevant details of any work experience or training followed during the pathway and, where appropriate, the skills acquired and the method of evaluation used;

(d) indicate the duration of the European pathway organised by the host partner during the work experience or training;

(e) identify the host partner;

(f) identify the mentor's function;

(g) be issued by the body responsible for organising the training in the Member State of provenance. It shall contain, for each European pathway, a record which shall form an integral part of the EUROPASS Training, completed by the host partner and signed by him/her and by the holder.

Article 5

Consistency and complementarity

With due regard for the procedures and resources specific to Community programmes and initiatives in education and vocational training, the Commission, in cooperation with the Member States, shall ensure overall consistency between the implementation of this Decision and those programmes and initiatives.

Article 6

Support measures and accompanying measures

1. The Commission shall be responsible for the production and appropriate dissemination and monitoring of the EUROPASS Training in close cooperation with the Member States. To that end, each Member State shall designate one or more bodies responsible for ensuring implementation at natioanl level, in close cooperation with the social partners and, where appropriate, with representative organisations for work-linked training.

2. To that end, each Member State shall take steps to:

(a) facilitate access to the EUROPASS Training by disseminating appropriate information;

(b) allow an evaluation of the actions implemented, and

(c) facilitate equal opportunities, in particular by raising awareness among all relevant actors.

3. In close cooperation with the Member States, the Commission shall set up a coordination and mutual information system.

4. In implementing the provisions of this Decision, the Commission and the Member States shall take account of the importance of SMEs and crafts and of their particular needs.

Article 7

Financing

The financial reference amount for the implementation of Article 6(1), (3) and (4) for the period 1 January 2000 to 31 December 2004 shall be ECU 7,3 million.

The annual appropriations shall be authorised by the budget authority within the limits of the financial perspective.

Article 8

This Decision shall apply from 1 January 2000.

Article 9

Evaluation

Three years after the adoption of this Decision the Commission shall submit to the European Parliament and the Council a report on its implementation, evaluate the impact of the Decision on the promotion of mobility in work-linked training, including apprenticeship, propose any further corrective measures designed to make it more effective and make any proposals it deems appropriate, including budgetary proposals.

Article 10

This Decision is addressed to the Member States.

Done at Brussels, 21 December 1998.

For the Council
The President
M. BARTENSTEIN

ANNEX

'EUROPASS TRAINING'

Description of the document

The document is in the form of an A5 booklet.

It comprises 12 pages in addition to the cover.

The outside front cover will bear:
— the words 'EUROPASS Training',
— the logo of the European Community.

Inside front cover:

General description of the 'Europass Training' (in the language in which the training has been followed in the Member State of provenance).

> *'This Community record, known as the "EUROPASS Training", is established in accordance with Council Decision 1999/51/EC on the implementation of European pathways in work-linked training, including apprenticeship (OJ L 17, 22. 1. 1999, p. 45). Its purpose (in accordance with Article 1 of the Decision) is to provide a Community record of the period(s) of training which a person in work-linked training, including apprenticeship, has completed in a Member State other than the one in which his/her training is based.*
>
> *It is issued by ... (body responsible for organising the training course in the Member State of provenance).*
>
> *(Date and signature)'*

Page 1 (in the language of the establishment of provenance)

Particulars of the holder:

— name,
— first name,
— signature.

All the headings will be given in the other official languages of the institutions of the European Union on the inside back cover.

Page 2 (in the language of the host partner):

European pathway 1

(a) vocational training followed;

(b) this European pathway forms part of the training followed in the Member State of provenance;

(c) content of the European pathway, providing relevant details of the work experience acquired or training followed during the pathway and, where appropriate, the skills acquired and the method of evaluation;

(d) duration of the European pathway;

(e) details of the host partner;

(f) name and function of the mentor;

(g) signatures of the host partner and the holder.

Page 3 (in the language of the establishment of provenance):

European pathway 1

Details given on page 2 repeated in the language of the establishment of provenance.

Page 4 (in the language of the holder):

European pathway 1

Details given on page 2 repeated in the language of the holder if different from that used on pages 1 and 2 and provided it is one of the official languages of the institutions of the European Union.

Pages 5, 6 and 7:

European pathway 2 (if appropriate)

Pages 8, 9 and 10:

European pathway 3 (if appropriate)

**Resolution of the Council
and the Ministers for Youth meeting within the Council
of 8 February 1999
on youth participation**

(OJ C 42, 17.2.1999)

I

(Information)

COUNCIL

RESOLUTION OF THE COUNCIL AND THE MINISTERS OF YOUTH MEETING WITHIN THE COUNCIL

of 8 February 1999

on youth participation

(1999/C 42/01)

THE COUNCIL AND THE MINISTERS OF YOUTH, MEETING WITHIN THE COUNCIL,

Taking due account of the United Nations Convention on the rights of the child, in particular Articles 12 to 15;

Considering the Conclusions of the European Council of Cardiff on 15 and 16 June 1998, which seek to bring the European Union closer to the people and make it more transparent;

Recalling the Lisbon Declaration on youth policies and programmes [1] which postulates that the active participation of youth is to be encouraged in all spheres of society and in decision-making processes;

Considering the resolution on measures to protect minors in the European Union, adopted by the European Parliament on 12 December 1996 [2], which calls upon the Member States to promote the political participation of young people and, in particular, to support the establishment of representative youth parliaments at the local, regional and national levels, and to encourage the participation of children in democratically governed organisations and associations;

Bearing in mind Recommendation R(97)3 of 4 February 1997 and Recommendation 1286 of the Council of Europe of 24 January 1996 which advocate a change in attitude to young people as individuals with rights of their own and favour their active and responsible participation in the familiy and in society;

Taking note of the debate which took place at the informal meeting of EU Ministers of Youth in Cork in 1996, which put the inclusion of youth in institutions of social, political, cultural and economic life and the promotion of personal development in the foreground,

NOTE that both the substance and the time horizons of the decisions taken at the Community level and at national levels have a long-term impact on the future prospects and opportunities for the young generation;

REGARD the increased active participation sought by young people as one of the central challenges in the process of shaping European society;

RECOGNISE the importance of young people having a say in all aspects of society, in particular in political, social, economic and cultural affairs;

Therefore CONSIDER it desirable to grant young people in the European Union a wider scope for active participation in European and national civic society and political affairs, the objective being to enable young people, on a step-by-step basis, to assume their share of both opportunities and responsibilities and to encourage them to become active citizens;

ENCOURAGE the European Institutions and the Member States of the European Union to consider how to associate the citizens more closely with the shaping of European policies, to enable young people to participate in all aspects of active citizenship, including their political participation and their mobility within the European Union, thereby involving the young citizens in the process of further European integration;

---

[1] Adopted at the World Conference of Ministers responsible for youth, Lisbon, August 1998.
[2] OJ C 20, 20.1.1997, p. 170.

CALL UPON young people to avail themselves of the existing participatory opportunities and to bring in their contributions to active citizenship;

Expressly INVITE the youth associations and youth organisations as well as the young people themselves to forward their views in general and specific proposals for the promotion of participatory projects;

Considering the above, the Council and the Ministers of Youth meeting within the Council HEREBY ADOPT the following Resolution:

Youth participation at the Community level

The Commission is invited:

— to focus on young people's interests as a guiding principle for action to be applied to all relevant policy areas and, where appropriate, to assess the potential effects of measures to be launched at the Community level on the living conditions of young people, and to show ways and means of taking the interests of young people into account,

— to promote the involvement of young people in the development, execution and evaluation of youth activities and programmes at the Community level by utilising the interest young people take in shaping the Europe of today and tomorrow,

— to promote the performance of studies to examine the possibilities and conditions of participation for young people in Europe, the exchange of experience, information and the documentation of activities in this field,

— to enter into dialogue with young people in the areas outlined above, and to take the opinion of young people into consideration in the development of Community programmes and activities in these areas,

— to enhance at Community level an exchange of experience on measures or projects aiming at promoting the participation of young people.

Youth participation in the Member States

The Council and the Ministers of Youth meeting within the Council advocate the full participation of Europe's youth in the political, economic, social and cultural potentials of the Member States, and strive to ensure this within their respective scope of action. They welcome and support the efforts made in the Member States to involve young people to a greater extent in decisions of relevance to the development of politics and society.

In the further pursuit of existing efforts, having regard to the competence of the Member States and in the context of their own legal system as regards the reception and implementation of the following objectives, the Council and the Ministers of Youth meeting within the Council agree to the importance of:

— supporting the creativity of young people to develop different forms of participatory dialogues in civic society,

— encouraging in the best possible way innovative participatory projects and structures,

— encouraging the participation of young people in democratic processes at local, regional and national level,

— promoting the integration of innovative participatory projects and learning opportunities in democratic decision-making structures,

— encouraging the active participation of young people in the development of the local community, in particular for young people with little experience of such involvement,

— facilitating adequate access for young people to participatory opportunities so as to strengthen the social involvement of youth initiatives and innovative networks and young people outside of organised structures,

— encouraging within existing youth associations and youth organisations opportunities for cooperation and participation with open access to all young people,

— recognising the valuable contribution provided by youth associations and organisations to the development of channels for youth participation at local, regional and national level.

The Member States are invited to focus on the young people's interests as a guiding principle of action to be applied to all relevant policy areas and, where appropriate, to assess the potential effects of measures to be launched on the living conditions of young people.

**Council Decision
of 26 April 1999
establishing the second phase of the Community vocational
training action programme "Leonardo da Vinci"**

(OJ L 146, 11.6.1999)

II

(Acts whose publication is not obligatory)

COUNCIL

COUNCIL DECISION

of 26 April 1999

establishing the second phase of the Community vocational training action programme 'Leonardo da Vinci'

(1999/382/EC)

THE COUNCIL OF THE EUROPEAN UNION,

Having regard to the Treaty establishing the European Community and in particular Article 127 thereof,

Having regard to the proposal from the Commission [1],

Having regard to the opinion of the Economic and Social Committee [2],

Acting in accordance with the procedure laid down in Article 189c of the Treaty [3],

(1) Whereas the Treaty establishing the European Community stipulates that the latter's action shall, *inter alia*, contribute to the development of quality education and vocational training;

(2) Whereas, by Decision 94/819/EC [4], the Council established an action programme for the implementation of a European Community vocational training policy; whereas it is appropriate, on the basis of the acquired experience of that programme, to ensure its extension, taking into account the results obtained to date;

(3) Whereas the extraordinary European Council on Employment held in Luxembourg on 20 and 21 November 1997 recognised that life-long education and vocational training can make an important contribution to Member States' employment policies in order to enhance employability, adaptability and entrepreneurship and to promote equal opportunities;

(4) Whereas life-long learning should be provided for persons of all ages and all occupational categories, not only because of technological change but also as a result of the reduction in the number of persons in active employment in the age pyramid;

(5) Whereas in its communication 'Towards a Europe of Knowledge' the Commission set out proposals for the creation of a European education area capable of achieving the objective of life-long education and vocational training, identifying the types of measures to be developed at Community level, all focusing on transnational cooperation and designed to bring added value to the action taken by the Member States, while fully respecting the principle of subsidiarity, and in a context of simplified procedures;

(6) Whereas in its White Paper 'Teaching and learning — Towards the learning society' the Commission states that the emergence of the learning society entails encouraging the acquisition of new knowledge and to this end providing motivation to learn at every opportunity; whereas in its Green Paper 'Education, vocational training, research: the obstacles to transnational mobility' the Commission highlighted the advantages of mobility for people and competitiveness in the European Union;

---

[1] OJ C 309, 9.10.1998, p. 9.
[2] OJ C 410, 30.12.1998, p. 6.
[3] Opinion, of the European Parliament of 5 November 1998 (OJ 359, 23.11.1998, p. 59), Council Common Position of 21 December 1998 (OJ C 49, 22.2.1999, p 65) and Decision of the European Parliament of 23 March 1999 (not yet published in the Official Journal).
[4] OJ L 340, 29.12.1994, p. 8.

(7) Whereas measures under this programme should serve the purpose of developing quality, fostering innovation and promoting the European dimension in vocational training systems and practices with a view to encouraging life-long learning; whereas, in the implementation of this programme, attention should be paid to fighting exclusion in all its forms, including racism and xenophobia; whereas special attention should be focused on removing all forms of discrimination and inequality, *inter alia* for people with a disability, and on promoting equal opportunities for women and men;

(8) Whereas it is necessary, in order to reinforce the added value of Community action, to ensure, at all levels, a coherence and complementarity between the actions implemented in the framework of this Decision and other Community interventions;

(9) Whereas, in view of their role in the maintenance and creation of jobs and the development of training, small and medium-sized enterprises (SMEs) and the craft industry should be more closely involved in the implementation of this programme;

(10) Whereas the Commission, in cooperation with the Member States, is seeking to secure coherence and complementarity between the actions under this programme and other relevant Community policies, instruments and actions, in particular the European Social Fund, by facilitating the transfer and dissemination, on a wider scale, innovatory approaches and methods developed under this programme; whereas the Commission, in partnership with social partners, is endeavouring to develop cooperation between this programme and the activities of the Community social dialogue;

(11) Whereas the Agreement on the European Economic Area ('EEA Agreement') provides for greater cooperation in the field of education, vocational training and youth between the European Community and its Member States, on the one hand, and the countries of the European Free Trade Association (EFTA) participating in the European Economic Area, ('EFTA/EEA countries'), on the other;

(12) Whereas provision should be made to open up this programme to participation of: the associated central and eastern European countries (CEEC), in accordance with the conditions established in the Europe Agreements, in their additional protocols and in the decisions of the respective Association Councils; Cyprus under the same conditions as those applied to the EFTA/EEA countries, funded by additional appropriations in accordance with the procedures to be agreed with that country; and Malta and Turkey, funded by additional appropriations in accordance with the Treaty;

(13) Whereas this programme should be regularly monitored and evaluated in cooperation between the Commission and the Member States in order to allow for readjustments, particularly in the priorities for implementing the measures;

(14) Whereas a financial reference amount, within the meaning of point 2 of the Declaration by the European Parliament, the Council and the Commission of 6 March 1995 ([1]), is included in this Decision for the entire duration of the programme, without thereby affecting the powers of the budgetary authority as they are defined by the Treaty;

(15) Whereas, in accordance with the principle of subsidiarity and the principle of proportionality as set out in Article 3b of the Treaty, since the objectives of the proposed action concerning the implementation of a vocational training policy at Community level cannot be sufficiently achieved by the Member States given the complexity of vocational training partnerships; they can therefore be better achieved by the Community owing to the transnational dimension of the Community actions and measures; whereas this Decision is limited to the minimum required to achieve these objectives and does not go beyond what is necessary to achieve these objectives,

HAS DECIDED AS FOLLOWS:

Article 1

Establishment of the programme

1. This Decision establishes the second phase of the action programme for the implementation of a Community vocational training policy 'Leonardo da Vinci', hereinafter referred to as 'this programme'.

2. This programme shall be implemented over the period starting on 1 January 2000 and ending on 31 December 2006.

3. This programme shall contribute to the promotion of a Europe of knowledge by developing a European area of cooperation in the field of education and vocational training. It shall support Member States' policies on life-long learning and the building up of the knowledge and skills and competences likely to foster active citizenship and employability.

4. This programme shall support and supplement action taken by, and in, the Member States while fully respecting their responsibility for the content and organisation of vocational training, and of their cultural and linguistic diversity.

([1]) OJ C 102, 4.4.1996, p. 4.

Article 2

Objectives of the programme

1. Within the framework of the objectives set out in Article 127 of the Treaty, this programme aims at developing the quality, innovation and European dimension in vocational training systems and practices, through transnational cooperation. The objectives of the programme shall be to:

(a) improve the skills and competences of people, especially young people, in initial vocational training at all levels; this may be achieved *inter alia* through work-linked vocational training and apprenticeship with a view to promoting employability and facilitating vocational integration and reintegration;

(b) improve the quality of, and access to, continuing vocational training and the life-long acquisition of skills and competences with a view to increasing and developing adaptability, particularly in order to consolidate technological and organisational change;

innovative counselling and guidance approaches are of particular importance for the fulfilment of the objectives set out in (a) and (b) and shall be given support;

(c) promote and reinforce the contribution of vocational training to the process of innovation, with a view to improving competitiveness and entrepreneurship, also in view of new employment possibilities; special attention shall be paid in this respect to fostering cooperation between vocational training institutions, including universities, and undertakings, particularly SMEs.

2. In implementing the objectives set out in paragraph 1, particular attention shall be paid to people at a disadvantage in the labour market, including disabled people, to practices facilitating their access to training, to the promotion of equality, to equal opportunities for women and men and to the fight against discrimination.

Article 3

Community measures

1. The objectives of this programme shall be pursued by means of the following measures, the operational content and application procedures thereof which are described in the Annexes and which may be combined:

(a) support for the transnational mobility of people undergoing vocational training, especially young people, and for those responsible for training ('Mobility');

(b) support for pilot projects based on transnational partnerships designed to develop innovation and quality in vocational training ('pilot projects');

(c) promotion of language competences, including for less widely used and taught languages, and understanding of different cultures in the context of vocational training ('language competences');

(d) support for the development of transnational cooperation networks facilitating the exchange of experience and good practice ('transnational networks');

(e) the development and updating of reference material through support for surveys and analyses, the establishment and updating of comparable data, the observation and dissemination of good practices and the comprehensive exchange of information ('reference material').

2. In carrying out the measures referred to in paragraph 1, specific support for transnational actions shall be available for the promotion and use of information and communication technologies (ICT) in vocational training.

Article 4

Access to the programme

Under the conditions and arrangements for implementation specified in the Annexes, access to this programme shall be open to all public and/or private bodies and institutions involved in vocational training and, in particular:

(a) vocational training establishments, centres and bodies at all levels, including universities;

(b) research centres and bodies;

(c) undertakings, particularly SMEs and the craft industry, or public or private sector establishments, including those involved in vocational training;

(d) trade organisations, including chambers of commerce, etc.;

(e) social partners;

(f) local and regional bodies and organisations;

(g) non profit making organisations, voluntary bodies and NGOs.

Article 5

Implementation of the programme and co-operation with the Member States

1. The Commission shall ensure the implementation of the Community actions covered by this programme.

2. Member States shall:

— take the necessary steps to secure, by means of appropriate structures, the coordination, an integrated management and the follow-up for the attainment of the objectives of this programme, involving all the parties concerned by vocational training, in accordance with national practice,

— ensure that relevant information and publicity is provided in respect of the actions of this programme,
— take the necessary steps to ensure the efficient running of this programme,
— endeavour, as far as possible, to adopt such measures as they deem necessary and desirable to remove obstacles to access to this programme.

3. In cooperation with Member States, the Commission shall:

— take the steps described in the Annexes to build upon the achievements of the first phase of this programme and the Community initiatives in the area of vocational training,
— ensure the smooth transition between those actions developed in the framework of the first phase of this programme and those to be implemented under the second phase.

Article 6

Joint actions

As part of the process of building up a Europe of knowledge, the measures contained in this programme may be implemented, in conformity with the procedure laid down in Article 7, as joint actions with related Community programmes and actions, particularly those in the fields of education and youth.

Article 7

Committee

1. The Commission shall be assisted by a committee composed of two representatives from each Member State and chaired by the representative of the Commission.

2. The Committee shall deliver opinions on the following points:

(a) the general guidelines for the implementation of this programme and the financial support to be supplied by the Community;

(b) the annual plan of work for the implementation of this programme's actions, including priorities, the themes for the thematic actions and the joint actions and the Commission proposals for project selection, including those under the joint actions;

(c) the annual budgets and distribution of funding between measures, as well as joint actions, accompanying measures and projects of European organisations;

(d) the criteria applicable for establishing the indicative breakdown of funds among the Member States for the purpose of the actions to be managed according to selection procedure A (Annex I, Section III);

(e) the arrangements for monitoring and evaluating the programme and for the dissemination and transfer of results.

3. As regards the points referred to in paragraph 2, the representative of the Commission shall submit to the Committee a draft of the measures to be taken. The Committee shall deliver its opinion on the draft within a time limit which the Chairman may lay down according to the urgency of the matter. The opinion shall be delivered by the majority laid down in Article 148(2) of the Treaty in the case of decisions which the Council is required to adopt on a proposal from the Commission. The votes of the representatives of the Member States within the Committee shall be weighted in the manner set out in that Article. The Chairman shall not vote.

4. (a) The Commission shall adopt measures which apply immediately.

(b) However, if these measures are not in accordance with the opinion of the Committee, they shall be communicated by the Commission to the Council forthwith. In that event,

— the Commission shall defer application of the measures which it has decided for a period of up to two months from the date of the communication,
— the Council, acting by a qualified majority, may take a different decision within the time limit referred to in the preceding indent.

5. The representative of the Commission shall consult the Committee on other appropriate matters concerning implementation of this programme. In that event, the representative of the Commission shall submit to the Committee a draft of the measures to be taken. The Committee shall deliver its opinion on the draft within a time limit which the Chairman may lay down according to the urgency of the matter, if necessary by taking a vote.

The opinion shall be recorded in the minutes; in addition, each Member State shall have the right to ask to have its position recorded in the minutes.

The Commission shall take the utmost account of the opinion delivered by the Committee. It shall inform the Committee of the manner in which its opinion has been taken into account.

6. The Committee shall draw up its rules of procedure.

7. The Commission, in cooperation with the Committee, shall establish regular and structured cooperation with the Committees established for the implementation of the European Community educational and youth programmes.

8. To ensure the consistency of this programme with other measures referred to in Article 9, the Commission shall keep the Committee regularly informed about Community initiatives taken in the fields of education, vocational training and youth, including cooperation with third countries and international organisations.

Article 8

Social partners

Without prejudice to the procedures described in Article 7(3), (4) and (5), the Commission may consult the Committee on any matter concerning the application of this Decision.

Whenever such consultation takes place, a number, equal to that of the representatives of the Member States, of representatives of the social partners, appointed by the Commission on the basis of proposals from the social partners at Community level, shall participate in the work of the Committee as observers.

They shall have the right to request that their position be recorded in the minutes of Committee meetings.

Article 9

Consistency and complementarity

1. The Commission shall, in cooperation with the Member States, ensure the overall consistency and complementarity with other relevant Community policies, instruments and actions, in particular the European Social Fund, in particular those contributing to a Europe of knowledge, in particular in the fields of education, vocational training, youth, research and technological development, and innovation.

2. In implementing the measures of this programme, the Commission and the Member States shall have regard to the priorities set out in the employment guidelines adopted by the Council, as part of a coordinated employment strategy.

3. In partnership with Community social partners, the Commission shall endeavour to develop the coordination between this programme and the social dialogue at Community level, including at sectoral levels.

4. The Commission shall secure the assistance of the European Centre for the Development of Vocational Training (Cedefop) in implementing this programme, in accordance with the arrangements set out in Regulation (EEC) No 337/75 ([1]) establishing the Cedefop. Subject to the same conditions and in the areas which lend themselves to it, coordination shall be established under the auspices of the Commission with the European Training Foundation as specified by Regulation (EEC) No 1360/90 ([2]).

5. The Commission shall keep the Advisory Committee on Vocational Training regularly informed of the progress of this programme.

Article 10

Participation of the EFTA/EEA countries, the associated central and eastern European countries (CEEC), Cyprus, Malta and Turkey

---
([1]) OJ L 39, 13.2.1975, p. 1. Regulation as last amended by Regulation (EC) No 354/95 (OJ L 41, 23.2.1995, p. 1).
([2]) OJ L 131, 23.4.1990, p. 1. Regulation as last amended by Regulation (EC) No 1572/98 (OJ L 206, 23.7.1998, p. 1).

This programme shall be open to the participation of:

— the EFTA/EEA countries in accordance with the conditions established in the EEA agreement,

— the associated central and eastern European countries (CEEC) in accordance with the conditions established in the Europe agreements, in their additional protocols and in the decisions of the respective Association Councils,

— Cyprus, under the same conditions as those applied to the EFTA/EEA countries, funded by additional appropriations in accordance with the procedures to be agreed with that country,

— Malta and Turkey, funded by additional appropriations, in accordance with the provisions of the Treaty.

Article 11

International cooperation

Under this programme, and in accordance with the procedure laid down in Article 7(2), (3) and (4), the Commission shall strengthen its cooperation with third countries and with the competent international organisations.

Article 12

Funding

1. The financial reference amount for the implementation of this programme for the period 2000 to 2006 shall be EUR 1 150 million.

2. The annual appropriations shall be authorised by the budgetary authority within the limits of the financial perspective.

Article 13

Monitoring and evaluation

1. The Commission shall regularly monitor this programme in cooperation with the Member States.

This monitoring shall include the reports referred to in paragraph 4 and specific activities.

2. The Commission shall regularly evaluate the implementation of this programme in cooperation with the Member States, in accordance with the procedure laid down in Article 7(2), (3) and (4) and on the basis of criteria devised in cooperation with the Member States. The main objective shall be the evaluation of the effectiveness and the impact of actions implemented in comparison with the objectives aimed at in Article 2. The evaluation shall also look at the dissemination of the results of actions under this programme, of good practiced and the impact of this programme as a whole in terms of its objectives.

This evaluation shall also examine the complementarity between actions under this programme and those pursued under other relevant Community policies, instruments and actions.

In accordance with criteria established using the procedure described in Article 7(2), (3) and (4), there shall be regular independent external evaluations of the results of the Community actions.

3. The findings of the monitoring and evaluation should be taken into account when implementing this programme.

4. Member States shall submit to the Commission by 31 December 2003 and 30 June 2007 respectively reports on the implementation and effectiveness of this programme and its impact on the vocational training systems and arrangements which exist in the Member States. The reports shall also take into account the promotion of equality, and of equal opportunities, between women and men.

5. The Commission shall submit to the European Parliament, the Council and the Economic and Social Committee:

— a first interim report on the initial operational implementation of this programme by 30 June 2002,
— a second interim report on the implementation of this programme by 30 June 2004,
— a communication on the continuation of this programme by 31 December 2004; where appropriate, that communication shall contain a suitable proposal,
— a final report on the implementation of this programme by 31 December 2007.

Article 14

Entry into force

This Decision shall enter into force on the date of its publication in the *Official Journal of the European Communities.*

Done at Luxembourg, 26 April 1999.

For the Council
The President
J. FISCHER

ANNEX I

COMMUNITY ACTIONS AND MEASURES

SECTION I: GENERAL PRINCIPLES

1. The objectives set out in Article 2 of the Decision will be implemented by means of transnational partnerships which submit proposals for action on the basis of the Community measures described in Article 3.

2. Each proposal submitted by a transnational partnership will pursue one or more of the objectives of the programme, and will indicate the measure(s) it intends to implement in order to achieve its aims. Proposals can be submitted for activities integrating various measures according to Article 3(1) and in a manner to be determined by the Committee referred to in Article 7 of the Decision. With the exception of measures 1 (Mobility) and 3 (Language competences) as described in Section II, each proposal must involve partners from at least three participating countries, of which at least one must be a Member State of the European Union. In the case of project proposals under Measures 1 and 3, each proposal must involve partners from at least two participating countries, of which at least one must be a Member State of the European Union.

3. Community calls for proposals will define the priorities for the objectives, the timetable, the conditions of submission, the common eligibility criteria, particularly in terms of transnationality, project evaluation and selection procedures. The indicative timetable will include Community annual deadlines for submission, selection and approval of project applications.

A first call for proposals will remain valid for three years. A second call for proposals, will be drawn up in 2002 valid for two years, a third in 2004 valid for two years on, the basis of the interim reports referred to in Article 13(5) of the Decision.

The Community calls for proposals will be published by the Commission after having sought the opinion of the Committee referred to in Article 7 of the Decision.

4. The proposals for action must set out clearly the aims established, the methods of implementation, the results anticipated, the mechanisms for evaluating the actual results, the plans for dissemination, the beneficiaries and the partners associated, as well as the nature and level of participation of these partners, including their financial contribution and the timetable of work.

5. The proposals can be sent in during the periods specified for each year by the call for proposals. Proposal selections will take place at least once yearly in accordance with the procedures defined in Section III.

6. Member States will take appropriate steps to promote interaction between the players taking part in this programme and in education and youth-related programmes.

7. Under no circumstances may the project partners' own resources derive from other Community funding.

SECTION II: MEASURES

1. **Mobility**

   Support for transnational mobility projects for people undergoing vocational training, especially young people, and for trainers.

   Community support will be provided for the following actions:

   (a) preparation and implementation of transnational placement projects for:

   — people undergoing initial vocational training (placements of normally three weeks to nine months in vocational training institutions and undertakings; these placements form an integral part of the vocational training programme for the people concerned),

- students (placements of three to twelve months in undertakings),

- young workers and recent graduates (placements of two to twelve months in vocational training institutions and undertakings);

Whenever possible, these placements should involve the validation of skills and competences acquired during the placement, according to the practices of the country of origin.

These placements may also include projects which are part of 'European pathways for work-linked vocational training and apprenticeship' within the meaning of Decision 1999/51/EC ([1]).

The transnational placement projects for people undergoing vocational training which involve SMEs and craft industry as host bodies will receive special financial support under the conditions described below.

(b) The organisation of transnational projects of exchanges

- between undertakings, on the one hand, and vocational training organisations or universities, on the other, targeting human resources managers in the business sector, and vocational training programme planners and managers, particularly trainers, and occupational guidance specialists,

- for trainers and mentors in the area of language competences (between the business sector, on the one hand, and the specialised language vocational training establishments, including universities, or vocational training bodies on the other).

Exchanges for these target groups will last between one week and a maximum of six weeks.

(c) Study visits for those responsible for vocational training on the themes proposed by the Commission can be provided by the cedefop.

The transnational placement and exchange projects may last up to two years. For the implementation of placement and exchange projects, measures for specific help for disabled participants are to be elaborated by the Committee referred to in Article 7 of the Decision.

Funding

The Community's financial contribution to the transnational placement and exchange projects defined under this measure may not exceed EUR 5 000 per beneficiary for a placement or an exchange - the maximum amount of this contribution corresponding to the maximum duration indicated in (a) and (b). This maximum amount may be exceeded in the case of participants with a disability.

For this measure, the Commission will allocate to each Member State an annual global grant the amount of which will be defined in accordance with the procedures described in Annex II.

Up to 10 % of this allocation will be set aside, in accordance with procedures agreed upon with the management structure concerned to help:

- SME promoters submitting their first application to the programme. The sum may not exceed EUR 500 per promoter,

- all promoters preparing the target group mentioned under (a). The sum allowed for the pedagogic, cultural and linguistic preparation of that target group, may not exceed EUR 200 per placement of less than three months duration or EUR 500 per placement of more than three months duration, with a ceiling of EUR 25 000 per promoter.

This amount is on top of that set aside for the sending organisation for the management and monitoring of transnational placement projects.

Any unused part of this allocation may be redeployed by the management structure elsewhere within this measure. The reasons for the redeployment must be communicated to the Commission.

2. **Pilot projects**

Support for transnational pilot projects to develop and transfer innovation and quality in vocational training, including actions aiming at the use of information and communication technologies (ICT) in vocational training.

Community support is available for the design, development, testing and assessment of transnational pilot projects to develop and/or disseminate innovation in vocational training.

---

[1] OJ L 17, 22.1.1999, p. 45.

Such transnational pilot projects may relate to the development of quality in vocational training, to the development of new methods of vocational training and to vocational guidance in the context of lifelong learning.

Transnational pilot projects may also aim at:

— developing the use of ICT in vocational training actions and products,

— promoting access for people undergoing vocational training to new tools, services and vocational training products which use ICT,

— supporting the development of transnational open and distance vocational training networks through the use of ICT (multimedia products, WEB sites, network transmission, etc.),

— designing, testing and validating new vocational training approaches arising from new work situations (e.g. teleworking).

Community support for projects under this measure may be available for up to three years.

Thematic actions

Special support will be given to a small number of projects on themes of particular interest at Community level, for example:

— the development of new methods of promoting transparency with an emphasis on new forms of certification or accreditation of skills and expertise learned on the job,

— actions in support of Member States' policies and initiatives to equip with appropriate skills those at a disadvantage in the labour market, particularly those young people who have no qualifications or people whose qualifications need updating,

— developing European arrangements for vocational guidance, counselling and vocational training in business-related services.

Funding

The Community may contribute up to 75 % of eligible expenditure for the transnational pilot projects, with a ceiling of EUR 200 000 per year and per project. For the thematic actions, the ceiling may be raised to EUR 300 000 per year and per project, if justified by the scope of the project concerned.

3. **Language competences**

Support for projects to promote language and cultural competences in vocational training

Community support is available for transnational pilot projects to develop language competences in a vocational training context. Special attention will be paid to projects on less widely used and taught languages.

The point of these projects is to design, test and validate, assess and disseminate teaching material as well as innovative pedagogical methods tailored to the specific needs of each occupational area and economic sector, including through the use of language audits, and also innovatory pedagogical approaches based on language self-tuition and the dissemination of their results.

Proposals for linguistic and cultural support may also be submitted under other actions and measures, particularly in order to improve language and cultural competences amongst the trainers and mentors responsible for the pedagogic supervision of people taking part in transnational mobility programmes.

Community support is also available for transnational programmes between the business sector on the one hand and the specialised language vocational training establishments or vocational training bodies on the other.

Community support for projects under this meaure may be available for up to three years.

Funding

The Community may contribute up to 75 % of eligible expenditure, with a ceiling of EUR 200 000 per project and per year.

4. **Transnational networks**

Support for transnational networks of European expertise and dissemination

Community support is available for the activities of multi-player vocational training networks, bringing together in the Member States, at the regional or sectoral level, the public and private players concerned. Those players include the local authorities, local chambers of commerce, trade organisations for employers and employees, undertakings and research and vocational training centres - including universities - as providers of services, advice and information on access to validated vocational training methods and products. These activities aim at:

(i) assembling, distilling and building on European expertise and innovatory approaches,

(ii) improving the analysis and anticipation of skills requirements,

(iii) disseminating the network outputs and project results throughout the Union in the appropriate circles.

Community support for transnational networks may be available for up to three years.

Funding

The Community may contribute up to 50 % of eligible expenditure for the activities of transnational networks, with a ceiling of EUR 150 000 per year and per network.

5. **Reference material**

Support for actions to establish, update and disseminate reference material

Community support is available for actions undertaken on a transnational basis on priority themes of common interest. Such actions shall make a contribution to:

— establishing comparable data on vocational training systems and arrangements, practices and various approaches to qualifications and competences in the Member States, or

— producing quantitative and/or qualitative information, analyses and observing best practices in support of policies and vocational training practices for lifelong learning that cannot be made available by Eurostat or Cedefop. Eurostat and Cedefop are closely associated with the production of statistical instruments within the procedures currently in place notably those defined by Council Regulation (EC) No 322/97 of 17 February 1997 on Community Statistics [1], taking into account Council Decision 99/126/EC of 22 December 1998 on the Community statistical programme 1998 to 2002 [2].

Community support for projects under this measure may be available for up to three years.

The Commission and the Member States will ensure that such reference material is disseminated as widely as possible, particularly in order to make it available to public and private decision-makers in vocational training.

Funding

The Community's financial contribution will be between 50 % and 100 % of eligible expenditure, with a ceiling of EUR 200 000 per year and per project. If justified by the scope of the project proposed, this ceiling could be raised to EUR 300 000.

6. **Joint actions**

1. For the joint actions described in Article 6 of the Decision, Community support may be provided for joint actions with other Community actions promoting a Europe of knowledge, particularly the Community programmes in the fields of education and youth.

---

[1] OJ L 52, 22.2.1997, p. 1.
[2] OJ L 42, 16.2.1999, p. 1.

2. Such joint actions may be carried out by common calls for proposals for selected themes of interest in fields of activity which are not exclusively covered by one single programme. The themes for joint actions will be agreed by the committees concerned, in accordance with the procedure laid down in Article 7(2), (3) and (4) of the Decision.

The common calls for proposals may also respond to new demands originating during the running of the programmes concerned.

Community support for projects under this measure may be available for up to three years.

Funding

The Community may contribute up to 75 % of eligible expenditure.

7. Accompanying measures

1. To attain the objectives set out in Article 2 of the Decision, Community support is available for:

   — management, coordination, monitoring and evaluation activities by the Member States as described in Articles 5 and 13 and of the Decision and in Section 1(6) of this Annex,

   — information, monitoring, assessment and dissemination activities by the Member States and the Commission to facilitate access to the programme and consolidate the transfer of methods, products and tools designed, and of the results obtained by this programme, among others through data banks accessible to a wide public,

   — the transnational network of national resource centres for vocational guidance,

   — cooperation activities with third countries and with relevant international organisations according to Article 11 of the Decision.

2. Community financial assistance shall be provided to support the activities of the appropriate structures set up by the Member States in accordance with Article 5 of the Decision.

3. In carrying out the programme, the Commission can have recourse to technical assistance organisations the financing of which shall be provided for within the overall envelope for the programme. It can, under the same conditions, have recourse to experts. Furthermore, the Commission will be able to organise seminars, colloquia or other meetings of experts, likely to facilitate the implementation of the programme and take forward information, publication and dissemination actions.

4. The respective roles and operational tasks of the technical assistance organisation(s) and the national management structures must be clearly defined, in accordance with Article 5.

SECTION III: SELECTION PROCEDURES

The proposals submitted by promoters under the calls for proposals shall be selected according to one of the following procedures:

1. Procedure A applicable to mobility actions (measure 1);

2. Procedure B applicable to:

   — pilot projects (measure 2) except for thematic actions,

   — language competences (measure 3),

   — transnational networks (measure 4);

3. Procedure C applicable to:

   — reference material (measure 5),

   — thematic actions (within measure 2),

   — joint actions (measure 6),

   — projects of European organisations (under all measures).

1. **Procedure A**

    This selection procedure consists of the following stages:

    (i) The Commission will allocate a global grant to each participating country according to the procedure defined in Annex II, after having sought the opinion of the Committee referred to in Article 7 of the Decision.

    (ii) Under the rules defined in the calls for proposals, proposals are to be submitted by the promoters to the management structure designated by the Member State.

    (iii) The management structure will assess the proposals on the basis of specifications established at Community level. The management structure will establish a list of the mobility programmes selected and circulate this list, for information, to the Commission and the management structures in the other Member States.

    (iv) The Member States, with the assistance of the respective management structures, shall be responsible for contracting and allocating the global grant to the individual promoters.

    (v) The Member States will submit to the Commission an annual report on the results of the mobility programmes. The report includes information *inter alia* on the following topics:

    — the target publics of the programme,

    — the contents and objectives in terms of skills and/or qualifications,

    — the duration of training and/or work learning experience in a training establishment and/or company,

    — the partners associated in the other Member State or States.

2. **Procedure B**

    This selection procedure consists of a two-step selection process:

    — selection of pre-proposals;

    — selection of full proposals.

    (i) Under the rules defined in the call for proposals, pre-proposals are to be submitted by the promoters to the management structure designated by the Member State.

    (ii) Member States will evaluate and select the pre-proposals. The promoters will be informed of the outcome of this selection. Only promoters of successful pre-proposals will be invited to submit a full proposal to the management structure in the respective Member State. The promoters will also send a copy of their full proposals to the Commission.

    (iii) Member States will evaluate and rank the full proposals and submit a report to the Commission, presenting the outcome of this pre-selection by objective and by measure, the assessment procedure, the parties involved in this procedure as well as a descriptive and reasoned list of proposals likely to be retained in order of priority. This report will also present the information and publicity measures taken to facilitate participation in the programme.

    (iv) The Commission, with the assistance of independent experts, will evaluate the proposals, with a view to assessing and ensuring their transnational and innovative nature. These independent experts will be appointed by the Commission, taking full account of the views of the Member States and the social partners. The Commission will examine the national reports and consult accordingly with each Member State.

    (v) The Commission will submit to the Committee a proposal on the allocation of the budgetary resources by measure and by Member State and will obtain its opinion in accordance with the procedure set out in Article 7 of the Decision.

    (vi) After receiving the opinion of the Committee, the Commission will establish the list of selected projects per Member State and allocate the funds for the implementation of the selected projects to each Member State.

    (vii) Member States, with the assistance of the respective management structures, will be responsible for contracting and allocating funds to the individual promoters.

    (viii) The selection of pre-proposals has to be carried out within two months after the end of the period for submission of proposals as specified in the call for proposals; the process on stages (iii) to (vi) should not take more than five months.

3. **Procedure C**

This procedure consists of a two-step selection process:

— selection of pre-proposals;

— selection of full proposals.

   (i) Under the rules defined in the call for proposals, pre-proposals are to be submitted by the promoters to the Commission. The promoters will also send a copy of their pre-proposals to the management structure in their Member States.

   (ii) The Commission will evaluate all the pre-proposals and, having sought the opinion of the programme Committee, make a selection. The promoters will be informed of the outcome of this selection.

   (iii) Only promoters of successful pre-proposals will be invited to submit a full proposal to the Commission. The promoters will also send a copy of their full proposals to the management structure of their Member States.

   (iv) The Commission, with the assistance of independent experts, will undertake a transnational appraisal of the proposals received and establish a short list of projects. These independent experts will be appointed by the Commission, taking full account of the views of the Member States and the social partners.

   (v) In accordance with the procedure set out in Article 7 of the Decision, the Commission shall seek the opinion of the Committee on this short-list.

   (vi) The Commission will establish the final list of proposals selected and inform the Committee. It will set out the conditions for monitoring these projects in conjunction with the management structures in the Member States.

   (vii) The Commission, with the appropriate technical assistance, will be responsible for contracting and allocating funds to the individual promoters.

   (viii) The selection of pre-proposals has to be carried out within three months after the end of the period for submission of proposals as specified in the call for proposals; the process on stages (iii) to (vi) should not take more than five months.

ANNEX II

SECTION I: OVERALL BUDGET BREAKDOWN

1. At the beginning of the operation, and no later than 1 March every year, the Commission will submit to the Committee an *ex ante* breakdown of budget resources by type of measure, by procedure and taking into account, to this end, the objectives set out in Article 2 of the Decision and will seek its opinion. The Commission will on this basis define an indicative budget for each Member State for the implementation of the actions covered by selection procedure A referred to in Annex I.

2. The funds available will be broken down internally subject to the following restrictions:

   (a) The funds allocated to mobility programmes may not be less than 39 % of the annual budget for the programme.

   (b) The funds allocated in support of devising, developing and testing transnational pilot projects may not be less than 36 % of the annual budget for the programme. Within this allocation the funds allocated in support of Thematic Action projects may not be more than 5 %.

   (c) The funds allocated in support of devising, developing and testing Language Competence projects may not be less than 5 % of the annual budget for the programme.

   (d) The remaining expenditure may not be less than 15 %. Within this expenditure, the funds allocated for the accompanying measures is not to exceed 9 %. The funds allocated for activities under Article 11 of the Decision is not to exceed 0,2 % of the annual budget of the programme.

3. All the percentages given above are indicative and can be adapted by the Committee according to the procedure laid down in Article 7(2), (3) and (4) of the Decision.

SECTION II: SPECIFIC REGULATIONS FOR MOBILITY GLOBAL GRANTS

1. Before the start of the transnational exchange and placement programmes, the Commission will allocate a global grant established on the basis of calculation criteria defined within the procedures described in Article 7 of the Decision, taking into account:

   — the population,

   — the difference in the cost of living between the Member State of origin of the sending organisation and the host Member State,

   — the geographical distance and the costs of transport,

   — the weight of the target public concerned in relation to the overall population, depending on the availability of data for all Member States.

   In any event, the application of these criteria cannot result in the exclusion of any Member State from funding of the transnational placement and exchange programmes described in Annex I.

2. The overall grant is allocated to each Member State on the basis of an operational plan which must set out clearly:

   — the arrangements for managing financial support,

   — the steps to be taken to assist placement and exchange organisers to identify potential partners,

   — appropriate measures to be taken in the interests of sound preparation, organisation and follow-up of placements and exchanges, also regarding the promotion of equal opportunities.

3. For the first year of programme implementation, Member States will submit this operational plan to the Commission no later than 31 March 2000. The Commission will on this basis allocate to each Member State an amount on the basis of which it can go ahead with transnational programmes. The amounts not used up within this allocation at 1 October 2000 will be incorporated in the final amount of the global grant.

ANNEX III

DEFINITIONS

For the purposes of this Decision and taking account of the differences which exist between the systems and arrangements in the Member States:

(a) *initial vocational training* means any form of initial vocational training, including technical and vocational teaching, apprenticeship and vocationally oriented education, which contributes to the achievement of a vocational qualification recognised by the competent authorities in the Member State in which it is obtained,

(b) *work-linked training* means vocational training, at any level including higher education. This vocational training, recognised or certified by the competent authorities of the Member State of provenance according to its own legislation, procedures or practices, involves structured periods of training in an undertaking and, where appropriate, in a vocational training establishment or centre,

(c) *continuing vocational training* means any vocational training undertaken by a worker in the Community during his or her working life,

(d) *life-long learning* means the education and vocational training opportunities offered to individuals throughout their lives to enable them continually to acquire, update and adapt their knowledge, skills and competences,

(e) *open and distance vocational training* means any form of flexible vocational training involving:

— the use of ICT techniques and services in traditional or modern form, and

— support in the form of individualised advice and mentoring,

(f) *European pathways for work-linked vocational training and apprenticeship* means any period which is completed by a person in a Member State other than the one where his or her work-linked vocational training is based, which forms part of the work-linked vocational training,

(g) *vocational guidance* means a range of activities such as counselling, information, assessment and advice, to assist people to make choices relating to initial and continuing vocational education and vocational training programmes, and to employment opportunities,

(h) *undertaking* means all undertakings in the public or private sector whatever their size, legal status or the economic sector in which they operate, and all types of economic activities, including the social economy,

(i) *workers* means all persons available on the labour market in accordance with national laws and practices, including the self-employed,

(j) *vocational training bodies* means any type of public, semi-public or private establishment which, in accordance with national laws and/or practices design or undertake vocational training, further vocational training, refresher vocational training or retraining, irrespective of the designation given to it in the Member States,

(k) *university* means any type of higher education institution, according to national legislation or practice, which offers qualifications or diplomas at that level, whatever such establishments may be called in the Member States,

(l) *students* means persons registered in universities as defined in this Annex, whatever their field of study, in order to follow higher education studies leading to a degree or diploma, up to and including the level of doctorate,

(m) *social partners* means, at national level, employers' and workers' organisations in conformity with national laws and/or practices and, at Community level, employers' and workers' organisations taking part in the social dialogue at Community level,

(n) *local and regional partners* means any player in regional and local life — local authority, association, local chambers of commerce and associations, consortia, advisory bodies, the media — participating in local or regional cooperation activities which include vocational training,

(o) *European organisations* means social partners at Community level, European employers' and trade union federations in specific sectors, and bodies and organisations with a European status or scope,

(p) *reference material* means all the analyses, studies, surveys and identification of good practice which make it possible to locate, at Community level, the relative position of the various Member States and the progress made on a given subject or in a given area.

**Council Decision No 1999/311/EEC
of 29 April 1999
adopting the third phase of the trans-European cooperation scheme
for higher education (Tempus III) (2000-2006)**

(OJ L 120, 8.5.1999)

II

(Acts whose publication is not obligatory)

COUNCIL

COUNCIL DECISION
of 29 April 1999
adopting the third phase of the trans-European cooperation scheme for higher education (Tempus III) (2000-2006)

(1999/311/EC)

THE COUNCIL OF THE EUROPEAN UNION,

Having regard to the Treaty establishing the European Community, and in particular Article 235 thereof,

Having regard to the proposal from the Commission [1],

Having regard to the opinion of the European Parliament [2],

Having regard to the opinion of the Economic and Social Committee [3],

Having regard to the opinion of the Committee of the Regions [4],

(1) Whereas the European Council meeting in Strasbourg on 8 and 9 December 1989 called on the Council to adopt, on the basis of a proposal from the Commission, measures aimed at enabling the central and eastern European countries to take part in programmes in the areas of education and/or training similar to the existing Community programmes;

(2) Whereas on 18 December 1989 the Council adopted Regulation (EEC) No 3906/89 on economic aid to the Republic of Hungary and the Polish People's Republic [5] (PHARE programme), which provides for aid to support the process of economic and social reform in central and eastern European countries in areas including training; whereas on 25 June 1996 the Council adopted Regulation (Euratom, EC) No 1279/96 concerning the provision of assistance to economic reform and recovery in the new independent States and Mongolia [6] (TACIS programme);

(3) Whereas on 29 April 1993 by Decision 93/246/EEC the Council adopted the second phase of the trans-European cooperation scheme for higher education (Tempus II) for a period of four years from 1 July 1994 [7]; whereas that Decision was amended on 21 November 1996 by Decision 96/663/EC [8] to extend to six years the duration of this programme (1994-2000);

(4) Whereas the countries of central and eastern Europe, the new independent States of the former Soviet Union and Mongolia, which are beneficiaries of the PHARE and TACIS programmes, consider higher education and training to be key areas for the process of economic and social reform;

(5) Whereas cooperation on higher education strengthens and deepens the whole fabric of relations existing between the peoples of Europe, brings out common cultural values, allows fruitful exchanges of views to take place and facilitates multinational activities in the scientific, cultural, artistic, economic and social spheres;

---

[1] OJ C 270, 29.8.1998, p. 9, and OJ C 87, 29.3.1999, p. 102.
[2] OJ C 98, 9.4.1999.
[3] OJ C 40, 15.2.1999, p. 23.
[4] OJ C 51, 22.2.1999, p. 86.
[5] OJ L 375, 23.12.1989, p. 11. Regulation as last amended by Regulation (EC) No 753/96 (OJ L 103, 26.4.1996, p. 5).
[6] OJ L 165, 4.7.1996, p. 1.
[7] OJ L 112, 6.5.1993, p. 34.
[8] OJ L 306, 28.11.1996, p. 36.

(6) Whereas the recent establishment of Tempus in the non-associated countries of central and eastern Europe, in the new independent States of the former Soviet Union and in Mongolia, whose needs are greater and whose areas are more extensive, fully warrants the continuation of the measures undertaken;

(7) Whereas Tempus can make an effective contribution to the structural development of higher education including the improvement of human resources and occupational skills adapted to economic reform and whereas there is no other instrument for achieving this objective;

(8) Whereas Tempus can also make an effective contribution, via universities and university staff, to the development of public administration and education structures in the eligible countries;

(9) Whereas Tempus can contribute to the restoration of cooperation, interrupted by recent events, between neighbouring regions of the Community and whereas this cooperation is a factor of peace and stability in Europe;

(10) Whereas the associated countries in the pre-accession phase which have taken part in Tempus I and Tempus II could now, thanks to the experience they have acquired, make a useful contribution alongside the Member States in assisting the partner countries who came into the programme at a much later stage to restructure their higher education systems;

(11) Whereas Article 11 of Decision 93/246/EEC stipulates that the Commission must carry out an evaluation of the implementation of the Tempus programme and submit no later than 30 April 1998 a proposal for the extension or the adjustment of the programme for the period commencing on 1 July 2000;

(12) Whereas the competent authorities in the countries of central and eastern Europe, the new independent States of the former Soviet Union and Mongolia, the users of the programme, the structures responsible for organising it in the eligible countries and in the European Community, and the experts and qualified representatives reflecting the views of the university world in Europe, share the findings of the evaluation report attesting to the capacity of Tempus to make an effective contribution in the eligible countries to the diversification of educational opportunities and to cooperation between universities, thereby paving the way for the development of scientific, cultural and economic and social cooperation;

(13) Whereas the possibility should be provided of creating effective coordination between the Tempus III programme and other Community programmes or activities with an educational and/or training-related dimension, thus stimulating synergies and increasing the added value of each of the Community activities;

(14) Whereas the Treaty does not provide, for the adoption of this Decision, powers other than those of Article 235; whereas the conditions for invoking that Article have been satisfied,

HAS DECIDED AS FOLLOWS:

Article 1

Duration of Tempus III

The third phase of the trans-European cooperation scheme for higher education (hereinafter referred to as 'Tempus III') is hereby adopted for a period of six years as from 1 July 2000.

Article 2

Eligible countries

Tempus III shall concern the non-associated countries of central and eastern Europe eligible for economic aid by virtue of Regulation (EEC) No 3906/89 (PHARE programme)[1], and the new independent States of the former Soviet Union and Mongolia mentioned in Regulation (Euratom, EC) No 1279/96 (TACIS programme), subject to these assistance programmes being prolonged for the period referred to. These countries are hereinafter referred to as 'eligible countries'.

On the basis of an evaluation of the specific situation of each country the Commission, in accordance with the procedures set out in the said Regulations, shall agree with the eligible countries concerned whether they should participate in Tempus III, and the nature and conditions of their participation in the national planning of Community assistance for social and economic reform.

Article 3

Involvement of associated countries

Actions under Tempus III are also open to the associated countries of central and eastern Europe so that what has been achieved through Tempus can be shared with the neighbouring countries and in order to develop regional and cross-border cooperation. Taking into account the respective financial rules and regulations, cooperation between Tempus and Erasmus projects should be encouraged.

[1] At present Albania, Bosnia-Herzegovina and the former Yugoslav Republic of Macedonia.

Article 4

Definitions

For the purposes of Tempus III:

(a) the term 'university' shall be used to cover all types of post-secondary educational and vocational training establishments which offer, within the framework of advanced education and training, qualifications or diplomas of that level, whatever such establishments may be called;

(b) the terms 'industry' and 'company' shall be used to cover all types of economic activity, irrespective of legal status, autonomous business organisations, chambers of commerce and industry and/or their equivalents, professional associations, and the training bodies of the institutions and organisations mentioned above;

(c) the term 'institution' shall be used to cover local and public authorities, and the social partners' and their training bodies.

Each Member State or eligible country may determine what types of establishment referred to in point (a) can participate in Tempus III.

Article 5

Aims

The aim of Tempus III is to promote, in line with the guidelines and general objectives of the PHARE and TACIS programmes for economic and social reform, the development of the higher education systems in the eligible countries through the most balanced cooperation possible with the partners from all the Member States of the Community.

More specifically, Tempus III is intended to facilitate the adaptation of higher education to the new socio-economic and cultural needs of the eligible countries by addressing:

(a) issues relating to the development and reshaping of curricula in the priority areas;

(b) reform of higher education structures and establishments and their management;

(c) the development of training leading to qualifications, with a view to making good the shortage of high-level skills needed in the context of economic reform, particularly by improving and increasing links with industry;

(d) the contribution of higher education and training to citizenship and the strengthening of democracy.

The Commission will, when pursuing the objectives of Tempus III, endeavour to adhere to the Community's general policy on equal opportunities for men and women. The Commission will also endeavour to ensure that no group of citizens is excluded or disadvantaged.

Article 6

Dialogue with the eligible countries

In agreement with the competent authorities in each country, the Commission will define the detailed priorities and objectives for the role of Tempus III in the national strategy for economic and social reform, on the basis of the programme's objectives and the provisions set out in the Annex, and in conformity in particular with:

(a) (i) the general objectives of the PHARE programme;
    (ii) the general objectives of the TACIS programme, with particular reference to its sectoral aspects;

(b) the policy of each eligible country on economic, social and educational reforms;

(c) the need to strike an appropriate balance between the priority areas selected and the resources allocated to Tempus III.

Article 7

Committee

1. The Commission shall implement the Tempus III programme in accordance with the provisions of the Annex, on the basis of detailed guidelines to be adopted annually and following the detailed objectives and priorities agreed with the competent authorities in each eligible country, as provided for in Article 6.

2. In the performance of that task, the Commission shall be assisted by a committee composed of two representatives appointed by each Member State and chaired by the Commission representative. The members of the committee may be assisted by experts and advisers.

The committee shall, in particular, assist the Commission in the implementation of the scheme having regard to the objectives set out in Article 5 and shall coordinate its work with that of other programme committees established in the field of education (Socrates) and training (Leonardo).

3. The Commission representative shall submit to the Committee drafts for measures concerning:

(a) the general guidelines governing Tempus III;

(b) the selection procedures and general guidelines for the Community's financial assistance (amounts, duration and beneficiaries);

(c) questions relating to the overall balance of Tempus III, including the breakdown between the various actions;

(d) the detailed priorities and objectives to be agreed with the competent authorities in each eligible country;

(e) the arrangements for monitoring and evaluating Tempus III.

4. The committee shall deliver its opinion on these draft measures within a time limit which the chairman may lay down according to the urgency of the matter. The opinion shall be delivered by the majority laid down in Article 148(2) of the Treaty in the case of decisions which the Council is required to adopt on a proposal from the Commission. The votes of the representatives of the Member States within the committee shall be weighted in the manner set out in that Article. The chairman shall not vote.

The Commission shall adopt measures which shall apply immediately. However, if these measures are not in accordance with the opinion of the committee, they shall be communicated by the Commission to the Council forthwith.

In that event the Commission may defer application of the measures which it has decided upon for a period of one month.

The Council, acting by a qualified majority, may take a different decision within the time limit referred to in the previous subparagraph.

5. In addition, the Commission may consult the committee on any other matter concerning the implementation of Tempus III, including the annual report.

The representative of the Commission shall submit to the committee a draft of the measures to be taken. The committee shall deliver its opinion on this draft, within a time limit which the chairman may lay down according to the urgency of the matter, if necessary by taking a vote.

The opinion shall be recorded in the minutes; in addition, each Member State shall have the right to ask to have its position recorded in the minutes.

The Commission shall take the utmost account of the opinion delivered by the committee. It shall inform the committee on the manner in which its opinion has been taken into account.

Article 8

Cooperation with the competent bodies

1. The Commission shall cooperate with the agencies of each of the eligible countries designated and set up to coordinate the relations and structures needed to implement Tempus III, including the allocation of funds earmarked by the eligible countries themselves.

2. In addition, for the implementation of Tempus III, the Commission shall cooperate closely with the competent national structures designated by the Member States. It shall take due account whenever possible of bilateral measures taken in this context by the Member States.

Article 9

Links with other Community actions

In line with the procedure set out in Article 7(3) of this Decision and, if applicable, the procedure defined in Article 9 of Regulation (EEC) No 3906/89 and in Article 8 of Regulation (Euratom, EC) No 1279/96, within the limits established by the annual budgetary decisions, the Commission shall ensure consistency and, where necessary, complementarity between Tempus III and other Community actions undertaken both in the Community and as part of assistance provided to eligible countries, particularly with regard to the activities of the European Training Foundation.

Article 10

Coordination with action taken in non-Community countries

1. The Commission shall organise appropriate coordination with actions undertaken by countries not members of the Community [1] or by universities and the business sector in these countries in the same field as Tempus III, including, where applicable, participation in Tempus III projects.

2. This participation may take a variety of forms, including one or more of the following:

— participation in Tempus III projects on a co-financing basis,

— using the opportunities available under Tempus III to channel exchange actions receiving bilateral funding,

— coordination between Tempus III and national initiatives which have the same aims but which are funded and managed separately,

— mutual exchange of information on all relevant initiatives in this field.

Article 11

Annual report

An annual report on the operation of Tempus III shall be forwarded by the Commission to the European Parliament, the Council, the Economic and Social Committee and the Committee of the Regions. This report shall also be forwarded to the eligible countries for information.

---

[1] These countries are the members of the Group of 24, other than the Member States of the Community, the Republic of Cyprus and Malta, and the associated countries of central and eastern Europe, and participation relates to projects with the non-associated countries of central and eastern Europe eligible under the PHARE programme.

Article 12

Monitoring and evaluation — reports

In accordance with the procedure set out in Article 7(3), the Commission shall supervise the arrangements for regular monitoring and external evaluation of experience gained with Tempus III, taking due account of the specific objectives in Article 5 and the national objectives defined in accordance with Article 6.

It shall submit by 30 April 2004 an interim report on the findings of the evaluation, together with any proposals for extending or adjusting Tempus for the period commencing on 1 July 2006.

The Commission shall submit a final report no later than 30 June 2009.

Done at Luxembourg, 29 April 1999.

For the Council
The President
W. MÜLLER

ANNEX

Joint European projects

1. The European Community will provide support for joint European projects (JEPs) of a maximum of three years' duration.

   The JEPs will associate at least one university in an eligible country, one university from a Member State and a partner establishment (university, company or institution as defined in Article 4) in another Member State.

2. Support for JEPs can be provided for activities according to the specific needs of the establishments concerned and in line with the priorities established, including:

   (i) joint education and training actions, particularly with a view to curriculum development and updating, boosting university capacity to provide continuing education and retraining, development of short intensive courses, and development of open and distance learning systems including information and communication technology;

   (ii) measures for the reform and development of higher education and its capacity, particularly by restructuring the management of higher education establishments and systems, by modernising existing infrastructures, by acquiring the equipment needed to implement a JEP and, where applicable, by providing technical and financial assistance to the authorities responsible;

   (iii) the promotion of cooperation between universities, industry and institutions as defined in Article 4 through JEPs;

   (iv) the development of mobility for teachers, administrative staff of universities and students under JEPs:

   (a) grants will be provided for teaching/administrative staff of universities or to trainers in companies in the Member States to carry out teaching/training assignments for periods lasting up to one year in eligible countries and vice versa;

   (b) grants will be awarded to teaching/administrative staff of universities in the eligible countries to undertake periods of retraining and updating in the European Community;

   (c) grants will be available for students up to and including postgraduate at doctoral level, targeting both students in the eligible countries undertaking a period of study in the European Community and European Community students undertaking a period of study in the eligible countries. These grants will normally be granted for a period of three months to one year;

   (d) grants will be available for students taking part in JEPs with the specific aim of promoting mobility, priority will go to students taking part in projects for which their university of origin will give full academic recognition to the period of study spent abroad;

   (e) support will be provided for practical or in-company training periods of one month to one year for teachers, trainers, students and graduates of the eligible countries between the end of their studies and their first job, so that they can undertake a period of practical training in companies in the Community and vice versa;

   (v) activities to ensure the success of a JEP involving two or more eligible countries.

Structural and/or complementary measures

Financial support will be provided for certain structural and/or complementary measures (particularly technical assistance, seminars, studies, publications, information activities) to support the objectives of the programme, particularly the development and restructuring of higher education systems in the eligible countries. Under the structural measures, financial aid will be granted to assist the eligible countries *inter alia* to:

— develop and strengthen the capacity for strategic planning and institutional development of higher education establishments at university or faculty level,

— establish a development plan for universities to help them build up international relations,
— support the spread of durable cooperation actions targeting the Tempus objectives,
— prepare a national strategy in a given eligible country to develop a specific aspect of higher education.

Individual grants

In addition to the JEPs and the structural and/or complementary measures, the European Community will also support the provision of individual grants to teachers, trainers, university administrators, senior ministerial officials, education planners and other experts in training from eligible countries or from the Community, for visits to promote the quality, development and restructuring of higher education and training in the eligible countries.

These visits could *inter alia* cover the following areas:

— the development of courses and teaching material,
— the development of staff, particularly through periods of refresher training and in-company placements,
— teaching and training assignments,
— activities to support the development of higher education,
— participation in the activities of European associations, in particular university associations.

Support actions

1. The Commission will receive the technical assistance needed to underpin the action taken pursuant to this Decision and to monitor programme implementation.

2. Support will be provided for appropriate external evaluation of Tempus III. Support will also be provided for dissemination in relation to JEPs, structural and/or complementary measures and individual mobility and for dissemination of successful outcomes from specific projects in earlier stages of the Tempus programme.

**Decision No 68/2000/EC of the European Parliament and of the Council
of 13 December 1999
amending the basic Decision relating to the Socrates programme
so as to include Turkey among the beneficiary countries**

(OJ L 10, 14.1.2000)

I

(Acts whose publication is obligatory)

DECISION No 68/2000/EC OF THE EUROPEAN PARLIAMENT AND OF THE COUNCIL
of 13 December 1999
amending the basic Decision relating to the Socrates programme so as to include Turkey among the beneficiary countries

THE EUROPEAN PARLIAMENT AND THE COUNCIL OF THE EUROPEAN UNION,

Having regard to the Treaty establishing the European Community, and in particular Articles 149 and 150 thereof,

Having regard to the proposal from the Commission [1],

Having regard to the opinion of the Economic and Social Committee [2],

Having regard to the opinion of the Committee of the Regions [3],

Acting in accordance with the procedure laid down in Article 251 of the Treaty [4],

Whereas:

(1) Decision No 819/95/EC of the European Parliament and of the Council of 14 March 1995 establishes the Community action programme Socrates [5] in which Turkey does not participate;

(2) Turkey is an associated country whose links with the Community have been substantially bolstered with the entry into force of the final phase of the Customs Union;

(3) the economic and trade links instituted by the Customs Union should be strengthened by closer cooperation in the field of education, training and youth;

(4) a considerable amount of time needs to be allowed, on the one hand, between the amendment of the Decision establishing the said programme, which is the subject of this Decison, enabling it to be opened up to Turkey and the end of the negotiations on the arrangements (particularly financial arrangements) for Turkey's participation and, on the other, between the end of those negotiations and its actual participation;

(5) the principle of such an opening-up, however, apart from giving a tangible sign of the European Union's oft-repeated willingness to develop sectoral cooperation with Turkey, makes it possible to undertake preparatory measures and measures to increase awareness, with a view to full participation in the said programme or in the future framework programme which is currently being drawn up,

HAVE DECIDED AS FOLLOWS:

Article 1

The second sentence of Article 7(3) of Decision No 819/95/EC shall be replaced by the following:

'This programme shall be open to the participation of Cyprus, Malta and Turkey on the basis of additional appropriations in accordance with procedures to be agreed with the countries in question, taking as a starting point the rules applied to the European Free Trade Association countries, and in compliance with the provisions of Article 3 of the current Financial Regulation.'

Article 2

This Decision concerns full or partial participation at the earliest possible date by Turkey in the Socrates programme in its current form, to the extent permitted by negotiations, as well as the launch of preparatory measures or measures to increase awareness with a view to such participation or to that provided for under the future framework programme (2000 to 2004).

Article 3

The purpose of the participation of Turkey in the Socrates programme is to enable genuine exchanges to take place between young people from both sides and the staff accompanying them, while respecting their linguistic, educational and cultural diversity, in accordance with Article 149(1) of the Treaty, and the rights of minorities.

---
[1] OJ C 186, 26.6.1996, p. 8.
[2] OJ C 158, 26.5.1997, p. 74.
[3] OJ C 293, 13.10.1999, p. 23.
[4] Opinion of the European Parliament of 25 February 1999 (OJ C 153, 1.6.1999, p. 19), common position of the Council of 12 July 1999 (OJ C 249, 1.9.1999, p. 1) and Decision of the European Parliament of 28 October 1999 (not yet published in the Official Journal).
[5] OJ L 87, 20.4.1995, p. 10.

Article 4

The European Parliament shall be kept informed of the various measures taken to implement this Decision.

Article 5

This Decision shall enter into force on the day of its publication in the *Official Journal of the European Communities*.

Done at Brussels, 13 December 1999.

For the European Parliament	*For the Council*
The President	*The President*
N. FONTAINE	S. HASSI

**Resolution of the Council and of the Ministers for Youth meeting within the Council
of 17 December 1999
on the non-formal education dimension of sporting activities
in the European Community youth programmes**

(OJ C 8, 12.1.2000)

RESOLUTION OF THE COUNCIL AND OF THE MINISTERS FOR YOUTH MEETING WITHIN THE COUNCIL

of 17 December 1999

on the non-formal education dimension of sporting activities in the European Community youth programmes

(2000/C 8/03)

THE COUNCIL OF THE EUROPEAN UNION AND THE MINISTERS FOR YOUTH MEETING WITHIN THE COUNCIL,

Having regard to Decision No 818/95/EC of the European Parliament and of the Council of 14 March 1995 adopting the third phase of the 'Youth for Europe' programme [1],

Having regard to Decision No 1686/98/EC of the European Parliament and of the Council of 20 July 1998 establishing the Community action programme 'European voluntary service for young people' [2],

Whereas:

(1) the Declaration on sport annexed to the Treaty of Amsterdam emphasises the social significance of sport, in particular its role in forging identity and bringing people together;

(2) the European Parliament Resolution on the role of the European Union in the field of sports [3] calls on the Commission, in particular, to take account of sport across the entire spectrum of its activities, especially in the regional, social, educational, youth training and health fields,

(1) NOTE that the European Community youth programmes aim, *inter alia*, at promoting young people's integration through non-formal education and that in this context sporting activities are a useful means and not an end, and emphasises that young people's sporting activities may have a pedagogical value and also promote active citizenship, participation, solidarity and tolerance;

(2) RECOGNISE that sporting activities form part of young people's everyday life in that, alongside traditional, organised youth sports, there are growing youth sporting activities stemming from young people's own needs, which are an integral part of the rich variety of youth cultures;

(3) CONSIDER that sporting activities with pedagogical aims and objectives may contribute to the strengthening of the civil society and play an important role in the socialisation and social integration of young people, in particular as regards disadvantaged and disaffected young people;

(4) ARE AWARE that sporting activities, with pedagogical aims and objectives can provide a useful means of preventing and combating chauvinistic and xenophobic attitudes and behaviour which are priority aims in youth work, promote dialogue between generations and help to overcome various forms of risk behaviour and promote social inclusion;

INVITE the Commission of the European Communities to devise, in cooperation with the Member States, a coherent approach with a view to exploiting the non-formal educational potential of sporting activities in the context of European cooperationg policy in the youth field. Such an approach could:

(i) encourage cooperation between youth and sports bodies with a view to promoting exchange of best practice in this field and to providing room for youth sporting activities which address the needs of young people in the area of non-formal education while ensuring the equal access of all young people;

(ii) capitalise on the potential inherent in sporting activities in terms of the implementation of the youth, education and training programmes and ensure that youth sporting projects are fully in line with the pedagogical aims and objectives, priorities and criteria of the programmes;

(iii) encourage the development of appropriate youth worker training schemes addressed to those involved in sporting activities so as to improve their knowledge and skills to carry out youth projects at European level;

(iv) identify priority themes in work with young people which can be promoted through sporting activities, such as democracy, participation, tolerance, mutual understanding, the dialogue between generations and sustainable social and environmental development.

---

[1] OJ L 87, 20.4.1995.
[2] OJ L 214, 31.7.1998.
[3] OJ C 200, 30.6.1997, p. 252.

**Council Resolution
of 17 December 1999
on "Into the new millennium": developing new working procedures
for European cooperation in the field of education and training**

(OJ C 8, 12.1.2000)

COUNCIL RESOLUTION

of 17 December 1999

on 'Into the new millennium': developing new working procedures for European cooperation in the field of education and training

(2000/C 8/04)

THE COUNCIL OF THE EUROPEAN UNION,

(1) NOTING that, according to the Treaty establishing the European Community, the Community is to contribute to the development of quality education by encouraging cooperation between Member States and, if necessary, by supporting and supplementing their activities, while respecting the principle of subsidiarity and the responsibility of Member States for the content and organisation of their own education systems. At the same time, the Commission has the right of initiative in the fields falling under Community competence;

(2) NOTING that both the Treaty of Amsterdam and the EU's Agenda 2000 document have resulted in an increase in the importance placed on education in skill and information-related policies, including those which contribute to economic competitiveness and employment in the European Union; that the development of a Europe of knowledge and the promotion of lifelong learning have become shared overall objectives;

(3) AWARE that the Socrates and Leonardo da Vinci programmes remain the most important instruments of cooperation in education and training within Europe; that it has however become clear that political cooperation at European level needs to be reinforced. In order to achieve this, new working procedures for the Council must be developed in the field of education and training so that the effectiveness of the Council's work can be further improved;

(4) STRESSES the need for a coherent approach to action to Community level in the field of education and training and believes that cooperation in these fields could be reinforced by creating a structured framework for political discussions and activities over the coming years;

(5) CONSIDERS that future work in the field of education and training could be organised around a 'rolling agenda', based on priority themes which would be included on the Council's agenda at regular intervals and which could therefore extend over several Presidencies. These priority themes would be discussed according to a cyclical model made up of a number of flexible steps:

— the Council discusses priority themes of common interest — submitted either by Member States or the Commission — and agrees, if appropriate, how to take forward individual themes,

— the Member States are invited to inform the Commission of relevant political initiatives and examples of best practice at national level in relation to the agreed priority themes,

— the Commission provides a summary analysis of the information supplied by Member States to the Council. This should also cover relevant Community action,

— the Council considers the Commission's analysis and, where appropriate, decides on future initiatives;

(6) STRESSES that the principal objective in developing such a framework would be to enable greater continuity, efficiency and effectiveness and a strengthening of the political impact of Community cooperation in the field of education and training. The new framework for cooperation would enable a more effective exchange of information and good practice. In addition, it could contribute to increased synergies between European cooperation in the field of education and training and other relevant policy fields;

(7) EMPHASISES the central role of the Presidency in the implementation of the rolling agenda, in particular by ensuring continuity and by maintaining the momentum of the process;

(8) STRESSES that this basic model and its components should be implemented whilst fully respecting the prerogatives of the Commission. It would need to be operated flexibly, taking into account new political developments as appropriate;

(9) UNDERLINES the importance of the European Parliament being regularly informed about the discussions and the progress achieved in the framework of the 'rolling agenda';

(10) CONSIDERS that the new framework of cooperation should be implemented from the beginning of 2000, especially where the basic elements of a 'rolling agenda' already exist as set out in the Annex;

(11) INVITES the Commission, in cooperation with the Member States, to work up more detailed measures for taking the 'rolling agenda' forward.

ANNEX

INDICATIVE THEMES TO BE CONSIDERED IN THE FRAMEWORK OF THE ROLLING AGENDA

Within the overall context of lifelong learning the abovementioned framework for cooperation could, in the first instance, be established in particular in the following fields:

— role of education and training in employment policies,

— develompent of quality education and training at all levels,

— promotion of mobility, including recognition of qualifications and periods of study.

Other areas for cooperation will be explored on a regular basis taking into account relevant political developments in future years.

**Council Conclusions
of 21 December 1999
on the implementation of measures to combat child sex tourism**

(OJ C 379, 31.12.1999)

I

(Information)

COUNCIL

COUNCIL CONCLUSIONS

of 21 December 1999

on the implementation of measures to combat child sex tourism

(1999/C 379/01)

THE COUNCIL OF THE EUROPEAN UNION,

1. DENOUNCES AND CONDEMS child sex tourism as a serious violation of the rights of the child and human dignity;

2. RECALLS the United Nations Convention of 1989 on the Rights of the Child on the occasion of its 10th anniversary and the Plan for Action adopted by the World Congress on Sexual Exploitation of children held in Stockholm in 1996;

3. CALLING for rapid progress in the work on the elaboration of the optional protocol to the Convention of the Rights of the Child on the sale of children, child prostitution and child pornography with a view to the successful conclusion of the work in the year 2000;

4. WELCOMES the Commission communication of 26 May 1999 on the implementation of measures to combat child sex tourism as a report on the progress achieved in the fight against sex tourism for the period 1997 to 1998 in the following four areas of action: improving knowledge of the phenomenon of child sex tourism; strengthening the effectiveness of laws and law enforcement, including extra-territorial criminal law; intensifying efforts to stem the flow of sex tourists from Member States; and developing measures to combat sex tourism in non-member countries;

5. EMPHASISES the cross-sectoral nature of the fight against child sex tourism, requiring at all levels of action a coordinated and integrated approach combining justice and home affairs, social affairs, health, education, tourism, new information technologies and internal market, as well as external policies and human rights;

6. WELCOMES the European Union initiatives to protect children in the context of Joint Action 97/154/JHA of 24 February 1997 concerning action to combat trafficking in human beings and sexual abuse of children [1], Common Position (EC) No 37/1999 of 13 September 1999 adopted by the Council with a view to adopting a Decision of the European Parliament and of the Council adopting a programme of Community action (the Daphne programme) (2000 to 2003) on preventive measures to fight violence against children, young people and women [2]; Joint Action 96/700/JHA of 29 November 1996 establishing an incentive and exchange programme for persons responsible for combating trade in human beings and the sexual exploitation of children [3] (the STOP programme, covering the period 1996 to 2000); and the actions aimed at combating child pornography on the Internet;

7. URGES the Commission and the Member States to continue and further develop appropriate initiatives to combat child sex tourism in the four areas of action outlined in the Commission communication, based on a cross-pillar approach;

8. CONSIDERS it necessary for the Commission and the Member States to continue supporting awareness-raising activities and encouraging the development of codes of conduct and other self-regulatory schemes in the tourism industry, placing a particular emphasis on their effective implementation;

9. WELCOMES all efforts to develop measures on combating child sex tourism through prevention, suppression, and support for the victims in those countries where children are specially prone to such abuse, and urges intensified efforts to stop the flow of child sex tourism from the Member States.

10. INVITES the Commission and the Member States to ensure that all development and cooperation policies support the fight against child sex tourism;

11. CALLS ON the Commission and the Member States to work together closely in a complementary and coordinated way, within their respective spheres of competence and in cooperation with relevant organisations, to combat child sex tourism as a specific contribution to the general objective of child protection.

---

[1] OJ L 63, 4.3.1997, p. 2.
[2] OJ C 317, 4.11.1999, p. 1.
[3] OJ L 322, 12.12.1996, p. 7.

**Decision No 253/2000/EC of the European Parliament and of the Council
of 24 January 2000
establishing the second phase of the Community action programme
in the field of education "Socrates"**

(OJ L 28, 3.2.2000)

I

(Acts whose publication is obligatory)

DECISION No 253/2000/EC OF THE EUROPEAN PARLIAMENT AND OF THE COUNCIL
of 24 January 2000
establishing the second phase of the Community action programme in the field of education 'Socrates'

THE EUROPEAN PARLIAMENT AND THE COUNCIL OF THE EUROPEAN UNION,

Having regard to the Treaty establishing the European Community and in particular Articles 149 and 150 thereof,

Having regard to the proposal from the Commission [1],

Having regard to the opinion of the Economic and Social Committee [2],

Having regard to the opinion of the Committee of the Regions [3],

Acting in accordance with the procedure laid down in Article 251 of the Treaty [4],

In the light of the joint text approved by the Conciliation Committee on 10 November 1999,

Whereas:

(1) the Treaty establishing the European Community provides that the latter's action shall contribute, *inter alia*, to the development of quality education and training; measures under this programme should promote the European dimension of education and contribute to the development of quality education with a view to encouraging life-long learning;

(2) by Decision No 819/95/EC the European Parliament and the Council established the Community action programme Socrates [5];

(3) the extraordinary European Council on employment held in Luxembourg on 20 and 21 November 1997 recognised that lifelong education and training can make an important contribution to the Member States' employment policies in order to enhance employability, adaptability and the culture of entrepreneurship and to promote equal opportunities;

(4) in its communication 'Towards a Europe of Knowledge', the Commission set out guidelines for the creation of an open and dynamic European education area capable of achieving the objective of life-long education and training;

(5) in its White Paper 'Teaching and learning — Towards the learning society', the Commission stated that the emergence of the learning society entails encouraging the acquisition of new knowledge and to this end providing motivation to learn at every opportunity; and in its Green Paper 'Education, training, research: the obstacles to transnational mobility', the Commission highlighted the advantages of mobility for people and competitiveness in the European Union;

(6) the Commission's aim, in line with the European Parliament's wish, is to attain a participation rate of around 10 % of schools under the Comenius action and of around 10 % of students in the mobility activities under the Erasmus action;

(7) there is a need to promote active citizenship and to step up the fight against exclusion in all its forms, including racism and xenophobia; special attention should be focused on promoting equality and furthering equal opportunities for women and men; whereas special attention should be given to persons with special needs;

(8) the European Parliament and the Council, in their Decision on youth, and the Council, in Decision 1999/382/EC on training [6], have established Community action programmes for the youth and training fields respectively, which contribute, together with the Socrates programme, to promoting a Europe of knowledge;

---
[1] OJ C 314, 13.10.1998, p. 5.
[2] OJ C 410, 30.12.1998, p. 2.
[3] OJ C 51, 22.2.1999, p. 77.
[4] Opinion of the European Parliament of 5 November 1998 (OJ C 359, 23.11.1998, p. 60), Council common position of 21 December 1998 (OJ C 49, 22.2.1999, p. 42), Decision of the European Parliament of 25 February 1999 (OJ C 153, 1.6.1999, p. 24) and Decision of the European Parliament of 15 December 1999 (not yet published in the Official Journal). Council Decision of 17 December 1999.
[5] OJ L 87, 20.4.1995, p. 10. Decision as amended by Decision No 576/98/EC (OJ L 77, 14.3.1998, p. 1).
[6] OJ L 146, 11.6.1999, p. 33.

(9) it is necessary, in order to reinforce the added value of Community action, that the Commission, in cooperation with the Member States, should ensure, at all levels, a coherence and a complementarity between the actions implemented in the framework of this Decision and other relevant Community policies, instruments and actions;

(10) it is necessary to provide for the possibility of organising joint activities involving the Socrates programme and other Community programmes or actions that have an educational dimension, thus encouraging synergies and reinforcing the added value of Community action;

(11) the Agreement on the European Economic Area (EEA Agreement) provides for greater cooperation in the field of education, training and youth between the European Community and its Member States, on the one hand, and the countries of the European Free Trade Association participating in the European Economic Area (EFTA/EEA countries), on the other;

(12) provision should be made to open up this programme to participation of the associated central and eastern European countries (CEEC), in accordance with the conditions established in the Europe agreements, in their additional protocols and in the decisions of the respective Association Councils, of Cyprus funded by additional appropriations in accordance with the procedures to be agreed with that country, as well as of Malta and Turkey, funded by additional appropriations in accordance with the provisions of the Treaty;

(13) this programme should be regularly monitored and evaluated in cooperation between the Commission and the Member States in order to allow for readjustments, particularly in the priorities for implementing the measures; whereas the evaluation should include an external evaluation to be conducted by independent, impartial bodies;

(14) in accordance with the principles of subsidiarity and proportionality as defined in Article 5 of the Treaty, since the objectives of the proposed action concerning the contribution of European cooperation to quality education cannot be sufficiently achieved by the Member States, *inter alia*, because of the need for multilateral partnerships, multilateral mobility and Community-wide exchanges of information, they can therefore be better achieved by the Community owing to the transnational dimension of the Community actions and measures; this Decision does not go beyond what is necessary to achieve those objectives;

(15) improvement of the European credit transfer system (ECTS) is an effective means of ensuring that mobility fully attains its objectives; universities participating in the programme are to be encouraged to make the widest possible use of the ECTS;

(16) this Decision lays down, for the entire duration of the programme, a financial framework constituting the prime reference, within the meaning of point 33 of the interinstitutional agreement of 6 May 1999 between the European Parliament, the Council and the Commission [1], on budgetary discipline and improvement of the budgetary procedure;

(17) the measures necessary for the implementation of this Decision should be adopted in accordance with Council Decision 1999/468/EC of 28 June 1999 laying down the procedures for the exercise of implementing powers conferred on the Commission [2],

HAVE DECIDED AS FOLLOWS:

Article 1

Establishment of the programme

1. This Decision establishes the second phase of the Community action programme in the field of education, 'Socrates', hereinafter referred to as 'this programme'.

2. This programme shall be implemented over the period starting on 1 January 2000 and ending on 31 December 2006.

3. This programme shall contribute to the promotion of a Europe of knowledge through the development of the European dimension in education and training by promoting life-long learning, based on formal and informal education and training. It shall support the building up of the knowledge, skills and competences likely to foster active citizenship and employability.

4. This programme shall support and supplement action taken by and in the Member States, while fully respecting their responsibility for the content of education and the organisation of education and training systems, and their cultural and linguistic diversity.

Article 2

Objectives of the programme

In order to contribute to the development of quality education and encourage life-long learning, while fully respecting the responsibility of the Member States, the objectives of the programme shall be:

(a) to strengthen the European dimension in education at all levels and to facilitate wide transnational access to educational resources in Europe while promoting equal opportunities throughout all fields of education;

(b) to promote a quantitative and qualitative improvement of the knowledge of the languages of the European Union, in particular those languages which are less widely used and less widely taught, so as to lead to greater understanding and solidarity between the peoples of the European Union and promote the intercultural dimension of education;

---
[1] OJ C 172, 18.6.1999, p. 1.
[2] OJ L 184, 17.7.1999, p. 23.

(c) to promote cooperation and mobility in the field of education, in particular by:

— encouraging exchanges between educational institutions,

— promoting open and distance learning,

— encouraging improvements in the recognition of diplomas and periods of study,

— developing the exchange of information,

and to help remove the obstacles in this regard;

(d) to encourage innovation in the development of educational practices and materials including, where appropriate, the use of new technologies, and to explore matters of common policy interest in the field of education.

Article 3

Community actions

1. The objectives of this programme as set out in Article 2 shall be pursued by means of the following actions, the operational content and the application procedures of which are described in the Annex:

Action 1 School education (Comenius);

Action 2 Higher education (Erasmus);

Action 3 Adult education and other educational pathways (Grundtvig);

Action 4 Teaching and learning of languages (Lingua);

Action 5 Open and distance learning; information and communication technologies in the field of education (Minerva);

Action 6 Observation and innovation;

Action 7 Joint actions;

Action 8 Accompanying measures.

2. These actions shall be implemented through the following types of measures, in the form of transnational operations which may combine several of the measures:

(a) support for the transnational mobility of people in the field of education in Europe;

(b) support for the use of information and communication technologies (ICT) in education;

(c) support for the development of transnational cooperation networks facilitating the exchange of experience and good practice;

(d) promotion of language skills and understanding of different cultures;

(e) support for innovatory pilot projects based on transnational partnerships designed to develop innovation and quality in education;

(f) constant improvement of Community reference material through the

— observation and analysis of national education policies,

— observation and dissemination of good practice and innovation,

— comprehensive exchange of information.

Article 4

Access to the programme

1. Under the conditions and arrangements for implementation specified in the Annex, this programme is aimed in particular at:

(a) pupils, students or other learners;

(b) staff directly involved in education;

(c) all types of educational institutions specified by each Member State;

(d) the persons and bodies responsible for education systems and policies at local, regional and national level within the Member States.

2. Public or private bodies cooperating with educational institutions may also take part in appropriate actions under this programme, in particular:

— local and regional bodies and organisations,

— associations working in the field of education, including students', pupils', teachers' and parents' associations,

— companies and consortia, trade organisations and Chambers of Commerce and Industry,

— social partners and their organisations at all levels,

— research centres and bodies.

Article 5

Implementation of the programme and cooperation with the Member States

1. The Commission shall

— ensure the implementation of the Community actions covered by this programme in conformity with the Annex,

— consult the social partners and relevant associations in the field of education at European level and shall inform the Committee referred to in Article 8(1) of their opinions.

2. The Member States shall

— take the necessary steps to ensure the efficient running of the programme at Member State level involving all the parties concerned in education in accordance with national practice,

— establish an appropriate structure for the coordinated management of the implementation of the programme's actions at Member State level (Socrates national agencies),

— endeavour to adopt such measures as they deem appropriate to remove legal and administrative obstacles to access to this programme,

— take steps to ensure that potential synergies with other Community programmes are realised at Member State level.

3. The Commission, in cooperation with the Member States, shall ensure

— the transition between those actions carried out within the framework of the preceding programme in the field of education (Socrates, established by Decision No 819/95/EC) and those to be implemented under this programme,

— the dissemination of the results of the actions undertaken within the framework of the preceding programme in the field of education (Socrates) and of those to be implemented under this programme,

— appropriate information, publicity and follow-up with regard to actions supported by this programme.

Article 6

Joint Actions

As part of the process of building up a Europe of knowledge, the measures contained in this programme may be implemented in accordance with the procedures laid down in Article 8(2) as joint actions with related Community programmes and actions, particularly Leonardo da Vinci and Youth as well as Community programmes in the field of research and development and new technologies.

Article 7

Implementing measures

1. The measures necessary for the implementation of this Decision relating to the matters referred to below shall be adopted in accordance with the management procedure referred to in Article 8(2).

(a) the annual plan of work, including priorities, themes for joint actions and the selection criteria and procedures;

(b) the financial support to be supplied by the Community (amounts, duration and recipients) and the general guidelines for implementing the programme;

(c) the annual budget and the breakdown of funds among the different actions of the programme;

(d) the breakdown of funds among the Member States for the actions to be managed on a decentralised basis;

(e) the arrangements for monitoring and evaluating the programme and for the dissemination and transfer of results;

(f) Commission proposals for project selection, including those under action 7 (Joint actions).

2. The measures necessary for the implementation of this Decision relating to all other matters shall be adopted in accordance with the advisory procedure referred to in Article 8(3).

Article 8

Committee

1. The Commission shall be assisted by a Committee.

2. Where reference is made to this paragraph, Articles 4 and 7 of Decision 1999/468/EC shall apply, having regard to the provisions of Article 8 thereof.

The period laid down in Article 4(3) of Decision 1999/468/EC shall be set at two months.

3. Where reference is made to this paragraph, Articles 3 and 7 of Decision 1999/468/EC shall apply, having regard to the provisions of Article 8 thereof.

4. The Committee shall adopt its rules of procedure.

Article 9

Cooperation with other programme committees and information on other Community initiatives

1. The Committee shall establish regular and structured cooperation with the Committee set up within the framework of the Leonardo da Vinci action programme for the implementation of a Community vocational training policy as well as with the Committee set up within the framework of the Youth Community action programme.

2. To ensure the consistency of this programme with other measures referred to in Article 11, the Commission shall keep the Committee regularly informed about Community initiatives taken in the fields of education, training and youth, including cooperation with third countries and international organisations.

Article 10

Funding

1. The financial framework for the implementation of this programme for the period specified in Article 1 is hereby set at EUR 1 850 million.

2. The annual appropriations shall be authorised by the budgetary authority within the limits of the financial perspective.

Article 11

Consistency and complementarity

1. The Commission shall, in cooperation with the Member States, ensure overall consistency and complementarity with other relevant Community policies, instruments and actions. The programme shall contribute to achieving the aims of Community policy in the areas of equality, equal opportunities for women and men and promotion of social inclusion.

The Commission shall ensure an efficient link-up between this programme and the programmes and actions in the area of education undertaken within the framework of the Community's cooperation with third countries and the competent international organisations.

2. In implementing the measures of this programme, the Commission and the Member States shall have regard to the priorities set out in the employment guidelines adopted by the Council, as part of a coordinated employment strategy.

Article 12

Participation of the EFTA/EEA countries, the associated central and eastern European countries (CEEC), Cyprus, Malta and Turkey

This programme shall be open to the participation of
— the EFTA/EEA countries in accordance with the conditions established in the EEA agreement,
— the associated central and eastern European countries (CEEC) in accordance with the conditions established in the Europe agreements, in their additional protocols and in the decisions of the respective Association Councils,
— Cyprus, funded by additional appropriations in accordance with procedures to be agreed with that country,
— Malta and Turkey, funded by additional appropriations in accordance with the provisions of the Treaty.

Article 13

International cooperation

Under this programme, and in accordance with the procedure laid down in Article 8(2), the Commission may cooperate with third countries and with the competent international organisations, in particular the Council of Europe.

Article 14

Monitoring and evaluation

1. The Commission shall regularly monitor this programme in cooperation with the Member States. The results of the monitoring and evaluation process should be utilised when implementing the programme.

This monitoring shall include the reports referred to in paragraph 3 and specific activities.

2. This programme shall be evaluated regularly by the Commission in cooperation with the Member States. This evaluation is intended to assess the relevance, effectiveness and impact of actions implemented with regard to the objectives referred to in Article 2. It will also look at the impact of the programme as a whole.

This evaluation will also examine the complementarity between action under this programme and that pursued under other relevant Community policies, instruments and actions.

In accordance with criteria established using the procedure described in Article 8(2), there will be regular independent external evaluations of this programme.

3. Member States shall submit to the Commission by 31 December 2003 and 30 June 2007, respectively, reports on the implementation and the impact of this programme.

4. The Commission shall submit to the European Parliament, the Council, the Economic and Social Committee and the Committee of the Regions:

— on the accession of new Member States, a report on the financial consequences of these accessions on the programme, followed, if appropriate, by financial proposals to deal with the financial consequences of these accessions on the programme, in accordance with the provisions of the interinstitutional Agreement of 6 May 1999 between the European Parliament, the Council and the Commission on budgetary discipline and improvement of the budgetary procedure and with the conclusions of the Berlin European Council of March 1999. The European Parliament and the Council will take a decision on such proposals as soon as possible,
— an interim evaluation report on the results achieved and on the qualitative and quantitative aspects of the implementation of this programme by 30 June 2004,
— a communication on the continuation of this programme by 31 December 2006,
— an *ex post* evaluation report by 31 December 2007.

Article 15

Entry into force

This Decision shall enter into force on the date of its publication in the *Official Journal of the European Communities*.

Done at Brussels, 24 January 2000.

For the European Parliament	*For the Council*
The President	*The President*
N. FONTAINE	J. GAMA

ANNEX

I. INTRODUCTION AND GENERAL PROVISIONS

1. The objectives laid down in Article 2 are to be implemented by means of the actions set out in this Annex on the basis of the Community measures described in Article 3.

2. The provisions relating to the timetable, the conditions for the submission of applications and the eligibility and selection criteria are to be determined in accordance with Article 8(2) and published regularly by the Commission in the 'Socrates Guidelines for Applicants'. In addition calls for proposals will be published, specifying all deadlines for the submission of proposals.

3. In the context of activities involving the mobility of persons, adequate linguistic preparation should be provided in order to ensure that the beneficiaries possess the necessary competence in the language(s) of instruction in the host establishment. Appropriate organisational arrangements should be made at the home and host establishments in order to ensure that maximum benefit is derived from the mobility activity in question.

4. The projects coordinated by universities under the various actions of the programme should form part of the 'institutional contract' of the institutions concerned provided for in Action 2.

5. Supporting measures may be taken to promote access and participation by persons with special educational needs. Where appropriate, positive actions may be taken in order to promote equal opportunities for women and men. Activities giving special emphasis to intercultural aspects or to promoting competence in other languages, in particular the less widely used and less taught languages of the Community, are to be particularly encouraged. The promotion of all types of open and distance learning, as well as the appropriate use of information and communication technology, is to be encouraged across all actions of the programme. Under all actions of the programme, particular attention will be paid to the dissemination of results.

II. COMMUNITY ACTIONS

This Annex contains two main types of actions:

— the first type, Actions 1 to 3, is aimed at the three basic stages of life-long education (school, university, other);

— the second type, Actions 4 to 8, concerns transversal measures in fields such as languages, information and communication technology (ICT) for educational purposes, including in particular educational multimedia and the exchange of information, as well as matters of horizontal interest such as innovation, the dissemination of results, joint actions and the evaluation of the programme.

ACTION 1:   'COMENIUS': SCHOOL EDUCATION

Action 1.1   **School partnerships**

Action 1.2   **Initial and in-service training of staff involved in school education**

Action 1.3   **Networks related to school partnerships and the training of staff involved in school education**

ACTION 2:   'ERASMUS': HIGHER EDUCATION

Action 2.1   **European interuniversity cooperation**

Action 2.2   **Mobility of students and university teachers**

Action 2.3   **Thematic networks**

ACTION 3:   'GRUNDTVIG': ADULT EDUCATION AND OTHER EDUCATIONAL PATHWAYS

ACTION 4:   'LINGUA': TEACHING AND LEARNING OF LANGUAGES

ACTION 5:   'MINERVA': OPEN AND DISTANCE LEARNING, INFORMATION AND COMMUNICATION TECHNOLOGIES IN THE FIELD OF EDUCATION

ACTION 6:   OBSERVATION AND INNOVATION

Action 6.1:   **Observation of education systems, policies and innovation**

Action 6.2:   **Innovatory initiatives responding to emerging needs**

ACTION 7:   JOINT ACTIONS

ACTION 8:   ACCOMPANYING MEASURES

ACTION 1: 'COMENIUS': SCHOOL EDUCATION

Comenius seeks to enhance the quality and reinforce the European dimension of school education, in particular by encouraging transnational cooperation between schools and contributing to improved professional development of staff directly involved in the school education sector, and to promote the learning of languages and intercultural awareness.

Action 1.1: **School partnerships**

1. The Community encourages the creation of multilateral partnerships between schools. Such partnerships may also involve other appropriate bodies, such as teacher training establishments, local institutions and authorities, businesses or cultural establishments as well as parents', pupils' and other relevant organisations.

2. Community financial assistance may be awarded for the following:

   (a) projects which focus on one or more topics of common interest to the participating schools, involving:

   — the participation of pupils in project preparation and project activities, including project-related mobility where appropriate,

   — the mobility of teachers to prepare and monitor a project or to teach in another Member State, including in-company placements,

   — the development of teaching material and the exchange of good practice;

   (b) projects aimed specifically at teaching and learning the official languages of the Community, together with Irish (one of the languages in which the Treaties establishing the European Communities are drawn up) and Lëtzeburgesch (a language spoken throughout the territory of Luxembourg), including in frontier regions of the Member States, the official languages of the Community in neighbouring regions of other Member States. The projects may be bilateral, especially where they target one of the less widely used or less widely taught of these languages and should include exchanges of pupils in addition to the activities referred to in point (a);

   (c) projects aimed at promoting intercultural awareness and in particular those designed to help combat racism and xenophobia or to address the specific needs of the children of migrant workers, gypsies and travellers and occupational travellers;

   (d) projects addressing issues related to pupils with special educational needs, with particular attention to the integration of such pupils into mainstream schooling.

3. Schools wishing to take part in this action shall submit a brief outline description of the activities which they plan to carry out during the coming school year within the framework of this programme ('Comenius Plan'). The Comenius Plan shall enable the Socrates national agencies to take into account the overall development of European activities of the respective school when carrying out the selection under this action.

Action 1.2: **Initial and in-service training of staff involved in school education**

1. The Community is to support multilateral projects undertaken by establishments and bodies active in the initial or in-service training of staff directly involved in school education. The participation of schools and other players involved in the field of education described in Article 4 of the Decision is to be encouraged, as is the involvement of supervisory bodies at regional and local level, where appropriate.

2. Community financial assistance may be awarded for the following:

   Mobility actions:

   (a) mobility undertaken for the purpose of initial training, including practical training periods, language assistantships and in-company placements;

   (b) mobility undertaken for the purpose of in-service training and updating the skills of trained school education staff;

   (c) mobility of limited duration, including immersion courses, for language teachers, staff retraining as language teachers, qualified teachers intending soon to return to employment as language teachers, and teaching staff of other disciplines required or wishing to teach in a foreign language;

   Multilateral cooperation projects concerning:

   (d) contributions to the development of curricula, courses, modules or teaching material in the context of reinforcing the European dimension of school education;

   (e) training activities and information exchange concerning school management and related services such as guidance and counselling;

(f) education and training activities and information exchange designed to enhance intercultural awareness in school education or to promote the integration and improved educational achievement of children of migrant workers, gypsies and travellers and occupational travellers;

(g) activities concerning the training and development of staff involved in the education of pupils at risk and of pupils with special educational needs.

Action 1.3: **Networks related to school partnerships and the training of staff involved in school education**

The Community is to promote the networking of school partnerships and of projects concerned with the training of staff involved in school education, supported within Actions 1.1 and 1.2 respectively, to enable cooperation to take place on subjects of mutual interest, the dissemination of results and good practice and discussion of qualitative and innovatory aspects of school education. The staff training networks are to be developed, where appropriate, in close cooperation with the university 'thematic networks' provided for in the Erasmus action.

ACTION 2: 'ERASMUS': HIGHER EDUCATION

Erasmus seeks to enhance the quality and reinforce the European dimension of higher education, to encourage transnational cooperation between universities, to boost European mobility in the higher education sector and to improve transparency and academic recognition of studies and qualifications throughout the Community.

Participating universities conclude 'institutional contracts' with the Commission covering all the Erasmus activities approved. Such contracts will normally be of three years' duration and will be renewable.

Action 2.1: **European interuniversity cooperation**

1. The Community supports interuniversity cooperation activities including the development of innovative projects, carried out by universities in conjunction with partners in other Member States, with the participation, where appropriate, of other players involved in education, as described in Article 4 of the Decision.

2. Community financial assistance may be awarded for the following:

   (a) the organisation of mobility of students and university teachers;

   (b) joint development and implementation of curricula, modules, intensive courses or other educational activities, including multidisciplinary activities and the teaching of subjects in other languages;

   (c) consolidation, extension and further development of the European credit transfer system (ECTS), which is designed to facilitate academic recognition in other Member States.

Action 2.2: **Mobility of students and university teachers**

1. The Community supports transnational mobility activities concerning:

   (a) students, in accordance with point 2;

   (b) university teachers, for the purpose of carrying out teaching assignments likely to enhance the European dimension or extend the range of courses offered by the universities concerned.

2. Students who, after completing at least their first year of studies, spend three to 12 months in another Member State within the framework of this Action, will be considered 'Erasmus students', regardless whether they have been awarded financial support in accordance with point 3. Such periods are fully recognised under the interuniversity agreements forming part of the institutional contracts and may include integrated in-company placements where appropriate. The host universities will not charge tuition fees to Erasmus students. Students with special needs will be given particular attention.

3. Community financial assistance may be awarded for:

   — the mobility of students. The Member States may, in awarding Community grants, take appropriate account of the economic situation of applicants. As the Community's contribution covers only part of the cost of students' mobility, Member States are invited to help provide the necessary funds. In this connection, grants or loans available to students in the Member State of origin shall continue to be paid during the period of study in a host Member State;

   — the mobility of university teachers;

   — preparatory measures, in accordance with Section IV B, point 4.

Action 2.3: **Thematic networks**

The Community promotes the development and consolidation of thematic networks, each enabling a large grouping of universities to cooperate on topics relating to one or more disciplines or on other matters of mutual interest in order to disseminate innovation, facilitate the spread of good practice, encourage discussion of qualitative and innovative aspects of higher education, improve teaching methods and stimulate the development of joint programmes and specialised courses. The involvement of representatives of learned societies, professional associations and socioeconomic circles is to be encouraged. Special attention will be paid to the dissemination of results.

ACTION 3: 'GRUNDTVIG': ADULT EDUCATION AND OTHER EDUCATIONAL PATHWAYS

1. As a complement to Action 1 (school education) and Action 2 (higher education), Grundtvig seeks to encourage the European dimension of life-long learning, to contribute — through enhanced transnational cooperation — to innovation and improved availability, accessibility and quality of other educational pathways, and to promote the learning of languages. The action is thus addressed to people who, at whatever stage of their life, seek access to knowledge and competences within the framework of formal or non-formal education or by means of autonomous learning, thereby increasing their intercultural awareness and employability and enhancing their capacity to progress in education and play a full and active role in society.

2. Community financial assistance may be awarded for transnational projects and initiatives seeking to promote:

    (a) adults' individual demand for and their participation in life-long learning activities;

    (b) acquisition or updating of competences for persons lacking basic education and qualifications;

    (c) the development, exchange and dissemination of innovative educational approaches and good practice, including the development and dissemination of modules and appropriate teaching material;

    (d) the development of information and support services for adult learners and for providers of adult education, including services related to guidance and counselling;

    (e) the development of tools and methods for the assessment, validation or certification of the knowledge, skills and competences acquired by adult learners, including by means of experiential or autonomous learning or through non-formal education;

    (f) improved competence in other Community languages or enhanced international awareness among adult learners and those involved in the provision of adult education;

    (g) the development of initial or in-service training for educational staff working in this sector;

    (h) visits and exchanges, for persons including those providing adult education or the training of adult educators;

    (i) projects addressing adult learners with special educational needs.

3. The Community encourages the creation of European networks to strengthen the links between the various parties involved in this area to enable them to cooperate on a more stable basis on matters of common interest, and to enhance their awareness of the European dimension of education.

ACTION 4: 'LINGUA': TEACHING AND LEARNING OF LANGUAGES

1. The aim of the Lingua action is to support transversal measures relating to the learning of languages, with a view to helping to promote and maintain linguistic diversity within the Community, to improve the quality of language teaching and learning and to facilitate access to life-long language learning opportunities tailored to individual requirements. Particular attention is to be given to intensifying transnational contacts in the language teaching profession and among those responsible for language teaching policies throughout the Community in all educational sectors. In this way, Lingua both complements and enriches measures related to the promotion of language-learning under other actions of this programme, in particular Actions 1, 2 and 3.

2. In this context, language teaching covers the teaching and learning as foreign languages of all the official languages of the Community, together with Irish (one of the languages in which the Treaties establishing the European Communities are drawn up) and Lëtzeburgesch (a language spoken throughout the territory of Luxembourg). Special attention shall be paid throughout the programme to promoting the less widely used and less widely taught of these languages.

3. Community financial assistance may be awarded to the following transnational language-learning projects and activities:

   (a) awareness-raising activities designed to draw attention to the importance of language-learning and the availability of language-learning opportunities;

   (b) activities seeking to promote and/or spread innovations and good practice, such as the early learning of languages or multilingual comprehension;

   (c) the development and exchange of curricula, production of new teaching material and improvement of methods and tools for the recognition of language competence;

   (d) exchange of information and transnational networking of resource centres;

   (e) the development of measures to promote competence in foreign languages as required in specific situations and contexts, and insofar as these are not related to specific professions;

   (f) addressing issues related to the teaching and learning of languages arising from further enlargement of the Community.

ACTION 5: 'MINERVA' OPEN AND DISTANCE LEARNING, INFORMATION AND COMMUNICATION TECHNOLOGIES IN THE FIELD OF EDUCATION

1. The aim of this action is to support transversal measures relating to open and distance learning (ODL) and the use of information and communication technologies (ICT), including multimedia, in the field of education. In so doing, it complements and enriches the corresponding measures provided for within the other actions of this programme.

   These measures serve a triple purpose:

   — to promote improved understanding among teachers, learners, educational decision-makers and the public at large of the implications of ODL and, in particular ICT for education, and the critical, responsible use of tools and methods which utilise such technologies for educational purposes,

   — to support awareness of the need to ensure that pedagogical considerations are given proper weight in the development of ICT-based educational products, notably multimedia, and

   — to promote access to improved methods and educational resources and to results achieved, in particular through transnational exchange of information, experience and good practice.

2. Community financial assistance may be awarded for the following:

   (a) projects and studies aimed at helping those involved in education to understand and exploit the innovative processes under way, in particular those relating to the use of ICT in teaching and learning, the development of innovative instruments and approaches, and methods for establishing criteria for quality assessment of ICT-based educational products and services;

   (b) projects to develop and test new methods, modules and resources for ODL and ICT;

   (c) projects for the development and interconnection of services and systems providing information for teachers, decision-makers and other actors involved in education on educational methods and resources which utilise ODL and ICT;

   (d) activities to support the exchange of ideas and experience relating to ODL and the use of ICT in education, in particular the networking of resource centres, teacher training institutions, experts, decision-makers and project coordinators on subjects of common interest.

ACTION 6: OBSERVATION AND INNOVATION

This action contributes to improving the quality and transparency of education systems and furthering the process of educational innovation in Europe through the exchange of information and experience, the identification of good practice, the comparative analysis of systems and policies in this field, and the discussion and analysis of matters of common educational policy interest to be determined by the Council.

Action 6.1: **Observation of education systems, policies and innovation**

1. Making optimal use of existing structures wherever possible, this action consists of the following:

    (a) collection of descriptive and statistical data, and comparative analysis of educational systems and policies in the Member States;

    (b) development of methods for evaluating the quality of education, including the development of appropriate criteria and indicators;

    (c) development and updating of databases and other information resources on innovatory experiments;

    (d) dissemination of experience resulting from relevant activities supported at Community and Member State level;

    (e) facilitation of the recognition of diplomas, qualifications and periods of learning at all educational levels in other Member States.

2. To this end, Community financial assistance may be awarded for:

    (a) the information network on education in Europe, 'Eurydice', comprising the European Unit set up by the Commission and units set up by the Member States to enable it to make a full contribution to the implementation of this action. The network will in particular be called upon to collect and exchange information on education systems and policies, to develop data bases, to produce comparative studies and to draw up indicators. Eurydice will seek, when necessary, relevant support from external experts;

    (b) the organisation of and participation in 'Arion' multilateral study visits for decision-makers and senior managers of educational institutions in any sector of education, designed to facilitate exchanges of information and experience on subjects of mutual interest to the Member States. The Commission and Member States will ensure appropriate dissemination of the results of the visits and promote their interactivity with other actions within this programme;

    (c) networking of institutes and other appropriately qualified bodies engaged in analysing educational systems and policies, as well as of the bodies involved in the evaluation of educational quality;

    (d) studies, analyses, pilot projects, seminars, exchanges of experts and other appropriate actions relating to matters of common educational policy interest bringing together decision-makers on the priority themes to be determined by the Council. The Commission may call upon the services of a group of experts to assist it in ensuring the reliability of the analytical work carried out within the framework of these activities. The arrangements for establishing the group will be determined in accordance with Article 8(2) of the Decision;

    (e) activities designed to promote the recognition of diplomas, qualifications and periods of learning, notably studies, analyses, pilot projects and the exchange of information and experience. The Community network of national academic recognition information centres (NARIC) will make a full contribution in this regard. In particular, it will collect and disseminate authenticated information which is necessary for the purpose of academic recognition, also bearing in mind synergies with the professional recognition of diplomas.

3. In implementing this action, close cooperation will be ensured in particular with the Statistical Office of the European Communities (Eurostat), the European Centre for the Development of Vocational Training (Cedefop), the European Training Foundation (ETF) and appropriate international organisations, notably the Council of Europe, the Organisation for Economic Cooperation and Development (OECD) and the United Nations Educational, Scientific and Cultural Organisation (UNESCO).

Action 6.2: **Innovatory initiatives responding to emerging needs**

In addition to the cooperation activities provided for in the other actions of the present programme, the Community may support transnational projects and studies aimed at helping to develop innovations in one or more specific sectors of education. The subjects to be given priority are to be determined by the Council and reviewed regularly to enable adaptation to the new requirements which emerge during the period covered by this programme.

ACTION 7: JOINT ACTIONS

1. In accordance with Article 6 of the Decision, Community support may be provided within the framework of this programme for Joint Actions with other Community programmes and actions promoting a Europe of knowledge, in particular the Leonardo da Vinci and Youth programmes.

2. Such joint actions may be carried out by common calls for proposals on selected themes of common interest which are not exclusively covered by any single programme concerned, to be determined in accordance with Article 8(2), of the Decision and agreed with the committees of the other programmes and actions involved.

3. Appropriate steps will be taken to promote regional and local contact and interaction between the players taking part in this programme and in the Leonardo da Vinci and Youth programmes.

ACTION 8: ACCOMPANYING MEASURES

1. Community financial assistance may be awarded to the following initiatives aimed at promoting the objectives of this programme, provided that such initiatives are not eligible for assistance under other actions of the programme:

    (a) awareness-raising activities to promote cooperation in the field of education, including support for appropriate competitions and other events designed to enhance the European dimension of education;

    (b) transnational activities carried out by associations and other non-governmental bodies active in the field of education, as well as bodies concerned with educational guidance and counselling;

    (c) conferences and symposia on innovations in the sectors targeted by the programme;

    (d) activities aimed at training persons involved in the management of European cooperation projects in the field of education;

    (e) measures to optimise and disseminate the results of projects and activities carried out with the support of this programme or its previous phase;

    (f) activities involving cooperation with third countries and with the competent international organisations, in particular the Council of Europe, in accordance with Article 13 of the Decision.

2. Community financial assistance will be provided to support the activities of the Socrates national agencies set up by the Member States in accordance with Article 5 of the Decision, and to ensure the effective monitoring and evaluation of this programme.

3. In carrying out the programme, the Commission may have recourse to experts and to technical assistance organisations, the financing of which may be provided for within the overall financial framework for the programme. Furthermore, the Commission may organise such seminars, colloquia or other meetings of experts as are likely to facilitate the implementation of the programme, and undertake appropriate information, publication and dissemination actions.

III. SELECTION PROCEDURES

Procedures for the proposal and selection of the activities referred to in this Annex are as follows:

1. **Decentralised actions**

    The following actions, under which the selection decisions are taken by the Member States, are to be considered 'decentralised':

    (a) — Action 1.1 (School partnerships)

    — Action 1.2, point 2(a), (b), (c) (Mobility actions within training partnerships for school educational staff)

    — Action 3, point 2(h) (Visits and exchanges in adult education)

    — Action 6.1, point 2(b) (Arion study visits)

    — preparatory visits under all actions.

    Requests for financial assistance submitted under these actions are to be submitted to the Socrates national agencies designated by the Member States in accordance with Article 5 of the Decision. The Member States, with the assistance of the Socrates national agencies, will carry out the selection and allocate financial assistance to the applicants selected in accordance with general guidelines to be established under Article 8(2) of the Decision.

    (b) Action 2.2, point 3 (Mobility of students and university teachers)

    The awarding of the financial assistance to students and university teachers for mobility assignments within the institutional contracts mentioned in Action 2.1 and for the organisation of the mobility of students and university teachers will be carried out by Member States with the assistance of the Socrates national agencies designated pursuant to Article 5 of the Decision, taking into account the past performance of the universities concerned, in accordance with general guidelines to be established under Article 8(2) of the Decision.

2. **Centralised actions**

The following actions, under which the selection decisions are taken by the Commission, are to be considered 'centralised':

(a) — Action 1.2, point 2(d), (e), (f), (g) (Multilateral cooperation activities)

   — Action 3, point 2(a) to (g) and (i) (Multilateral cooperation activities)

   — Action 4 (Lingua)

   — Action 5 (Minerva)

   — Action 6.2 (Innovatory initiatives).

For the selection of projects under these actions, the following procedure will apply:

   (i) project coordinators will submit a project proposal to the Commission and send a copy to the Socrates national agency designated by the respective Member State;

   (ii) the Commission, with the assistance of independent experts will assess the project proposals. National agencies may provide the Commission with their assessment of these proposals;

   (iii) in cases where the Commission's assessment is at variance with the assessment received from the national agency in the coordinating country concerning the quality or appropriateness of the project, the Commission shall, upon request of the Member State, consult with the Member State concerned. The duration of this consultation process shall not exceed two weeks;

   (iv) the Commission will submit to the committee a proposal on the final selection (projects to be supported and amounts to be awarded) in accordance with the procedure set out in Article 8(2) of the Decision;

   (v) after receiving the opinion of the committee, the Commission will establish the list of selected projects and allocate the amounts to be awarded.

In certain cases, owing in particular to the scale and nature of the activities in question, a two-phase procedure may be adopted. In such cases, the procedure set out above is preceded by the submission and selection of pre-proposals. The decision in this regard and the arrangements for the pre-selection will be determined in accordance with Article 8(2) of the Decision.

(b) — Action 1.3 (Networks related to school partnerships and the training of staff involved in school education)

   — Action 2.1 (European inter-university cooperation)

   — Action 2.3 (Erasmus thematic networks)

   — Action 3.3 (Networks in adult education)

   — Action 6.1, points 2(a), (c), (d), (e) (Observation)

   — Action 8 (Accompanying Measures)

Project proposals under these actions will be submitted to the Commission. The Commission, in the case of Actions 1.3, 2.3 and 3.3 with the assistance of independent experts, will assess the project proposals. Decisions on the project proposals will be taken by the Commission after receiving the opinion of the committee in accordance with Article 8(2) of the Decision.

The two-phase procedure referred to in the final paragraph of Section III.2(a) will apply to Actions 1.3, 2.3 and 3.3 under the same conditions as set out in that paragraph.

3. **Joint actions**

Procedures for selection under Action 7 of the programme (Joint Actions) will be determined in accordance with Article 8(2) of the Decision. Where appropriate, the procedures set out above may be adapted in order to meet the special requirements of the Joint Actions in question. The Commission will make every effort to ensure optimal coordination between these procedures and those adopted within the other Community programmes or actions with which the Joint Actions in question are implemented.

4. The Commission, assisted by the Member States, will endeavour to ensure that the selection decisions are made known to applicants at the latest five months after the closing date for submission of applications under the action in question. For projects selected in accordance with the two-phase procedure provided for under point 2(a) and (b), this will only refer to the second stage of the selection (full project proposal).

5. The Commission and, in the case of decentralised actions, the Member States will seek to ensure optimal coordination between the procedures and deadlines for submitting and selecting applications for support within this programme and the Community programmes in the fields of vocational training and youth respectively.

IV. FINANCIAL PROVISIONS

A. Decentralised actions

1. The Community funds intended to provide financial support under the actions identified as decentralised in Section III, point I, are to be allocated among the Member States in accordance with the following formulae:

    (a) a minimum amount to be determined in accordance with budgetary availability for the action concerned will be allocated to each Member State;

    (b) the remainder will be allocated to the various Member States on the basis of:

        (i) the difference in the cost of living between the Member State of origin and the host Member State;

        (ii) the distance and cost of travel between the Member State of origin and the host Member State to be calculated taking into account the lowest travel price for the journey concerned;

        (iii) the country's total number of:

            — pupils and teachers in school education for Action 1.1 (School partnerships) and Action 1.2 point 2(a), (b), (c) (Mobility actions within training partnerships for school education staff);

            — students in higher education for Action 2.2, point 3 (Mobility of students). The number of graduates should be limited in its scope as a subsidiary and complementary factor to be determined in accordance with Article 8(2) of the Decision to qualify, where appropriate, the allocation to the Member States;

            — university teachers for Action 2.2 point 3 (Mobility of university teachers).

2. The Community funds thus distributed are to be administered by the Member States with the assistance of the Socrates national agencies provided for in Article 5 of the Decision.

3. The Commission, acting in cooperation with the Member States, will take the necessary measures to encourage balanced participation at Community, national and, where appropriate, regional level, and, in the case of higher education, across the various fields of study. The proportion allocated to these measures must not exceed 5 % of the annual budget for financing each of the Actions in question.

4. The arrangements for the allocation of funds to each Member State for the mobility activities provided for in Action 3, point 2(h) (Adult education visits and exchanges) and 6.1, point 2, second indent (Arion), for the organisation of the mobility of students and university teachers in accordance with Section III. I.(b), for the support of preparatory visits and for the preparatory measures referred to in Section IV, point B.4 will be decided upon by the Commission after receiving the opinion of the committee in accordance with Article 8(2) of the Decision.

B. Other provisions

1. Having due regard to the quality and quantity of applications for financial support, the following guidelines will be taken into account when allocating resources in accordance with Article 8(2) of the Decision:

    (a) the resources to be committed under Action 1 (Comenius) will not be less than 27 % of the total budget available for this programme;

    (b) the resources to be committed under Action 2 (Erasmus) will not be less than 51 % of the total budget available for this programme;

    (c) the resources to be committed under Action 3 (Grundtvig) will not be less than 7 % of the total budget available for this programme;

    (d) the resources to be committed for financial assistance for the Socrates national agencies under Action 8.2 and for technical assistance under Action 8.3 will not exceed 4,5 % of the total annual budget available for this programme.

    The above percentages are indicative and may be adapted in accordance with Article 8(2) of the Decision.

2. As a general rule, Community financial assistance granted for projects under this programme is intended partially to offset the estimated cost necessary to carry out the activities concerned and may cover a maximum period of three years, subject to a periodic review of progress achieved. The Community contribution will not normally exceed 75 % of the total cost of any specific project, except in the case of accompanying measures. Assistance may be granted in advance to enable preparatory visits to take place in respect of the projects in question.

    The amount to be made available in the annual budget of the programme for activities under Action 8.1 (f) shall not exceed EUR 250 000.

3. The specific situation of persons with special needs will be taken into account when determining the amount of Community financial assistance to be awarded.

4. With regard to activities involving the mobility of persons, Community financial assistance may be awarded to help ensure adequate preparation for the period to be spent in another Member State. Such preparatory measures may include in particular language courses, information on social and cultural aspects of the host Member State, etc.

V. DEFINITIONS

For the purposes of this Decision:

1. 'company' means all companies in the public or private sector whatever their size, legal status or the economic sector in which they operate, and all types of economic activities, including the social economy;

2. 'decision-makers' means any category of staff with managerial, assessment, training, guidance and inspection duties in the field of education and persons responsible for this area at local, regional and national level and within ministries;

3. 'guidance and counselling' means a range of activities such as information, assessment, orientation and advice to assist learners to make choices relating to education and training programmes or employment opportunities;

4. 'life-long learning' means the education and training opportunities offered to individuals throughout their lives to enable them continually to acquire, update and adapt their knowledge, skills and competences;

5. 'open and distance learning' means any form of flexible education, whether or not involving the use of information and communication technologies;

6. 'project' means transnational cooperation activity developed jointly by a formal or informal grouping of organisations or institutions;

7. 'pupil' means persons enrolled in that capacity at a 'school' as defined in this Annex;

8. 'resource centre' means a body engaged in the production, collection or dissemination of documentation, materials or methodologies relating to a sector of activity addressed by this programme, such as languages or information and communication technologies related to education;

9. 'school' means all types of institutions providing general (nursery, primary or secondary), vocational or technical education and, exceptionally, in the case of measures to promote language learning, non-school institutions providing apprenticeship training;

10. 'social partners' means, at national level, employers' and workers' organisations in conformity with national laws and/or practices and, at Community level, employers' and workers' organisations taking part in the social dialogue at Community level;

11. 'student' means persons registered in 'universities' as defined by this Annex, whatever their field of study, in order to follow higher education studies leading to a degree or diploma, up to and including the level of doctorate;

12. 'teacher/educational staff' means persons who, through their duties, are involved directly in the educational process in the Member States, in accordance with the organisation of their respective education system;

13. 'university' means any type of higher education institution, according to national legislation or practice, which offers qualifications or diplomas at that level, whatever such establishments may be called in the Member States;

14. 'university teacher' means any category of personnel employed in that capacity at a 'university' as defined in this Annex.

**Decision No 293/2000/EC of the European Parliament and of the Council
of 24 January 2000
adopting a programme of Community action (the Daphne programme)
(2000 to 2003) on preventive measures to fight violence against children,
young persons and women**

(OJ L 34, 9.2.2000)

I

(Acts whose publication is obligatory)

DECISION No 293/2000/EC OF THE EUROPEAN PARLIAMENT AND OF THE COUNCIL
of 24 January 2000
adopting a programme of Community action (the Daphne programme) (2000 to 2003) on preventive measures to fight violence against children, young persons and women

THE EUROPEAN PARLIAMENT AND
THE COUNCIL OF THE EUROPEAN UNION,

Having regard to the Treaty establishing the European Community, and in particular Article 152 thereof,

Having regard to the proposal from the Commission [1],

Having regard to the opinion of the Economic and Social Committee [2],

Having regard to the opinion of the Committee of the Regions [3],

Acting in accordance with the procedure laid down in Article 251 of the Treaty [4],

Whereas:

(1) Physical, sexual and psychological violence against children, young persons and women constitutes a breach of their right to life, safety, freedom, dignity and physical and emotional integrity and a serious threat to the physical and mental health of the victims of such violence; the effects of such violence are so widespread throughout the Community as to constitute a major health scourge.

(2) It is important to recognise the serious immediate and long-term implications for health, psychological and social development, and for the equal opportunities of those concerned, that violence has for individuals, families and communities and the high social and economic costs to society as a whole.

(3) According to the World Health Organisation's definition, health is a state of complete physical, mental and social well-being and not merely the absence of disease or infirmity; in accordance with Article 3(p) of the Treaty, Community action is to include a contribution to the attainment of a high level of health protection.

(4) These principles are recognised in the United Nations Convention of 1979 on the elimination of all forms of discrimination against women, the United Nations Convention of 1989 on the rights of the child, the Vienna Declaration of 1993 on the elimination of violence against women, the Declaration and Platform of Action adopted at the IVth Conference on women held in Beijing in 1995, the Declaration and the Plan of Action against the sex trade and the exploitation of minors adopted at the Stockholm Conference in 1996, and the Lisbon Declaration of 1998 on youth policies and programmes of the world conference of ministers of youth.

(5) The European Union has taken action in the field of justice and home affairs in particular by the Joint Action of 24 February 1997 concerning action to combat trafficking in human beings and sexual exploitation of children [5]; the criminal law aspects of violence are a matter for the Member States.

(6) The European Parliament, in its Resolutions of 18 January 1996 on trafficking in human beings [6], of 19 September 1996 on minors who are victims of violence [7], of 12 December 1996 on measures to protect minors in the European Union [8] and of 16 September 1997 on the need to establish a European Union-wide campaign for zero tolerance of violence against women [9] and of 16 December 1997 on trafficking in women for the purpose of sexual exploitation [10] has called upon the Commission to draw up and implement action programmes to combat such violence.

---

[1] OJ C 259, 18.8.1998, p. 2,
OJ C 89, 30.3.1999, p. 42 and
OJ C 162, 9.6.1999, p. 11.
[2] OJ C 169, 16.6.1999, p. 35.
[3] OJ C 89, 30.3.1999, p. 42.
[4] Opinion of the European Parliament of 16 April 1999 (OJ C 219, 30.7.1999, p. 497); Council common position of 13 September 1999 (OJ C 317, 4.11.1999, p. 1); Decision of the European Parliament of 17 November 1999 (not yet published in the Official Journal) and Council Decision of 13 December 1999.

[5] OJ L 63, 4.3.1997, p. 2.
[6] OJ C 32, 5.2.1996, p. 88.
[7] OJ C 320, 28.10.1996, p. 190.
[8] OJ C 20, 20.1.1997, p. 170.
[9] OJ C 304, 6.10.1997, p. 55.
[10] OJ C 14, 19.1.1998, p. 39.

(7) The Commission, in its Communication of 24 November 1993 on the framework for action in the field of public health, identified, *inter alia*, the prevention of injuries as an important area for action in the public health field; in this framework on 8 February 1999 Decision No 372/1999/EC of the European Parliament and of the Council was adopted on a programme of Community action on injury prevention [1].

(8) By providing support for acquiring better knowledge and understanding of, and wider dissemination of information about violence against children, young persons and women and by developing actions complementary to existing Community programmes and actions, while avoiding unnecessary duplication, this programme will contribute greatly to curbing exploitation and ensuring a high level of human health protection, taking into account its physical, mental and social aspects, and a high quality of life.

(9) Direct action concerning violence against children, young persons and women is in essence part of Member States' activity at national, regional or local level.

(10) The Community can provide added value to the actions of Member States concerning the prevention of violence, including violence in the form of sexual exploitation and abuse perpetrated against children, young persons and women through the dissemination and the exchange of information and experience, promoting an innovative approach, the joint establishment of priorities, the development of networking as appropriate, the selection of Community-wide projects and the motivation and mobilisation of all parties concerned.

(11) This programme can bring added value by identifying and stimulating good practice, by encouraging innovation and by exchanging relevant experience of actions undertaken in the Member States, including an exchange of information relating to the various laws and the results achieved.

(12) Therefore, in accordance with the principles of subsidiarity and proportionality as set out in Article 5 of the Treaty, the objectives of the proposed measure can be better achieved by the Community; this Decision confines itself to the minimum required in order to achieve those objectives and does not go beyond what is necessary for that purpose.

(13) Active partnership between the Commission, the Member States and non-governmental organisations (NGOs) and in particular organisations concerned with the welfare and quality of life of children, young persons and women needs to be promoted in this area and synergy between all the relevant policies and measures encouraged by promoting cooperation between NGOs, other organisations and national, regional and local authorities.

(14) In order to achieve the objectives of the programme and use the resources available in the most efficient way, the areas in which work is to be done must be carefully chosen by selecting projects which offer a greater Community added value and show the way towards trying out and disseminating innovative ideas to prevent violence, in the context of a multidisciplinary approach.

(15) Cooperation with the international organisations competent in the fields covered by the programme and with third countries should be fostered, as well as with all those likely to be involved in preventing violence.

(16) Provision should be made for opening up this programme to participation by the applicant countries in the pre-accession phase, in accordance with the conditions established in the relevant agreements, particularly the Association Agreements and the additional protocols to those Agreements.

(17) In order to increase the value and impact of the programme, a continuous assessment of the actions undertaken should be carried out, with particular regard to their effectiveness and the achievement of the objectives set and with a view, where appropriate, to making the necessary adjustments.

(18) This programme should be of a four-year duration in order to allow sufficient time for actions to be implemented to achieve the objectives set.

(19) The measures necessary for the implementation of this Decision should be adopted in accordance with Council Decision 1999/468/EC of 28 June 1999 laying down the procedures for the exercise of implementing powers conferred on the Commission [2].

(20) This Decision lays down for the entire duration of the programme a financial framework constituting the prime reference, within the meaning of point 33 of the Interinstitutional Agreement between the European Parliament, the Council and the Commission of 6 May 1999 on budgetary discipline and improvement of the budgetary procedure [3],

HAVE DECIDED AS FOLLOWS:

Article 1

Establishment of the programme

1. A programme of Community action to fight violence towards children, young persons and women, is hereby adopted for the period 1 January 2000 to 31 December 2003.

---

[1] OJ L 46, 20.2.1999, p. 1.
[2] OJ L 184, 17.7.1999, p. 23.
[3] OJ C 172, 18.6.1999, p. 1.

2. This programme aims to contribute towards ensuring a high level of protection of physical and mental health by the protection of children, young persons and women against violence (including violence in the form of sexual exploitation and abuse), by the prevention of violence and by the provision of support for the victims of violence, in order, in particular, to prevent future exposure to violence. It further aims to assist and encourage NGOs and other organisations active in this field. By so doing, the programme will contribute to social well-being.

3. The actions to be implemented under the programme, as set out in the Annex, are intended to promote:

(a) transnational actions to set up multidisciplinary networks and to ensure exchange of information, best practice and cooperation at Community level;

(b) transnational actions aimed at raising public awareness;

(c) complementary actions.

Article 2

Implementation

1. The Commission shall ensure implementation, in close cooperation with the Member States, of the actions referred to in Article 1(3) in accordance with Article 5.

2. The Commission shall, after consultations with the Member States, cooperate with institutions and organisations active in the field of prevention of and protection against violence against children, young persons and women, and of the support of victims. It shall encourage, in particular, transnational cooperation between NGOs and national, regional and local authorities.

3. The Commission shall take account of activities carried out in this field at national, regional and local level. It shall also ensure a balanced approach in respect of the target groups.

4. The actions undertaken shall involve a significant number of Member States.

Article 3

Budget

1. The financial framework for the implementation of the four-year programme (2000 to 2003) is hereby set at EUR 20 million.

2. The annual appropriations shall be established by the Budgetary Authority within the limits of the financial perspectives.

3. The Community contribution shall vary according to the nature of the action. It may not exceed 80 % of the total cost of the action.

Article 4

Consistency and complementarity

The Commission shall ensure that there is consistency and complementarity between the Community actions to be implemented under the programme and those implemented under other relevant Community programmes and measures, including future developments in the field of public health.

Article 5

Implementing measures

1. The measures necessary for the implementation of this Decision relating to the matters referred to below shall be adopted in accordance with the management procedure referred to in Article 6(2):

(a) the annual plan of work for the implementation of the measures in the programme, including the budgetary implications and selection criteria;

(b) the general balance between the various sections of the programme;

(c) the procedures for coordination with programmes and initiatives which are of direct relevance to achievement of the aim of this programme;

(d) the arrangements for cooperating with the third countries and international organisations referred to in Article 8;

(e) the procedures for monitoring and evaluating the programme.

2. The measures necessary for the implementation of this Decision relating to all other matters shall be adopted in accordance with the advisory procedure referred to in Article 6(3).

Article 6

Committee

1. The Commission shall be assisted by a Committee.

2. Where reference is made to this paragraph, Articles 4 and 7 of Decision 1999/468/EC shall apply, having regard to the provisions of Article 8 thereof.

The period laid down in Article 4(3) of Decision 1999/468/EC shall be set at two months.

3. Where reference is made to this paragraph, Articles 3 and 7 of Decision 1999/468/EC shall apply, having regard to the provisions of Article 8 thereof.

4. The Committee shall adopt its rules of procedures.

Article 7

Participation of the EFTA/EEA countries, the associated central and eastern European countries, Cyprus, Malta and Turkey

This programme shall be open to the participation of:

— the EFTA/EEA countries, in accordance with the conditions established in the EEA Ageement,

— the associated central and eastern European countries, in accordance with the conditions established in the Europe Agreements, in their additional protocols and in the decisions of the respective Association Councils,
— Cyprus, funded by additional appropriations in accordance with procedures to be agreed with that country,
— Malta and Turkey, funded by additional appropriations in accordance with the provisions of the Treaty.

Article 8

International cooperation

Subject to Article 300 of the Treaty, in the course of implementing the programme, cooperation with third countries and with international organisations competent in the fields covered by the programme shall be fostered as well as with all those likely to be involved in preventing and protecting against all forms of violence.

Article 9

Monitoring and evaluation

1. In the implementation of this Decision, the Commission shall take the necessary measures to ensure the monitoring and continuous evaluation of the programme taking account of the general and specific objectives referred to in Article 1 and in the Annex.

2. During the second year of the programme, the Commission shall present an evaluation report to the European Parliament and to the Council.

3. The Commission shall submit a final report to the European Parliament and the Council on completion of the programme.

4. The Commission shall incorporate into the reports referred to in paragraphs 2 and 3 information on Community financing in the various fields of action and on complementarity with the other actions referred to in Article 4, as well as the results of the evaluations. It shall also send the reports to the Economic and Social Committee and the Committee of the Regions.

Article 10

Entry into force

This Decision shall enter into force on the date of its publication in the *Official Journal of the European Communities*.

Done at Brussels, 24 January 2000.

For the European Parliament	*For the Council*
The President	*The President*
N. FONTAINE	J. GAMA

ANNEX

SPECIFIC OBJECTIVES AND ACTIONS

I. TRANSNATIONAL ACTIONS TO SET UP MULTIDISCIPLINARY NETWORKS AND TO ENSURE EXCHANGE OF INFORMATION, BEST PRACTICE AND COOPERATION AT COMMUNITY LEVEL

Objective: *To support and encourage both non-governmental organisations (NGOs) and other organisations including public authorities active in the fight against violence to work together*

1. Support for the establishment and strengthening of multidisciplinary networks and the encouragement and support of cooperation between NGOs and the various organisations and public bodies at national, regional and local level, in order to improve on both sides the level of knowledge and understanding of each other's role and to facilitate the exchange of relevant information.

2. Stimulation and exchange of best practice, including pilot projects, at Community level on the prevention of violence and on the support and protection of children, young persons and women.

The networks shall in particular carry out activities to address the problems of violence that will:

1. produce a common framework for analysis of violence, including the definition of different types of violence, the causes of violence and all its consequences;

2. measure the real impact of the different types of violence within Europe on victims and society, in order to establish an appropriate response;

3. assess the types and effectiveness of measures and practices to prevent and detect violence including violence in the form of sexual exploitation and abuse and to provide support for victims of violence, in order, in particular, to prevent future exposure to violence.

II. TRANSNATIONAL ACTIONS AIMED AT RAISING PUBLIC AWARENESS

Objective: *To support the raising of public awareness of violence and the prevention of violence against children, young persons and women, including the victims of trafficking for the purpose of sexual exploitation, commercial sexual exploitation and other sexual abuse*

1. Encouragement of information campaigns in cooperation with the Member States and pilot projects with European added-value and awareness-raising activities among the general public and in particular, among children and young persons, educators and other categories involved as well as among the media about potential risks of violence and of ways of avoiding them, including knowledge of legislative measures, health education and training in the context of the fight against violence.

2. Development of a Community-wide information source to assist and inform NGOs and public bodies of publicly available information compiled by governmental, NGO and academic sources relevant to the field of violence, its prevention and the support of victims, and the means to prevent violence, as well as the provision of information about all measures and programmes on this subject under the auspices of the Community. This should enable information to be integrated into all relevant information systems.

3. Studies in the field of violence and sexual abuse and the means of their prevention with the aim, *inter alia*, of identifying the most effective procedures and policies for preventing violence, for supporting victims of violence, in order, in particular, to prevent future exposure to violence, and for examining the social and economic costs, in order to establish appropriate responses to this phenomenon.

4. Improvement of recognition, reporting and management of the consequences of violence.

III. COMPLEMENTARY ACTIONS

In carrying out the programme, the Commission, in compliance with Articles 2 and 5 of the Decision, can have recourse to technical assistance organisations the financing of which shall be provided for within the overall financial framework for the programme. It can, under the same conditions, have recourse to experts. Furthermore, the Commission will be able to organise seminars, colloquia or other meetings of experts, likely to facilitate the implementation of the programme and enhance information, publication and dissemination actions.

**Decision No 1031/2000/EC of the European Parliament and of the Council
of 13 April 2000
establishing the "Youth" Community action programme**

(OJ L 117, 18.5.2000)

I

(Acts whose publication is obligatory)

DECISION No 1031/2000/EC OF THE EUROPEAN PARLIAMENT AND OF THE COUNCIL
of 13 April 2000
establishing the 'Youth' Community action programme

THE EUROPEAN PARLIAMENT AND THE COUNCIL OF THE EUROPEAN UNION,

Having regard to the Treaty establishing the European Community and in particular Article 149 thereof,

Having regard to the proposal from the Commission [1],

Having regard to the opinion of the Economic and Social Committee [2],

Having regard to the opinion of the Committee of the Regions [3],

Acting in accordance with the procedure laid down in Article 251 of the Treaty [4], in the light of the joint text approved on 9 March 2000 by the Conciliation Committee,

Whereas:

(1) The Treaty establishing the European Community provides that the latter's action shall, *inter alia*, contribute to the development of quality education and training. This was resolutely reiterated by the Treaty of Amsterdam signed on 2 October 1997 which states that the Community is also to promote the development of the highest possible level of knowledge for its peoples through a wide access to education and through a continuous updating of knowledge.

(2) By their Decision No 818/95/EC of 14 March 1995 adopting the third phase of the 'Youth for Europe' programme [5], the European Parliament and the Council set up an action programme regarding cooperation in the field of youth. It is appropriate to pursue and strengthen cooperation and Community action in that field on the basis of the experience acquired from that programme.

(3) The extraordinary European Council on employment held in Luxembourg on 20 and 21 November 1997 adopted a coordinated employment strategy in which lifelong education and training have a fundamental role to play in implementing the guidelines set out in the Council resolution of 15 December 1997 [6] for the Member States' employment policies in order to enhance employability, adaptability and the culture of entrepreneurship and to promote equal opportunities.

(4) The Commission in its communication 'Towards a Europe of knowledge' set out guidelines on the creation of an open and dynamic European education area capable of achieving the objective of lifelong education and training.

(5) In its White Paper 'Teaching and learning — Towards the learning society', the Commission stated that the emergence of the learning society entails encouraging the acquisition of new knowledge and to this end providing motivation to learn at every opportunity. In its Green Paper 'Education, training, research: the obstacles to transnational mobility', the Commission highlighted the advantages of mobility for people and competitiveness in the European Union.

(6) There is a need to promote active citizenship, to strengthen the links between measures pursued under this programme and to step up the fight for respect for human rights and against exclusion in all its forms, including racism and xenophobia. Special attention should be focused on removing discrimination and on promoting equal opportunities for women and men.

(7) The actions of this programme should reach young people in general and not just the initiated and/or those who belong to youth organisations. The Commission and the Member States should therefore undertake to provide an adequate flow of information and appropriate dissemination for those actions.

---

[1] OJ C 311, 10.10.1998, p. 6.
[2] OJ C 410, 30.12.1998, p. 11.
[3] OJ C 51, 22.2.1999, p. 77.
[4] Opinion of the European Parliament of 5 November 1998 (OJ C 359, 23.11.1998, p. 75), Council common position of 28 June 1999 (OJ C 210, 22.7.1999, p. 1) and Decision of the European Parliament of 28 October 1999 (not yet published in the Official Journal). Decision of the Council of 10 April 2000 and Decision of the European Parliament of 12 April 2000 (not yet published in the Official Journal).
[5] OJ L 87, 20.4.1995, p. 1.
[6] OJ C 30, 28.1.1998, p. 1.

(8) This Decision establishes a Community framework intended to contribute to the development of transnational voluntary service activities. The Member States should endeavour to adopt appropriate and coordinated measures to remove legal and administrative obstacles in order to further improve young people's access to the programme and facilitate recognition of the specific nature of voluntary service for young people.

(9) Youth exchanges in particular contribute to mutual trust, the strengthening of democracy, tolerance, a willingness to cooperate and solidarity between young people, and they are therefore crucial for the cohesion and further development of the Union.

(10) The participation of young people in voluntary service activities is a type of informal education leading to the acquisition of additional knowledge, whose quality should be largely based on appropriate preparatory measures, including those of a linguistic and cultural nature. It helps to determine the future direction of their lives, to broaden their horizons and to develop their social skills, active citizenship and balanced integration into society from the economic, social and cultural points of view, including preparation for working life, and promotes awareness of true European citizenship.

(11) In its resolution of 14 May 1998 on the information and communication policy in the European Union ([1]), the European Parliament stated that, with regard to support and action programmes, the selection of projects should be more transparent and the reasons for the choice should be clearer to those who submit the projects.

(12) The Commission and Member States should seek to guarantee complementarity between European voluntary service activities and the various similar national schemes.

(13) The European Parliament and the Council, in their Decision No 253/2000/EC on education, and the Council, in Decision 1999/382/EC of 26 April 1999 on training, have established Community action progammes for the education and training fields respectively, which contribute together with the youth programme to a Europe of knowledge.

(14) The policy of cooperation in the youth field contributes to the promotion of informal education, and therefore to lifelong learning, and this policy needs to be further developed.

(15) The integration of young people into the world of work is an essential part of their integration into society, and this also calls for all their skills and competences acquired as part of their experience of informal education to be recognised and for a high premium to be put on their importance.

(16) It is necessary, in order to reinforce the added value of Community action that the Commission, in cooperation with the Member States, should ensure coherence and a complementarity at all levels between the actions implemented within the framework of this Decision and other relevant policies, instruments and actions.

(17) It is important that the Youth programme committee should consult, on the basis of arrangements to be defined, with the committees responsible for the implementation of the Community vocational training and educational programmes (Leonardo da Vinci and Socrates). It is important that the Youth programme committee be kept regularly informed about Community initiatives taken in the fields of education, vocational training and youth.

(18) The European Councils of Essen (9 and 10 December 1994) and Cannes (26 and 27 June 1995) stressed the need for further action to enhance the social and vocational integration of young people in Europe. The conclusions of the European Council of Florence (21 and 22 June 1996) emphasised the importance of making it easier for young people to enter the labour force. The European Council meeting in Amsterdam (15 to 17 June 1997) expressed its support for non-profit-making activities. The European Parliament and Council adopted Decision No 1686/98/EC on 20 July 1998 establishing the Community action programme 'European voluntary service for young people' ([2]).

(19) European voluntary service activities are not a substitute for military service, for the alternative service formulas provided in particular for conscientious objectors or for the compulsory civilian service existing in several Member States, and should not restrict or be a substitute for potential or existing paid employment.

(20) The grant of residence permits and any visas required falls within the competence of the authorities in the Member States, and the concept of legal resident is defined by national law.

(21) The European Parliament adopted a resolution on 2 July 1998 on promoting the role of voluntary organisations and foundations in Europe ([3]). The voluntary sector should also play an important role in enabling all young people, particularly those with the greatest difficulties, to participate in these programmes.

(22) The Commission and the Member States are to ensure that they foster cooperation with non-governmental organisations active in the youth and social fields, as well as in the areas of the environment, culture, sport and combating the various forms of exclusion.

([1]) OJ C 167, 1.6.1998, p. 230.

([2]) OJ L 214, 31.7.1998, p. 1.
([3]) OJ C 226, 20.7.1998, p. 66.

(23) The Agreement on the European Economic Area (EEA Agreement) provides for greater cooperation in the field of education, training and youth between the European Community and its Member States, on the one hand, and the States of the European Free Trade Association (EFTA) participating in the European Economic Area, on the other. The EEA Agreement lays down procedures for the participation of the EFTA States participating in the EEA in Community programmes in the field of education, training and youth.

(24) Provision should be made to open up this programme to participation of the associated central and east European countries (CEEC) in accordance with the conditions established in the Europe Agreements, in their additional protocols and in the decisions of the respective Association Councils, of Cyprus, funded by additional appropriations in accordance with the procedures to be agreed with that country, as well as of Malta and Turkey, funded by additional appropriations, in accordance with the provisions of the Treaty.

(25) This programme should be monitored and continually evaluated in cooperation between the Commission and the Member States in order to allow for readjustments, particularly in the priorities for implementing the measures.

(26) In accordance with the principles of subsidiarity and proportionality as defined in Article 5 of the Treaty, since the objectives of the proposed action concerning the development and strengthening of a cooperation policy in the youth field, including European voluntary service and youth exchanges both within the Community and with third countries, cannot be sufficiently achieved by the Member States because of the complexity and diversity of the youth field, they can therefore be better achieved by the Community owing to the transnational dimension of Community actions and measures. This Decision does not go beyond what is necessary to achieve those objectives.

(27) This Decision lays down, for the entire duration of the programme, a financial framework constituting the prime reference for the budgetary authority during the annual budgetary procedure, within the meaning of point 33 of the Interinstitutional Agreement of 6 May 1999 between the European Parliament, the Council and the Commission, on budgetary discipline and improvement of the budgetary procedure [1].

(28) The measures necessary for the implementation of this Decision should be adopted in accordance with Council Decision 1999/468/EC of 28 June 1999 laying down the procedures for the exercise of implementing powers conferred on the Commission [2],

HAVE DECIDED AS FOLLOWS:

Article 1

Establishment of the programme

1. This decision establishes the 'Youth' Community action programme, hereinafter referred to as 'this programme', concerning cooperation policy in the youth field, including European voluntary service and youth exchanges both within the Community and with third countries.

2. This programme shall be implemented over the period starting on 1 January 2000 and ending on 31 December 2006.

3. This programme shall contribute to the promotion of a Europe of knowledge by developing a European area of cooperation in the field of youth policy, based on informal education and training. It shall promote lifelong learning and the building up of the knowledge and skills and competences likely to foster active citizenship and employability.

4. This programme shall support and supplement action taken by and in the Member States while fully respecting their cultural and linguistic diversity.

Article 2

Objectives of the programme

1. In order to allow young people to acquire knowledge, skills and competences which may be one of the foundations of their future development, and to exercise responsible citizenship so as to become an active part of society and bearing in mind the importance of promoting equal opportunities, the objectives of this programme are as follows:

(a) to promote an active contribution by young people to the building of Europe through their participation in transnational exchanges within the Community or with third countries so as to develop understanding of the cultural diversity of Europe and its fundamental common values, thus helping to promote respect for human rights and to combat racism, anti-Semitism and xenophobia;

(b) to strengthen their sense of solidarity through more extensive participation by young people in transnational community-service activities within the Community or with third countries, in particular those with which the Community has concluded cooperation agreements;

---
[1] OJ C 172, 18.6.1999, p. 1.
[2] OJ L 184, 17.7.1999, p. 23.

(c) to encourage young people's initiative, enterprise and creativity so that they may take an active role in society and, at the same time, to stimulate recognition of the value of informal education acquired within a European context;

(d) reinforce cooperation in the field of youth by fostering the exchange of good practice, the training of youth workers/leaders and the development of innovative actions at Community level.

2. This programme shall also contribute to attaining the objectives of other relevant areas of Community policy.

Article 3

Community actions

1. The objectives of this programme as set out in Article 2 shall be pursued by means of the following actions, the operational content and the application procedures of which are described in the Annex:

— Youth for Europe,
— European voluntary service,
— youth initiatives,
— joint actions,
— support measures.

2. These actions shall be implemented through the following types of measures, which may, where appropriate, be combined:

(a) support for the transnational mobility of young people;

(b) support for the use of information and communication technologies (ICT) in the youth field;

(c) support for the development of cooperation networks at the European level permitting mutual exchange of experience and good practice;

(d) support for transnational projects to promote citizenship of the Union and the commitment of young people to the development of the Union;

(e) promotion of language skills and understanding of different cultures;

(f) support for pilot projects based on transnational partnerships designed to develop innovation and quality in the youth field;

(g) development, at a European level, of methods of analysis and follow-up of youth policies and their evolution (e.g. databases, key figures, mutual knowledge of 'systems') and of methods of disseminating good practice.

Article 4

Access to the programme

1. This programme is aimed at young people, in principle between the ages of 15 and 25, as well as those involved in youth work, who are legal residents of a Member State. The age limits may be slightly adjusted, where justified by the specific circumstances of certain projects.

Within the framework of actions 1.2, 2.2 and 5 set out in the Annex, this programme may also be aimed at young people, in principle aged from 15 to 25, and those involved in youth work who reside in third countries, without prejudice to the competences of the Member States.

2. Particular attention should be paid to ensuring that all young people, without discrimination, have access to the activities of this programme.

3. The Commission and the Member States shall ensure that special efforts are made to assist young people who, for cultural, social, physical, mental, economic or geographical reasons, find it more difficult to participate in relevant action programmes at Community, national, regional or local level, as well as to assist small local groups. The Commission shall accordingly take account of the difficulties faced by these target groups, thus contributing to combating exclusion.

4. The Member States shall endeavour to take appropriate measures so that participants in the programme can have access to health care in accordance with the provisions of Community law. The Member State of origin shall endeavour to take appropriate measures so that participants in the European voluntary service can retain their social protection.

Article 5

Implementation of the programme and cooperation with the Member States

1. The Commission shall ensure the implementation of the Community actions covered by this programme in accordance with the Annex.

2. The Commission, in cooperation with the Member States, shall take the steps described in the Annex (action 5) in order to make the best use of what has been achieved through Community cooperative action in the youth field.

3. The Commission and Member States shall take appropriate action to develop structures established at Community and national level to achieve the objectives of the programme, in a user-friendly way, so as to facilitate access to the programme for young people and other partners at local level, to evaluate and monitor actions called for under the programme and to apply transparent consultation and selection arrangements.

The Commission and the Member States shall ensure that they take measures to facilitate young people's access to transnational mobility through measures designed adequately to inform them and raise their awareness of this subject. The Commission and the Member States shall ensure that appropriate information and publicity is provided about actions supported by the programme.

4. The Member States shall take the necessary steps to ensure the efficient running of the programme; they shall also endeavour, as far as possible, to adopt such measures as they deem necessary and desirable to remove legal and administrative obstacles to access to this programme.

5. The Commission, in cooperation with the Member States, shall ensure the transition between those actions carried out within the framework of the previous Community programmes in the youth field (Youth for Europe III and European voluntary service) and the actions to be implemented under this programme.

Article 6

Joint actions

As part of the process of building up a Europe of knowledge, the measures of this programme may be implemented in accordance with the procedures laid down in Article 8 as joint actions with related Community programmes and actions in the areas of youth, education and vocational training.

Article 7

Implementing measures

1. The measures necessary for the implementation of this Decision relating to the matters referred to below shall be adopted in accordance with the management procedure referred to in Article 8(2):

(a) the arrangements for implementing this programme, including the annual plan of work for the implementation of the programme's actions;

(b) the general balance between the different actions of the programme;

(c) the criteria applicable for establishing the indicative breakdown of funds among the Member States for the purpose of the actions to be managed on a decentralised basis;

(d) the arrangements for implementing the joint actions;

(e) the arrangements for evaluating the programme;

(f) the arrangements for attesting to participation of young volunteers.

2. The measures necessary for the implementation of this Decision relating to all other matters shall be adopted in accordance with the advisory procedure referred to in Article 8(3).

Article 8

Committee

1. The Commission shall be assisted by a committee.

2. Where reference is made to this paragraph, Articles 4 and 7 of Decision 1999/468/EC shall apply, having regard to the provisions of Article 8 thereof.

The period laid down in Article 4(3) of Decision 1999/468/EC shall be set at two months.

3. Where reference is made to this paragraph, Articles 3 and 7 of Decision 1999/468/EC shall apply, having regard to the provisions of Article 8 thereof.

4. The committee shall adopt its rules of procedure.

Article 9

Funding

1. The financial framework for the implementation of this programme for the period specified in Article 1 is hereby set at EUR 520 million.

2. The annual appropriations shall be authorised by the budgetary authority within the limits of the financial perspective.

Article 10

Consistency and complementarity

1. The Commission, in cooperation with the Member States and without prejudice to the individual character and specificity of each programme, shall ensure overall consistency and complementarity with other relevant Community policies, instruments and actions. Particular attention shall be paid to the promotion of equality and to equal opportunities for women and men.

2. The Commission, in cooperation with the Member States, shall ensure consistency between the implementation of this programme and the other Community activities relating to youth, in particular in the area of culture and the audiovisual sector, the completion of the internal market, the information society, environment, consumer protection, SMEs, social policy, employment, and public health.

3. The Commission and the Member States shall ensure that the measures of this programme have regard to the employment guidelines adopted by the Council as part of a coordinated strategy for employment.

4. The Commission shall ensure an efficient link-up between this programme and the programmes and actions in the youth field undertaken as part of the Community's external relations.

Article 11

Participation of the EFTA/EEA countries, the associated central and east European countries (CEEC), Cyprus, Malta and Turkey

This programme shall be open to the participation of:

— the EFTA/EEA countries in accordance with the conditions established in the EEA Agreement,

— the associated central and east European countries (CEEC) in accordance with the conditions established in the Europe Agreements, in their additional protocols and in the decisions of the respective Association Councils,

— Cyprus, funded by additional appropriations in accordance with the procedures to be agreed with that country,

— Malta and Turkey, funded by additional appropriations in accordance with the provisions of the Treaty.

Article 12

International cooperation

Under this programme, the Commission, acting in accordance with the procedures laid down in Article 7, shall strengthen its cooperation with non-Community countries and relevant international organisations, in particular the Council of Europe.

Article 13

Monitoring and evaluation

1. The Commission shall regularly monitor this programme in cooperation with the Member States.

This monitoring shall include the reports referred to in paragraph 3 and specific activities.

2. This programme shall be evaluated regularly by the Commission in cooperation with the Member States. This evaluation is intended to increase the effectiveness of actions implemented with regard to the objectives referred to in Article 2 and to ensure that equality of access to the programme as laid down in Article 4(2) and (3) is guaranteed.

This evaluation will also examine the complementarity between actions under this programme and those pursued under other relevant Community policies, instruments and actions.

In accordance with criteria established using the procedure described in Article 8(2), there will be regular external evaluations of the results of the Community actions.

3. Member States shall submit to the Commission by 31 December 2004 and 30 June 2007, respectively, reports on the implementation and the impact of this programme.

4. The Commission shall submit to the European Parliament, the Council, the Economic and Social Committee and the Committee of the Regions:

— on the accession of new Member States, a report on the financial consequences of these accessions on the programme, followed, if appropriate, by financial proposals to deal with the financial consequences of these accessions on the programme, in accordance with the provisions of the Interinstitutional Agreement of 6 May 1999 between the European Parliament, the Council and the Commission on budgetary discipline and improvement of the budgetary procedure and with the conclusions of the Berlin European Council of March 1999. The European Parliament and the Council will take a decision on such proposals as soon as possible,

— an interim evaluation report on the qualitative and quantitative aspects of the implementation of this programme by 30 June 2005,

— a final report on the implementation of this programme by 31 December 2007.

Article 14

Entry into force

This Decision shall enter into force on the date of its publication in the *Official Journal of the European Communities*.

Done at Luxembourg, 13 April 2000.

For the European Parliament	*For the Council*
The President	*The President*
N. FONTAINE	A. VARA

ANNEX

Funding approved under the programme is to observe the principles of co-financing and additionality. In accordance with Article 4(3) of the Decision, efforts must be made to facilitate access to the programme for young people who face difficulties of a cultural, social, physical, mental, economic or geographical nature, as well as for small local groups. The committee referred to in Article 8 of the Decision is to lay down the specific form these efforts should take. Community funding is to be distributed in such a way as to take account of the need to ensure balance between the mobility actions undertaken and an equal opportunity of participation for the young people of every Member State; that is to say, Article 4(3) is to be taken into account.

Initiatives designed to encourage tolerance and the acceptance of differences, as well as measures combating all forms of exclusion, should be given specific encouragement and stimulation. The Community will be receptive to activities giving a prominent position to culture and sport in the context of informal education for young people.

In order to achieve the objectives of the programme, five categories of action are to be implemented on the basis of the measures described in Article 3 of the Decision:

— Youth for Europe

— European voluntary service

— Youth initiatives

— Joint actions

— Support measures.

ACTION 1 — YOUTH FOR EUROPE

Action 1.1: Intra-Community exchanges for young people

The Community will support mobility activities for young people provided that the activities in question last at least one week, are carried out on the basis of joint projects within the Community and involve groups of young people aged in principle between 15 and 25 years and legally resident in a Member State. The age limits may be slightly adjusted where justified by the specific circumstances of certain projects.

Those activities, based on transnational partnerships between groups of young people, are to involve their active participation and be designed to make it possible for them to discover and become aware of different social and cultural realities and to encourage them to participate in, or initiate, other activities at European level. Particular attention is to be paid to participation by young people for whom it is their first European activity and to small-scale or local groups without experience at European level.

In order to move towards a better balance between bilateral and multilateral activities, Community support will be progressively focused on multilateral group-mobility activities. Bilateral group mobility will receive funding if this is justified in terms of the target groups or a specific pedagogical approach.

Activities designed to strengthen the active involvement of young people in group mobility projects may receive funding under this action, particularly in the form of activities to provide the young people in question with linguistic and intercultural preparation.

Action 1.2: Exchanges of young people with third countries

The Community will support mobility activities for young people provided that the activities in question last at least one week, are carried out on the basis of joint projects and involve groups of young people aged in principle between 15 and 25 years and legally resident in a Member State or in a third country. These mobility activities are to involve at least two Member States.

Those activities, based on transnational partnerships between groups of young people are to involve their active participation and be designed to make it possible for them to discover and become aware of different social and cultural realities and to encourage them to participate in, or initiate, other activities at European level. Moreover, these projects are to make it possible for partners in the third countries to gain experience of this kind of activity in the field of informal education and to contribute to the development of youth work and associations in those countries.

Activities designed to strengthen the active involvement of young people in group mobility projects may receive funding, particularly in the form of activities to provide the young people in question with linguistic and intercultural preparation before their departure.

ACTION 2 — EUROPEAN VOLUNTARY SERVICE

For the purposes of this programme, 'young volunteer' is taken to be a person aged in principle between 18 and 25 years and legally resident in a Member State.

Young volunteers will undertake, as active citizens, to carry out an activity which gives tangible form to solidarity, with the view to acquiring social and personal abilities and skills thus laying the foundations for their future development, while at the same time contributing to society. To this end, young volunteers will participate, in a Member State other than the one in which they reside, or in a third country, in a non-profit-making and unpaid activity of importance to the community and of a limited duration (12 months maximum) in the context of a project recognised by the Member State and the Community, in compliance with the aims of this programme set out in Article 2. In particular it should not result in job substitution. Full board and lodging as well as mentoring will be provided. The voluntary service project will ensure that young volunteers are covered by health and appropriate insurance. Young volunteers will receive an allowance/pocket money.

European voluntary service is based on a partnership and shared responsibilities between the young volunteers, the sending organisation and the host organisation.

In accordance with the provisions relating to the programme committee referred to in Article 8, a document, issued by the Commission, will attest to the participation of the young volunteers in European voluntary service and to the experience and skills that they have acquired during the relevant period.

Action 2.1: Intra-Community European voluntary service

The Community will support transnational projects (for a limited period ranging in principle from three weeks to one year) which involve young people, actively and personally, in activities designed to help meet the needs of society in a wide range of fields (social, sociocultural, environmental, cultural, etc.) which constitute at the same time an experience of informal education with a view to acquiring social and cultural skills. These projects are designed to bring young people into contact with other cultures and other languages and to experience new ideas and projects in a multicultural civil society.

The Community may support schemes, particularly those with a linguistic or intercultural element, which aim at preparing young volunteers for their departure and easing their social integration during those activities as well as when they have completed their period of European voluntary service. Particular attention is to be paid to pedagogical support and mentoring.

Action 2.2: European voluntary service with third countries

The Community will support transnational projects with third countries (for a limited period ranging in principle from three weeks to one year) which involve young people, actively and personally, in activities designed to help meet the needs of society in a wide range of fields (social, sociocultural, environmental, cultural, etc.) which constitute at the same time an experience of informal education with a view to acquiring social and cultural skills. These projects are designed to bring young people into contact with other cultures and other languages and to experience new ideas and projects in a multicultural civil society.

Support may be given to action laying or consolidating the necessary foundations for developing transnational European voluntary service projects with third countries.

The Community may support schemes, particularly those with a linguistic or intercultural element, which aim at preparing young volunteers for their departure and easing their social integration during those activities as well as when they have completed their period of European voluntary service. Particular attention is to be paid to pedagogical support and mentoring.

ACTION 3 — YOUTH INITIATIVES

In order to encourage initiative and creativity among young people, the Community will support projects in which young people actively and directly participate in innovative and creative schemes and in schemes which focus on the social commitment of young people at local, regional, national or European level. These projects will allow young people to develop their initiative and to put into practice activities of their own devising in which they play the key roles.

The Community will support initiatives designed to help young volunteers to make the best possible use of the experience they have gained during their period of voluntary service and to encourage their active integration into society. Those initiatives taken by young people after completing their European voluntary service will allow them to launch and promote activities of a social, cultural, sociocultural and economic nature and/or aim at their personal development. Priority access will be given to those young people most in need.

Support will aim at encouraging extension of these projects to include similar initiatives conducted in other Member States in order to strengthen their transnational nature and greatly expand exchanges of experience and cooperation between young people. This aid may include organising meetings of young promoters of Europe-wide initiatives. Financial aid may be granted towards the effective establishment of stable, transnational partnerships between such projects.

ACTION 4 — JOINT ACTIONS

Having regard to the need for a flexible and creative approach as a precondition for cooperation between sectors, Community aid may be granted for the actions referred to in Article 6 of the Decision and for activities to be undertaken jointly with other Community schemes relating to the Europe of knowledge, in particular Community programmes in the field of education and vocational training.

The Commission, in cooperation with the Member States, will aim at developing a common system of information, observation and dissemination concerning good practice in the field of knowledge and lifelong learning, alongside joint actions with regard to multimedia for educational and training purposes. Those projects will cover a range of schemes from a number of different sectors including youth. They may be funded in a complementary manner by a number of different Community programmes, and may be implemented by means of calls for joint projects.

Appropriate measures may be adopted to promote, at regional and local level, contact and interaction between those participating in this programme and in programmes dealing with vocational training and education. In this context, activities increasing awareness of the opportunities provided by the Community to young people may be supported.

ACTION 5 — SUPPORT MEASURES

Action 5.1: Training and cooperation in relation to those involved in youth policy

Funding shall be granted to:

1. Activities designed to give further training to persons involved in youth work, particularly European voluntary service instructors, youth workers/leaders, those running European projects and youth initiative counsellors, who take part in schemes directly involving young people, of the kind described in actions 1, 2 and 3 of the programme, the aim being to ensure that such schemes are of an appropriately high quality. Particular attention is to be paid to activities seeking to encourage the participation of those young people who find it most difficult to participate in Community actions.

2. Activities designed to develop European modules fulfilling the requirements for transnational cooperation.

3. Activities, such as study visits, feasibility studies, seminars, work-experience, which focus particularly on exchanges of experience and good practice in relation to joint actions or issues of common interest or which are designed to facilitate and promote the establishment of sustainable transnational partnerships and/or multilateral networks between those active in the field of youth work.

4. Experimental activities which comprise a source of innovation and enrichment of youth policy through the implementation of new approaches and new forms of cooperation, as well as through the shared efforts of participants from differing backgrounds.

5. Community support may also be given to conferences and seminars which seek to promote cooperation and the exchange of good practice in the field of youth, as well as to other promotion and dissemination measures regarding the results of the projects and activities supported within the framework of Community actions related to youth.

Activities associated with these measures may be solely intra-Community in nature or involve non-member countries. Particular attention is to be paid to those who work with youth at a regional or local level and who have no or little experience of, or scope for, contacts at European level, as well as to activities in which young people play the key roles.

Action 5.2: Information for young people and youth studies

1. In line with the objectives of the programme and in particular to improve access for all young people and to enhance their initiative and active participation in society, the Commission will encourage those active in the field of youth work to become involved in informing young people at European level, as well as boosting cooperation between the information and communication systems for young people established in the Member States and at Community level. In this context, particular stress is to be laid on broadening cooperation to include the fields of education and training, as well as on the dialogue both between and with young people.

2. Accordingly, funding is to be provided for initiatives involving:

   — the acquisition of the necessary experience and skills to carry out youth information projects based on transnational cooperation and projects which provide information and, in particular, advisory services for young people,

   — cooperative projects focusing on information dissemination, enhancing the awareness among young people of the field covered by the programme and giving young people access to all necessary information to achieve the objectives of the programme,

   — the implementation, as part of transnational cooperation projects, of mechanisms permitting dialogue both between and with young people, particularly through the use of youth-oriented media and new technologies.

3. With regard to the youth studies associated with the programme objectives, the Commission will support studies focusing, among other subjects, on the impact of measures taken on behalf of young people and, in particular, measures that seek to promote cooperation in this field. Such studies shall analyse the impact of other policies on the world of youth and shall seek to provide a clearer and more comprehensive picture of young people's needs and of the circumstances in which they live.

Priority shall be given to studies concerning the paths taken by less-favoured and marginalised young people; they shall analyse, in particular, the factors which have promoted or hampered the social integration of young people, and shall bring to the fore input from the informal education sector and from the third sector in general. Priority shall also be given to comparative studies of measures designed to promote the spirit of initiative, including their impact on local development, particularly through the creation of activities (creation of jobs, creation of cultural or social enterprises, etc.). This research may take the form of case studies, the most relevant of which shall be made public.

Action 5.3: Information and visibility of measures

The Commission shall take all necessary measures to, *inter alia*, collect information on measures in the youth field from a range of sources, draw benefits from EU youth projects and increase the visibility of the actions aimed at young people at Community level by developing appropriate means of dialogue with them, including through the Internet.

Action 5.4: Support measures

1. *National agencies*

    Community assistance may be provided to support the activities of the structures set up by Member States, in accordance with Article 5 of the Decision.

2. *Technical assistance and operational support*

    In carrying out the programme, the Commission may have recourse to technical-assistance organisations the financing of which may be provided for within the overall financial framework for the programme. It may have recourse to experts under the same conditions. Furthermore, the Commission will be able to undertake evaluation studies and organise such seminars, colloquia or other meetings of experts as are likely to facilitate the implementation of the programme, including application of Article 12 of the Decision. The Commission may also undertake information, publication and dissemination actions.

**Council Decision
of 17 July 2000
amending Decision 1999/311/EC adopting the third phase
of the trans-European cooperation scheme for higher education
(Tempus III) (2000 to 2006)**

(OJ L 183, 22.7.2000)

COUNCIL

COUNCIL DECISION
of 17 July 2000
amending Decision 1999/311/EC adopting the third phase of the trans-European cooperation scheme for higher education (Tempus III) (2000 to 2006)

(2000/460/EC)

THE COUNCIL OF THE EUROPEAN UNION,

Having regard to the Treaty establishing the European Community, and in particular Article 308 thereof,

Having regard to the proposal of the Commission,

Having regard to the opinion of the European Parliament [1],

Having regard to the opinion of the Economic and Social Committee [2],

Having regard to the opinion of the Committee of the Regions [1],

Whereas:

(1) By Decision 1999/311/EC [3] the Council adopted the third phase of the trans-European cooperation scheme for higher education (Tempus III) (2000 to 2006).

(2) This programme is intended for the non-associated countries of central and eastern Europe eligible for economic aid by virtue of Regulation (EEC) No 3906/89 (PHARE programme) [4] or the programme intended to replace it and the new independent states of the former Soviet Union and Mongolia as laid down in Council Regulation (EC, Euratom) No 99/2000 of 29 December 1999 concerning the provision of assistance to the partner States in Eastern Europe and Central Asia [5] (which replaces the old TACIS programme).

(3) The footnote inserted in Article 2 states that 'at present' the programme relates to Albania, Bosnia-Herzegovina and the former Yugoslav Republic of Macedonia.

(4) It is important to be able to extend the Tempus III programme to other countries in the region in future, in particular Croatia,

HAS DECIDED AS FOLLOWS:

Article 1

Decision 1999/311/EC is hereby amended as follows:

1. In Article 2, the first paragraph shall be replaced by the following:

'Tempus III concerns the non-associated countries of central and eastern Europe designated as eligible for economic aid by virtue of Regulation (EEC) No 3906/89 (PHARE programme) or the programme intended to replace it, and the new independent states of the former Soviet Union and Mongolia mentioned in Regulation (EC, Euratom) No 99/2000 (which replaces the old TACIS programme). These countries are hereinafter referred to as "eligible countries".'

2. Footnote 1 shall be deleted.

Article 2

This Decision shall take effect on the day of its publication in the *Official Journal of the European Communities*.

Done at Brussels, 17 July 2000.

For the Council
The President
L. FABIUS

---

[1] Opinion delivered on 14 June 2000 (not yet published in the Official Journal).
[2] Opinion delivered on 29 May 2000 (not yet published in the Official Journal).
[3] OJ L 120, 8.5.1999, p. 30.
[4] OJ L 375, 23.12.1989, p. 11. Regulation as last amended by Regulation (EC) No 1266/1999 (OJ L 161, 20.6.1999, p. 68).
[5] OJ L 12, 18.1.2000, p. 1.

**Decision No 1934/2000/EC of the European Parliament and of the Council
of 17 July 2000
on the European Year of Languages 2001**

(OJ L 232, 14.9.2000)

I

(Acts whose publication is obligatory)

DECISION No 1934/2000/EC OF THE EUROPEAN PARLIAMENT AND OF THE COUNCIL
of 17 July 2000
on the European Year of Languages 2001

THE EUROPEAN PARLIAMENT AND THE COUNCIL OF THE EUROPEAN UNION,

Having regard to the Treaty establishing the European Community and in particular to Articles 149 and 150 thereof,

Having regard to the proposal from the Commission [1],

Having regard to the opinion of the Economic and Social Committee [2],

Having regard to the opinion of the Committee of the Regions [3],

Acting in accordance with the procedure laid down in Article 251 of the Treaty [4],

Whereas:

(1) In the preamble to the Treaty, it is stated that the Member States are: 'Determined to promote the development of the highest possible level of knowledge for their peoples through a wide access to education and through its continuous updating'.

(2) Article 18 of the Treaty establishes the right of every citizen of the European Union 'to move and reside freely within the territory of the Member States'. The ability to use foreign languages is essential in order in practice fully to exercise that right.

(3) Article 151 of the Treaty states that the Community shall contribute to the flowering of the cultures of the Member States while respecting their national and regional diversity, and shall take cultural aspects into account in its action under other provisions of the Treaty. Among the cultural aspects, matters pertaining to languages are of great importance.

(4) All the European languages, in their spoken and written forms, are equal in value and dignity from the cultural point of view and form an integral part of European cultures and civilisation.

(5) The languages question is a challenge that must be tackled as part of the European integration process and the European Year of Languages may therefore prove to be highly instructive as far as the formulation of measures to encourage cultural and linguistic diversity is concerned.

(6) Article 6 of the Treaty on European Union states that the Union shall respect fundamental rights, as guaranteed by the European Convention for the Protection of Human Rights and Fundamental Freedoms.

(7) Access to the vast literary heritage in the languages in which it was originally produced would contribute to developing mutual understanding and giving a tangible content to the concept of European citizenship.

(8) It is important to learn languages as it enhances awareness of cultural diversity and helps eradicate xenophobia, racism, anti-Semitism and intolerance.

(9) In addition to the human, cultural and political advantages, learning languages is also of considerable potential economic benefit.

(10) A command of the respective mother tongue and knowledge of the classical languages, in particular Latin and Greek, can make it easier to learn other languages.

(11) It is important to raise awareness among public and private decision-makers of the importance of easy access to language learning facilities.

(12) The Council Conclusions of 12 June 1995 on linguistic diversity and multilingualism in the European Union emphasised that linguistic diversity must be preserved and multilingualism promoted in the Union, with equal respect for the languages of the Union and with due regard to the principle of subsidiarity. Decision No 2493/95/EC of the European Parliament and Council [5] of 23 October 1995 establishing 1996 as the 'European Year of Lifelong Learning' highlighted the importance of the role of lifelong learning in developing competencies, including linguistic, throughout an individual's lifetime.

---

[1] OJ C 56 E, 29.2.2000, p. 62.
[2] OJ C 51, 23.2.2000, p. 53.
[3] Opinion delivered on 17 February 2000 (not yet published in the Official Journal).
[4] Opinion of the European Parliament of 13 April 2000 (not yet published in the Official Journal). Council Decision of 8 June 2000.

[5] OJ L 256, 26.10.1995, p. 45.

(13) The Commission's 1995 White Paper 'Education, training, research: Teaching and learning: towards a learning society' established as its Objective Four proficiency for all in three Community languages. The Commission's 1996 Green Paper 'Education, Training, Research: The obstacles to transnational mobility' concluded that 'learning at least two Community languages has become a precondition if citizens of the European Union are to benefit from occupational and personal opportunities open to them in the single market'.

(14) Council Resolution of 31 March 1995 on improving and diversifying language learning and teaching within the education systems of the European Union [1] states that pupils should as a general rule have the opportunity of learning two languages of the European Union other than their mother tongue(s) for a minimum of two consecutive years during compulsory schooling and if possible for a longer period.

(15) The measures in the Lingua programme, adopted by Council Decision 89/489/EEC [2], were reinforced and partially integrated as horizontal measures into the Socrates programme adopted by Decision 819/95/EC of the European Parliament and the Council [3]. Those measures have promoted the improvement of knowledge of the languages of the Union and have thus contributed to greater understanding and solidarity between the peoples of the Union. The European Parliament and Council in their Decision No 253/2000/EC [4] propose that those measures be further developed and reinforced in the second phase of the Socrates programme.

(16) The Leonardo da Vinci programme, adopted by Decision 94/819/EC [5] of the European Parliament and the Council, has, building on the results achieved under the Lingua programme, supported activities aimed at developing linguistic skills as part of vocational training measures. That support will be further developed and reinforced in the second phase of the Leonardo da Vinci programme, adopted by Council Decision 1999/382/EC [6].

(17) The Culture 2000 programme adopted by Decision No 508/2000/EC [7] also contributes to improving mutual understanding of the cultural achievements of the European peoples, especially by highlighting cultural diversity and multilingualism.

(18) A multiannual programme to promote the linguistic diversity of the Community in the information society was established by Council Decision 96/664/EC [8].

(19) The Report of the High Level Panel on the Free Movement of Persons presented to the Commission on 18 March 1997, considered 'the multiplicity of European languages [to be] ... a treasure to be safeguarded' and suggested measures to foster language training and the use of languages in the Community.

(20) In accordance with the principle of subsidiarity as defined in Article 5 of the Treaty, the objectives of the proposed action cannot be sufficiently achieved by the Member States, inter alia because of the need for a coherent Community-wide information campaign avoiding duplication and achieving economies of scale. Those objectives can be better achieved by the Community, owing to the transnational dimension of Community actions and measures. This Decision does not go beyond what is necessary to achieve those objectives.

(21) However, it is also important that there should be close cooperation and coordination between the Commission and the Member States, so as to ensure that measures undertaken at European level are underpinned by small-scale measures undertaken at local, regional and national level which are likely to be more suited to the needs of target groups and specific situations, and that cultural diversity is strengthened as a result.

(22) It is important to develop appropriate cooperation between the European Community and the Council of Europe so as to ensure consistency between measures undertaken at Community level and those undertaken by the Council of Europe, and such cooperation is expressly mentioned in Article 149 of the Treaty.

(23) It is important to take into account the fact that the European Year of Languages will take place against the background of preparations for the enlargement of the Union.

(24) This Decision lays down for the entire duration of the programme, a financial framework constituting the prime reference, within the meaning of point 33 of the Interinstitutional Agreement of 6 May 1999 between the European Parliament, the Council and the Commission [9], for the budgetary authority, during the annual budgetary procedure.

(25) The Joint Declaration of 4 May 1999 by the European Parliament, the Council and the Commission [10] sets out the arrangements for the implementation of the co-decision procedure laid down in Article 251 of the Treaty.

(26) The measures necessary for the implementation of this decision should be adopted in accordance with the Council Decision 1999/468/EC of 28 June 1999 laying down the procedures for the exercise of implementing powers conferred on the Commission [11],

---

[1] OJ C 207, 12.8.1995, p. 1.
[2] OJ L 239, 16.8.1989, p. 24.
[3] OJ L 87, 20.4.1995, p. 10. Decision as last amended by Decision 576/98/EC (OJ L 77, 14.3.1998, p. 1).
[4] OJ L 28, 3.2.2000, p. 1.
[5] Council Decision 94/819/EC of 6 December 1994 establishing an action programme for the implementation of a European Community vocational training policy (OJ L 340, 29.12.1994, p. 8).
[6] OJ L 146, 11.6.1999, p. 33.
[7] OJ L 63, 10.3.2000, p. 1.
[8] OJ L 306, 28.11.1996, p. 40.
[9] OJ C 172, 18.6.1999, p. 1.
[10] OJ C 148, 28.5.1999, p. 1.
[11] OJ L 184, 17.7.1999, p. 23.

HAVE DECIDED AS FOLLOWS:

Article 1

Establishment of the European Year of Languages

1. The year 2001 shall be designated as the 'European Year of Languages'.

2. During the European Year of Languages, information and promotional measures will be undertaken on the theme of languages, with the aim of encouraging language learning by all persons residing in the Member States. These measures will cover the official languages of the Community, together with Irish, Letzeburgesch, and other languages in line with those identified by the Member States for the purposes of implementing this Decision.

Article 2

Objectives

The objectives of the European Year of Languages shall be:

(a) to raise awareness of the richness of linguistic and cultural diversity within the European Union and the value in terms of civilisation and culture embodied therein, acknowledging the principle that all languages must be recognised to have equal cultural value and dignity;

(b) to encourage multilingualism;

(c) to bring to the notice of the widest possible public the advantages of competencies in several languages, as a key element in the personal and professional development of individuals (including in finding one's first job), in intercultural understanding, in making full use of the rights conferred by citizenship of the Union and in enhancing the economic and social potential of enterprises and society as a whole. The target public referred to above shall include, among others: pupils and students, parents, workers, job seekers, the speakers of certain languages, the inhabitants of border areas, the peripheral regions, cultural bodies, deprived social groups, migrants, etc.;

(d) to encourage the lifelong learning of languages, where appropriate, starting at preschool and primary school age and related skills involving the use of languages for specific purposes, particularly in a professional context by all persons residing in the Member States, whatever their age, background, social situation or previous educational experiences and achievements;

(e) to collect and disseminate information about the teaching and learning of languages, and about skills, methods (especially innovative methods) and tools, including those developed within other Community measures and initiatives, which assist that teaching and learning including those that are developed in the framework of other Community measures and initiatives and/or facilitate communication between users of different languages.

Article 3

Content of measures

The measures designed to meet the objectives set out in Article 2 include, in particular:

— the use of a common logo and of slogans together with the Council of Europe in accordance with the provisions of Article 10;

— a Community-wide information campaign;

— the organisation of meetings, competitions, prizes and other activities.

Details of these measures are set out in the Annex.

Article 4

Implementation of the Decision and cooperation with the Member States

1. The Commission shall ensure the implementation of the Community measures pursued under this Decision.

2. Each Member State shall designate one or more appropriate bodies to be responsible for participation in the European Year of Languages, the coordination and implementation at national level of the measures provided for in this Decision, including thorough assistance with the selection procedure described in Article 7.

Article 5

Committee

1. The Commission shall be assisted by a Committee.

2. Where reference is made to this paragraph, Articles 3 and 7 of Decision 1999/468/EC shall apply having regard to the provisions of Article 8 thereof.

3. The Committee shall adopt its rules of procedure.

Article 6

Financial arrangements

1. Measures as described in Part I, Section A of the Annex, may be financed up to 100 % by the general budget of the European Union.

2. Measures as described in Part I, Section B of the Annex, may be co-financed by the general budget of the European Union up to a maximum of 50 % of the total cost.

Article 7

Application and selection procedure

1. Applications for the co-financing of measures from the general budget of the European Union under Article 6(2) shall be submitted to the Commission through the body or the bodies designated under Article 4(2). They shall include information enabling the outcome to be assessed on the basis of objective criteria. The Commission shall take the utmost account of the assessment provided by the bodies concerned.

2. Decisions on the financing and co-financing of measures under Article 6 shall be taken by the Commission in accordance with the procedure set out in Article 5(2). The Commission shall ensure a balanced distribution among Member States, where appropriate, among the various languages referred to in Article 1 and among the different fields of activity involved.

ANNEX

I. **Nature of the measures referred to in Article 3**

A. *Measures which may be financed up to 100 % from the general budget of the European Union* (The indicative allocation for these measures shall be 40 % of the overall budget which may be adjusted by the Commission in accordance with the procedure set out in Article 5(2)).

   1. Meetings and events:

      (a) organisation of meetings at Community level and of events to raise awareness of linguistic diversity, including the opening and closing events of the Year;

      (b) organisation in each Member State of one or more presentations of the European Year of Languages, deemed to reach large numbers of people from different social backgrounds.

   2. Information and promotional campaigns involving:

      (a) the development of a logo and slogans for the European Year of Languages, for use in the framework of all activities linked to the Year;

      (b) an information campaign on a Community-wide scale, including, among other things, the setting-up of an interactive Web site and the dissemination of information on projects (including those referred to in section C);

      (c) the production of information materials, for use throughout the Community, which are also accessible to socially vulnerable groups, on effective teaching and learning techniques and on the conditions for successful language learning;

      (d) the organisation of European competitions highlighting achievements and experiences on the themes of the European Year of Languages.

   3. Other measures:

      Surveys and studies on a Community-wide scale, having, *inter alia*, the aim of:

      — better defining the situation in Europe with regard to languages (including sign languages and the classical languages), their use (including in scientific and university research) and language teaching and learning and the acquisition of related skills; as far as possible, all the languages referred to in Article 1 are concerned,

      — better defining the expectations of different target groups (including those in bilingual areas) with regard to language learning and the way in which the Community could fulfil those expectations,

      — carrying out evaluation studies concerning the effectiveness and impact of the European Year of Languages, examining best practice in the field of language teaching and training and disseminating the results throughout the Member States.

B. *Measures which may be co-financed by the general budget of the European Union* (The indicative allocation for these measures shall be 60 % of the overall budget which may be adapted by the Commission in accordance with the procedure set out in Article 5(2)).

   Measures at local, regional, national or transnational level may qualify for financing from the general budget of the European Union up to a maximum of 50 % of the cost, according to the nature and circumstances of what is proposed. These may include, inter alia:

   1. Events around the objectives of the European Year of Languages;

   2. Information measures and measures disseminating examples of good practice, other than those described in Section A;

   3. The organisation of prizes or competitions;

   4. Surveys and studies other than those mentioned in Section A;

   5. Other measures promoting language teaching and learning, provided that those measures would be ineligible for funding under existing Community programmes and initiatives.

C. *Measures receiving no financial aid from the general budget of the European Union*

   The Community will offer its moral support, including written authorisation to use the logo and other material associated with the European Year of Languages, for initiatives undertaken by public or private organisations, where those organisations can demonstrate to the satisfaction of the Commission that the intitiatives involved are or will be in progress during the year 2001 and are likely to contribute significantly to one or more of the objectives of the European Year.

II. **Technical assistance**

   In carrying out these measures, the Commission may have recourse to technical assistance organisations, funding for which may be provided for within the overall budget for the programme. It may, under the same conditions, have recourse to experts. The Commission shall consult the committee referred to in Article 5 on the financial impact of this assistance.

3. The Commission (in particular through its national and regional contact points), in cooperation with the bodies referred to in Article 4(2), shall ensure that calls for proposals are made in sufficient time and circulated as widely as possible.

Article 8

Consistency

The Commission, in cooperation with the Member States, shall ensure:

— consistency between the measures provided for in this Decision and other Community measures and initiatives, in particular those in the field of education, training and culture,

— optimal complementarity between the European Year of Languages and other existing Community, national and regional initiatives and resources, where these can contribute to fulfilling the objectives of the European Year of Languages.

Article 9

Budget

1. The financial framework for the implementation of this programme for the period 1 January to 31 December 2001 is hereby set at EUR 8 million.

2. The annual appropriations shall be authorised by the budgetary authority within the limits of the financial perspective.

Article 10

International cooperation

In the framework of the European Year of Languages, and in accordance with the procedure laid down in Article 5(2), the Commission may cooperate with relevant international organisations. In particular, there shall be close cooperation and coordination as well as joint initiatives with the Council of Europe, in order to strengthen links between the peoples of Europe.

Article 11

Monitoring and evaluation

The Commission shall submit, by 31 December 2002 at the latest, a detailed report containing objective information to the European Parliament, the Council, the Economic and Social Committee and the Committee of the Regions on the implementation, results and overall assessment of all the measures provided for in this Decision.

Article 12

Entry into force

This Decision shall be published in the *Official Journal of the European Communities*. It shall take effect on the day of its publication.

Done at Brussels, 17 July 2000.

For the European Parliament	*For the Council*
The President	*The President*
N. FONTAINE	J. GLAVANY

**Council Decisio
of 28 September 2000
concerning the conclusion of an Agreement between the European Community
and Malta adopting the terms and conditions for the participation of Malta
in Community programmes in the fields of training, education and youth**

(OJ L 267, 20.10.2000)

II

(Acts whose publication is not obligatory)

COUNCIL

COUNCIL DECISION

of 28 September 2000

concerning the conclusion of an Agreement between the European Community and Malta adopting the terms and conditions for the participation of Malta in Community programmes in the fields of training, education and youth

(2000/630/EC)

THE COUNCIL OF THE EUROPEAN UNION,

Having regard to the Treaty establishing the European Community, and in particular Articles 149 and 150, in conjunction with Article 300(2) and (3), first subparagraph thereof,

Having regard to the proposal from the Commission,

Having regard to the opinion of the European Parliament [1],

Whereas:

(1) The participation of Malta in Community programmes is an important element of the pre-accession strategy for Malta as set out in Council Regulation (EC) No 555/2000 of 13 March 2000 on the implementation of operations in the framework of the pre-accession strategy for the Republic of Cyprus and the Republic of Malta [2].

(2) Council Decision 1999/382/EC of 26 April 1999 establishing the second phase of the Community vocational training action programme 'Leonardo da Vinci' [3], and in particular Article 10 thereof, Decision No 253/2000/EC of the European Parliament and of the Council of 24 January 2000 establishing the second phase of the Communiy action programme in the field of education 'Socrates' [4], and in particular Article 12 thereof, and Decision No 1031/2000/EC of the European Parliament and of the Council of 13 April 2000 establishing the 'Youth' Community action programme [5], and in particular Article 11 thereof, provide that these programmes are to be open to the participation of Malta.

(3) In conformity with the negotiating guidelines adopted by the Council on 14 February 2000, the Commission has negotiated, on behalf of the Community, an agreement to enable Malta to participate in these programmes.

(4) This Agreement should be approved,

HAS DECIDED AS FOLLOWS:

Article 1

The Agreement between the European Community and Malta adopting the terms and conditions for the participation of Malta in Community programmes in the fields of training, education and youth is hereby approved on behalf of the Community.

The text of the Agreement is attached to this Decision.

Article 2

The President of the Council is hereby authorised to appoint the person(s) empowered to sign the Agreement in order to bind the Community.

Article 3

The President of the Council shall, on behalf of the Community, give the notifications provided for in Article 4 of the Agreement.

Done at Brussels, 28 September 2000.

For the Council
The President
D. VAILLANT

---

[1] Opinion delivered on 6 September 2000 (not yet published in the Official Journal).
[2] OJ L 68, 16.3.2000, p. 3.
[3] OJ L 146, 11.6.1999, p. 33.
[4] OJ L 28, 3.2.2000, p. 1.
[5] OJ L 117, 18.5.2000, p. 1.

**Resolution of the Council and of the Representatives of the Governments
of the Member States, meeting within the Council,
of 14 December 2000
concerning an action plan for mobility**

(OJ C 371, 23.12.2000)
–   **Corrigendum D (OJ C 66, 1.3.2001)**

RESOLUTION OF THE COUNCIL AND OF THE REPRESENTATIVES OF THE GOVERNMENTS OF THE MEMBER STATES, MEETING WITHIN THE COUNCIL

of 14 December 2000

concerning an action plan for mobility

(2000/C 371/03)

THE COUNCIL OF THE EUROPEAN UNION AND THE REPRESENTATIVES OF THE GOVERNMENTS OF THE MEMBER STATES, MEETING WITHIN THE COUNCIL;

CONVINCED that the construction of a genuine European area of knowledge is a priority for the European Community and that it is through education that Europeans will acquire the shared cultural references that are the basis of European citizenship and of a political Europe.

SURE that this belief is based on mutual discovery of our diversity and complementarity and involves increased personal contacts and exchange of knowledge and experience.

CONVINCED, that it is therefore essential to target intelligible action, shared by all of the Member States, at young people, schoolchildren, students, researchers, all those being educated and their teachers; that it is by building the Europe of intelligence that we will bring about a true feeling of being part of Europe.

AWARE that the Europe of knowledge is also an economic necessity; that in an internationalised economy increasingly founded on knowledge, openness to foreign cultures and the ability to educate oneself and work in a multilingual environment are essential to the competitiveness of the European economy.

CONVINCED that increasing the mobility of young people, schoolchildren, students, researchers, all those being educated and their teachers in Europe is thus a major political goal and that it requires simultaneous commitment and effort by the European Community and the Member States.

NOTE that to attain this goal Europe already has a wealth of resources: the Community's Socrates, Leonardo da Vinci and Youth programmes represent appreciable progress and play an essential role which will increase with the second generation of programmes.

CONVINCED that this progress must be taken further; that even if the number of people choosing mobility is on the increase, it is still small; that, for example, among students it concerns only a small percentage; that substantial obstacles remain: unequal access to information, obstacles of a financial nature, administrative difficulties as regards tax and social benefits, complex residence procedures, disadvantages in terms of status and career.

NOTE that the Extraordinary European Council in Lisbon of 23 and 24 March 2000 recognised the urgency of removing obstacles and promoting mobility and that, in its conclusions, it invited the Council and Commission to define 'by the end of 2000, the means for fostering the mobility of students, teachers and training and research staff both through making the best use of existing Community programmes, by removing obstacles and through greater transparency in the recognition of qualifications and periods of study and training' (paragraph 26).

UNDERTAKE, to meet the great expectations of their fellow citizens, that with the support of the Commission, each in its field, and in full compliance with the principle of subsidiarity it will take the steps necessary to remove obstacles to mobility and to promote it.

CONSIDER that this Resolution, far from prejudging the substantial amount of work already done by the Commission and the Council towards providing a suitable legal framework for promoting mobility and in particular the proposal for a Recommendation on mobility which it is hoped will be adopted soon aims, on the contrary, to facilitate the implementation of Community initiatives in this area by suggesting possible specific initiatives. These initiatives will be implemented in close cooperation with all the participants and institutions concerned, in particular universities, whose participation is a key to success.

WELCOME the mobility action plan set out in the Annex which was submitted to the Ministers for Education at the Sorbonne on 30 September 2000. That plan has three major objectives:

— to define and democratise mobility in Europe;

— to promote appropriate forms of funding;

— to increase mobility and improve the conditions for it.

The measures mentioned in the Action Plan are conceived as a 'toolbox' of 42 measures divided into four main chapters which, in their individual scope and combination, are designed to identify and deal with the obstacles encountered by those who, no matter where, seek to implement a mobility measure.

The first chapter concerns actions to promote mobility through measures to train people who help to implement mobility, to develop multilingual skills and to access useful information.

The second chapter covers the funding of mobility and seeks to identify a series of measures that will mobilise all possible financial resources.

The third chapter aims to increase and improve mobility by multiplying the forms that it may take and by improving reception facilities and the organisation of timetables.

Lastly, the fourth chapter describes measures to make the most of periods of mobility and gain recognition of the experience acquired.

CONVINCED that if all Member States, with the assistance of the Commission, make use on a voluntary basis of those actions which they consider will best enable the obstacles encountered by those requesting mobility in their countries to be overcome, all agree from the outset that the following measures in the action plan are of particular importance:

— developing multilingualism,

— establishment of a portal giving access to the different European sources of information on mobility,

— recognition of periods of mobility in diploma courses,

— training of the teachers and administrative staff involved to become true mobility organisers able to provide advice and guidance and draft mobility projects,

— definition and adoption of a quality charter on reception facilities for foreign nationals on training courses,

— drawing up of an inventory of existing mobility circuits and good practices, exchanges of students, trainees and trainers,

— creating linkage between mobility funding from the Union, the Member States and local authorities, the public sector and the private sector.

PROPOSE that, as part of rolling programming instituted by the Council in its Resolution of 17 December 1999 (¹) and for the sake of regular assessment of progress in achieving the targets set, the Council, in collaboration with the other European institutions concerned, regularly take stock of the situation, in principle every two years.

RECALL that the plan also identifies measures of broader scope coming under larger-scale coordination within each Member State and between the Commission and the Member States' administrations.

In accordance with the conclusions of the Extraordinary European Council in Lisbon, this Resolution is submitted to the European Council in Nice.

(¹) Council Resolution of 17 December 1999 on 'Into the new millenium': developing new working procedures for European cooperation in the field of education and training (OJ C 8, 12.1.2000, p. 6).

ANNEX

MOBILITY ACTION PLAN

Objectives and measures proposed

A. GENERAL OBJECTIVE

Central objective	Adopt a European mobility strategy	Implementation
measure A	**Define**: establishment of a common definition of the concept of mobility and the target groups concerned — age, circuit, geographical scope, length of stay	Commission, Member States
measure B	**Democratise**: democratisation of access to mobility measures	Member States

B. PARTICULAR OBJECTIVES

I. PROMOTING MOBILITY IN EUROPE

Objective 11	Train people to act as contacts for mobility in Europe	Implementation
measure 111	**Proper guidance**: preparation of teachers and the relevant administrative staff to become mobility organisers, able to provide advice and guidance and draft mobility projects: training on the mobility circuits, the different education systems in the Union, the rights of those opting for mobility	Commission, Member States
measure 112	**More exchanges**: development of exchanges between mobility organisers from the countries taking part in Community programmes	Member States
measure 113	**More resources**: encouragement of educational establishments and universities to devote more resources to international relations in order to cope with the new demands of mobility	Member States

Objective 12	Develop multilingualism	Implementation
measure 121	**Specific training**: promotion of training in the relevant foreign language and culture before and during the mobility period, making use of the public sector and of private initiatives	Member States
measure 122	**Instructor placements**: opportunity for language teachers to go on long-term training placements abroad	Member States
measure 123	**Exchange of good practice**: exchange of good language-teaching practice, particularly as regards vocational or adult courses	Commission, Member States
measure 124	**Common indicators**: use of common indicators to evaluate the language skills of pupils, students and trainees	Commission, Member States
measure 125	**Quality commitment**: follow up to the Council Resolution of 31 March 1995 on improving and diversifying language learning and teaching within the education systems of the European Union (OJ C 207, 12.8.1995, p. 1)	Commission, Member States

Objective 13	Make it easier to find information on mobility	Implementation
measure 131	**A 'mobility' portal site**: creation of a portal site providing access to the various European sources of information on mobility	Commission, Member States, National Agencies for Socrates, Leonardo da Vinci and Youth
measure 132	**Ad hoc forums**: introduction in educational establishments and universities of electronic chat rooms for mobility organisers, students, trainees and young volunteers to exchange information	Commission, Member States, National Agencies for Socrates, Leonardo da Vinci and Youth

Objective 14	Draw up a mobility chart	Implementation
measure 141	**Identification of circuits**: joint definition of a methodology enabling each Member State which so wishes gradually to compile reliable statistics on mobility and make as full as possible an inventory of the student, trainee and instructor exchange circuits	Commission, Member States, National Agencies for Socrates, Leonardo da Vinci and Youth
measure 142	**Programme awareness**: creation of a database of all the bilateral or multilateral mobility programmes operating in Europe, perhaps limited to public programmes	Commission, Member States
measure 143	**Advertising of posts**: encouraging the advertising of posts for higher education teaching staff and researchers throughout the Union, using the thematic circuits, particularly EURES	Commission, Member States

II. PROMOTING THE FINANCING OF MOBILITY

Objective 21	Look into the financing of mobility: towards financial partnerships	Implementation
measure 211	**A partnership framework**: strengthening coordination between the various players, for example by means of a framework for partnerships: the European Union, the State, local authorities and universities, and making best use of financing	Commission, Member States
measure 212	**Bigger budgets**: study of possible ways of making better use of or increasing national and local mobility budgets	Member States
measure 213	**Encouragement of the public sector**: examine the desirability and possibility of loans at preferential rates for those intending to take a period of mobility	Member States
measure 214	**Multiple partnerships**: encouragement of the private sector, businesses, foundations and social partners to become involved in financing mobility (for example by means of establishing foundations, seals of approval for bank loans)	Member States, Commission
measure 215	**Looking ahead**: study of ways of redeploying the mobility appropriations in the Community budget and programmes when they come up for review	Commission, Member States

Objective 22	Democratise mobility by making it financially and socially accessible to all	Implementation
measure 221	**An information campaign**: launching of an information campaign on: — the mobility assistance available and how to apply for it; — the practical administrative aspects of mobility at the time of going abroad and during the period spent there	Commission
measure 222	**Retention of benefits**: assure people who take mobility that they will continue to receive the benefits provided for by national and Community provisions in force; regularly review any problems that persist and take suitable steps to remedy them	Member States
measure 223	**Equal treatment**: study of the possibility of offering young people opting for mobility the same preferential tariffs as young people in the host country; regularly review any problems that persist and take suitable steps to remedy them	Member States

III. INCREASING AND IMPROVING MOBILITY

Objective 31	Introduce new forms of mobility	Implementation
measure 311	**Summer universities**: organisation of more European summer universities for students, academic or vocational trainees and mobility organisers	Commission, Member States
measure 312	**Courses on the Internet**: making academic and vocational training modules available on the Internet	Commission, Member States
measure 313	**Develop circuits**: creation or strengthening of bilateral or multilateral exchange circuits, in particular mobility partnerships between universities	Member States

Objective 32	Improve reception facilities for people opting for mobility	Implementation
measure 321	**A quality charter**: definition and adoption by players of a quality charter covering reception facilities for trainees who are foreign nationals and providing in particular for the necessary means of ensuring equal reception facilities for people opting for mobility (for example one-stop information shops or free services)	Commission, Member States
measure 322	**On-line information**: provision of on-line information on the reception facilities for people opting for mobility	Commission, Member States, National Agencies for Socrates, Leonardo da Vinci and Youth

Objective 33	Simplify the mobility calendar	Implementation
measure 331	**Clear dates**: wide dissemination of information on university calendars and school years	Member States, National Agencies for Socrates, Leonardo da Vinci and Youth
measure 332	**A European calendar**: with due regard to the autonomy of universities, drafting of a European academic calendar showing the core periods of term time, and in appropriate cases concentration of mobility training modules in those periods	Commission, Member States, National Agencies for Socrates, Leonardo da Vinci and Youth
measure 333	**Adoption of semesters**: study of the possibility of dividing the university year into semesters and of enrolling and paying fees by semester	Member States

Objective 34	A proper status for people opting for mobility	Implementation
measure 341	**Mobility as a priority**: declaration by the relevant authorities that mobility is a priority which will ultimately become an important component of instruction given or received by students and trainees, by teachers right through from primary to higher education, and by instructors	Member States
measure 342	**A specific youth card**: creation of a European card for young people opting for mobility	Commission, Member States
measure 343	**Mobility for teachers undergoing training**: opportunity for teachers to take all or part of their initial or continuing training in another Member State	Member States
measure 344	**One status for all**: examine the possibility of extending the current higher-education post of associate member of the teaching staff to other levels and to other circuits of education, in Member States where it seems appropriate to do so	Member States

IV. GAINING MORE FROM PERIODS OF MOBILITY

Objective 41	Increase crossover opportunities by developing the system of recognition and equivalence of diplomas and training	Implementation
measure 411	**Equivalence**: encouragement for all universities to generalise systems of diploma equivalence, the European Community Course Credit Transfer System (ECTS), the Sorbonne and Bologna process particularly via the European Network of National Information Centres on academic mobility and recognition (ENIC network) and the National Academic Recognition Information Centres (NARIC)	Commission, Member States, National Agencies for Socrates, Leonardo da Vinci and Youth
measure 412	**An addendum**: generalisation of academic and vocational diploma supplements to make them recognisable in all Member States	Member States

Objective 42	Recognise the experience acquired	Implementation
measure 421	**Recognised experience**: issue by the relevant authorities of the host State of a document certifying the skills acquired during the period of mobility, with particular reference to languages, and taking into account by the relevant authorities of the country of origin of periods of study or training successfully completed abroad	Member States
measure 422	**An ad hoc document**: generalisation of the Europass training [1]	Commission, Member States
measure 423	**Voluntary work**: taking into account of voluntary work in the Member State of origin	Member States

[1] Council Decision of 21 December 1998 on the promotion of European partnerships in work-linked training, including apprenticeship (OJ L 17, 22.1.1999, p. 45).

Objective 43	Gain more from periods of mobility	Implementation
measure 431	**Professional incentives**: examine the desirability and possibilities in national law and practice of making the best use of the experience gained by teaching staff who have taken a period of mobility	Member States
measure 432	**Suitable methodology**: devise a methodology for measuring the professional impact of periods of mobility	Commission, Member States

**Resolution of the Council and of the Representatives of the Governments
of the Member States, meeting within the Council,
of 14 December 2000
on the social inclusion of young people**

(OJ C 374, 28.12.2000)

RESOLUTION OF THE COUNCIL AND OF THE REPRESENTATIVES OF THE GOVERNMENTS OF THE MEMBER STATES, MEETING WITHIN THE COUNCIL,

of 14 December 2000

on the social inclusion of young people

(2000/C 374/04)

THE COUNCIL AND THE REPRESENTATIVES OF THE GOVERNMENTS OF THE MEMBER STATES, MEETING WITHIN THE COUNCIL

Whereas:

(1) Article 2 of the Treaty establishing the European Community gave the Community the task of promoting throughout the Community a harmonious, balanced and sustainable development of economic activities and a high level of employment and of social protection and the raising of the standard of living and quality of life.

(2) Article 136 of the said Treaty assigned to the Community and the Member States the particular objectives of the promotion of employment, improved living and working conditions and the combating of exclusion.

(3) Article 149 of the said Treaty provides for action by the Community to be aimed in particular at encouraging the development of youth exchanges and of exchanges of socio-educational instructors.

(4) The Lisbon declaration on youth policies and programmes defined guidelines for developing youth policy, in particular in the areas of education, employment, participation and health [1].

(5) The European Parliament and the Council, in their Decision No 253/2000/EC of 24 January 2000 establishing the second phase of the Community action programme in the field of education 'Socrates' [2] and their Decision No 1031/2000/EC of 13 April 2000 establishing the 'Youth' Community action programme [3], and the Council in its Decision 1999/382/EC of 26 April 1999 establishing the second phase of the Community vocational training action programme 'Leonardo da Vinci' [4], established Community action programmes contributing to the construction of a Europe of knowledge open to all.

(6) On 8 February 1999 the Council and the Ministers responsible for Youth adopted a resolution on youth participation, which emphasises the importance of young people taking an active part in social, political, cultural and economic life.

(7) The 'Youth' Council on 23 November 1999 established guidelines including a cross-sectoral approach to youth questions and a policy based on involving young people which are to underpin the policy of cooperation regarding youth.

(8) The European Council meeting in Lisbon on 23 and 24 March 2000 set a strategic goal for the European Union linking economic progress with social progress. In pursuit of that goal the European Council advocated an open method of coordination and called for the setting of appropriate targets for the fight against poverty and social exclusion to be approved by the end of the year, while emphasising that the best safeguard against social exclusion is a job and that the improvement of skills, education and lifelong training, voluntary service activities and universal access to knowledge, play an important part in combating social exclusion.

(9) The Commission has adopted a communication on a social policy agenda in preparation for the European Council in Nice, based on recognition of the interaction between economic, employment and social policies,

TAKE THE VIEW that the process of European construction cannot succeed without the involvement of young people.

---

[1] Declaration adopted at the World Conference of Ministers Responsible for Youth, held in Lisbon in August 1998.
[2] OJ L 28, 3.2.2000, p. 1.
[3] OJ L 117, 18.5.2000, p. 1.
[4] OJ L 146, 11.6.1999, p. 33.

AFFIRM that, with their wealth of experience, capabilities and critical acumen, young people must be more closely associated with the policies which concern them. Similarly, social and institutional players dealing with young people should have an opportunity to give their views and make their contribution to a policy of cooperation in the youth field.

CONSIDER that exchanges of young people in Europe help, on the one hand, to make young people more aware of what is at stake in Europe by making Europe more real for them, and, on the other, to encourage a better understanding among them of Europe's cultural diversity, as well as of its common fundamental values, based on the endeavour to ensure respect for human rights and to combat racism, anti-semitism, xenophobia and other forms of discrimination, to increase a sense of solidarity and to develop their spirit of initiative.

NOTE that young people, particularly the most vulnerable, are particularly susceptible to social, political and cultural exclusion.

STRESS the difficulties encountered by many young people in gaining autonomy and attaining social and occupational inclusion.

WELCOME what has been done under the Luxembourg process, through the guidelines on employment and the initiative launched by the Lisbon European Council for a Community action programme to fight social exclusion, which have all, in their own field, contributed to the social inclusion of young people.

ENCOURAGE the Community institutions and Member States, in line with the principle of subsidiarity and further to the Lisbon European Council, to launch Europe-wide cooperation initiatives in conjunction with national and, as appropriate, regional and local youth policies, and INVITE, in this context, the Commission and the Member States, each within its own sphere of competence, to:

(i) make the improvement of the socioeconomic situation of young people and their social inclusion, as well as preventing and tackling their exclusion, a priority common to all relevant European Union policies;

(ii) promote broad access by a wide range of young people to Community and national initiatives and programmes designed for their benefit, particularly with regard to mobility;

(iii) study common objectives directed at:

— developing for all young people residing legally in a Member State conditions which enable them to play a full part in economic and social life (standard of living, quality of life, employment, training, education, housing, healthcare, culture, sport and leisure),

— fighting discriminatory behaviour against young people, whether based on sex, race or ethnic origin, religion or beliefs, disability, age or sexual orientation,

— preventing breakdowns in conditions of existence which could lead to situations of marginalisation and the risk of exclusion, particularly by developing capabilities for occupational inclusion and by promoting policies aimed at ensuring that no one is excluded from the information society,

— assisting the mobilisation of institutional, social and economic players to help the social inclusion of young people,

— encouraging young people to participate in drawing up the policies which concern them.

(iv) develop exchanges of information and good practice in the field of combating the social exclusion of young people;

ENCOURAGE the Member States to:

(a) promote measures to prevent young people being excluded, unemployed and leading a precarious existence, and develop new training opportunities for young people excluded from education and training systems;

(b) foster access and return to work for those young people having the greatest difficulty in entering the world of work;

(c) develop accompanying measures suited to situations of job and training rotation;

(d) fight discrimination against young people in employment, particularly as regards access to and conditions of employment;

(e) promote access to quality education and initiate support measures for young people in particular difficulty, and, under the guidelines for employment, for young people who drop out of the school system early;

(f) encourage access to information for young people and take steps to ensure that young people are not excluded from new information technologies, so that they can fully utilise them;

(g) encourage young people to obtain and hold on to housing;

(h) strengthen the shelter and support structures for young people from broken homes who have been the victims of or threatened with violence;

(i) seek a high level of health protection for young people and develop preventive health care and information, particularly on contraception and sexuality, taking into account their specific needs and the requirement of confidentiality, and on substance abuse;

(j) develop leisure-time sporting, cultural and educational activities directed at young people, particularly by encouraging incentive pricing policies;

(k) support non-governmental youth organisations and youth associations, both in the measures they take to help young people and in the opportunities they offer young people of playing an active role in civil society;

(l) develop information suited to young people, particularly by using qualified staff;

(m) create the conditions for young people to become involved in the decisions taken concerning them.

WISH THIS RESOLUTION to contribute to the development of the policy of cooperation in the youth field, in particular by defining common objectives to work towards and to be taken into consideration when targets for combating poverty and social exclusion are being determined and implemented.

**Council Decision
of 22 December 2000
concerning the conclusion of an Agreement between
the European Community and the Republic of Cyprus
adopting the terms and conditions for the participation
of the Republic of Cyprus in Community programmes
in the fields of training, education and youth**

(OJ L 29, 31.1.2001)

II

(Acts whose publication is not obligatory)

COUNCIL

COUNCIL DECISION
of 22 December 2000
concerning the conclusion of an Agreement between the European Community and the Republic of Cyprus adopting the terms and conditions for the participation of the Republic of Cyprus in Community programmes in the fields of training, education and youth

(2001/84/EC)

THE COUNCIL OF THE EUROPEAN UNION,

Having regard to the Treaty establishing the European Community, and in particular Articles 149 and 150, in conjunction with Article 300(2), first sentence, and (3), first sub-paragraph thereof,

Having regard to the proposal from the Commission,

Having regard to the opinion of the European Parliament [1],

Whereas:

(1) The participation of Cyprus in Community programmes is an important element of the pre-accession strategy for Cyprus as set out in Council Regulation (EC) No 555/2000 of 13 March 2000 on the implementation of operations in the framework of the pre-accession strategy for the Republic of Cyprus and the Republic of Malta [2].

(2) Council Decision 1999/382/EC of 26 April 1999 establishing the second phase of the Community vocational training action programme 'Leonardo da Vinci' [3], and in particular Article 10 thereof, Decision No 253/2000/EC of 24 January 2000 of the European Parliament and of the Council establishing the second phase of the Community action programme in the field of education 'Socrates' [4], and in particular Article 12 thereof, and Decision No 1031/2000/EC of 13 April 2000 of the European Parliament and of the Council establishing the 'Youth' Community action programme [5], and in particular Article 11 thereof, provide that these programmes shall be open to the participation of Cyprus.

(3) In conformity with the negotiating guidelines adopted by the Council on 14 February 2000, the Commission has negotiated, on behalf of the European Community, an agreement to enable Cyprus to participate in these programmes.

(4) The Agreement should be approved,

HAS DECIDED AS FOLLOWS:

Article 1

The Agreement between the European Community and the Republic of Cyprus adopting the terms and conditions for the participation of the Republic of Cyprus in Community programmes in the fields of training, education and youth is hereby approved on behalf of the Community.

The text of the Agreement is attached to this Decision.

Article 2

The President of the Council is hereby authorised to appoint the person(s) empowered to sign the Agreement in order to bind the Community.

---
[1] Opinion delivered on 13 December 2000 (not yet published in the Official Journal).
[2] OJ L 68, 16.3.2000, p. 3.
[3] OJ L 146, 11.6.1999, p. 33.
[4] OJ L 28, 3.2.2000, p. 1.
[5] OJ L 117, 18.5.2000, p. 1.

Article 3

The President of the Council shall, on behalf of the Community, give the notifications provided for in Article 4 of the Agreement.

Done at Brussels, 22 December 2000.

For the Council
The President
C. PIERRET

AGREEMENT

between the European Community and the Republic of Cyprus adopting the terms and conditions for the participation of the Republic of Cyprus in Community programmes in the fields of training, education and youth

THE EUROPEAN COMMUNITY,

of the one part, and

THE REPUBLIC OF CYPRUS, hereinafter referred to as Cyprus,

of the other part,

Whereas:

(1) Council Decision 1999/382/EC of 26 April 1999 establishing the second phase of the Community vocational training action programme 'Leonardo da Vinci' [1], and in particular Article 10 thereof, and Decision No 253/2000/EC of 24 January 2000 of the European Parliament and of the Council establishing the second phase of the Community action programme in the field of education 'Socrates' [2], and in particular Article 12 thereof, and Decision No 1031/2000/EC of 13 April 2000 of the European Parliament and of the Council establishing the 'Youth' Community action programme [3], and in particular Article 11 thereof, provide that these programmes shall be open to the participation of Cyprus.

(2) Cyprus has expressed the wish to participate in these programmes.

(3) The participation of Cyprus in these programmes constitutes a significant step in the pre-accession strategy of Cyprus as set out in Council Regulation (EC) No 555/2000 of 13 March 2000 on the implementation of operations in the framework of the pre-accession strategy for the Republic of Cyprus and the Republic of Malta [4],

HAVE AGREED AS FOLLOWS:

Article 1

Cyprus shall participate, from 2001, in the second phase of the European Community action programmes Leonardo da Vinci and Socrates ('Leonardo da Vinci II' and 'Socrates II') and in the 'Youth' Community action programme ('Youth') according to the terms and conditions set out in Annexes I and II which shall form an integral part of this Agreement.

Article 2

This Agreement shall apply from 1 January 2001 until the end of the programmes.

Article 3

This Agreement shall apply, on the one hand, to the territories in which the Treaty establishing the European Community is applied and under the conditions laid down in that Treaty and, on the other, to the territory of Cyprus.

Article 4

This Agreement shall enter into force on the day of the notification by the Contracting Parties of the completion of their respective procedures.

Article 5

This Agreement is drawn up in duplicate in the Danish, Dutch, English, French, Finnish, German, Greek, Italian, Portuguese, Spanish and Swedish languages, each of these texts being equally authentic.

Done at Brussels, 22 December 2000.

For the European Community

For the Republic of Cyprus

---

[1] OJ L 146, 11.6.1999, p. 33.
[2] OJ L 28, 3.2.2000, p. 1.
[3] OJ L 117, 18.5.2000, p. 1.
[4] OJ L 68, 16.3.2000, p. 3.

ANNEX I

Terms and conditions for the participation of Cyprus in Leonardo da Vinci II, Socrates II and Youth

1. Cyprus will participate in Leonardo da Vinci II, Socrates II and Youth ('Programmes') in conformity, unless otherwise provided in this Agreement, with the objectives, criteria, procedures and deadlines as defined in Decision 1999/382/EC, Decision No 253/2000/EC and Decision No 1031/2000/EC. It will participate in all the activities of the Programmes, with the exception of certain activities within Youth which are devoted to cooperation with third countries which are not full participants in that programme.

2. In conformity with the terms of respective Articles 5 of the said Decisions and with the provisions relating to the responsibilities of the Member States and of the Commission of the European Communities concerning the Leonardo da Vinci, Socrates and Youth National Agencies adopted by the Commission, Cyprus shall establish the appropriate structures for the coordinated management of the implementation of the programme actions at national level and take the measures needed to ensure the adequate funding of these Agencies, which will receive programme grants for their activities. Cyprus will take all other necessary steps for the efficient running of the Programmes at national level.

3. To participate in the Programmes, Cyprus will pay each year a contribution to the general budget of the European Union according to the detailed arrangements described in Annex II.

   If necessary in order to take into account programme developments, or the evolution of Cyprus's absorption capacity, the Association Council is entitled to adapt this contribution, so as to avoid budgetary imbalance in the implementation of the programmes.

4. The terms and conditions for the submission, assessment and selection of applications related to eligible institutions, organisations and individuals of Cyprus will be the same as those applicable to eligible institutions, organisations and individuals of the Community.

   Cypriot experts may be taken into consideration by the Commission when appointing independent experts according to the relevant provisions of the decisions establishing the programmes to assist it in the project evaluation.

5. With a view to ensuring the Community dimension of the Programmes, to be eligible for Community financial support, projects and activities will have to include at least a partner from one of the Member States of the Community.

6. For the mobility activities referred to in Annex I, section III.1 of the Leonardo da Vinci II decision, and for the actions to be managed on a decentralised basis within Socrates and Youth, as well as for financial support to the activities of the National Agencies set up in accordance with point 2 of this Annex, funds will be allocated to Cyprus on the basis of the annual programme budget breakdown decided at Community level and Cyprus's contribution to the programme. The maximum amount of financial support to the activities of the National Agencies will not exceed 50 % of the budget for the National Agencies' work programmes.

7. The Member States of the Community and Cyprus will make every effort, within the framework of existing provisions, to facilitate the free movement and residence of students, teachers, trainees, trainers, university administrators, young people and other eligible persons moving between Cyprus and the Member States of the Community for the purpose of participating in activities covered by this Agreement.

8. Activities covered by this Agreement shall be exempt from imposition by Cyprus of indirect taxes, customs duties, prohibitions and restrictions on imports and exports in respect of goods and services intended for use under such activities.

9. Without prejudice to the responsibilities of the Commission of the European Communities and the Court of Auditors of the European Communities in relation to the monitoring and evaluation of the programmes pursuant to the decisions concerning Leonardo da Vinci II, Socrates II and Youth (Articles 13, 14 and 13 respectively), the participation of Cyprus in the programmes will be continuously monitored on a partnership basis involving the Commission of the European Communities and Cyprus. Cyprus will submit to the Commission relevant reports and take part in other specific activities set out by the Community in that context.

10. In conformity with the Community's financial regulations, contractual arrangements concluded with, or by, entities of Cyprus shall provide for controls and audits to be carried out by, or under the authority of, the Commission and the Court of Auditors. As far as financial audits are concerned, they may be carried out with the purpose of controlling such entities' income and expenditures, related to the contractual obligations towards the Community. In a spirit of cooperation and mutual interest, the relevant authorities of Cyprus shall provide any reasonable and feasible assistance as may be necessary or helpful under the circumstances to perform such controls and audits.

    The provisions relating to the responsibilities of the Member States and of the Commission concerning the Leonardo da Vinci, Socrates and Youth National Agencies adopted by the Commission will apply to the relations between Cyprus, the Commission and the Cypriot National Agencies. In the event of irregularity, negligence or fraud imputable to the Cypriot National Agencies, the Cypriot authorities shall be responsible for the funds not recovered.

11. Without prejudice to the procedures referred to in Article 7 of the Decision on Leonardo da Vinci II and respective Articles 8 of the Decisions on Socrates II and Youth, representatives of Cyprus will participate as observers in the Programme Committees, for the points which concern them. These committees shall meet without the presence of representatives of Cyprus for the rest of the points, as well as at the time of voting.

12. The language to be used in all contacts with the Commission, as regards the application process, contracts, reports to be submitted and other administrative arrangements for the programmes, will be any of the official languages of the Community.

13. The Community and Cyprus may terminate activities under this Agreement at any time upon twelve months' notice in writing. Projects and activities in progress at the time of termination shall continue until their completion under the conditions laid down in this Agreement.

ANNEX II

Financial contribution of Cyprus to Leonardo da Vinci II, Socrates II and Youth

1. Leonardo da Vinci

The financial contribution to be paid by Cyprus to the general budget of the European Union to participate in the Leonardo da Vinci II programme will be the following (in euro):

Year 2001	Year 2002	Year 2003	Year 2004	Year 2005	Year 2006
497 000	529 000	552 000	574 000	603 000	626 000

2. Socrates

The financial contribution to be paid by Cyprus to the general budget of the European Union to participate in the Socrates II programme will be the following (in euro):

Year 2001	Year 2002	Year 2003	Year 2004	Year 2005	Year 2006
681 000	697 000	712 000	731 000	753 000	780 000

3. Youth

The financial contribution to be paid by Cyprus to the general budget of the European Union to participate in the Youth programme will be the following (in euro):

Year 2001	Year 2002	Year 2003	Year 2004	Year 2005	Year 2006
533 000	565 000	598 000	627 000	658 000	698 000

4. Cyprus will pay the contribution mentioned above partly from the Cypriot national budget, and partly from Cyprus's pre-accession funds. Subject to a separate programming procedure within the framework of Regulation (EC) No 555/2000, the requested pre-accession funds will be transferred to Cyprus by means of a separate Financing Memorandum. Together with the part coming from Cyprus's State budget, these funds will constitute Cyprus's national contribution, out of which it will make payments in response to annual calls for funds from the Commission.

5. The pre-accession funds will be requested according to the following schedule:
— for the contribution to the Leonardo da Vinci II programme, the following yearly amounts (in euro)

Year 2001	Year 2002	Year 2003	Year 2004	Year 2005	Year 2006
200 000	200 000	200 000	200 000	200 000	150 000

— for the contribution to the Socrates II programme, the following yearly amounts (in euro)

Year 2001	Year 2002	Year 2003	Year 2004	Year 2005	Year 2006
400 000	350 000	300 000	300 000	200 000	150 000

— for the contribution to the Youth programme, the following yearly amounts (in euro)

Year 2001	Year 2002	Year 2003	Year 2004	Year 2005	Year 2006
400 000	300 000	250 000	200 000	200 000	150 000

The remaining part of the contribution of Cyprus will be covered from the Cypriot State budget.

6. The financial regulation applicable to the general budget of the European Union will apply, notably to the management of the contribution of Cyprus.

   Travel costs and subsistence costs incurred by representatives and experts of Cyprus for the purposes of taking part as observers in the work of the committees referred to in Annex I, Point 11 or other meetings related to the implementation of the Programmes shall be reimbursed by the Commission on the same basis as and in accordance with the procedures currently in force for nongovernmental experts of the Member States.

7. After the entry into force of this Agreement and at the beginning of each following year, the Commission will send to Cyprus a call for funds corresponding to its contribution to each of the respective programmes under this Agreement.

   This contribution shall be expressed in euros and paid into an euro bank account of the Commission.

   Cyprus will pay its contribution according to the call for funds:
   — by 1 May for the part financed from its national budget, provided that the call for funds is sent by the Commission before 1 April, or at the latest one month after the call for funds is sent if later;
   — by 1 May for the part financed from the pre-accession funds, provided that the corresponding amounts have been sent to Cyprus by this time, or at the latest in a period of 30 days after these funds have been sent to Cyprus.

   Any delay in the payment of the contribution shall give rise to the payment of interest by Cyprus on the outstanding amount from the due date. The interest rate corresponds to the rate applied by the European Central Bank, on the due date, for its operations in euro, increased by 1,5 percentage points.

**Recommendation of the European Parliament and of the Council
of 12 February 2001
on European cooperation in quality evaluation in school education**

(OJ L 60, 1.3.2001)

II

(Acts whose publication is not obligatory)

EUROPEAN PARLIAMENT AND COUNCIL

RECOMMENDATION OF THE EUROPEAN PARLIAMENT AND OF THE COUNCIL

of 12 February 2001

on European cooperation in quality evaluation in school education

(2001/166/EC)

THE EUROPEAN PARLIAMENT AND THE COUNCIL OF THE EUROPEAN UNION,

Having regard to the Treaty establishing the European Community, and in particular Article 149(4) and Article 150(4) thereof,

Having regard to the proposal from the Commission,

Having regard to the opinion of the Economic and Social Committee [1],

Having regard to the opinion of the Committee of the Regions [2],

Acting in accordance with the procedure referred to in Article 251 of the Treaty [3],

Whereas:

(1) There is a need to promote a European dimension in education as it is an essential objective in building a people's Europe.

(2) Quality education is one of the principal objectives of primary and secondary education, including vocational education, for all Member States in the context of the learning society.

(3) The quality of school education must be assured at all levels and in all areas of education, regardless of any differences in educational objectives, methods and needs, and regardless of school excellence rankings where they exist.

(4) The resources devoted to education have increased in all industrialised countries during the last decades. Education is seen not only as a personal enrichment but also as a contribution towards social cohesion, social inclusion and the solution to problems of employment. Lifelong learning is an important means of controlling one's future on a professional and personal level. Quality education is essential in the light of labour market policies, the free movement of workers within the Community and the recognition of diplomas and teaching qualifications.

(5) It is the responsibility of the Member States to ensure, when they have the possibility, that school syllabuses take account of developments in society.

(6) Member States should help the educational establishments to meet the educational and social requirements in the new millennium and to keep pace with the developments arising from them. Member States should therefore support the educational establishments in order to improve the quality of the services they provide by helping them to develop new initiatives geared to ensure the quality of teaching and by helping them to encourage both the movement of persons between countries and the transfer of knowledge.

(7) In the area of labour market policies, the Council adopts each year a set of employment guidelines building on quantitative targets and indicators. Guideline 7 of the employment guidelines for 2000, set out in the Annex to Decision/2000/228/EC [4], states that Member States will 'improve the quality of their school systems in order to reduce substantially the number of young people who drop out of the school system early. Particular attention should also be given to young people with learning difficulties'.

(8) In guideline 8 of the said guidelines, specific reference is made to developing computer literacy, to equipping schools with computer equipment and to facilitating student access to the Internet by the end of 2002, which should have a positive impact on the quality of education and prepare young people for the digital age.

---

[1] OJ C 168, 16.6.2000, p. 30.
[2] OJ C 317, 6.11.2000, p. 56.
[3] Opinion of the European Parliament of 6 July 2000 (not yet published in the Official Journal), Council Common Position of 9 November 2000 (OJ C 375, 28.12.2000, p. 38) and Decision of the European Parliament of 16 January 2001 (not yet published in the Official Journal).

[4] OJ L 72, 21.3.2000, p. 15.

(9) The promotion of mobility enshrined as an objective of the Community in Articles 149 and 150 of the Treaty should be encouraged by quality education.

(10) European cooperation and transnational exchanges of experiences will contribute to identifying and disseminating effective and acceptable methods of evaluating quality.

(11) Systems designed to ensure quality must remain flexible and be adaptable to the new situation created by changes in the structure and objectives of educational establishments, taking into account the cultural dimension of education.

(12) Systems to ensure quality vary from one Member State and one educational establishment to another, given the diversity in the sizes, structures, financial circumstances, institutional character and educational approach of different establishments.

(13) Quality evaluation and school self-evaluation in particular are tools well suited to the aim of combating the number of young people who drop out of the school system early and social exclusion in general.

(14) In order to achieve the objective of quality education, a whole range of means are available. Quality evaluation is one of them and is a valuable contribution to securing and developing the quality of education within general and vocational schools. The quality evaluation of education must seek, *inter alia*, to assess the capacity of schools to take account of the use of the new information technologies which are becoming more widespread.

(15) The networking at European level of institutions involved in quality evaluation in school education is of fundamental importance. Existing networks such as the European network of policy makers for the evaluation of education systems set up by the Member States in 1995 can provide invaluable aid to the implementation of this recommendation.

(16) The Commission conducted a pilot project on quality evaluation in higher education in 1994 and 1995. Council Recommendation 98/561/EC of 24 September 1998 on European cooperation in quality assurance in higher education (¹) underlines the importance of the exchange of information and experiences and cooperation regarding quality assurance between other Member States.

(17) The Socrates programme (²), in particular Action 6.1., invites the Commission to promote the exchange of information and experience on questions of common interest. Evaluating quality in school education is one of the priority themes of the said Action.

(18) The Commission has, since March 1996, launched various studies and operational activities to examine the question of evaluation from different perspectives with the aim of describing the wide variety and wealth of approaches and education evaluation methodologies used at different levels.

(19) The Commission conducted a pilot project during the academic year 1997/1998 in 101 upper and lower secondary schools in the countries participating in the Socrates programme, which raised awareness of quality issues and helped to improve the quality of education in those schools. The final report, June 1999, entitled 'Evaluation quality in school education, A European pilot project' emphasises a range of methodological elements as important elements for successful self-evaluation.

(20) In its conclusions of 16 December 1997 (³), the Council stated that evaluation is also an important element for assuring and, where appropriate, improving quality.

(21) The Council Presidency declared in its conclusions at the Extraordinary European Council held in Lisbon on 23 and 24 March 2000 that European education and training systems must adapt both to the needs of the information society and to the need to raise levels of employment and improve its quality.

(22) With a view to the enlargement of the Union, the accession countries should be involved in European cooperation in the field of quality evaluation.

(23) It is necessary to take account of the principle of subsidiarity and Member States' exclusive responsibilities for the organisation and structure of their education systems, so that the particular cultural character and educational traditions of each State can flourish,

I. RECOMMEND THAT MEMBER STATES:

within their specific economic, social and cultural context while taking due account of the European dimension, support the improvement of quality evaluation in school education, by:

1. supporting and, where appropriate, establishing transparent quality evaluation systems with the following aims:

   (a) to secure quality education, whilst promoting social inclusion, and equal opportunities for girls and boys,

   (b) to safeguard quality of school education as a basis for lifelong learning,

---
(¹) OJ L 270, 7.10.1998, p. 56.
(²) OJ L 28, 3.2.2000, p. 1.

(³) OJ C 1, 3.1.1998, p. 4.

(c) to encourage school self-evaluation as a method of creating learning and improving schools, within a balanced framework of school self-evaluation and any external evaluations,

(d) to use techniques aimed at improving quality as a means of adapting more successfully to the requirements of a world in rapid and constant change,

(e) to clarify the purpose and the conditions for school self-evaluation, and to ensure that the approach to self-evaluation is consistent with other forms of regulation,

(f) to develop external evaluation in order to provide methodological support for school self-evaluation and to provide an outside view of the school encouraging a process of continuous improvement and taking care that this is not restricted to purely administrative checks;

2. encouraging and supporting, where appropriate, the involvement of school stakeholders, including teachers, pupils, management, parents and experts, in the process of external and self-evaluation in schools in order to promote shared responsibility for the improvement of schools;

3. supporting training in the management and the use of self-evaluation instruments with the following aims:

(a) to make school self-evaluation function effectively as an instrument strengthening the capacity of schools to improve,

(b) to ensure an efficient dissemination of examples of good practice and new instruments within self-evaluation;

4. supporting the capacity of schools to learn from one another nationally and on a European scale, with the following aims:

(a) to identify and to disseminate good practice and efficient tools such as indicators and benchmarks in the field of quality evaluation in school education,

(b) to form networks between schools, at all appropriate levels, to support each other and provide outside impetus to the evaluation process;

5. encouraging cooperation between all the authorities involved in quality evaluation in school education and promoting their European networking.

This cooperation could cover some of the following areas:

(a) the exchange of information and experience, in particular on methodological developments and examples of good practice, especially by using modern information and communication technologies, and, when appropriate, by organising European conferences, seminars and workshops,

(b) the collection of data and the development of tools such as indicators and benchmarks of particular relevance for quality evaluation in schools,

(c) publication of results of school evaluation in accordance with the relevant policies of each Member State and its educational establishments, to be made available to authorities in the Member States,

(d) promoting contacts between experts in order to build European expertise in the area,

(e) making use of the results of international surveys for the development of quality evaluation in schools.

II. INVITE THE COMMISSION:

1. to encourage, in close cooperation with the Member States, and on the basis of existing Community programmes, the cooperation referred to in points 4 and 5 of Section I, also involving relevant organisations and associations with the necessary experience in this field.

In doing this, the Commission should ensure that full benefit is drawn from the expertise of the Eurydice network referred to in Action 6.1. of the Socrates programme;

2. to establish, on the basis of the existing Community programmes, a database for the dissemination of effective tools and instruments of school quality evaluation. The database should also contain examples of good practice and be accessible on the Internet; interactive use thereof should be ensured;

3. to make use of the resources within existing Community programmes, to incorporate the experience already gained into these programmes and to develop the existing networks;

4. to make, as a first step, an inventory of the instruments and strategies for quality evaluation in primary and secondary education already in use in the various Member States. When the inventory has been compiled, the Commission will work with the Member States on appropriate follow-up. The European Parliament, the Council, the Economic and Social Committee and the Committee of the Regions should be fully informed on a regular basis of the follow-up;

5. to present on the basis of contributions from the Member States triennial detailed reports to the European Parliament, the Council, the Economic and Social Committee and the Committee of the Regions in relation to the implementation of this Recommendation;

6. to draw conclusions and make proposals on the basis of these reports.

Done at Brussels, 12 February 2001.

For the European Parliament	*For the Council*
The President	*The President*
N. FONTAINE	T. ÖSTROS

**Council Decision
of 26 February 2001
concerning the conclusion of an Agreement between
the European Community and the United States of America
renewing a programme of cooperation in higher education
and vocational education and training**

(OJ L 71, 13.3.2001)

II

(Acts whose publication is not obligatory)

COUNCIL

COUNCIL DECISION
of 26 February 2001
concerning the conclusion of an Agreement between the European Community and the United States of America renewing a programme of cooperation in higher education and vocational education and training

(2001/196/EC)

THE COUNCIL OF THE EUROPEAN UNION,

Having regard to the Treaty establishing the European Community, and in particular Articles 149 and 150 in conjunction with Article 300(3), first subparagraph thereof,

Having regard to the proposal from the Commission,

Having regard to the opinion of the European Parliament,

Whereas:

(1) By its Decision of 22 May 2000 the Council authorised the Commission to negotiate Agreements for cooperation in higher education and vocational training between the European Community, Canada and the United States of America.

(2) The Community and the United States of America expect to obtain mutual benefit from such cooperation, which must, on the Community's side, be complementary to the bilateral programmes between the Member States and the United States of America and provide a European added value.

(3) The Agreement between the European Community and the United States of America renewing a programme of cooperation in higher education and vocational education and training should be approved,

HAS DECIDED AS FOLLOWS:

Article 1

The Agreement between the European Community and the United States of America renewing a programme of cooperation in higher education and vocational education and training is hereby approved on behalf of the Community.

The text of the Agreement is attached to this Decision.

Article 2

The delegation of the European Community to the Joint Committee referred to in Article 6 of the Agreement shall consist of a representative from the Commission assisted by a representative from each Member State.

Article 3

The President of the Council shall carry out the notification provided for in Article 12 of the Agreement.

Done at Brussels, 26 February 2001.

For the Council
The President
A. LINDH

AGREEMENT

between the European Community and the United States of America renewing a programme of cooperation in higher education and vocational education and training

THE EUROPEAN COMMUNITY,

of the one part, and

THE UNITED STATES OF AMERICA,

of the other part,

hereinafter collectively referred to as 'the Parties',

NOTING that the Transatlantic Declaration adopted by the European Community and its Member States and the Government of the United States of America in November 1990 makes specific reference to strengthening mutual cooperation in various fields which directly affect the present and future wellbeing of their citizens, such as exchanges and joint projects in education and culture, including academic and youth exchanges;

CONSIDERING that the adoption and the implementation of the 1995 Agreement Between the European Community and the United States of America establishing a cooperation programme in higher education and vocational education and training give effect to the commitments of the Transatlantic Declaration and constitute examples of highly successful and cost-effective cooperation;

NOTING that the new Transatlantic Agenda adopted at the EU-US Summit in December 1995 in Madrid refers under Action IV - Building bridges across the Atlantic - to the EC/US Agreement establishing a cooperation programme in education and vocational training as a potential catalyst for a broad spectrum of innovative cooperative activities of direct benefit to students and teachers and refers to the introduction of new technologies into classrooms, linking educational establishments in the United States of America with those in the European Union and encouraging teaching of each other's languages, history and culture;

ACKNOWLEDGING the crucial contribution of education and training to the development of human resources capable of participating in the global knowledge-based economy;

RECOGNISING that cooperation in education and vocational training should complement other relevant cooperation initiatives between the European Community and the United States of America;

NOTING that the 1997 'Bridging the Atlantic: people to people links' Transatlantic Conference underlined the potential for cooperation between the European Community and the United States of America in the field of non-formal education;

ACKNOWLEDGING the importance of ensuring complementarity with relevant initiatives carried out in the field of higher education and vocational training by international organisations active in these fields such as OECD, Unesco and the Council of Europe;

RECOGNISING that the Parties have a common interest in cooperation in higher education and vocational education and training between them;

EXPECTING to obtain mutual benefit from cooperative activities in higher education and vocational education and training;

RECOGNISING the need to widen access to the activities supported under this Agreement, in particular those activities in the vocational education and training sector; and

DESIRING to establish a formal basis for continued cooperation in higher education and vocational education and training,

HAVE AGREED AS FOLLOWS:

Article 1

Purpose

This Agreement renews the cooperation programme in higher education and vocational education and training (hereinafter referred to as 'the Programme'), originally established under the 1995 Agreement Between the European Community and the United States of America establishing a cooperation programme in higher education and vocational education and training.

Article 2

Definitions

For the purpose of this Agreement:

1. 'higher education institution' means any establishment according to the applicable laws or practices which offers qualifications or diplomas at the higher education level, whatever such establishment may be called;

2. 'vocational education and training institutions' means any type of public, semi-public or private body, which, irrespective of the designation given to it, in accordance with the applicable laws and practices, designs or undertakes vocational education or training, further vocational training, refresher vocational training or retraining; and

3. 'students' means all those persons following learning or training courses or programmes which are run by higher education or vocational education and training institutions as defined in this Article.

Article 3

Objectives

The objectives of the Programme shall be to:

1. promote mutual understanding between the peoples of the European Community and the United States of America including broader knowledge of their languages, cultures and institutions;

2. improve the quality of human resource development in both the European Community and the United States of America, including the acquisition of skills required to meet the challenges of the global knowledge-based economy;

3. encourage an innovative and sustainable range of student-centered higher education and vocational education and training cooperative activities between the different regions in the European Community and in the United States of America that have a durable impact;

4. improve the quality of transatlantic student mobility by promoting transparency, mutual recognition of periods of study and training, and, where appropriate, portability of credits;

5. encourage the exchange of expertise in e-learning and open and distance learning and their effective use to broaden Programme impact;

6. promote or enhance partnerships among higher education and vocational education and training institutions, professional associations, public authorities, private sector and other associations as appropriate in both the European Community and the United States of America;

7. reinforce a European Community and United States dimension to transatlantic cooperation in higher education and vocational education and training; and

8. complement relevant bilateral programmes between the Member States of the European Community and the United States of America as well as other European Community and United States programmes and initiatives.

Article 4

Principles

Cooperation under this Agreement shall be guided by the following principles:

1. full respect for the responsibilities of the Member States of the European Community and the States of the United States of America and the autonomy of higher education and vocational education and training institutions;

2. mutual benefit from activities undertaken through this Agreement;

3. effective provision of seed-funding for a diverse range of innovative projects that build new structures and links, that have a multiplying effect through consistent and effective dissemination of results, that are sustainable over the longer term without on-going Programme support and that, where student mobility is involved, provide mutual recognition of periods of study and training and, where appropriate, portability of credits;

4. broad participation across the different Member States of the European Community and the United States of America;

5. recognition of the full cultural, social, and economic diversity of the European Community and the United States of America; and

6. selection of projects on a competitive basis, taking account of the foregoing principles.

Article 5

Programme actions

The Programme shall be pursued by means of the actions described in the Annex, which forms an integral part of this Agreement.

Article 6

Joint Committee

1. A Joint Committee is hereby established. It shall comprise an equal number of representatives of each Party.

2. The functions of the Joint Committee shall be to:

(a) review the cooperative activities envisaged under this Agreement; and

(b) provide a report annually to the Parties on the level, status and effectiveness of cooperative activities undertaken under this Agreement.

3. The Joint Committee shall meet at least every second year, with such meetings being held alternately in the European Community and the United States of America. Other meetings may be held as mutually determined.

4. Decisions of the Joint Committee shall be reached by consensus. Minutes, comprising a record of the decisions and principal points, shall be taken at each meeting. These Minutes shall be approved by those persons selected from each side to jointly chair the meeting, and shall, together with the annual report, be made available to appropriate Minister-level officials of each Party.

Article 7

Monitoring and evaluation

The Programme shall be monitored and evaluated as appropriate on a cooperative basis. This shall permit, as necessary, the reorientation of activities in the light of any needs or opportunities becoming apparent in the course of its operation.

Article 8

Funding

1. Activities under this Agreement shall be subject to the availability of funds and to the applicable laws and regulations, policies and programmes of the European Community and the United States of America. Financing will be, to the extent possible, on the basis of an overall matching of funds between the Parties. The Parties shall attempt to offer Programme activities of comparable benefit and scope.

2. Costs incurred by or on behalf of the Joint Committee shall be met by the Party to whom the members are responsible. Costs, other than those of travel and subsistence, which are directly associated with meetings of the Joint Committee, shall be met by the host Party.

Article 9

Entry of personnel

Each Party shall use its best efforts to facilitate entry to and exit from its territory of personnel, students, material and equipment of the other Party engaged in or used in cooperative activities under this Agreement.

Article 10

Other agreements

This Agreement shall not replace or otherwise affect other agreements or activities undertaken in the fields covered between any Member State of the European Community and the United States of America.

Article 11

Territorial application of this Agreement

This Agreement shall apply, on the one hand, to the territories in which the Treaty establishing the European Community is applied and under the conditions laid down in that Treaty and, on the other hand, to the territory of the United States of America.

Article 12

Entry into force and termination

1. This Agreement shall enter into force on 1 January 2001 or on the first day of the month following the date on which the Parties shall have notified each other in writing that their legal requirements for the entry into force of this Agreement have been fulfilled, whichever is the later date. This Agreement replaces the 1995 Agreement Between the European Community and the United States of America establishing a cooperation programme in higher education and Vocational education and training in its entirety.

2. This Agreement shall remain in force for five years and may be extended or amended by mutual written agreement. Amendments or extensions shall enter into force on the first day of the month following the date on which the Parties shall have notified each other in writing that their requirements for entry into force of the agreement providing for the amendment or extension in question have been fulfilled.

3. This Agreement may be terminated at any time by either Party by twelve months' written notice. The expiration or termination of this Agreement shall not affect the validity or duration of any pre-existing arrangements made under it.

Article 13

This Agreement is drawn up in duplicate in the Danish, Dutch, English, Finnish, French, German, Greek, Italian, Portuguese, Spanish and Swedish languages, each of these texts being equally authentic.

EN FE DE LO CUAL, los abajo firmantes, debidamente autorizados, suscriben el presente Acuerdo.

TIL BEKRÆFTELSE HERAF har undertegnede behørigt befuldmægtigede underskrevet denne aftale.

ZU URKUND DESSEN haben die Unterzeichneten, hierzu gehörig befugten Bevollmächtigten dieses Abkommen unterschrieben.

ΕΙΣ ΠΙΣΤΩΣΗ ΤΩΝ ΑΝΩΤΕΡΩ, οι υπογράφοντες πληρεξούσιοι, δεόντως εξουσιοδοτημένοι προς τούτο, έθεσαν την υπογραφή τους κάτω από την παρούσα συμφωνία.

IN WITNESS WHEREOF the undersigned, being duly authorised, have signed the present Agreement.

EN FOI DE QUOI, les soussignés, dûment mandatés, ont apposé leur signature au bas du présent accord.

IN FEDE DI CHE i sottoscritti, muniti di regolari poteri, hanno firmato il presente accordo.

TEN BLIJKE WAARVAN de ondergetekenden, naar behoren gemachtigd, hun handtekening onder deze overeenkomst hebben geplaatst.

EM FÉ DO QUE os abaixo assinados, com os devidos poderes para o efeito, apuseram as suas assinaturas no presente Acordo.

TÄMÄN VAKUUDEKSI jäljempänä mainitut täysivaltaiset edustajat ovat allekirjoittaneet tämän sopimuksen.

TILL BEVIS HÄRPÅ har undertecknade befullmäktigade undertecknat detta avtal.

Hecho en Washington D.C., el dieciocho de diciembre del año dos mil.

Udfærdiget i Washington D.C. den attende december to tusind.

Geschehen zu Washington D.C. am achtzehnten Dezember zweitausend.

Έγινε στην Ουάσιγκτον D.C., στις δέκα οκτώ Δεκεμβρίου δύο χιλιάδες.

Done at Washington D.C. on the eighteenth day of December in the year two thousand.

Fait à Washington D.C., le dix-huit décembre deux mille.

Fatto a Washington D.C., addì diciotto dicembre duemila.

Gedaan te Washington D.C., de achttiende december tweeduizend.

Feito em Washington D.C., em dezoito de Dezembro de dois mil.

Tehty Washington D.C.:ssä kahdeksantenatoista päivänä joulukuuta vuonna kaksituhatta.

Som skedde i Washington D.C. den artonde december tjugohundra.

Por la Comunidad Europea
For Det Europæiske Fællesskab
Für die Europäische Gemeinschaft
Για την Ευρωπαϊκή Κοινότητα
For the European Community
Pour la Communauté européenne
Per la Comunità europea
Voor de Europese Gemeenschap
Pela Comunidade Europeia
Euroopan yhteisön puolesta
På Europeiska gemenskapens vägnar

Por los Estados Unidos de América
For Amerikas Forenede Stater
Für die Vereinigten Staaten von Amerika
Για τις Ηνωμένες Πολιτείες της Αμερικής
For the United States of America
Pour les États-Unis d'Amérique
Per gli Stati Uniti d'America
Voor de Verenigde Staten van Amerika
Pelos Estados Unidos da América
Amerikan yhdysvaltojen puolesta
På Amerikas förenta staters vägnar

ANNEX

ACTIONS

ACTION 1

Joint European Community/United States consortia projects

1. The Parties shall provide support to higher education and vocational education and training institutions which form joint EC/US consortia for the purpose of undertaking joint projects in the area of higher education and vocational education and training. The European Community will provide support for the use of the European Community consortia partners; the United States of America will provide support for United States consortia partners.

2. Each joint consortium must have a minimum of three active partners on each side from at least three different Member States of the European Community and three different States of the United States of America.

3. Each joint consortium should, as a rule, involve transatlantic mobility of students, with a goal of parity in the flows in each direction, and should foresee adequate language and cultural preparation.

4. The structural cooperative activities of a consortium will be supported by seed-funding for a maximum period of three years. Preparatory or project development activities may be supported for a period of up to one year.

5. Appropriate authorities on each side will mutually agree upon the eligible subject areas for joint EC/US consortia.

6. Project activities eligible for support may include:

    (a) preparatory or project development activities;

    (b) development of organisational frameworks for student mobility, including work placements, which provide adequate language preparation and full recognition by the partner institutions;

    (c) structured exchanges of students, teachers, trainers, administrators, and other relevant specialists;

    (d) joint development and dissemination of innovative curricula, including teaching materials, methods and modules;

    (e) joint development and dissemination of new methodologies in higher education and vocational education and training, including the use of information and communication technologies, e-learning, and open and distance learning;

    (f) short intensive programmes of a minimum of three weeks, provided they are an integral part of the programme of study or training;

    (g) teaching assignments at a transatlantic partner institution that support the project's curriculum development; and

    (h) other innovative projects which aim to improve the quality of transatlantic cooperation in higher education and vocational education and training and meet at least one of the objectives specified in Article 3 of this Agreement.

ACTION 2

Fulbright/European Union programme

The Parties shall provide scholarships for the study of, and research and lecturing on, European Community affairs and EC/US relations. Grants will be provided under the Fulbright/European Union programme.

ACTION 3

Complementary activities

The Parties may support a limited number of complementary activities in accordance with the objectives of the Agreement, including exchanges of experience or other forms of joint action in the fields of education and training.

PROGRAMME ADMINISTRATION

Administration of the Actions shall be implemented by the competent officials of each Party. These tasks may include:

1. deciding upon the rules and procedures for the presentation of proposals including the preparation of a common set of guidelines for applicants;
2. establishing a timetable for publication of calls for proposals, submission and selection of proposals;
3. providing information on the Programme and its implementation;
4. appointing academic advisors and experts;
5. recommending to the appropriate authorities of each Party which projects to finance;
6. providing financial management; and
7. promoting a cooperative approach to programme monitoring and evaluation.

TECHNICAL SUPPORT MEASURES

Under the present Programme, funds may be used for the purchase of services necessary to the implementation of the Programme. In particular, the Parties may have recourse to experts; may organise seminars, colloquia or other meetings likely to facilitate the implementation of the Programme; and may undertake evaluation, information, publication and dissemination activities.

**Council Decision of 26 February 2001
concerning the conclusion of an Agreement between the European Community
and the Government of Canada renewing a cooperation programme
in higher education and training**

(OJ L 71, 13.3.2001)

COUNCIL DECISION
of 26 February 2001
concerning the conclusion of an Agreement between the European Community and the Government of Canada renewing a cooperation programme in higher education and training

(2001/197/EC)

THE COUNCIL OF THE EUROPEAN UNION,

Having regard to the Treaty establishing the European Community, and in particular Articles 149 and 150 in conjunction with Article 300(3), first subparagraph thereof,

Having regard to the proposal from the Commission,

Having regard to the opinion of the European Parliament,

Whereas:

(1) By its Decision of 22 May 2000 the Council authorised the Commission to negotiate Agreements for cooperation in higher education and vocational training between the European Community, Canada and the United States of America.

(2) The Community and Canada expect to obtain mutual benefit from such cooperation, which must, on the Community's side, be complementary to the bilateral programmes between the Member States and Canada and provide a European added value.

(3) The Agreement between the European Community and the Government of Canada renewing a cooperation programme in higher education and training should be approved,

HAS DECIDED AS FOLLOWS:

Article 1

The Agreement between the European Community and the Government of Canada renewing a cooperation programme in higher education and training is hereby approved on behalf of the Community.

The text of the Agreement is attached to this Decision.

Article 2

The delegation of the European Community to the Joint Committee referred to in Article 6 of the Agreement shall consist of a representative from the Commission assisted by a representative from each Member State.

Article 3

The President of the Council shall carry out the notification provided for in Article 12 of the Agreement.

Done at Brussels, 26 February 2001.

For the Council
The President
A. LINDH

AGREEMENT

between the European Community and the Government of Canada renewing a cooperation programme in higher education and training

THE EUROPEAN COMMUNITY,

of the one part, and

THE GOVERNMENT OF CANADA,

of the other part,

hereinafter collectively referred to as 'the Parties',

NOTING that the Transatlantic Declaration adopted by the European Community and its Member States and the Government of Canada on 22 November 1990 makes specific reference to strengthening mutual cooperation in various fields which directly affect the present and future well-being of their citizens, such as exchanges and joint projects in education and culture, including academic and youth exchanges;

NOTING that the Joint Declaration on EU-Canada relations adopted on 17 December 1996 remarks that in order to renew their ties based on shared cultures and values, the Parties will encourage contacts between their citizens at every level, especially among their youth; and that the Joint Action Plan attached to the Declaration encourages the Parties to further strengthen their cooperation through the Agreement on higher education and training;

CONSIDERING that the adoption and the implementation of the 1995 Agreement on higher education and training materialises the commitment of the Transatlantic Declaration and that the experience of its implementation has been highly positive to both Parties;

ACKNOWLEDGING the crucial contribution of higher education and training to the development of human resources capable of participating in the global knowledge-based economy;

RECOGNISING that cooperation in higher education and training should complement other relevant cooperation initiatives between the European Community and Canada;

ACKNOWLEDGING the importance of taking into account the work done in the field of higher education and training by international organisations active in these fields such as the OECD, Unesco and the Council of Europe;

RECOGNISING that the Parties have a common interest in cooperation in higher education and training, as part of the wider cooperation that exists between the European Community and Canada;

EXPECTING to obtain mutual benefit from cooperative activities in higher education and training;

RECOGNISING the need to widen access to the activities supported under this Agreement, in particular those activities in the training sector;

DESIRING to renew the basis for the continuing conduct of cooperative activities in higher education and training,

HAVE AGREED AS FOLLOWS:

Article 1

Purpose

This Agreement renews the cooperation programme in higher education and training between the European Community and Canada, established in 1995.

Article 2

Definitions

For the purpose of this Agreement:

1. 'higher education institution' means any establishment according to the applicable laws or practices which offers qualifications or diplomas at higher education level, whatever such establishment may be called;

2. 'training institution' means any type of public, semi-public or private body, which, irrespective of the designation given to it, in accordance with the applicable laws and practices, designs or undertakes vocational education or training, further vocational training, refresher vocational training or retraining contributing to qualifications recognised by the competent authorities;

3. 'students' means all those persons following learning or training courses or programmes which are run by higher education or training institutions as defined in this Article, and which are recognised or financially supported by the competent authorities.

Article 3

Objectives

The objectives of the Cooperation Programme shall be to:

1. promote closer understanding between the peoples of the European Community and Canada, including broader knowledge of their languages, cultures and institutions;

2. improve the quality of human resource development in both the European Community and Canada, including the acquisition of skills required to meet the challenges of the global knowledge-based economy;

3. encourage an innovative and sustainable range of student-centred higher education and training cooperative activities between the different regions in the European Community and in Canada that have a durable impact;

4. improve the quality of transatlantic student mobility by promoting transparency, mutual recognition of qualifications and periods of study and training, and where appropriate, portability of credits;

5. encourage the exchange of expertise in e-learning and open and distance education and their effective use by project consortia to broaden Programme impact;

6. form or enhance partnerships among higher education and training institutions, professional associations, public authorities, private sector and other associations as appropriate in both the European Community and Canada;

7. reinforce a European Community and a Canadian value-added dimension to Transatlantic cooperation in higher education and training;

8. complement bilateral programmes between the Member States of the European Community and Canada as well as other European Community and Canadian programmes and initiatives.

Article 4

Principles

Cooperation under this Agreement shall be conducted on the basis of the following principles:

1. full respect for the responsibilities of the Member States of the European Community and the Provinces and Territories of Canada and the autonomy of the higher education and training institutions;

2. overall balance of benefits from activities undertaken through this Agreement;

3. effective provision of seed-funding for a diverse range of innovative projects, that build new structures and links, that have a multiplying effect through consistent and effective dissemination of results, that are sustainable over the longer term without on-going Cooperation Programme support, and where student mobility is involved, provide mutual recognition of periods of study and training and, where appropriate, portability of credits;

4. broad participation across the different Member States of the European Community and the Provinces and Territories of Canada;

5. recognition of the full cultural, social and economic diversity of the European Community and Canada; and

6. selection of projects on a competitive and transparent basis, taking account of the foregoing principles.

Article 5

Programme actions

The Cooperation Programme shall be pursued by means of the actions described in the Annex, which forms an integral part of this Agreement.

Article 6

Joint Committee

1. A Joint Committee is hereby established. It shall comprise representatives of each Party.

2. The functions of the Joint Committee shall be to:

(a) review the cooperative activities envisaged under this Agreement;

(b) provide a report at least biennially to the Parties on the level, status and effectiveness of cooperative activities undertaken under this Agreement.

3. The Joint Committee shall meet at least every second year, with such meetings being held alternately in the European Community and Canada. Other meetings may be held as mutually determined.

4. Minutes shall be agreed by those persons selected from each side to jointly chair the meeting, and shall, together with the biennial report, be made available to the joint Cooperation Committee established under the 1976 Framework Agreement for commercial and economic cooperation between the European Community and Canada and appropriate Ministers of each Party.

Article 7
Monitoring and evaluation

The Cooperation Programme shall be monitored and evaluated as appropriate on a cooperative basis. This shall permit, as necessary, the reorientation of the Cooperation Programme in the light of any needs or opportunities becoming apparent in the course of its operation.

Article 8
Funding

1. Cooperative activities shall be subject to the availability of funds and to the applicable laws and regulations, policies and programmes of the European Community and Canada. Financing will be on the basis of an overall matching of funds between the Parties.

2. Each Party shall provide funds for the direct benefit of: for the European Community, citizens of one of the European Community Member States or persons recognised by a Member State as having official status as permanent residents; for Canada, its own citizens and permanent residents as defined in the Immigration Act.

3. Costs incurred by or on behalf of the Joint Committee shall be met by the Party to whom the members are responsible. Costs, other than those of travel and subsistence, which are directly associated with meetings of the Joint Committee, shall be met by the host Party.

Article 9
Entry of personnel

Each Party shall take all reasonable steps and use its best efforts to facilitate entry to and exit from its territory of personnel, students, material and equipment of the other Party engaged in or used in cooperative activities under this Agreement in accordance with laws and regulations of each Party.

Article 10
Other agreements

1. This Agreement is without prejudice to cooperation which may be taken pursuant to other agreements between the Parties.

2. This Agreement is without prejudice to existing or future bilateral agreements between individual Member States of the European Community and Canada in the fields covered herein.

Article 11
Territorial application of this Agreement

This Agreement shall apply, on the one hand, to the territories in which the Treaty establishing the European Community is applied and under the conditions laid down in that Treaty and, on the other hand, to the territory of Canada.

Article 12
Final clauses

1. This Agreement shall enter into force on the first day of the month following the date on which the Parties shall have notified each other in writing that their legal requirements for the entry into force of this Agreement have been fulfilled. The Agreement shall enter into force on the first day of the month following the later notification.

2. This Agreement shall be in force for a period of five years, following which it may be renewed by agreement of the Parties.

3. This Agreement may be amended or extended by agreement of the Parties. Amendments or extensions shall be in writing and shall enter into force on the first day of the month following the date on which the Parties shall have notified each other in writing that their legal requirements for the entry into force of the Agreement providing for the amendment or extension in question have been fulfilled.

4. This Agreement may be terminated at any time by either Party upon twelve months written notice. The expiration or termination of this Agreement shall not affect the validity or duration of any arrangements made under it or the obligations established pursuant to the Annex to this Agreement.

Article 13
Authentic texts

This Agreement is drawn up in duplicate in the Danish, Dutch, English, Finnish, French, German, Greek, Italian, Portuguese, Spanish and Swedish languages, each of these texts being equally authentic.

EN FE DE LO CUAL, los abajo firmantes suscriben el presente Acuerdo.

TIL BEKRÆFTELSE HERAF har undertegnede befuldmægtigede underskrevet denne aftale.

ZU URKUND DESSEN haben die Unterzeichneten dieses Abkommen unterschrieben.

ΕΙΣ ΠΙΣΤΩΣΗ ΤΩΝ ΑΝΩΤΕΡΩ, οι υπογράφοντες πληρεξούσιοι έθεσαν την υπογραφή τους κάτω από την παρούσα συμφωνία.

IN WITNESS WHEREOF the undersigned, have signed this Agreement.

EN FOI DE QUOI, les soussignés ont apposé leur signature au bas du présent accord.

IN FEDE DI CHE i sottoscritti hanno firmato il presente accordo.

TEN BLIJKE WAARVAN de ondergetekenden hun handtekening onder deze overeenkomst hebben geplaatst.

EM FÉ DO QUE os abaixo assinados apuseram as suas assinaturas no presente Acordo.

TÄMÄN VAKUUDEKSI jäljempänä mainitut ovat allekirjottaneet tämän sopimuksen.

TILL BEVIS HÄRPÅ har undertecknade befullmäktigade undertecknat detta avtal.

Hecho en Ottawa, el diecinueve de diciembre del año dos mil.

Udfærdiget i Ottawa den nittende december to tusind.

Geschehen zu Ottawa am neunzehnten Dezember zweitausend.

Έγινε στην Οτάβα, στις δέκα εννέα Δεκεμβρίου δύο χιλιάδες.

Done at Ottawa on the nineteenth day of December in the year two thousand.

Fait à Ottawa, le dix-neuf décembre deux mille.

Fatto a Ottawa addì diciannove dicembre duemila.

Gedaan te Ottawa, de negentiende december tweeduizend.

Feito em Otava, em dezanove de Dezembro de dois mil.

Tehty Ottawassa yhdeksäntenätoista päivänä joulukuuta vuonna kaksituhatta.

Som skedde i Ottawa den nittonde december tjugohundra.

Por la Comunidad Europea
For Det Europæiske Fællesskab
Für die Europäische Gemeinschaft
Για την Ευρωπαϊκή Κοινότητα
For the European Community
Pour la Communauté européenne
Per la Comunità europea
Voor de Europese Gemeenschap
Pela Comunidade Europeia
Euroopan yhteisön puolesta
På Europeiska gemenskapens vägnar

Por el Gobierno de Canadá
For Canadas regering
Für die Regierung Kanadas
Για την Κυβέρνηση του Καναδά
For the Government of Canada
Pour le gouvernement du Canada
Per il governo del Canada
Voor de regering van Canada
Pelo Governo do Canadá
Kanadan hallituksen puolesta
På Kanadas regerings vägnar

ANNEX

ACTIONS

ACTION 1

Joint EC/Canada consortia projects

1. The Parties will provide support to higher education institutions and training institutions which form joint EC/Canada consortia for the purpose of undertaking joint projects in the area of higher education and training. The European Community will provide support for the use of the European Community consortia partners, Canada will provide support for Canadian consortia partners.

2. Each joint consortium must involve at least three active partners on each side from at least three different Member States of the European Community and from at least two different Provinces or Territories of Canada.

3. Each joint consortium should as a rule involve transatlantic mobility of students, with a goal of parity in the flows in each direction, and foresee adequate language and cultural preparation.

4. Financial support may be awarded to joint consortia projects for innovative activities with objectives which can be accomplished within a time-scale of up to a maximum of three years. Preparatory or project development activities may be supported for a period of up to one year.

5. The eligible subject areas for joint EC/Canada consortia cooperation shall be agreed by the Joint Committee as established by Article 6.

6. Activities eligible for support may include:
   — preparatory or project development activities,
   — development of organisational frameworks for student mobility, including work placements, which provide adequate language preparation and full recognition by the partner institutions,
   — structured exchanges of students, teachers, trainers, administrators, human resource managers, vocational training programme planners and managers, trainers and occupational guidance specialists in either higher education institutions or vocational training organisations,
   — joint development of innovative curricula including the development of teaching materials, methods and modules,
   — joint development of new methodologies in higher education and training including the use of information and communication technologies, e-learning, open and distance learning,
   — short intensive programmes of a minimum of three weeks,
   — teaching assignments forming an integral part of the curriculum in a partner institution,
   — other innovative projects, which aim to improve the quality of transatlantic cooperation in higher education and training and meet one or more of the objectives specified in Article 3 of this Agreement.

ACTION 2

Complementary activities

The Parties may support a limited number of complementary activities in accordance with the objectives of the Agreement, including exchanges of experience or other forms of joint action in the fields of education and training.

PROGRAMME ADMINISTRATION

1. Each Party may provide financial support for the activities provided for under this Programme.

2. Administration of the Actions shall be implemented by the competent officials of each Party. These tasks will comprise:
   — deciding the rules and procedures for the presentation of proposals including the preparation of a common set of guidelines for applicants,
   — establishing the timetable for publication of calls for proposals, submission and selection of proposals,
   — providing information on the programme and its implementation,
   — appointing academic advisors and experts, including for independent appraisal of proposals,
   — recommending to the appropriate authorities of each Party which projects to finance,
   — financial management,
   — a cooperative approach to programme monitoring and evaluation.

TECHNICAL SUPPORT MEASURES

Under the Cooperation Programme, funds will be made available for purchasing of services to ensure optimal programme implementation; in particular the Parties may organise seminars, colloquia or other meetings of experts, conduct evaluations, produce publications or disseminate programme-related information.

**Declaration by the Council and the Representatives
of the Governments of the Member States, meeting within the Council,
of 28 June 2001
on combating racism and xenophobia on the Internet by intensifying
work with young people**

(OJ C 196, 12.7.2001)

I

(Information)

COUNCIL

DECLARATION BY THE COUNCIL AND THE REPRESENTATIVES OF THE GOVERNMENTS OF THE MEMBER STATES, MEETING WITHIN THE COUNCIL

of 28 June 2001

on combating racism and xenophobia on the Internet by intensifying work with young people

(2001/C 196/01)

The European Union is founded on the principles of liberty, democracy, respect for human rights, fundamental freedoms and the rule of law. Diversity and tolerance are democratic values unanimously recognised and respected in each Member State.

Anti-democratic influences exploit the Internet to communicate and disseminate their messages of racism, xenophobia and other expressions of intolerance, taking advantage of the fact that young people in Europe are frequent Internet consumers. The initiative, enterprise, creativity and social solidarity of youth should be harnessed to counteract these anti-democratic attitudes on the Internet wherever they appear.

Europe must combat all forms of racicm, xenophobia and related expressions of intolerance, at local, national, European and worldwide level.

Therefore:

THE COUNCIL AND THE REPRESENTATIVES OF THE GOVERNMENTS OF THE MEMBER STATES, MEETING WITHIN THE COUNCIL:

— WELCOME the European Commission's communication entitled 'Creating a safer information society by improving the security of information infrastructures and combating computer-related crime (Europe 2002)' and especially welcome the European Commission's initiative to examine the scope for action against racist and xenophobic activity on the Internet;

— EMPHASISE the importance and responsibilities of schools, other relevant institutions and youth organisations in encouraging young people's direct involvement in the development of democratic values, as well as in creating opportunities for promotion of democracy, human rights and tolerance;

— EMPHASISE the need, among young people, to create an understanding of the current laws concerning publication and dissemination of racist and xenophobic materal on the Internet and of the importance of a critical review of material found on the web, stressing the importance of schools and other relevant institutions and organisations in creating this understanding;

— STRESS the need to involve and educate those working with young people in order to increase their awareness and understanding of problems related to intolerance and increase their ability to apply democratic values when working with young people;

— EMPHASISE the importance and the need for an exchange of experience and information among the Member States, by promoting the development of the existing programmes, networks and institutions such as the European Monitoring Centre on Racism and Xenophobia involving authorities at national and local level as well as professionals in order to develop best practice in this area and the Community action plan on promoting the safer use of Internet;

— STRESS that efforts should be employed to harness the initiative and creativity of young people with a view to rejecting and counteracting racism, xenophobia and related expressions of intolerance to be found on the web;

— EMPHASISE the need of encourage Internet service providers based in the Union to provide means for the public to report racist and xenophobic contents that they encounter on the Internet;

— EMPHASISE the need to encourage cooperation between Internet service providers — i.e. access providers and web hosts — and police and legal authorities in the Member States, in order to combat racist and xenophobic material on the Internet.

**Resolution of the Council and of the Representatives
of the Governments of the Member States meeting within the Council,
of 28 June 2001
on promoting young people's initiative, enterprise and creativity:
from exclusion to empowerment**

(OJ C 196, 12.7.2001)

RESOLUTION OF THE COUNCIL AND OF THE REPRESENTATIVES OF THE GOVERNMENTS OF THE MEMBER STATES MEETING WITHIN THE COUNCIL

of 28 June 2001

on promoting young people's initiative, enterprise and creativity: from exclusion to empowerment

(2001/C 196/02)

I

THE COUNCIL OF THE EUROPEAN UNION AND THE REPRESENTATIVES OF THE GOVERNMENTS OF THE MEMBER STATES OF THE EUROPEAN COMMUNITY, MEETING WITHIN THE COUNCIL,

Bearing in mind that:

1. The Treaty establishing the European Community provides for Community action to be aimed at encouraging the development of youth exchanges and of exchanges of socio-educational instructors.

2. The Community has been assigned the task among others of promoting harmonious, balanced and sustainable development of economic activities, a high level of employment and social protection, and a rise in living standards and in the quality of life.

3. The promotion of employment, improvement of living and working conditions, and combating exclusion are mentioned among the specific objections of the social provisions of the Treaty.

4. The European Parliament and the Council have by Decision No 1031/2000/EC of 13 April 2000 ([1]) established the 'Youth' Community action programme. One objective of this programme is to encourage young people's initiative, enterprise and creativity so that they can play an active role in society.

5. On 9 November 2000 the Council and the Representatives of the Governments of the Member States, meeting within the Council, adopted a Resolution on the social inclusion of young people ([2]).

6. On 8 February 1999, the Council and the Ministers of Youth, meeting within the Council, adopted a Resolution on youth participation ([3]) which puts the inclusion of youth in institutions of social, political, cultural and economic life in the foreground.

7. In a Resolution on a youth policy for Europe ([4]), adopted by the European Parliament on 9 March 1999, the Member States and the Commission were encouraged to act promptly to approve knowledge acquired through non-formal learning, and to ensure that it is recognised in the labour market.

8. In the Presidency conclusions of the European Council meeting in Lisbon on 23 and 24 March 2000 one of the targets set was for the Member States, in accordance with their constitutional provisions, and also the Council and the Commission to take certain necessary steps within their areas of competence to fulfil inter alia the target of developing a common European format for curriculum vitae to be used on a voluntary basis in order to facilitate mobility by helping the assessment by both educational and training institutions and employers of knowledge acquired. The achievement of the priority objective of mobility will be based in particular on the action plan for mobility, approved by the Heads of State or Government at the European Council in Nice, and on a draft recommendation on mobility within the Community for students, persons undergoing training, volunteers, teachers and trainers which, according to the conclusions of the European Council in Stockholm, it is intended to adopt by June 2001.

9. The memorandum on lifelong learning presented by the Commission to the Council (Education/Youth) of 9 November 2000, proposed consulting all the relevant public and private actors on six main topics including non-formal learning and the need to invest more in human resources.

10. Under its Decision 2000/819/EC of 20 December 2000 ([5]), the Council established a multiannual programme for enterprise and entrepreneurship, and in particular for small and medium-sized enterprises (2001 to 2005).

11. In the conclusions of the European Council meeting in Lisbon on 23 and 24 March 2000 entrepreneurship is mentioned as one of the five basic skills which should be provided through lifelong learning.

12. In Council Decision 2001/63/EC of 19 January 2001 on guidelines for Member States' employment policies for the year 2001 ([6]), the development of entrepreneurship and job creation is identified as one of the four pillars,

---

([1]) OJ L 117, 18.5.2000, p. 1.
([2]) OJ C 374, 28.12.2000, p. 5.
([3]) OJ C 42, 17.2.1999, p. 1.
([4]) OJ C 175, 21.6.1999, p. 48.

([5]) OJ L 333, 29.12.2000, p. 84.
([6]) OJ L 22, 24.1.2001, p. 18.

THEREFORE.

II

13. ARE OF THE VIEW that young people's initiative, enterprise and creativity are a key resource that should be better promoted in various spheres of society for the development of their own personal and social skills as well as being an important precondition for attaining the Union's strategic goal of becoming the world's most competitive and dynamic knowledge-based economy in the world, capable of sustainable economic growth, more and better job opportunities and greater social cohesion.

14. WELCOME in this context the emphasis placed by the Lisbon Conclusions on lifelong learning as a basic component of the European social model.

15. EMPHASISE the importance of young people's own initiative and creativity in combating racism, xenophobia and intolerance.

16. EMPHASISE the importance of young people's initiative, enterprise and creativity when it comes to their ability to prevent social, political and cultural exclusion and the importance of strengthening young people's power and influence over their life situation.

17. CONSIDER the results of the questionnaire survey on non-formal education on which the French Presidency, in the light of the discussions initiated by the Portuguese Presidency during the year 2000, took the initiative on 8 December 2000.

18. CONSIDER that the promotion of young people's initiative, enterprise and creativity is one of the objectives of cooperation in youth issues,

III

INVITE the Commission to emphasis the importance of young people's initiative, enterprise and creativity in European cooperation in youth issues and in particular:

(i) in the preparation of Community cooperation policy in the youth field, to associate young people themselves and to consider their initiative, enterprise and creativity as a resource in society;

(ii) to ensure that the youth dimension is taken into account in Community activities concerning initiative, enterprise and creativity;

(iii) in the forthcoming evaluation of the Youth programme, to report to what extent young people's initiative, enterprise and creativity are promoted within the framework of the programme;

(iv) to involve young people in the development of European cooperation in the youth field and non-formal learning initiatives;

(v) to take particular note of young people's own initiative, enterprise and creativity in drawing up new strategies for lifelong learning,

IV

INVITE the Member States:

(i) to encourage and make more visible in all fields the spirit of initiative, enterprise and creativity of the young people;

(ii) to improve young people's information of available opportunities and support in starting and developing activities, including cultural and business activities;

(iii) to promote pupil participation and their initiative and creativity as a valuable resource in teaching and other school activities, and to contribute so that the education system stimulates active citizenship;

(iv) to promote student participation in higher education, and vocational training where young people's initiative, enterprise and creativity are a resource not only in education but also in research and other knowledge-developing activities;

(v) to take particular note of young people's own initiative, enterprise and creativity in drawing up new strategies for both lifelong learning and innovative methods of teaching and learning;

(vi) to integrate young people's initiative, enterprise and creativity in practical national level labour-market policy measures in the youth sector;

(vii) to develop and promote the sharing of experience and dissemination of best practice with respect to both boys' and girls' initiative, enterprise and creativity in clubs and associations, including Youth organisations,

V

INVITE the Commission and Member States, within their respective spheres of competence:

(i) to integrate and promote young people's initiative, enterprise and creativity in combating exclusion;

(ii) to encourage young people's initiative and creativity in combating racism, xenophobia and intolerance;

(iii) to promote sharing of experience and dissemination of best practice with respect to activities and projects developed on the basis of young people's initiative, enterprise and creativity;

(iv) to encourage young people's initiative, enterprise and creativity as a key driving force in the context of the strategy for creating more and better jobs in Europe;

(v) to take into account the views of pupils and students in the further implementation of Community education programmes notably Socrates and Leonardo da Vinci, in order to put young people's initiative and creativity to use;

(vi) to promote research and sharing of experience in order to increase knowledge of young people's initiative, enterprise and creativity;

(vii) to emphasise the importance of non-formal learning as a means of expressing and developing young people's initiative, enterprise and creativity and encourage those engaged in non-formal learning to share their experience;

(viii) to promote existing cooperation between the Member States, the Commission and international organisations, especially the Council of Europe, with respect to research, methodology and assessment models concerning non-formal learning;

(ix) to clarify to what extent and how young people's initiative, enterprise and creativity are put to use as a resource in projects conducted with the support of the EU Structural Funds;

(x) to educate young people as critical consumers, and take particular note in this context of their important role as consumers as well as practitioners in sectors such as music, film and other creative industries and to promote their enterprise, initiative and creativity in these sectors.

**Recommendation of the European Parliament and of the Council
of 10 July 2001
on mobility within the Community for students, persons undergoing
training, volunteers, teachers and trainers**

(OJ L 215, 9.8.2001)

II

(Acts whose publication is not obligatory)

COUNCIL

RECOMMENDATION OF THE EUROPEAN PARLIAMENT AND OF THE COUNCIL
of 10 July 2001
on mobility within the Community for students, persons undergoing training, volunteers, teachers and trainers

(2001/613/EC)

THE EUROPEAN PARLIAMENT AND THE COUNCIL OF THE EUROPEAN UNION,

Having regard to the Treaty establishing the European Community, and in particular Article 149(4) and Article 150(4) thereof,

Having regard to the proposal from the Commission,

Having regard to the opinion of the Economic and Social Committee [1],

Having regard to the opinion of the Committee of the Regions [2],

Acting in accordance with the procedure laid down in Article 251 of the Treaty [3],

Whereas:

(1) The transnational mobility of people contributes to enriching different national cultures and enables those concerned to enhance their own cultural and professional knowledge and European society as a whole to benefit from those effects. Such experience is proving to be increasingly necessary given the current limited employment prospects and an employment market which requires more flexibility and a greater ability to adapt to change.

(2) Mobility for students, persons undergoing training, volunteers, teachers and trainers – whether in the context of a Community programme or not – is an integral part of freedom of movement for people. This is one of the fundamental freedoms protected by the Treaty. The right to move and reside freely is moreover recognised for any citizen of the Union under the conditions provided for by Article 18 of the Treaty.

(3) Council Directive 68/360/EEC of 15 October 1968 on the abolition of restrictions on movement and residence within the Community for workers of Member States and their families [4], recognises the right of residence for workers and their families. Council Directive 93/96/EEC of 29 October 1993 on the right of residence for students [5] obliges Member States to recognise the right of residence for any student who is a national of another Member State and who has been accepted on a vocational training course, and for the student's spouse and their dependent children who do not enjoy this right under other provisions of Community law. Furthermore, Council Directive 90/364/EEC of 28 June 1990 on the right of residence [6] recognises the right of residence more generally, in certain conditions, for citizens of the Union.

---

[1] OJ C 168, 16.6.2000, p. 25.
[2] OJ C 317, 6.11.2000, p. 53.
[3] Opinion of the European Parliament of 5 October 2001 (not yet published in the Official Journal), Council Common Position of 19 January 2001 (OJ C 70, 2.3.2001, p. 1) and Decision of the European Parliament of 15 May 2001 (not yet published in the Official Journal). Council Decision of 26 June 2001.
[4] OJ L 257, 19.10.1968, p. 13. Directive as last amended by the 1994 Act of Accession.
[5] OJ L 317, 18.12.1993, p. 59.
[6] OJ L 180, 13.7.1990, p. 26.

(4) Mobility for students, persons undergoing training, volunteers, teachers and trainers is also an integral part of the principle of non-discrimination on grounds of nationality as provided for in Article 12 of the Treaty. That principle applies to the areas covered by the Treaty, as has been held in the case law of the Court of Justice. It therefore applies to the fields of education, training and youth.

(5) The Council and the Representatives of the Governments of the Member States, meeting within the Council, adopted on 14 December 2000 a resolution concerning an Action Plan for mobility [1], which was also approved at the Nice European Council.

(6) Council Regulation (EEC) No 1408/71 of 14 June 1971 on the application of social security schemes to employed persons, to self-employed persons and to members of their families moving within the Community [2] has in part become applicable to students under Council Regulation (EC) No 307/1999 [3].

(7) Council Regulation (EEC) No 1612/68 of 15 October 1968 on freedom of movement for workers within the Community [4] provides for equality of treatment as regards access to education and vocational training for workers and their families who have exercised their right to freedom of movement.

(8) The recognition of professional qualifications for entering and exercising regulated professions, such as teaching, is governed in the Community by the general system established by Council Directives 89/48/EEC [5] and 92/51/EEC [6].

(9) Council Resolution of 3 December 1992 on the transparency of qualifications [7], and Council Resolution of 15 July 1996 on the transparency of vocational training certificates [8], called on the Commission and the Member States to take steps to improve mutual understanding of the qualifications systems of the various Member States and of the qualifications themselves, by making them clearer and more readable, and therefore more transparent. A European Forum in the field of transparency of vocational qualifications has been created to make concrete proposals for implementing those Resolutions. The first proposals were submitted in February 2000.

(10) Involvement in transnational voluntary activities helps to shape young people's future careers, develop their social skills and smooth their integration into society, thereby fostering the development of an active citizenship. In addition, since voluntary work is an activity which specifically involves solidarity, is non-profit-making and unpaid, it should not be treated, under national legislation, as employment.

(11) Furthermore, the Council has invited the Commission to study the feasibility of introducing, on a voluntary basis, a European administrative annex to the diploma in order to establish synergies between academic recognition and professional recognition of qualifications [9]. The work undertaken along those lines by the Commission together with the Council of Europe and UNESCO has been completed and will soon be followed up with a public awareness campaign.

(12) Despite the provisions quoted above, the Green Paper on 'Education, training, research: the obstacles to transnational mobility', adopted by the Commission in October 1996, noted the existence of obstacles to mobility. The diversity of the status in the Member States of students, persons undergoing training, teachers and trainers, particularly with regard to provisions on the right of residence, employment law, social security and taxation, is an obstacle to mobility. Similarly, not recognising the specific nature of voluntary work is a hindrance to the mobility of volunteers.

(13) Persons wishing to undertake mobility in the areas of education, training and youth, particularly students, persons in training, volunteers and teachers and trainers, are often discouraged by the many obstacles they encounter, as evidenced by the petitions they address to the European Parliament. In this context, the Community's action should cater for the aspirations of its citizens in terms of mobility in education and training.

---

[1] OJ C 371, 23.12.2000, p. 4.
[2] OJ L 149, 5.7.1971, p. 2. Regulation as last amended by Regulation (EC) No 1399/1999 (OJ L 164, 30.6.1999, p. 1).
[3] OJ L 38, 12.2.1999, p. 1.
[4] OJ L 19, 24.1.1989, p. 16.
[5] OJ L 19, 24.1.1989, p. 16.
[6] OJ L 209, 24.7.1992, p. 25. Directive as last amended by Commission Directive 2000/5/EC (OJ L 54, 26.2.2000, p. 42).
[7] OJ C 49, 19.2.1993, p. 1.
[8] OJ C 224, 1.8.1996, p. 7.
[9] OJ C 195, 6.7.1996, p. 6.

(14) In the context of Article 293 of the Treaty which provides in particular for the Member States, so far as is necessary, to enter into negotiations with each other with a view to securing for the benefit of their nationals the abolition of double taxation within the Community, it should be noted that this network of bilateral agreements is still not complete, with the result that obstacles to mobility still remain.

(15) The Green Paper proposed a series of actions to eliminate those obstacles. They have been largely approved in the context of the debates which have been organised on this subject in all Member States. It is therefore necessary to remove those obstacles to mobility. Special attention should be paid to the needs of the most disadvantaged and most vulnerable groups, such as the disabled.

(16) The European Council in Lisbon on 23 and 24 March 2000 declared its support for mobility as an essential feature of the new knowledge society and in promoting lifelong education. It called on the Member States, the Council and the Commission to:

— take the necessary steps within their areas of competence to foster the mobility of students, teachers and training staff, in particular by removing obstacles, through greater transparency in the recognition of qualifications and periods of study and training, and through specific measures for removing obstacles to the mobility of teachers by 2002;

— develop a common European format for curricula vitae to encourage mobility by helping to improve assessment, by education and training establishments and employers, of knowledge acquired.

The European Council also called on the Council and the Commission to create a European database on jobs and learning opportunities to facilitate mobility, while improving employability and reducing the skills shortage.

(17) Mobility fosters the discovery of new cultural and social environments. There is therefore a need to facilitate the cultural preparation and initiation of the persons concerned into living, learning and working practices in different European countries, as well as their return under appropriate conditions, namely by training relevant contact persons of the target groups (university teachers and administrators, vocational teachers and trainers, teachers and head teachers, staff of sending and hosting organisations) interculturally, and to encourage educational and training establishments to appoint staff to coordinate and facilitate their intercultural training.

(18) This Recommendation conforms to the principle of subsidiarity referred to in Article 5 of the Treaty insofar as Community action, complementing action by the Member States, is necessary for the obstacles to mobility to be removed. It is important to that end to emphasise that mobility requires Community intervention because by its nature it entails transnational aspects. This Recommendation also conforms to the principle of proportionality referred to in that Article because it does not go beyond what is necessary to achieve the objectives pursued.

(19) This Recommendation seeks to encourage cooperation between Member States on the subject of mobility by supporting their activities and fully respecting their responsibilities within the framework of their national legislation in particular as regards the implementation of the invitations which it contains.

(20) This Recommendation is aimed at Member State nationals who would like to experience living in a Member State other than the home Member State. Nevertheless, it should also be noted that the European Council stated at Tampere on 15 and 16 October 1999 that the European Union must ensure 'equal treatment for third country nationals who are legally resident in a Member State' and that a more vigorous integration policy should aim at granting them rights and imposing on them obligations comparable to those citizens of the Union. Third country nationals who are legally resident in a Member State should be granted a number of rights in that Member State which come as close as possible to those enjoyed by the citizens of the Union.

(21) Community education, training and youth programmes are open to the countries of the European Free Trade Association participating in the European Economic Area and the associated countries of Central and Eastern Europe (CCEE), in accordance with the conditions set out in the Europe Agreements, in their additional protocols and in the decisions of the relevant Association Councils, and to Cyprus, Malta and Turkey. This Recommendation should accordingly be brought to the attention of these countries and mobility should be facilitated for any nationals from those countries who pursue studies or training, take part in voluntary activities, or provide teaching or training within the European Union under a Community programme.

(22) The Community programmes, including those mentioned above, have enabled the development at Community level of good practice and of important tools which aim to facilitate mobility for students, persons undergoing training, volunteers, teachers and trainers. The widest possible application of those good practices and tools should be envisaged,

I. HEREBY RECOMMEND that Member States:

1. Measures which concern all categories of people covered by this Recommendation:

(a) take the measures they consider appropriate to remove the legal and administrative obstacles to the mobility of persons undertaking a course of studies, a period of training or a voluntary activity, or providing teaching or training in another Member State, particularly in the context of Community programmes (including Socrates, Leonardo da Vinci and Youth) but also outside them; to cooperate with the Commission in the promotion of the exchange of experience and good practice relating to the transnational mobility of the persons concerned and the various aspects of this Recommendation;

(b) take the measures they consider appropriate to reduce linguistic and cultural obstacles, for example:

— to encourage the learning of at least two Community languages, and to make young people aware, in particular, of Union citizenship and respect for cultural and social differences;

— to encourage linguistic and cultural preparation before any mobility measure;

(c) promote the development of various arrangements for financial support for mobility (grants, scholarships, subsidies, loans, etc.) and in particular:

— facilitate the portability of scholarships and national aids;

— take the measures they consider appropriate so that the procedures for transferring and paying grants and other assistance abroad are facilitated and simplified;

(d) take the measures they consider appropriate to promote a European qualification area, i.e. to enable those concerned to report on the qualifications obtained and the experience acquired in the host State to the relevant authorities, particularly the academic and professional authorities in their home State; that might be carried out by promoting the objectives of the 1992 and 1996 Resolutions on the transparency of qualifications and training certificates, by encouraging the use of the Europass Training document as provided for in Council Decision 1999/51/EC of 21 December 1998 on the promotion of European pathways in work-linked training, including apprenticeship [1] and of the European diploma supplement, and by implementing the conclusions of the Lisbon European Council of 23 and 24 March 2000, in particular by establishing a European framework of basic skills and a common European format for curricula vitae;

(e) consider to what extent the persons covered by this Recommendation can benefit from the arrangements for support available to the same categories of persons in the host State, such as for example reductions for public transport, financial assistance with accommodation and meals, as well as access to libraries and museums, with the exception of benefits available under social security. In this context discussions on introducing a 'mobility card' should be initiated;

---

[1] OJ L 17, 22.1.1999, p. 45.

(f) help to enable people interested in mobility to have easy access to any useful information concerning opportunities for studying, training, volunteering, or providing teaching or training in the other Member States, by extending the work of the National Academic Recognition Information Centres, the European Network of Information Centres and Europe Direct, in particular by:

— improving the dissemination of information regarding the possibilities and conditions (especially the arrangements for financial support) concerning transnational mobility;

— ensuring that their citizens are aware of their entitlements under Regulation (EEC) No 1408/71 and under existing reciprocal arrangements concerning social security cover while they are temporarily resident in another Member State;

— encouraging the training of, and regular provision of information to, those at all administrative levels regarding the Community acquis on mobility;

— taking part in the work on the creation of a database on jobs and learning opportunities, in the context of decentralised procedures and taking full advantage of existing structures and mechanisms such as the European Employment Services (EURES);

(g) take the measures they consider appropriate so that the categories of persons concerned by this Recommendation are not subjected to discrimination in their home Member State in relation to the same categories of persons who do not undertake a transnational mobility experience;

(h) take measures they consider appropriate to remove obstacles to the mobility of third country nationals who, when participating in Community programmes, including Socrates, Leonardo da Vinci and Youth, pursue study or training, do voluntary work or provide teaching or training.

2. Measures which specifically concern students:

(a) facilitate the recognition, for academic purposes, in the home Member State of the period of study undertaken in the host Member State; for this purpose the use of the European Credit Transfer System (ECTS) throughout the Community should be encouraged which, based on the transparency of curricula, guarantees the recognition of academic experience as a result of a contract drawn up in advance between the student and the home and host establishments;

(b) take, furthermore, appropriate measures so that the decisions of the authorities responsible for academic recognition are adopted within reasonable timescales, are justified and can be subject to administrative and/or legal appeal;

(c) encourage educational establishments to issue a European supplement as an administrative annex to the diploma, the aim of which is to describe the studies undertaken in order to facilitate their recognition;

(d) encourage students and pupils to complete a part of their studies in another Member State and to facilitate the recognition of periods of study completed in this context in another Member State;

(e) take or to encourage appropriate measures to enable students more easily to prove that they have health cover or insurance in order to obtain their residence permits;

(f) facilitate the integration (academic guidance, educational psychology, etc.), of students undergoing mobility into the education system of the host Member State, as well as their reintegration into the education system of the home Member State, following the example of the Socrates programme.

3. Measures which specifically concern persons undergoing training:

(a) promote the consideration in the home Member State of attested training undertaken in the host Member State; to this end, the use of the 'Europass Training' document, amongst others, should be encouraged;

(b) encourage the use of more transparent models for vocational training certificates, as provided for in the 1996 Resolution on the transparency of vocational training certificates and in the proposals submitted by the European Forum on the transparency of vocational qualifications. These proposals aim in particular at:

— issuing, with official national certificates, a translation of such certificates and/or a European certificate supplement;

— designating national reference points responsible for providing information on national vocational qualifications;

(c) take the measures they consider appropriate, in accordance with Community law and in the framework of their national law, so that persons travelling to another Member State for the purpose of undergoing recognised training there are not subject, because of their mobility to discrimination with respect to relevant social protection, including the administrative formalities for this protection, such as in the area of health care and other relevant areas;

(d) take the measures they consider appropriate from the administrative point of view to make it easier to obtain proof that a person undergoing training in another Member State has sufficient resources, as provided for in Directive 90/364/EEC.

4. Measures which specifically concern volunteers:

(a) ensure that the specific nature of voluntary activity is taken into account in national legal and administrative measures;

(b) promote the consideration, in the home Member State, of voluntary activity undertaken in the host Member State by means of a certificate that persons have taken part in voluntary activity projects, describing the experience gained, within the framework of the objective of bringing about a common European format for curricula vitae;

(c) take the measures they consider appropriate, in accordance with Community law and in the framework of their national law, so that volunteers and their families are not discriminated against because of their mobility with respect to relevant social protection, such as health care and social welfare policies;

(d) take the measures they consider appropriate, under national legislation, to ensure that recognised voluntary activities are not treated as employment.

5. Measures which specifically concern teachers and trainers:

(a) take into account as far as possible the problems facing teachers and trainers on short-term mobility covered by the legislation of several Member States and encourage cooperation in this respect;

(b) take the measures they consider appropriate to facilitate teachers' and trainers' mobility to other Member States, for example:

— by making arrangements for the temporary replacement of teachers and trainers on European mobility;

— by ensuring that arrangements are made to facilitate their integration in the host establishment;

— by considering the introduction, in accordance with procedures established at national level, of European training periods to make mobility easier.

(c) encourage the introduction of a European dimension into the professional environments of teachers and trainers, in particular:

— in the content of the programmes for the training of teachers and trainers;

— by encouraging contacts between establishments for the training of teachers and trainers in different Member States, including exchanges and courses in other Member States;

(d) promote consideration of European mobility experience as a component of the careers of teachers and trainers.

II. HEREBY INVITE Member States:

— to draw up and forward to the Commission, within two years of the adoption of this Recommendation and thereafter every two years, an evaluative report on the action they have taken in response to the recommendations set out above and in the Action Plan for mobility.

III. HEREBY INVITE the Commission:

(a) to set up a group of experts who represent all Member States and comprise the officials responsible for coordinating, at national level, the implementation of these recommendations and of the measures in the Action Plan for mobility, in order to enable the exchange of information and experience on these;

(b) to continue to cooperate with the Member States and the social partners, within *inter alia* the European Forum on the transparency of professional qualifications, so that useful information and experience concerning the implementation of the measures advocated in this Recommendation may be exchanged;

(c) to submit to the European Parliament, the Council, the Economic and Social Committee and the Committee of the Regions, at the latest two years and six months after the adoption of this Recommendation and thereafter every two years, an analytical summary of the reports from the Member States referred to in II above; and to include in such a summary an indication of the areas of activity in which Community action may be needed to complement measures which have been taken by Member States;

(d) to study the procedures for introducing a pass for schoolchildren/students/trainees/volunteers within the Community giving holders entitlement to different concessions during their period of mobility;

(e) to draw up proposals for improved cooperation in promoting the transparency of qualifications, in particular for making the EUROPASS available to third countries participating in Community programmes, and with regard to certificates of completion of vocational training;

(f) to study appropriate procedures for the adoption of measures, in cooperation with the Member States, for the exchange of information on opportunities for education, training or voluntary work, or providing teaching or training in the other Member States.

Done at Brussels, 10 July 2001.

For the European Parliament	*For the Council*
The President	*The President*
N. FONTAINE	D. REYNDERS

ANNEX

CATEGORIES OF PEOPLE COVERED BY THIS RECOMMENDATION

The people mentioned below are covered by this Recommendation only if they move from one State (the home State) to another (the host State) for a temporary stay and return to the home State at the end of their stay. Such persons keep their legal residence, as defined by the law of each Member State, in the home State.

I. Students

People who study in educational establishments such as those covered by the third indent of Article 149(2) of the Treaty.

II. Persons undergoing training

People who, regardless of their age and professional conditions, attend vocational training at any level including higher education.

III. Volunteers

People, especially young people, who, in the context of the 'European Voluntary Service' section of the Community 'Youth' programme or of transnational voluntary projects similar to the 'European Voluntary Service', undertake an activity which specifically involves solidarity, is nonprofit making and unpaid and helps them acquire social and personal skills.

IV. Teachers

People who provide teaching in educational establishments such as those covered by the third indent of Article 149(2) of the Treaty.

V. Trainers

People who provide training in educational or vocational training centres such as those referred to in the fourth indent of Article 150(2) of the Treaty and/or in training centres or undertakings.

**Council Resolution
of 13 July 2001
on the role of education and training in employment
related policies**

(OJ C 204, 20.7.2001)

I

(Information)

COUNCIL

COUNCIL RESOLUTION

of 13 July 2001

on the role of education and training in employment related policies

(2001/C 204/01)

THE COUNCIL OF THE EUROPEAN UNION,

bearing in mind:

(1) The Conclusions of the European Council in Lisbon of 23 and 24 March 2000, where the European Union set itself a new strategic goal for the next decade and emphasised the fundamental role of education and training in the successful transition to a knowledge-based economy and society. In particular, the European Council invited the Council (Education) to contribute to the Luxembourg and Cardiff processes.

(2) The opinion of the Council (Education) of 9 November 2000 on the proposal for a Council Decision on guidelines for Member States' employment policies for the year 2001 which recommends that from 2001 the Commission should, when drafting guidelines for employment policies for the following year, take into account the opinion the Ministers for Education will forward to it.

(3) The Conclusions of the Stockholm European Council of 23-24 March 2001 which reaffirmed the Lisbon strategic goal and stressed the importance of basic skills, particularly IT and digital skills, and the role of strong general education in order to support labour mobility and lifelong learning.

(4) The 'Employment Package 2000', which was endorsed by the European Council in Nice of 7 and 8 December 2000, and Council Decision 2001/63/EC of 19 January 2001 on Guidelines for Member States' employment policies for the year 2001 [1] which give priority to lifelong learning as a horizontal objective around which Member States should define coherent strategies.

(5) The European Social Agenda, also approved by the Nice European Council, which amongst other things underlines the need to improve access to lifelong learning and which implies integrated policy formulation and implementation at European and national levels.

[1] OJ L 22, 24.1.2001, p. 18.

(6) The report from the Council (Education) on the concrete future objectives of education and training systems, which was submitted to the Stockholm European Council as a contribution to the Luxembourg and Cardiff processes, and the request by the Stockholm European Council for a new report to the spring European Council in 2002.

(7) The Communication from the Commission on 'New labour markets, open to all, with access for all' which underlines the importance of increasing the level of skills and their transferability from one country to another and of the strengthening of education skills and lifelong learning policies, as well as the endorsement by the Stockholm European Council of the setting-up of a high-level task force on skills and mobility, drawing on expertise from business, education and the social partners.

(8) The Commission's memorandum on lifelong learning which has launched a wide debate at European level and in the Member States on how to implement comprehensive and coherent strategies for lifelong learning, and the e-Learning action plan for the period 2001 to 2004 which aims to involve education and training players, as well as the relevant social, industrial and economic players, in order to rectify the shortage of skills associated with the new economy and to improve social inclusion,

RECOGNISES the importance placed on education and training policies in the European Employment Strategy and the significant role attached to education and training for achieving the new strategic goal set in Lisbon that Europe should become the most competitive and dynamic knowledge-based economy in the world;

ACKNOWLEDGES the importance of addressing education and training policy-related issues in a wide context, taking full account of all the general aims that society attributes to education and training: the development of society and the individual as well as the development of the economy;

UNDERLINES the relevance and the complementarity to the objectives of the Luxembourg process of the three main objectives set out in the Report on the concrete future objectives of education and training systems:

— increasing quality and effectiveness of education and training systems in the European Union,

— facilitating the access of all to the education and training systems,

— opening up education and training systems to the wider world;

EMPHASISES that several sub-objectives stated in this report are related to facilitating access to the labour market and to improving adaptability of the workface, in particular:

— developing skills for the knowledge society,

— ensuring access to information and communications technologies (ICTs) for everyone,

— open learning environment,

— strengthening links with working life, research and society at large,

— developing the spirit of enterprise,

— improving foreign language learning,

— increasing mobility and exchanges;

STRESSES therefore that the drawing up and implementation of the work programme resulting from the Report on the concrete future objectives of the education and training systems is a process in its own right;

EMPHASISES THAT THE FOLLOW-UP OF THAT REPORT will make a significant contribution to the Luxembourg process and to the development of employment policies at both European and national level;

NOTES the Commission's document 'Education and training in employment policies' which highlights in this context:

— the need for more intensive efforts to ensure quality initial education to provide young people with the basic skills needed to meet the demands of the knowledge society,

— the importance of coherent education and training strategy to link the various education and training systems and to promote recognition of formal and informal training,

— the importance of comparable statistics and availability of indicators to analyse and monitor the contribution of Member States' education and training policies;

LOOKS FORWARD TO the Commission's forthcoming action plan on lifelong learning, due to be released in November 2001, which should make an important contribution to existing processes and initiatives for achieving a knowledge-based society and economy;

LOOKS FORWARD TO the report to be submitted by the high-level task force on skills and mobility by December 2001 and to the opportunity to contribute to the preparation of the action plan for developing and opening up new European labour markets, to be presented to the spring European Council in 2002;

REAFFIRMS its intention to participate actively in the implementation of the European social agenda, particularly in relation to the orientation 'More and better jobs' by promoting effective lifelong learning strategies, the development of skills in information and communication technologies and the mobility of students, teachers and trainees;

STRESSES the need for those responsible for education and training to be actively involved in the different processes in place at European level to promote full employment, given the vital contribution that education and training systems are expected to make to them and the importance of a coherent approach to activities and initiatives relating to education and training;

CALLS UPON THE COMMISSION AND THE MEMBER STATES

within their respective areas of competence,

— to ensure that the follow-up to the Report on the concrete future objectives of the education and training systems contributes to the Luxembourg and Cardiff processes and places education and training in the centre of Community cooperation in employment and related policy areas,

— to ensure that the Council (Education) is actively involved in the examination of the Commission's proposal for the employment guidelines and in the definition of policy relevant and comparable indicators with a view to presenting a timely contribution to the preparation of the guidelines and relevant areas dealing with education and training as well as within a lifelong learning perspective,

— to strengthen the exchange of experience and examples of good practice in the field, based on comparative analysis of the national action plans for employment such as the Commission's document 'Education and training in employment policies'.

**Council Resolution
of 13 July 2001
on e-Learning**

(OJ C 204, 20.7.2001)

COUNCIL RESOLUTION

of 13 July 2001

on e-Learning

(2001/C 204/02)

THE COUNCIL OF THE EUROPEAN UNION,

Bearing in mind:

(1) The conclusions of the European Council in Lisbon of 23 and 24 March 2000 which set the strategic goal of creating a competitive, dynamic and knowledge-based economy as well as specific targets with regard to information and communications technology (ICT) and education, as well as the conclusions of the Stockholm European Council of 23 and 24 March 2001 which reaffirmed that improving basic skills, particularly IT and digital skills is a top priority for the Union.

(2) The report from the Council (Education) to the Stockholm European Council on the concrete future objectives of education and training systems which underlines, *inter alia*, the importance of developing skills for the knowledge society and achieving the targets set by the Lisbon European Council to ensure access to ICTs for everyone.

(3) The request at the Stockholm European Council for a new report for the spring European Council in 2002, containing a detailed work programme on the follow-up of the objectives of education and training systems.

(4) The important commitment to the use of ICT in education and training already present in the Socrates and Leonardo Programmes as well as other existing Community instruments.

(5) The guidelines for Member States' employment policies for 2001 [1] which stress that in connection with developing skills for the new labour market in the context of lifelong learning, Member States will aim at developing e-Learning for all citizens.

(6) The Council resolution of 6 May 1996 relating to educational multimedia software in the fields of education and training and the Council conclusions of 22 September 1997 on education, information and communication technology and teacher training for the future [2].

---

[1] Council Decision 2001/63/EC of 19 January 2001 (OJ L 22, 24.1.2001, p. 18).
[2] OJ C 303, 4.10.1997, p. 5.

(7) The Commission's communication on 'e-Learning: designing tomorrow's education' of 24 May 2000 which sets out objectives in the light of the Lisbon conclusions and as a complement to the Commissions comprehensive 'e-Europe action plan'.

(8) The Commission's communication entitled 'e-Learning action plan — designing tomorrow's education' of 28 March 2001 which defines common activity areas and specific measures with regard to using new multimedia technologies and the internet to improve the quality of learning and which covers infrastructure, training, high-quality multimedia services and content and dialogue and cooperation at all levels,

(9) INVITES the Member States:

(i) to continue their efforts concerning the effective integration of ICT in education and training systems, as an important part of the adaptation of the education and training systems requested by the Lisbon European Council Conclusions and by the Report on concrete future objectives of education systems;

(ii) to capitalise on the potential of Internet, multimedia and virtual learning environments for a better and faster realisation of lifelong learning as a basic educational principle and for providing access to educational and training opportunities for all, in particular for those who have access problems for social, economic, geographical or other reasons;

(iii) to promote the necessary provision of ICT learning opportunities within education and training systems by accelerating integration of ICT and revision of school and higher education curricula in all relevant subject areas without losing sight of the long-term objectives and the critical approach required by educational systems;

(iv) to continue their efforts in the initial and in-service training of teachers and trainers in the pedagogical use of ICT, given the need to develop the digital culture as one essential element in the teacher's basic skills and to motivate teachers and trainers to make the best pedagogical use of ICT in their own teaching;

(v) to encourage those responsible for educational and training establishments as well as local, regional and national decision-makers and other relevant stakeholders to acquire the necessary understanding of the potential offered by ICT for enhancing new ways of learning and pedagogical development in order to integrate and manage ICT effectively;

(vi) to accelerate the provision of equipment and of a quality infrastructure for education and training, taking into account technical progress: hardware, software and Internet access within educational and training establishments, and relevant human resources for ensuring help, support and maintenance services;

(vii) to encourage the development of high-quality digital teaching and learning materials to ensure quality of online offers; to provide appropriate support mechanisms to facilitate the choice of quality products for teachers and managers of educational and training establishments;

(viii) to take advantage of the opportunities that digitisation and documentary standardisation offer for facilitating access and increasing the educational and pedagogical use of public cultural resources, such as libraries, museums and archives;

(ix) to support the development and adaptation of innovative pedagogy that integrates the use of technology within broader cross-curriculum approaches; to foster new approaches, based on a more extensive use of innovative pedagogical methods and software and the use of new devices and experiences in order to stimulate learners' knowledge and motivation and so foster, as a part of teaching, critical attitudes among learners to content on the Internet and other media;

(x) to exploit the communication potential of ICT to foster European awareness, exchanges, and collaboration at all eductation and training levels, and especially in schools; to consider the possibility of integrating these European experiences in curricula, and to support and strengthen physical and virtual mobility as an important part of education, developing the new skills and competencies required to live and work in a multilingual and multicultural society;

(xi) to support and stimulate virtual meeting places for cooperation and exchange of information, experience and good practice, which will take into account new pedagogic approaches and new forms of cooperation between learners, and between teachers or trainers and to stimulate European networking at all levels in the field of educational multimedia, educational use of Internet, ICT-mediated collaboration and learning, and other uses of ICT in education and training;

(xii) to capitalise and build on the experiences gained in the framework of initiatives such as the European School-net and European Network of Teacher Education Policies (ENTEP);

(xiii) to foster the European dimension of joint development of ICT-mediated and ICT-complemented curricula in higher education, by encouraging further common approaches in higher education certification models and quality assurance (following the Sorbonne/Bologna process); to provide incentives to establishments, faculties or departments achieving innovative and pedagogically sound work at European level, in this area;

(xiv) to enhance research in e-Learning, in particular on how to improve learning performance through ICT, pedagogical development, implications of ICT-based teaching and learning and to stimulate international cooperation in this regard;

(xv) to promote partnership between the public and private sectors as a contribution to the development of e-Learning in order to encourage exchange of experiences, the dialogue on future requirements for multimedia learning materials; and technology transfer;

(xvi) to monitor and analyse the process of integration and use of ICT in teaching, training and learning, to provide existing quantitative and qualitative information, and to develop improved observation and evaluation methods, in order to share experiences and to exchange good practices with a view to contributing to the follow-up to the Report on the concrete future objectives of education and training systems;

(10) INVITES the Commission:

(i) to pay particular attention in its implementation of the e-Learning Action Plan, to the work related to the key priorities expressed in the Report on the concrete future objective of education and training systems such as exchange of good practice and experiences between Member States, including experiences from other countries;

(ii) to continue supporting existing European portals and to encourage the development of other portals to facilitate access to educational content and to promote collaboration and exchange of experiences in the area of e-Learning and pedagogical development, especially with a view to:

— supporting transnational virtual meeting places,

— stimulating European networking at all levels and in this context establish and provide networks for the benefit of teacher training,

— supporting directories of existing quality Internet resources.

(iii) to implement support actions at European level, in particular to share experience and information about products and services in the field of multimedia educational software and, in this context, to propose methods for assistance and advice in the selection of qualitative and pedagogical multimedia resources; the establishment of cross-border links between producers, users and managers of education and training systems in order to promote quality in products and services and better correspondence between supply and demand; to support information and communication actions and European-wide debate in all the above matters;

(iv) to examine together with Member States whether the 'eSchola, a week for e-Learning in Europe', could develop into an on-going activity that includes an annual high-profile event;

(v) to support the testing of new learning environments and approaches in order to take into account the growing differentiation of learners' styles, cultures and languages, and to foster, in cooperation with Member States, virtual mobility and transnational virtual campus projects, especially in the field of languages, science and technology, art and culture;

(vi) to undertake strategic studies on innovative approaches in education, on the pedagogical aspects of new technologies, on the strengths and weaknesses of the European educational multimedia sector, and on the potential of cultural institutions and science centres as new learning environments;

(vii) to intensify, in the framework of Community programmes, research, experimentation and evaluation on pedagogical, socioeconomic and technological dimensions of new ICT-mediated approaches, and on their adaptation to users' needs; to actively disseminate the results of this research with a view to facilitating its transfer to the education and training systems and to professional publishers and providers;

(viii) to support the development of European multilingual educational resources, platforms and services, taking into account, when necessary, education and training-related aspects of intellectual property rights and the use of new distribution methods, and the development and promotion of internationally aspected standards and open source software;

(ix) to report to the Council on the results of the abovementioned activities no later than December 2002, in order to facilitate an overall evaluation of their results and decisions on further actions. An interim report shall also be presented to the Council in November 2001.

**Council Conclusions
of 13 July 2001
on the follow-up of the report on concrete future objectives
of education and training systems**

(OJ C 204, 20.7.2001)

COUNCIL CONCLUSIONS

of 13 July 2001

on the follow-up of the report on concrete future objectives of education and training systems

(2001/C 204/03)

THE COUNCIL OF THE EUROPEAN UNION,

1. RECALLS that the Council (Education) adopted the report on the concrete future objectives of education and training systems on 12 February 2001 for transmission to the Stockholm European Council, following the mandate given by the Lisbon European Council in March 2000, with a very clear message to all those involved in its follow-up that there should be rapid progress in working out how to take its implementation forward, and in selecting priorities.

2. RECALLS that the Stockholm European Council underlined that the joint report, which the Council and the Commission will present to the European Council in Barcelona in spring 2002, should contain 'a detailed work programme on the follow-up of the objectives of education and training systems, including an assessment of their achievement in the framework of the open method of coordination and in a worldwide perspective'.

3. AGREES that the main objectives of the follow-up of the Objectives Report of 12 February 2001 will be to:

   — assess the achievement of the objectives stated in the report so that the Council (Education) can report back to the European Council whenever this is seemed appropriate,

   — provide support for the improvement of education and training policy design and implementation at all levels,

   — promote further development of cooperation and exchange of good practice between Member States, thus enhancing efficiency and effectiveness of this work.

   As stated in the objectives report consideration will have to be given throughout the follow-up process to other processes at European level affecting the work of the Council (Education). Similarly, account should be taken within those processes of the follow-up work on the objectives of education and training systems.

4. AGREES upon the following milestones leading up to the Barcelona European Council:

   — a draft work programme, including a further elaborated methodology, to be discussed by the Council at its meeting on 29 November 2001,

   — a joint report by the Commission and the Council containing a detailed work programme to be adopted at the Council meeting on 14 February 2002 and transmitted to the Barcelona European Council.

5. EMPHASISES that the work programme should cover in sufficient detail the period up to 2004, the aim being that work should have started by then in all areas contained in the Objectives Report, and also cover in broad terms developments foreseen up to 2010. Similarly, this work programme should aim at a strong general education in order to strengthen lifelong learning in accordance with a permanently evolving society.

6. FURTHER AGREES that work will start in the following three areas which were also highlighted in the conclusions of the Stockholm European Council:

   — basic skills,

   — information and communications technology (ICT),

   — mathematics, science and technology.

7. UNDERLINES that work should start without delay in all three agreed areas so that progress could be accounted for in the joint report by the Council and the Commission to Barcelona.

8. STRESSES that indicators, although, only one element of the follow-up progress, represent an important tool for measuring and comparing performance, and that if the process is to be successful and credible, the indicators need to be underpinned by clearly defined, comparable and, above all, policy-relevant data.

9. REAFFIRMS that the objectives of the follow-up process can only be achieved with active involvement and contribution from Member States, *inter alia*, through:

   — provision of the necessary support to the national statistical offices,

— provision of up-to-date data and, when available, their national forecasts and objectives,

— information on relevant changes in national policies and instruments, influencing the education and training systems,

— contribution to all other aspects of the following work, e.g. provision of qualitative information, involvement in studies and nomination of experts to working groups.

10. RECALLS moreover that the Commission will be fully involved in all phases of the work. The Commission should therfore take the necessary initiatives to support the process.

**Council opinion
of 14 February 2002
concerning education and training issues
in the proposal for a Council Decision on guidelines
for Member States' employment policies for 2002**

(OJ C 47, 21.02.2002)

I

(Information)

COUNCIL

COUNCIL OPINION

of 14 February 2002

concerning education and training issues in the proposal for a Council Decision on guidelines for Member States' employment policies for 2002

(2002/C 47/01)

THE COUNCIL OF THE EUROPEAN UNION,

Whereas:

(1) The Lisbon European Council of 23 and 24 March 2000 acknowledged the important role played by the education and training sector in living and working in the knowledge society and that the Council (Education) should contribute to the Luxembourg and Cardiff processes by reflecting on the concrete future objectives of education systems.

(2) The Stockholm European Council of 23 and 24 March 2001 confirmed that role and requested the Council and the Commission to present a joint report to the spring 2002 European Council containing a detailed work programme on the follow-up of the objectives of education and training systems.

(3) The Council (Education) adopted a favourable opinion on 9 November 2000 on the proposal for a Council Decision on guidelines for Member States' employment policies for the year 2001, where lifelong learning is a horizontal objective.

(4) The Council Resolution of 13 July 2001 on the role of education and training in employment related policies [1] invited the Commission and the Member States, *inter alia*, to ensure that the Council (Education) is actively involved in the examination of the Commission's proposal for employment guidelines and the identification of policy relevant and comparable indicators with a view to a timely contribution to the preparation of the guidelines and relevant areas dealing with education and training as well as within a lifelong learning perspective.

RECALLS that the role of education and training policies in support of employment is recognised within the current structure of the employment guidelines in four pillars — employability, entrepreneurship, adaptability and equal opportunities. The introduction in 2000 into the employment guidelines for 2001 of the 'horizontal objective on lifelong learning' was an important step towards a greater coherence and understanding of this role. However, a better representation of education and training policies should be pursued;

STRESSES the fact that lifelong learning, which has already become a key issue (in education and training) at Member State and Community level, has become a clear priority in national employment policies;

NOTES that lifelong learning is still dispersed among several guidelines and pillars and that a new horizontal objective on quality in work has been added to the employment guidelines (building on the Commission Communication 'Employment and social policies: framework for investing in quality') covering skills and lifelong learning. While welcoming this objective it would be helpful if the more distinctive features in relation to lifelong learning could be indicated;

WELCOMES the fact that there has been increased involvement of those responsible for education and training in the different phases of implementation of the European employment strategy;

EMPHASISES that through its own processes and instruments, the Council will increasingly contribute to the Lisbon goals and the Luxembourg process as well as to the successful transition to a knowledge-based economy and society.

In this context, there is a need to strengthen cooperation and synergy between the different and complementary processes and initiatives, in particular the follow-up of the report on the concrete future objectives of education and training systems, the follow-up of the Commission's Memorandum on lifelong learning and the action plan on eLearning;

NOTES that the Member States and the Commission are currently carrying out an impact evaluation of the European employment strategy which will be reflected in the employment Guidelines 2003. In this context, it is important that the Council and the authorities responsible for education and training be closely associated in this evaluation process, at national and European level, in view of a more effective involvement in the evaluation before political conclusions are drawn.

---

[1] OJ C 204, 20.7.2001, p. 1.

**Council Resolution
of 14 February 2002
on the promotion of linguistic diversity and language learning
in the framework of the implementation of the objectives
of the European Year of Languages 2001**

(OJ C 50, 23.02.2002)

I

(Information)

COUNCIL

COUNCIL RESOLUTION

of 14 February 2002

on the promotion of linguistic diversity and language learning in the framework of the implementation of the objectives of the European Year of Languages 2001

(2002/C 50/01)

THE COUNCIL OF THE EUROPEAN UNION,

RECALLING:

(1) the Council Resolution of 31 March 1995 on improving and diversifying language learning and teaching within the education systems of the European Union ([1]), according to which pupils should, as a general rule, have the opportunity of learning two languages of the Union other than their mother tongue(s);

(2) the responsibility of Member States for the content of teaching and the organisation of education systems and their cultural and linguistic diversity;

(3) the Commission's 1995 White Paper entitled Teaching and learning: Towards the learning society;

(4) the Council Conclusions of 12 June 1995 on linguistic diversity and multilingualism in the European Union;

(5) the Council Resolution of 16 December 1997 on the early teaching of European Union languages ([2]);

(6) the Presidency conclusions of the Lisbon European Council of 23 and 24 March 2000 which include foreign languages within a European framework for the definition of basic skills;

(7) Decision No 1934/2000/EC of the European Parliament and of the Council of 17 July 2000 on the European Year of Languages 2001 ([3]);

(8) Article 22 of the Charter of Fundamental Rights of the European Union of 7 December 2000 ([4]), welcomed by the Nice European Council, which states that the Union shall respect cultural, religious and linguistic diversity;

(9) the Resolution of the Council and of the representatives of the Governments of the Member States, meeting within the Council, of 14 December 2000 on the social inclusion of young people ([5]), which was approved by the Nice European Council;

(10) the Council Decision of 19 January 2001 on Guidelines for Member States' employment policies for the year 2001 ([6]) and in particular the horizontal objective concerning lifelong learning;

(11) the Report of the Education Council of 12 February 2001 on the concrete future objectives of education and training systems which was submitted to the Stockholm European Council and which explicitly includes improving foreign language learning as one of its objectives, and the Council Conclusions of 28 May 2001 on the follow-up to be given to the Report;

(12) the Commission's 2000 Memorandum on lifelong learning which has given an impetus to a broad discussion, both at European level and in the Member States, on how to implement broad and coherent strategies for lifelong learning, *inter alia* in the field of language learning;

(13) the Recommendation of the European Parliament and of the Council of 10 July 2001 on mobility within the Community for students, persons undergoing training, volunteers, teachers and trainers ([7]);

(14) the activities developed by the Council of Europe in the field of the promotion of linguistic diversity and language learning.

([1]) OJ C 207, 12.8.1995, p. 1.
([2]) OJ C 1, 3.1.1998, p. 2.
([3]) OJ L 232, 14.9.2000, p. 1.
([4]) OJ C 364, 18.12.2000, p. 1.
([5]) OJ C 374, 28.12.2000, p. 5.
([6]) OJ L 22, 24.1.2001, p. 18.
([7]) OJ L 215, 9.8.2001, p. 30.

EMPHASISES THAT:

(1) the knowledge of languages is one of the basic skills which each citizen needs to acquire in order to take part effectively in the European knowledge society and therefore facilitates both integration into society and social cohesion; a thorough knowledge of one's mother tongue(s) can facilitate the learning of other languages;

(2) knowledge of languages plays an important role in facilitating mobility, both in an educational context as well as for professional purposes and for cultural and personal reasons;

(3) knowledge of languages is also beneficial for European cohesion, in the light of EU enlargement;

(4) all European languages are equal in value and dignity from the cultural point of view and form an integral part of European culture and civilisation.

RECALLS THAT:

the European Year of Languages 2001, organised in cooperation with the Council of Europe, is stimulating awareness of linguistic diversity and the promotion of language learning;

the Report of the Education Council of 12 February 2001 on the concrete future objectives of education and training systems, which explicitly includes improving foreign language learning as one of its objectives, should be implemented via a detailed work programme to be defined in a joint report which the Council and Commission will present to the Barcelona European Council.

REAFFIRMS:

the objectives set out in Article 2 of Decision No 1934/2000/EC of the European Parliament and of the Council of 17 July 2000 on the European Year of Languages 2001, with a view to the further implementation of these objectives.

INVITES the Member States within the framework, limits and priorities of their respective political, legal, budgetary, educational and training systems:

(1) to take the measures they deem appropriate to offer pupils, as far as possible, the opportunity to learn two, or where appropriate, more languages in addition to their mother tongues, and to promote the learning of foreign languages by others in the context of lifelong learning, taking into account the diverse needs of the target public and the importance of providing equal access to learning opportunities. In order to promote cooperation and mobility across Europe, the supply of languages should be as diversified as possible, including those of neighbouring countries and/or regions;

(2) to ensure that study programmes and educational objectives promote a positive attitude to other languages and cultures and stimulate intercultural communication skills from an early age;

(3) to promote the learning of languages in vocational training, thereby taking into account the positive impact of language knowledge on mobility and employability;

(4) to facilitate the integration of non-native speakers in the educational system and in society as a whole, including through-measures to improve their knowledge of the official language(s) of instruction, respecting the languages and cultures of their country of origin;

(5) to promote the application of innovative pedagogical methods, in particular also through teacher training;

(6) to encourage future language teachers to take advantage of relevant European programmes to carry out part of their studies in a country or region of a country where the language which they will teach later is the official language;

(7) to set up systems of validation of competence in language knowledge based on the common European framework of reference for languages developed by the Council of Europe, taking sufficient account of skills acquired through informal learning;

(8) to stimulate European cooperation in order to promote transparency of qualifications and quality assurance of language learning;

(9) to bear in mind the wealth of linguistic diversity within the European Community in the context of the abovementioned objectives, and thus to encourage, *inter alia*, cooperation between official centres or other cultural institutions for the dissemination of the languages and cultures of the Member States.

INVITES the Commission:

(1) to support the Member States in their implementation of the abovementioned recommendations;

(2) to take into account, in this context, the principle of linguistic diversity in its relations with third and candidate countries;

(3) to draw up proposals by early 2003 for actions for the promotion of linguistic diversity and language learning while ensuring consistency with the implementation of the report on concrete future objectives of education and training systems.

Resolution of the Council and of the Representatives of the Governments of the Member States, meeting within the Council, of 14 February 2002 on the added value of voluntary activity for young people in the context of the development of Community action on youth

(OJ C 50, 23.02.2002)

RESOLUTION

of the Council and of the Representatives of the Governments of the Member States, meeting within the Council,

of 14 February 2002

on the added value of voluntary activity for young people in the context of the development of Community action on youth

(2002/C 50/02)

THE COUNCIL OF THE EUROPEAN UNION AND THE REPRESENTATIVES OF THE GOVERNMENTS OF THE MEMBER STATES, MEETING WITHIN THE COUNCIL,

Whereas:

(1) The Treaty provides that Community action is to be aimed at encouraging the development of exchange programmes for young people and youth workers.

(2) The European Parliament and the Council adopted the 'Youth' Community action programme by Decision No 1031/2000/EC [1]. This programme, which has been increasingly successful in all the Member States, contains an important component devoted to 'European voluntary service', which provides a clear definition of transnational voluntary work.

(3) The Umeå Conference (16 to 18 March 2001) on 'Conditions for young people in Europe', organised by the Swedish Presidency and the Commission, underlined in its recommendations the importance of assigning voluntary activity by young people a clearly defined position at European level.

(4) The United Nations has proclaimed 2001 as 'International Year of Volunteers'.

(5) The conclusions of the Lisbon European Council on 23 and 24 March 2000 state that the European Union requires an overall strategy aimed at preparing the transition to a knowledge-based economy and society and that as a consequence existing models for learning and working must be adapted.

(6) The Commission Memorandum on lifelong learning of 30 October 2000 and the Commission's preparatory activities with a view to its communication for lifelong learning are of particular importance. In the discussions on progress conducted over the past six-month periods, attention has been clearly drawn to the added value of informal and non-formal learning resulting from voluntary activity.

(7) The Resolution of the Council and of the Representatives of the Governments of the Member States, meeting within the Council, of 14 December 2000 on the social inclusion of young people [2] invites the Commission and the Member States, each within its own sphere of competences, to study common objectives directed at developing the conditions to enable all young people lawfully residing in a Member State to play a full part in economic and social life.

(8) The action plan on mobility approved by the Nice European Council and the Recommendation of the European Parliament and of the Council of 10 July 2001 on mobility within the Community for students, persons undergoing training, volunteers, teachers and trainers [3], listed a series of measures to promote mobility. In particular, the European Parliament and the Council identified in the Recommendation on mobility a series of measures which Member States consider appropriate to remove obstacles to mobility for volunteers.

(9) The Resolution of the Council and of the Representatives of the Governments of the Member States, meeting within the Council, of 28 June 2001 on promoting young people's initiative, enterprise and creativity — from exclusion to empowerment [4], points to the importance of the creative environment as a valuable source of support.

(10) Declaration 38 on voluntary service activities, which is attached to the Final Act of the Treaty of Amsterdam, recognises the important contribution made by voluntary service activities to developing social solidarity and states that the Community will encourage the European dimension of voluntary organisations with particular emphasis on the exchange of information and experience as well as on the participation of the young and the elderly in voluntary work,

FIND AND ACKNOWLEDGE THAT:

1. In all the Member States, countless young people are active in various forms of voluntary activity. Despite differences between the Member States, young people everywhere represent a significant proportion of the total number of volunteers active in the Community in initiatives, projects and in non-governmental organisations of a mainly social and humanitarian nature and for the benefit of a democratic society and sustainable development.

---

[1] OJ L 117, 18.5.2000, p. 1.
[2] OJ C 374, 28.12.2000, p. 5.
[3] OJ L 215, 9.8.2001, p. 30.
[4] OJ C 196, 12.7.2001, p. 2.

2. Various forms of voluntary activity for young people, including those in the context of the European Union action entitled 'European voluntary service' forming part of the 'Youth' action programme, have added social value because:

   (a) they transmit universal values with regard to human rights, democracy, anti-racism and solidarity, and sustainable development;

   (b) they promote social participation, voluntary engagement and active citizenship and strengthen civil society at all levels;

   (c) they promote the social inclusion of young people, contribute to the development of young people's creativity, enterprise and social innovation.

3. Youth voluntary activity provides the opportunity for young people to develop a number of personal and professional skills, and as such contributes to their greater employability and to their participation in society in general.

4. Youth organisations and projects have significant potential as informal and non-formal learning environments for young people, and, partly on account of their diversity, contribute to the realisation of life-long and life-wide learning in all its aspects.

5. Non-governmental organisations, youth organisations and all other organisations active in the area of youth voluntary activity play a specific role as environments where voluntary activities by young people are given shape, at local, national and European level.

6. Young volunteers themselves play an important role in the development and implementation of projects in the framework of various actions of the 'Youth' Community action programme.

INVITE THE MEMBER STATES:

To take the measures they deem appropriate to remove legal and administrative obstacles so as to provide every opportunity for youth voluntary activity in a national and international context.

To prevent voluntary activity for young people from restricting or being used as a substitute for potential or existing paid employment.

INVITE THE COMMISSION AND THE MEMBER STATES, WITHIN THEIR RESPECTIVE SPHERES OF COMPETENCE:

1. To take measures to strengthen and to further develop the role of voluntary activity for young people, and in so doing to take as their guide, where appropriate, the strategic objectives formulated by the United Nations in the framework of the International Year of Volunteers.

2. To develop policy on voluntary activity for young people and strengthen European cooperation in this area, using the following elements which result from the strategic objectives of the UN Resolution proclaiming 2001 the International Year of Volunteers:

   (a) the accessibility and promotion of information provision on voluntary activity, with a view to reinforcing a positive image;

   (b) recognition and support for voluntary activity, *inter alia* by authorities at all levels, public opinion, media, commerce, employers and civil society;

   (c) support for voluntary activity through incentives and the training of volunteers, their mentors and their associations;

   (d) networking between all parties involved, with special attention to the perspective of young people themselves;

   (e) quality care with regard to youth voluntary activity, including health and safety aspects.

3. To recognise the importance of experience gained in the context of youth voluntary activity and to collate and exchange good practice with regard to youth voluntary activity.

4. To support all the parties involved in the implementation of voluntary activity for young people.

5. To make voluntary activity more easily accessible to young people and to avoid all forms of social exclusion or discrimination.

6. To promote and support research into voluntary activity for young people via regular monitoring of developments in the field and by appropriate policy decisions.

7. To involve non-governmental organisations, youth organisations and all other organisations active in the area of voluntary activity for young people, as well as young volunteers themselves, in drawing up and implementing policy for supporting youth voluntary activity, in an atmosphere of participation and making use of the experience of volunteers and their associations.

8. To incorporate these policy objectives or measures in the follow-up which may result from the European White Paper 'Youth' published by the Commission of the European Communities.

INVITE THE COMMISSION:

1. To develop synergies between the initiatives of the European Community, the Council of Europe and initiatives of other international organisations, at both strategic and operational levels.

2. To take account of the important contribution of young volunteers to the activities of the 'Youth' programme, and to examine how youth voluntary activity can be further encouraged when the programme is evaluated and further developed.

EXPRESS THE WISH THAT:

This Resolution contribute to the development of the policy of cooperation in the youth field, in line with the principle of subsidiarity, particularly through recognition of the added value of voluntary activity with and by young people.

**Council Conclusions
of 14 February 2002
on the follow-up to the Report on the concrete future objectives of education
and training systems in view of the preparation of a joint Council/Commission report
to be presented to the Spring 2002 European Council**

(OJ C 50, 23.02.2002)

I

(Information)

COUNCIL

COUNCIL CONCLUSIONS

of 14 February 2002

on the follow-up to the Report on the concrete future objectives of education and training systems in view of the preparation of a joint Council/Commission report to be presented to the Spring 2002 European Council

(2002/C 58/01)

THE COUNCIL OF THE EUROPEAN UNION,

Recalling:

(1) The new strategic goal for the European Union set by the Lisbon European Council on 23 and 24 March 2000 and reaffirmed by the Stockholm European Council on 23 and 24 March 2001 'to become the most competitive and dynamic knowledge-based economy in the world, capable of sustainable economic growth with more and better jobs and greater social cohesion'.

(2) The Lisbon European Council's affirmation that Europe's education and training systems need to adapt both to the demands of the knowledge society and to the need for an improved level and quality of employment.

(3) The mandate from the Lisbon European Council to the Education Council 'to undertake a general reflection on concrete future objectives of education systems, focusing on common concerns and priorities while respecting national diversity with a view to contributing to the Luxembourg and Cardiff processes, and presenting a broader report to the European Council in the Spring of 2001' (Presidency Conclusions, No 27).

(4) The Report on the concrete future objectives of the education and training systems (hereafter referred to as the Report) adopted by the Education Council of 12 February 2001 which took into account a Commission proposal and which included three concrete strategic objectives together with 13 associated objectives and takes account of the general aims which society attributes to education and training.

(5) The Stockholm European Council which re-emphasised the importance of education and training stating: 'Improving basic skills, particularly IT and digital skills, is a top priority to make the Union the most competitive and dynamic knowledge-based economy in the world. This priority includes education policies and lifelong learning as well as overcoming the present shortfall in the recruitment of scientific and technical staff. A knowledge-based economy necessitates a strong general education in order to further support labour mobility and lifelong learning'.

(6) The Stockholm European Council also mandated the Council and the Commission to 'present a report to the Spring European Council in 2002 containing a detailed work programme on the follow-up of the objectives of education and training systems including an assessment of their achievement in the framework of the open method for coordination and in a worldwide perspective'.

(7) The conclusions of the Council of 13 July 2001 concerning the follow-up of the Report, which indicated that in particular work would start without delay in the areas of basic skills (objective 1.2); information and communication technologies (objective 1.3) and mathematics, science and technology (Objective 1.4) which were also highlighted in the conclusions of the Stockholm European Council.

(8) The Communication 'Draft detailed work programme for the follow-up of the report on the concrete objectives of education and training systems' adopted on 7 September 2001 which the Commission presented in response to the mandate of the Stockholm European Council provides useful input to the joint report which will be put to the Council for adoption on 14 February 2002 and forwarded to the Barcelona European Council,

REAFFIRMS:

That the follow-up to the Report adopted on 12 February 2001 should:

— assess the achievement of the objectives stated in the Report so that the Council (Education) can report back to the European Council whenever this is deemed appropriate,

— provide support for the improvement of education and training policy design and implementation at all levels,

— provide further development of cooperation and exchange of good practice between Member States, thus enhancing efficiency and effectiveness of this work,

ACKNOWLEDGES:

The setting up of three working groups by the Commission with the aim of contributing to the implementation of the open method of coordination with respect to three of the associated objectives of the Report,

STRESSES:

The need for synergy between the follow-up to the Report and:

1. the European Employment strategy, the effective implementation of the Luxembourg and Cardiff processes and the broad economic policy guidelines;

2. the ongoing work of the Commission's high-level task force on skills and mobility. On the basis of a report which the task force had to submit in December 2001, the Commission will prepare, for the Barcelona European Council, an action plan with a view to opening up the European labour markets to everyone by 2005;

3. the activities in the framework of the evaluation of the progress on mobility in the follow-up work of the Recommendation and the Action Plan for Mobility;

4. the Commission's forthcoming communication on making a European area of lifelong learning a reality following the consultation on the Memorandum on Lifelong Learning;

5. the Commission's forthcoming Action Plan on Science and Society as a contribution to the European Research area following an invitation by the joint informal meeting of Education and Research Ministers at Uppsala on 1 to 3 March 2001;

6. the Commission's communication entitled *e*-Learning action plan: designing tomorrow's education of 28 March 2001, which complements its comprehensive *e*-Europe action plan and is designed to be a key element in the European employment strategy,

REAFFIRMS:

Bearing in mind the worldwide perspective of this follow-up, the current international situation and its impact on the European Union:

1. the role of education and training in the prevention of discrimination, racism and xenophobia at all levels and the value of education and training to promote citizenship, social cohesion, tolerance and respect for human rights;

2. the willingness to further the promotion of an open European area for mobility in education and training, thus ensuring non-discriminatory access to education and training;

3. that international openness is integral to the quality and relevance of education and training in Europe and to their competitiveness and attractiveness in the world,

AGREES TO THE FOLLOWING PRINCIPLES CONCERNING THE FOLLOW-UP:

1. The Council, the Member States and the Commission have the responsibility for ensuring the outcome of the follow-up work, each within their respective areas of competence. The Council, in cooperation with the Commission, has responsibility for deciding on the main subjects of the educational and training objectives as well as on whether and where to use indicators, peer-reviews, exchange of good practices and benchmarks.

2. The three concrete strategic objectives and the 13 associated objectives from the Report need to be made operational. The annexed Interim Report therefore contains a proposal for a series of key issues linked to those objectives.

3. Measurement and other follow-up instruments for the implementation of the different objectives should be determined in a manner that is justified in terms of policy relevance. The appropriate application of the open method of coordination to the various objectives requires relevant technical expertise to identify appropriate indicators and other follow-up instruments in the field of education and training. Comparable data is a prerequisite for the application of indicators and benchmarks.

4. Apart from the measuring instruments mentioned above and for general reference, the follow-up can be supported by methods generally applied in the context of international cooperation, inter alia the use of surveys, exchange of views with experts in a specific field and pilot projects on the implementation of a particular associated objective from the Report.

5. In the follow-up, specific attention has to be paid to ongoing processes, existing expertise and monitoring tools and networks that policy makers should use in a more systematic way. It might be appropriate to group the follow-up activities for several key issues.

6. The candidate countries should be invited to take part in the work follow-up in due course,

AGREES, WITH REGARD TO THE TIMETABLE FOR THE PERIOD 2001 TO 2004 THAT:

(a) this timetable is proposed in the context of the developments in broad terms foreseen up to 2010 which will be covered in the joint report to be presented to the Spring 2002 European Council. The timetable of reports based on the results of the follow-up work will be included in the report to the Barcelona European Council;

(b) the work for all objectives should have started by 2004;

(c) the follow-up work will be organised in three stages, as set out in the timetable proposed in the annexed Interim Report. Stage one having already started;

(d) work in the following five areas will start during the first half of 2002:

— improving education and training for teachers and trainers (Objective 1.1)

— making the best use of resources (Objective 1.5)

— supporting active citizenship, equal opportunities and social cohesion (Objective 2.3)

— increasing mobility and exchange (Objective 3.4)

— strengthening European cooperation (Objective 3.5);

(e) a review of progress achieved shall be carried out in 2004.

INVITES THE COMMISSION, in the context of their joint work on the follow-up of the report on objectives of the education and training systems in Europe, to report regularly on its relevant activities, including on the progress by its working groups.

ANNEX

INTERIM REPORT

DETAILED WORK PROGRAMME FOR THE IMPLEMENTATION OF THE 13 ASSOCIATED OBJECTIVES

Strategic objective 1

IMPROVING THE QUALITY AND EFFECTIVENESS OF EDUCATION AND TRAINING SYSTEMS IN THE EUROPEAN UNION

ASSOCIATED OBJECTIVE 1.1 — IMPROVING EDUCATION AND TRAINING FOR TEACHERS AND TRAINERS

A. **Key issues**

1. **Providing the conditions which adequately support teachers and trainers as they respond to the challenges of the knowledge society, including through initial and in-service training in the perspective of lifelong learning**

2. **Identifying the skills, that teachers and trainers should have, given their changing roles in knowledge society**

3. **Securing a sufficient level of entry to the teaching profession, across all subjects and levels, as well as providing for the long-term needs of the profession by making teaching and training even more attractive**

4. **Attracting recruits to teaching and training who have professional experience in other fields**

B. **Organisation of the follow-up**

(a) *Starting period:* during 2002 (second stage)

(b) *Current/Future activities (indicative list)*

— Activities (seminars, surveys) of the European Network of Teacher Education Policies (ENTEP)

— Eurydice survey on teachers (teaching and teaching profession) launched in 2001 will provide a rich source of information based on quantitative and qualitative data (final report to be expected end 2002)

— CEDEFOP actions within the teachers and training network

(c) *Specific goals already agreed:* —

(d) *Key issues where quantitative measuring instruments could be applied (indicative list):* Key issue 3

(e) *Key issues particularly suitable for qualitative approach, including exchange of good practice (indicative list):* Key issues 1, 2, 4.

ASSOCIATED OBJECTIVE 1.2 — DEVELOPING SKILLS FOR THE KNOWLEDGE SOCIETY

A. **Key issues**

1. **Identifying new basic skills, and how these skills together with the traditional basic skills can be better integrated in the curricula, learned and maintained**
2. **Making attainment of basic skills genuinely available to everyone, including those less advantaged, those with special needs, school drop-outs and to adult learners**
3. **Promoting official validation of basic skills**

B. **Organisation of the follow-up**

(a) *Starting period:* second half of 2001 (first stage)

(b) *Current/Future activities (indicative list):*

Commission working group on basic skills was established September 2001

(c) *Specific goals already agreed*

Halving by 2010 the number of 18 to 24 years old with only lower-secondary level education (Employment guidelines 2001, No 4)

(d) *Key issues where quantitative measuring instruments could be applied (indicative list):* Key issue 2

(e) *Key issues particularly suitable for qualitative approach, including exchange of good practice (indicative list):* Key issues 1, 2, 3.

ASSOCIATED OBJECTIVE 1.3 — ENSURING ACCESS TO ICT FOR EVERYONE

A. **Key issues**

1. **Providing adequate equipment and educational software so that ICT and e-Learning processes can be best applied in teaching and training practices**
2. **Encouraging the best use of innovative teaching and learning techniques based on ICT**

B. **Organisation of the follow-up**

(a) *Starting period:* second half of 2001 (first stage)

(b) *Current/Future activities (indicative list)*

— Commission working group on ICT was established October 2001

— e-Learning initiatives and Commission action plan

— Eurydice surveys:

— ICT@Europe.edu: Information and Communication Technology in European Education Systems (2001)

— Information and Communication technology systems in Europe. National Education policies, curricula, teacher training (2000)

(c) *Specific goals already agreed*

All schools to have access to the internet and multimedia resources by the end of 2001 (Employment guidelines 2001, No 5)

All teachers needed are skilled in the use of these technologies by the end of 2002 in order to provide pupils with a broad digital literacy (Employment guidelines 2001, No 5)

(d) *Key issues where quantitative measuring instruments could be applied (indicative list):* Key issue 1

(e) *Key issues particularly suitable for qualitative approach, including exchange of good practice (indicative list):* Key issue 2.

ASSOCIATED OBJECTIVE 1.4 — INCREASING THE RECRUITMENT TO SCIENTIFIC AND TECHNICAL STUDIES

A. **Key issues**

1. **Increasing the interest in mathematics, science and technology from an early age**
2. **Motivating more young people to choose studies and careers in the fields of mathematics, science and technology in particular research careers and scientific disciplines where there are shortages of qualified personnel, in a short and medium term perspective**
3. **Improving gender balance among people learning mathematics, science and technology**
4. **Securing a sufficient numbers of qualified teachers in mathematics and scientific and technical subjects**

B. **Organisation of the follow-up**

(a) *Starting period:* second half of 2001 (first stage)

(b) *Current/Future activities (Indicative list):*

— Commission working group on MST has been installed September 2001

— Follow-up reports of the Commission Communication 'Towards a European Research Area'

(c) *Specific goals already agreed* —

(d) *Key issues particularly suitable for qualitative approach, including exchange of good practice (indicative list):* Key issues 2, 3, 4

(e) *Key issues particularly suitable for qualitative approach, including exchange of good practice (indicative list):* Key issue 1.

ASSOCIATED OBJECTIVE 1.5 — MAKING THE BEST USE OF RESOURCES

A. **Key issues**

1. **Increasing investment in human resources while ensuring an equitable and effective distribution of available means in order to facilitate general access to, and enhance the quality of, education and training**

2. **Supporting the development of compatible quality assurance systems respecting diversity across Europe**

3. **Developing the potential of public/private partnerships**

B. **Organisation of the follow-up**

(a) *Starting period:* during 2002 (second stage)

(b) *Current/Future activities (indicative list)*

— Follow-up to be carried out at national (regional and even local) level in the first place since the appreciation of making the best use of resources is heavily dependent on the actual concrete socio-economic and cultural context. This objective is transversal, i.e. it will accompany the implementation of all other objectives from an overall perspective. It has also to be noted that some issues are also subject to international cooperation in other than strictly EU framework (e.g. OECD)

— Existing network: ENQA

(c) *Specific goals already agreed*

A substantial annual increase per capita investment in human resources (Lisbon European Council conclusions No 26)

(d) *Key issues where quantitative measuring instruments could be applied (indicative list):* Key issue 1

(e) *Key issues particularly suitable for qualitative approach, including exchange of good practice (indicative list):* Key issues 1, 2, 3.

Strategic objective 2

FACILITATING ACCESS OF ALL TO EDUCATION AND TRAINING SYSTEMS

ASSOCIATED OBJECTIVE 2.1 — OPEN LEARNING ENVIRONMENT

A. **Key issues**

1. **Broadening access to lifelong learning by providing information, advice and guidance, on the full range of learning opportunities available**

2. **Delivering education and training so that adults can effectively participate and combine their participation in learning with other responsibilities and activities**

3. **Ensuring that learning is accessible for all, in order to better respond to the challenges of the knowledge society**

4. **Promoting flexible learning paths for all**

B. **Organisation of the follow-up**

(a) *Starting period:* between second half of 2002 and end of 2003 (third stage)

(b) *Current/Future activities (indicative list)*

Activities should be launched in relation to the follow-up of the Commission memorandum on Lifelong Learning and should be combined with those of 2.2 below.

(c) *Specific goals already agreed* —

(d) *Key issues where quantitative measuring instruments could be applied (indicative list):* Key issues 2, 3

(e) *Key issues particularly suitable for qualitative approach, including exchange of good practice (indicative list):* Key issues 1, 4.

ASSOCIATED OBJECTIVE 2.2 — MAKING LEARNING MORE ATTRACTIVE

A. **Key issues**

1. **Encouraging young people to remain in education or training after the end of compulsory education; and motivating and enabling adults to participate in learning through later life**
2. **Developing ways for the official validation of non-formal learning experiences**
3. **Finding ways of making learning more attractive, both within the formal education and training systems and outside them**

B. **Organisation of the follow-up**

(a) *Starting period:* between second half of 2002 and end of 2003 (third stage)

(b) *Current/Future activities (indicative list)*

Activities should be launched in relationship to the follow-up of the Commission memorandum on Lifelong Learning and should be combined with those of 2.1 above

(c) *Specific goals already agreed*

Halving the number of 18 to 24 years old with only lower secondary education who are not in education and training by 2010 (Employment Guidelines 2001, No 4)

(d) *Key issues where quantitative measuring instruments could be applied (indicative list):* Key issue 1

(e) *Key issues particularly suitable for qualitative approach, including exchange of good practice (indicative list):* Key issue 1, 2, 3.

ASSOCIATED OBJECTIVE 2.3 — SUPPORTING ACTIVE CITIZENSHIP, EQUAL OPPORTUNITIES AND SOCIAL COHESION

A. **Key issues**

1. **Ensuring that the learning of democratic values and democratic participation by all school partners is effectively promoted in order to prepare people for active citizenship**
2. **Integrating fully equal opportunity considerations in the objectives and functioning of education and training**
3. **Ensuring fair access to acquisition of skills for the less privileged or those currently less well served and motivating them to participate in learning**

B. **Organisation of the follow-up**

(a) *Starting period:* During 2002 (second stage)

(b) *Current/Future activities (indicative list)*

Lisbon follow-up (social inclusion)

(c) *Specific goals already agreed*

Halving the number of 18 to 24 years old with only lower secondary education who are not in education and training by 2010 (Employment Guidelines 2001, No 4)

(d) *Key issues where quantitative measuring instruments could be applied (indicative list):* Key issue 3

(e) *Key issues particularly suitable for qualitative approach, including exchange of good practice (indicative list):* Key issues 1, 2, 3.

Strategic objective 3

OPENING UP EDUCATION AND TRAINING SYSTEMS TO THE WIDER WORLD

ASSOCIATED OBJECTIVE 3.1 — STRENGTHENING THE LINKS WITH WORKING LIFE AND RESEARCH, AND SOCIETY AT LARGE

A. **Key issues**

1. **Promoting close cooperation between education and training systems and society at large**
2. **Establishing partnerships between all types of education and training institutions, firms and research facilities for their mutual benefit** [1]

B. **Organisation of the follow-up**

(a) *Starting period:* between second half of 2002 and end of 2003 (third stage)

(b) *Current/Future activities (indicative list)*

Many actions will have to be taken at local level in the first place due to the impact of the concrete socio-economic context involving relevant stakeholders including the social partners

(c) *Specific goals already agreed* —

(d) *Key issues where quantitative measuring instruments could be applied (indicative list):* Key issues 1, 2

(e) *Key issues particularly suitable for qualitative approach, including exchange of good practice (indicative list):* Key issues 1, 2.

---

[1] See Lisbon Conclusions, point 26.

ASSOCIATED OBJECTIVE 3.2 — DEVELOPING THE SPIRIT OF ENTERPRISE

A. **Key issues**

1. **Promoting the sense of initiative and creativity throughout the education and training system in order to develop the spirit of enterprise (entrepreneurship)**

2. **Facilitating the acquisition of skills needed to set up and run a business** [1]

B. **Organisation of the follow-up**

(a) *Starting period:* between second half of 2002 and end of 2003 (third stage)

(b) *Current/Future activities (indicative list)*

There might be no need for the setting-up of a separate follow-up structure for this objective. Follow-up could be included in that for basic skills (objective 1.2, starting second half of 2001)

(c) *Specific goals already agreed*

Promoting education for entrepreneurship and self-employment (Employment guidelines 2001, No 9)

(d) *Key issues where quantitative measuring instruments could be applied (indicative list)* —

(e) *Key issues particularly suitable for qualitative approach, including exchange of good practice (indicative list):* Key issues 1, 2.

ASSOCIATED OBJECTIVE 3.3 — IMPROVING FOREIGN LANGUAGE LEARNING

A. **Key issues**

1. **Encouraging everyone to learn two, or where appropriate, more languages in addition to their mother tongues, and increasing awareness of the importance of foreign language learning at all ages**

2. **Encouraging schools and training institutions in using efficient teaching and training methods and motivating continuation of language learning at a later stage of life**

B. **Organisation of the follow-up**

(a) *Starting period:* between second half of 2002 and end of 2003 (third stage)

(b) *Current/Future activities (indicative list)*

Follow-up of the European Year of Languages, in the cooperation with the Council of Europe. The Commission will draw up proposals by early 2003 for the promotion of linguistic diversity and language learning while ensuring consistency with the implementation of the report on the concrete future objectives of education and training systems

(c) *Specific goals already agreed*

Pupils should, as a general rule, have the opportunity of learning two languages of the Union other than their mother tongue(s) for a minimum of two consecutive years during compulsory schooling and if possible for longer periods (Council Resolution of 31 March 1995)

---

[1] See Objective Report, page 14, point 2.3.2 (5980/01).

(d) *Key issues where quantitative measuring instruments could be applied (indicative list)*: Key issue 1

(e) *Key issues particularly suitable for qualitative approach, including exchange of good practice (indicative list)*: Key issues 1, 2.

ASSOCIATED OBJECTIVE 3.4 — INCREASING MOBILITY AND EXCHANGE

A. **Key issues**

1. **Providing the widest access to mobility to individuals and to education and training organisations, including those serving a less privileged public and reducing the remaining obstacles to mobility**

2. **Monitoring the volume, direction, participation rates as well as qualitative aspects of mobility flows across Europe**

3. **Facilitating validation and recognition of competencies acquired during mobility**

B. **Organisation of the follow-up**

(a) *Starting period*: During 2002 (second stage)

(b) *Current/Future activities (indicative list)*

— Community mobility programmes: Socrates, Leonardo and Youth, EU assistance provided for research worker mobility

— Commission High Level Task Force on skills and mobility

— Commission working group to be set up for the monitoring of the implementation of the mobility action plan (proposed by the Nice European Council) and of the recommendation on mobility

(c) *Specific goals already agreed*

Conclusions of the Lisbon European Council No 13 concerning mobility of researchers and No 26 concerning mobility of students, teachers and training and research staff

(d) *Key issues where quantitative measuring instruments could be applied (indicative list)*: Key issues 1, 2

(e) *Key issues particularly suitable for qualitative approach, including exchange of good practice (indicative list)*: Key issues 1, 2, 3.

ASSOCIATED OBJECTIVE 3.5 — STRENGTHENING EUROPEAN COOPERATION

A. **Key issues**

1. **Enhancing the effectiveness and timeliness of recognition processes for the purpose of further study, training and employment throughout Europe**

2. **Promoting cooperation between responsible organisations and authorities in view of more compatibility in quality assurance and accreditation**

3. **Promoting transparency of information on education and training opportunities and structures in view of the creation of an open European area for education**

B. **Organisation of the follow-up**

(a) *Starting period*: during 2002 (second stage)

(b) *Current/Future activities (indicative list)*

As a transversal objective, it concerns the implementation of all objectives and the activities of the Education Council itself. Synergy is to be sought with other activities, in particular those concerning transparency, recognition and quality assurance (Europass, NARIC/ENIC and ENQA) as well as those carried out in a non-EU context, like the Bologna process or the Convention on the Recognition of Qualifications concerning Higher Education in the European Region (Lisbon Recognition Convention)

(c) *Specific goals already agreed* —

(d) *Key issues where quantitative measuring instruments could be applied (indicative list)*: Key issue 1

(e) *Key issues particularly suitable for qualitative approach, including exchange of good practice (indicative list)*: Key issue 1, 2, 3.

TIMETABLE TO START FOLLOW-UP WORK FOR ASSOCIATED OBJECTIVES

Stage 1 (starting: second half of 2001)

Objective 1.2. — Developing skills for the knowledge society

Objective 1.3. — Ensuring access to ICT for everyone

Objective 1.4. — Increasing the recruitment to scientific and technical studies

Stage 2 (starting: during 2002)

Objective 1.1. — Improving education and training for teachers and trainers

Objective 1.5. — Making the best use of resources

Objective 2.3. — Supporting active citizenship, equal opportunities and social cohesion

Objective 3.4. — Increasing mobility and exchange

Objective 3.5. — Strengthening European cooperation

Stage 3 (starting: between second half of 2002 and end of 2003)

Objective 2.1. — Open learning environment

Objective 2.2. — Making learning more attractive

Objective 3.1. — Strengthening the links with working life and research, and society at large

Objective 3.2. — Developing the spiret of enterprise

Objective 3.3. — Improving foreign language learning

ANNEXES

**Decision No 182/1999/EC of the European Parliament and of the Council
of 22 December 1998
concerning the fifth framework programme of the European Community
for research, technological development
and demonstration activities (1998 to 2002)**

(OJ L 26, 1.2.1999)

I

(Acts whose publication is obligatory)

DECISION No 182/1999/EC OF THE EUROPEAN PARLIAMENT AND OF THE COUNCIL

of 22 December 1998

concerning the fifth framework programme of the European Community for research, technological development and demonstration activities (1998 to 2002)

THE EUROPEAN PARLIAMENT AND THE COUNCIL OF THE EUROPEAN UNION,

Having regard to the Treaty establishing the European Community, and in particular Article 130i(1) thereof,

Having regard to the proposal from the Commission [1],

Having regard to the opinion of the Economic and Social Committee [2],

Having regard to the opinion of the Committee of the Regions [3],

Acting in accordance with the procedure laid down in Article 189b of the Treaty [4] and in the light of the joint text approved by the Conciliation Committee on 25 November 1998,

(1) Whereas, in accordance with Articles 130f(3) and 130i(1) of the Treaty, a multiannual framework programme covering all Community activities in the field of research and technological development including demonstration activities, hereinafter referred to as RTD, should be adopted;

(2) Whereas it has been considered appropriate to adopt a new framework programme for the period 1998 to 2002 in order to ensure continuity of Community research;

(3) Whereas, in accordance with Article 4(2) of Decision No 1110/94/EC of the European Parliament and of the Council of 26 April 1994 concerning the fourth framework programme of the European Community activities in the field of research, technological development and demonstration (1994 to 1998) [5], the Commission is required to have an external assessment conducted into the management of and progress with Community activities carried out during the five years preceding the assessment, prior to presenting its proposal for a fifth framework programme; whereas that assessment, the conclusions thereof and the Commission's comments have been communicated to the European Parliament, the Council, the Economic and Social Committee and the Committee of the Regions;

(4) Whereas, in accordance with Article 130f(1) of the Treaty, the Community's research and technological development policy should address, as a matter of priority, problems of society, improving the international competitiveness of Community industry, sustainable development, job creation, the quality of life and globalisation of knowledge, contributing to the development and implementation of the Community's policies and

---

[1] OJ C 173, 7.6.1997, p. 10, and OJ C 291, 25.9.1997, p. 15.
[2] OJ C 355, 21.11.1997, p. 38, and OJ C 73, 9.3.1998, p. 133.
[3] OJ C 379, 15.12.1997, p. 26.
[4] Opinion of the European Parliament of 18 December 1997 (OJ C 14, 19.1.1998, p. 171), Council Common Position of 24 March 1998 (OJ C 178, 10.6.1998, p. 49) and Decision of the European Parliament of 17 June 1998 (OJ C 210, 6.7.1998, p. 131). Decision of the European Parliament of 15 December 1998 and Decision of the Council of 22 December 1998.

[5] OJ L 126, 18.5.1994, p. 1. Decision as last amended by Decision No 2535/97/EC (OJ L 347, 18.12.1997, p. 1).

the role of the Community in the world as a focal point of scientific and technological excellence;

(5) Whereas appropriate steps should be taken to promote cooperation and coordination between Member States;

(6) Whereas the RTD activities undertaken in the context of the first activity referred to in Article 130g of the Treaty should focus on a limited number of topics; whereas those activities, in the context of indirect actions, should be implemented through 'key actions', which bring together the activities (ranging from basic research through applied and generic research to development and demonstration) in a coherent whole in order to target them strategically on a common European challenge or problem; research and technological development activities of a generic nature; and activities designed to encourage the optimum use of research infrastructures and improve access thereto;

(7) Whereas the activities undertaken in the context of the second (cooperation with third countries and international organisations), third (dissemination and optimisation of RTD results) and fourth (training and mobility of researchers) activities referred to in Article 130g of the Treaty should complement, support and interact with each other and the abovementioned RTD activities;

(8) Whereas this approach presupposes that the potential for scientific and technological excellence existing within the Community is maintained and reinforced, whilst taking full account of the efforts made by its main international partners;

(9) Whereas it is appropriate, in this same context, to place special emphasis on the needs of small and medium-sized enterprises (SMEs), so as to promote their effective participation in Community programmes and their ability to benefit from them; on the dissemination and transfer of results; on innovation; and on the training and mobility of researchers, thereby encouraging the emergence of a new generation of enterprising researchers with innovative ideas;

(10) Whereas research and technological development can stimulate economic growth and, as a result, lead to the creation of lasting employment;

(11) Whereas researchers, industry and users have contributed substantially to the definition of actions to be undertaken in the fifth framework programme and should be involved in its implementation;

(12) Whereas the formulation and implementation of the Community's policies and actions must take into account objectives related to economic and social cohesion; whereas, in accordance with this principle, the framework programme must contribute to the harmonious development of the Community while encouraging RTD activities of high quality; whereas it is therefore necessary to respect the complementary roles of RTD activities and the action undertaken by the Community through other relevant instruments;

(13) Whereas it is necessary to promote and facilitate the participation of ultraperipheral regions in Community RTD actions through appropriate mechanisms adapted to their particular situation;

(14) Whereas, in accordance with the principles of subsidiarity and proportionality as enshrined in Article 3b of the Treaty, the objectives of Community research and technological development policy reflected in the fifth framework programme warrant activities at Community level in so far as the objectives cannot be sufficiently achieved by the Member States; whereas there is a need to establish a 'critical mass' in human and financial terms, in particular through the combination of the complementary expertise and resources available in the various Member States; whereas these objectives can therefore be better achieved at Community level; whereas this Decision does not go beyond what is necessary to achieve these objectives;

(15) Whereas the Community's financial participation in the actions of the framework programme may, in accordance with the principles set out in this framework programme, be varied at the level of the specific programmes according to the nature of the activities concerned and the proximity to the market, in specific and duly justified cases and in compliance with the provisions of the Community framework for State aid for research and development ([1]), in particular points 5.12 and 5.13 thereof, and with international rules;

([1]) OJ C 45, 17.2.1996, p. 5.

(16) Whereas the maximum overall amount of the fifth framework programme would need to be revised should new Member States accede before the framework programme expires;

(17) Whereas Community participation in the framework programme should correspond to the financial perspective in force for the whole period of the programme; whereas account should be taken of the fact that a new financial perspective will be negotiated during the course of the fifth framework programme; whereas, if the maximum overall amount were inconsistent with the amount available for research within the financial perspective then in force, or if there were no financial perspective in force, it would be necessary to decide on a new amount under the conditions provided for in the Treaty; whereas there should be equivalent arrangements for the specific programmes; whereas, in the absence of such arrangements, the specific programmes could not be implemented since they would have been deprived of a legal base for the expenditures which they foresee;

(18) Whereas the administrative expenditure arising from research activities has to be financed within the general amount allocated to the framework programme and should be included in the budget in a transparent fashion;

(19) Whereas the criteria which have been laid down to choose the topics covered by the fifth framework programme and the related scientific and technological objectives take into account the abovementioned principles; whereas those criteria should also be applied when the fifth framework programme is implemented, in order to ensure consistency;

(20) Whereas the Joint Research Centre (JRC) will implement direct RTD actions through research and scientific and technical support activities of an institutional character where it has special or even unique expertise and facilities in the Community or where it is entrusted with activities necessary for the framing and implementation of Community policies and tasks incumbent on the Commission pursuant to the Treaty which require the JRC's impartiality; whereas in addition, it will participate progressively in a competitive approach, as a member of consortia, in carrying out research activities foreseen by way of indirect actions;

(21) Whereas it is necessary to take into account the ethical aspects of advances in knowledge and technologies and their application and to conduct research activities in compliance with fundamental ethical principles and with the protection of privacy;

(22) Whereas the Community equal opportunities policy must be taken into account in implementing the fifth framework programme whereas, therefore, participation of women in the field of RTD should be encouraged;

(23) Whereas, in addition to the annual report to be submitted to the European Parliament and the Council pursuant to Article 130p of the Treaty, arrangements should be adopted, in accordance with recommendations to be implemented in respect of transparency and sound and efficient management, for the systematic examination of the progress of the fifth framework programme and its evaluation;

(24) Whereas the European Parliament, as one of the decision-making bodies for future research programmes, intends to follow the progress of the framework programme during its implementation by the Commission, while not impinging on or constraining the Commission's implementation role;

(25) Whereas a *modus vivendi* between the European Parliament, the Council and the Commission concerning the implementing measures for acts adopted in accordance with the procedure laid down in Article 189b of the Treaty ([1]) was concluded on 20 December 1994;

(26) Whereas it is necessary to reinforce the phasing-in within the framework Programme, in accordance with the eligibility criteria, of certain coal and steel research activities currently being carried out on the basis of the Treaty establishing the European Coal and Steel Community, which expires in 2002;

(27) Whereas, in order to ensure consistency between research activities undertaken under the Treaty establishing the European Community and those carried out under the Treaty establishing the European Atomic Energy Community, the Decision concerning the framework programme for nuclear research and training activities should be adopted at the same time and for the same period as this framework programme;

([1]) OJ C 102, 4.4.1996, p. 1.

(28) Whereas the Scientific and Technical Research Committee (CREST) has been consulted,

HAVE DECIDED AS FOLLOWS:

Article 1

1. A multiannual framework programme for all Community activities, including demonstration activities, in the field of research and technological development, hereinafter referred to as the 'fifth framework programme', is hereby adopted for the period 1998 to 2002.

2. The fifth framework programme shall, in accordance with Article 130g of the Treaty, comprise four Community activities:

(a) implementation of research, technological development and demonstration programmes;

(b) promotion of cooperation in the field of Community research, technological development and demonstration with third countries and international organisations;

(c) dissemination and optimisation of the results of activities in Community research, technological development and demonstration;

(d) stimulation of the training and mobility of researchers in the Community.

The first Community activity shall relate to the following four themes:

1. quality of life and management of living resources;

2. user-friendly information society;

3. competitive and sustainable growth;

4. energy, environment and sustainable development.

The second, third and fourth Community activities shall relate to the following three themes respectively:

1. confirming the international role of Community research;

2. promotion of innovation and encouragement of participation of SMEs;

3. improving human research potential and the socioeconomic knowledge base.

Activities undertaken within the thematic programmes of the first Community activity will also contribute, in coordination and interaction with the horizontal programmes, to the achievement of the objectives of those three themes.

Complementarity with relevant initiatives of the Member States, and initiatives such as COST and Eureka, will be sought.

3. The criteria for selecting the themes referred to in paragraph 2 and the related objectives are set out in Annex I. They shall apply for the purposes of the implementation of the fifth framework programme.

4. The general outlines of the Community activities, their scientific and technological objectives and the related priorities are set out in Annex II.

Article 2

1. (a) The maximum overall amount for Community participation in the fifth framework programme shall be ECU 13 700 million.

   Of this amount:

   to ECU 3 140 million is for the period 1998 to 1999,

   to ECU 10 560 million is for the period 2000 to 2002.

(b) The figure of ECU 10 560 million shall be deemed to be confirmed if it is consistent with the financial perspective in force in the period 2000 to 2002. In the case of any new financial perspective in force, this condition shall be met only if:

   — the financial perspective indicates the share of expenditure available for research, and

   — that share permits Community participation of ECU 10 560 million in the period 2000 to 2002.

(c) If the figure of ECU 10 560 million is not consistent with the financial perspective in force in the period 2000 to 2002, or if there is no financial perspective in force in those years,

   — the European Parliament and the Council, acting under the conditions provided for in Article 130i(1) of the Treaty, shall set a new maximum overall amount and adjust the amounts in Annex III accordingly,

— the Council, acting under the conditions provided for in Article 130i(4) of the Treaty, shall adapt the amounts deemed necessary for the specific programmes referred to in Article 3, so as to ensure their consistency with the new maximum overall amount.

Pending the decisions provided for in the first and second indents above, the specific programmes shall not be implemented beyond the provision in the first indent of subparagraph (a) of this paragraph.

2. The amount referred to in paragraph 1 shall be subject to revision should new Member States accede before this framework programme expires.

3. Annex III fixes the respective amounts earmarked for each of the Community activities envisaged in Article 1 and indicates the breakdown between the themes of the first Community activity defined in Article 1(2).

4. All administrative expenditure arising from the research activities shall be paid from the overall amount of the programme. It shall be dealt with in the general budget of the European Communities according to the usual procedures applicable to other comparable administrative expenditure.

Article 3

1. The fifth framework programme shall be implemented through eight specific programmes, four of which correspond to the four themes of the first Community activity, three are linked to the second, third and fourth Community activities respectively, and the eighth is a programme specific to the Joint Research Centre. The scientific, industrial and user communities will be closely involved throughout this implementation process.

Each specific programme shall specify its precise objectives having regard to the scientific and technological objectives set forth in Annex II, define the detailed rules for its implementation, fix its duration and provide for the means deemed necessary.

The Commission will establish and publish under its own responsibility a detailed manual of operational procedures and guidelines for the selection of research and technological development actions.

2. Implementation of the fifth framework programme may give rise, where necessary, to supplementary programmes within the meaning of Article 130k of the Treaty, to Community participation in research and development programmes undertaken by several Member States within the meaning of Article 130l or to the setting-up of joint undertakings or any other structure within the meaning of Article 130n. It may also give rise to cooperation with third countries or international organisations within the meaning of Article 130m.

Article 4

The detailed rules for financial participation by the Community in the fifth framework programme shall be those laid down in accordance with the special provisions concerning research and technological development appropriations set out in the Financial Regulation applicable to the general budget of the European Communities ([1]), as supplemented by Annex IV to this Decision.

Article 5

1. The Commission shall continually and systematically monitor each year, with the help of independent qualified experts, the implementation of the fifth framework programme and its specific programmes in the light of the criteria set out in Annex I and the scientific and technological objectives set out in Annex II. It shall assess, in particular, whether the objectives, priorities and financial resources are still appropriate to the changing situation. Where appropriate, it shall submit proposals to adapt or supplement the framework programme and/or the specific programmes, taking account of the results of this assessment.

2. Before submitting its proposal for a sixth framework programme, the Commission shall have an external assessment conducted by independent highly qualified experts into the implementation and achievements of Community activities carried out during the five years preceding that assessment in the light of the criteria set out in Annex I, the scientific and technological objectives set out in Annex II and the implementation of this Decision via the specific programmes based thereon. The Commission shall communicate the conclusions thereof, accompanied by its comments, to the European Parliament, the Council, the Economic and Social Committee and the Committee of the Regions.

3. The independent qualified experts referred to in paragraphs 1 and 2 shall be drawn in particular from scientific, industrial and user communities and chosen by the Commission, which shall take account, in a balanced fashion, of the various research players.

([1]) OJ L 356, 31.12.1977, p. 1. Regulation as last amended by Regulation (EC, ECSC, Euratom) No 2548/98, OJ L 320, 28.11.1998, p. 1.

The Commission shall make known the full list of experts and their individual qualifications following their appointment.

4. The Commission shall regularly inform the European Parliament and the Council of the overall progress of the implementation of the framework programme and the specific programmes.

Article 6

Halfway through the term of the fifth framework programme, the Commission shall review progress with the programme and shall submit to the European Parliament and tho the Council, on the basis of the assessments of the various specific programmes, a communication accompanied, if appropriate, by a proposal for the adaptation of this Decision.

Article 7

All research activities conducted pursuant to the fifth framework programme shall be carried out in compliance with fundamental ethical principles, including animal welfare requirements, in conformity with Community law.

Done at Brussels, 22 December 1998.

For the European Parliament	*For the Council*
The President	*The President*
J.M. GIL-ROBLES	C. EINEM

ANNEX I

CRITERIA FOR SELECTING THE THEMES AND OBJECTIVES OF COMMUNITY ACTIVITIES

1. The European Community's RTD policy is directed towards strengthening the scientific and technological bases of Community industry and encouraging it to become more competitive at international level, while promoting all the research activities deemed necessary by virtue of other Chapters of the Treaty. It shall also contribute to promoting the quality of life of the Community's citizens and to the sustainable development of the Community as a whole, including the ecological aspects. Its implementation is based on the twin principles of scientific and technological excellence and relevance to the abovementioned objectives.

   Moreover, in pursuit of a cost-benefit approach dictated by concern for optimum allocation of European public funding and in accordance with the subsidiarity principle, themes for the fifth framework programme and the related objectives are selected on the basis that the Community shall take action only if and in so far as the objectives cannot be sufficiently achieved by the Member States.

2. In application of the foregoing principles, the framework programme shall be defined on the basis of a set of common criteria, divided into three categories:

   — *Criteria related to the Community 'value added' and the subsidiarity principle*

     — need to establish a 'critical mass' in human and financial terms, in particular through the combination of the complementary expertise and resources available in the various Member States,

     — significant contribution to the implementation of one or more Community policies,

     — addressing of problems arising at Community level, or questions relating to aspects of standardisation, or questions connected with the development of the European area,

   so as to select only objectives which are more efficiently pursued at the Community level by means of research activities conducted at that level.

   — *Criteria related to social objectives*

     — improving the employment situation,

     — promoting the quality of life and health,

     — preserving the environment,

   in order to further major social objectives of the Community reflecting the expectations and concerns of its citizens.

   — *Criteria related to economic development and scientific and technological prospects*

     — areas which are expanding and create good growth prospects,

     — areas in which Community businesses can and must become more competitive,

     — areas in which prospects of significant scientific and technological progress are opening up, offering possibilities for dissemination and exploitation of results in the medium or long term,

   in order to contribute to the harmonious and sustainable development of the Community as a whole.

3. The criteria referred to in paragraph 2 will be used, and where necessary supplemented, for the purposes of the implementation of the fifth framework programme, in order to define the specific programmes and select research and technological development activities, including demonstration activities. The three categories of criteria will supply simultaneously and must all be met, although to a different extent from case to case.

ANNEX II

GENERAL OUTLINES OF COMMUNITY ACTIVITIES, SCIENTIFIC AND TECHNOLOGICAL OBJECTIVES AND RELATED PRIORITIES

I. THEMES AND ORGANISATION

With regard to the themes and organisation of the fifth framework programme, it is recalled that, in accordance with Article 130g of the EC Treaty, the fifth framework programme will comprise four activities:

— the first activity covers research, technological development and demonstration programmes,

— the second activity is aimed at promoting cooperation on research, technological development and demonstration with third countries and international organisations,

— the third activity concerns the dissemination and optimisation of the results of research, technological development and demonstration activities,

— the fourth activity is intended to stimulate the training and mobility of researchers.

1. CONTENT AND ORGANISATION OF THE FIRST ACTIVITY

The research, technological development and demonstration programmes will comprise:

— 'key actions',

— research and technological development activities of a generic nature,

— activities in support of research infrastructures.

These programmes will, where appropriate, include studies and research activities on relevant ethical and legal aspects, within a context of fundamental respect for human values. Community funding for research projects unter this programme will be used exclusively for civil purposes, including research on the detection and clearance of landmines.

Within these programmes, particular account will be taken of the socioeconomic implications of the implementation, use, and effects of the technologies, processes and scenarios covered by each of these programmes. As an integral part of actions within the first activity, relevant socioeconomic research will be carried out. A particular effort will be made to ensure coherence between these activities in order to optimise the exploitation and dissemination of results by users. These actions will be complemented by socioeconomic research on horizontal issues carried out within the fourth activity.

Particular account will be taken of the need to encourage the participation of women in the fields of research and technological development.

In addition, in the framework of a coherent approach involving also the second, third and fourth activities, these programmes will implement, in their respective areas, actions contributing to the aims of these activities.

A particular effort will be made to encourage genuine participation of SMEs in the programme, especially in shared-cost actions.

Synergy will be sought with other relevant Community instruments.

(a) *'Key actions'*

Key actions will be problem-oriented and clearly defined corresponding to the criteria and specifically targeted to the objectives of each programme and to the desired results, taking into account the views of users. They will have a clear European focus. The 'key action' is regarded as a cluster of small and large, applied, generic and, as appropriate, basic research projects directed towards a common European challenge or problem not excluding global issues.

The research activities carried out in this context will integrate the entire spectrum of activities and disciplines needed to achieve the objectives, and range from basic research through development to demonstration. Appropriate links with relevant national and international initiatives (including complementary European RTD frameworks) will be given proper attention.

(b) *Research and technological development activities of a generic nature*

These activities, which are essential to achieve the objectives of the thematic programmes, will be carried out in a limited number of areas not covered by the key actions. They will complement the key actions. Their main aim is to help the Community maintain and improve its scientific and technological capability in those areas of research and enabling technologies which should be used widely.

(c) *Support for research infrastructures*

Since the construction and operation of research infrastructure is the responsibility of national authorities, Community support for research infrastructures in line with the objectives of the thematic programmes should contribute to cover two essential requirements at Community level: (1) the need for an optimum use of existing research infrastructures and (2) the need for transnational cooperation in the rational and cost-effective development of research infrastructures.

The role of the Community should be to provide added value, complementary to national or multinational initiatives. Community support may enhance access to infrastructures and will in particular be provided for research infrastructure networks leading to further complementarity, pooling of efforts and/or specialisation at the European level (including the compatibility of databases).

2. CONTENT AND ORGANISATION OF THE SECOND, THIRD AND FOURTH ACTIVITIES

The horizontal themes are at the crossroads of the Community's research policy and its policies for external relations, innovation, SMEs and human resources, and for social and employment issues.

Each of them comprises:

— specific activities, including, where necessary, key actions, linked to the general objectives of the Community's policy with regard to external relations, innovation, SMEs and human resources which are not carried out as part of the themes of the first activity,

— activities essentially in the form of coordination, support and accompanying activities to ensure the coherence of equivalent activities carried out under the themes of the first activity.

In coordination and interaction with the horizontal programmes, the thematic programmes will take the necessary measures to make an active contribution, in the context of their own activities, towards the achievement of the general objectives of the horizontal programmes.

Community support for research infrastructures in the context of the fourth activity will concentrate in particular on measures enhancing access to such infrastructures.

3. THE JOINT RESEARCH CENTRE

The direct RTD actions to be implemented by the Joint Research Centre (JRC) will comprise research and scientific and technical support activities of an institutional character. The JRC may provide support where it has special or even unique expertise and facilities in the Community or where it is entrusted with activities necessary for the framing and implementation of Community policies and tasks incumbent on the Commission pursuant to the Treaty which require the JRC's impartiality (for example in the case of standardisation). The JRC will carry out its activities in close cooperation with the scientific community and enterprises in Europe. Exchanges between the JRC and universities, research institutes and industry will be encouraged.

The JRC is also progressively involved in competitive activities.

The appropriations made available to the JRC constitute a maximum amount. In addition, the JRC may endeavour to secure funds from other sources. The relevant JRC management rules and regulations will apply to these allocations.

II. SCIENTIFIC AND TECHNOLOGICAL OBJECTIVES

1. FIRST ACTIVITY

THEME 1

QUALITY OF LIFE AND MANAGEMENT OF LIVING RESOURCES

> Improving the quality of life and health is a major challenge and the Community plans to tackle it by helping to increase knowledge and develop technologies in the field of the life sciences.
>
> In this context, the need is to improve the quality of life of all Europe's citizens, taking into account the particular problems of certain sectors of the population such as the ageing and the disabled.
>
> At the same time, progress in this area will help to increase the competitiveness of the Community's enterprises by opening up new prospects in areas in which the Community already has a strong hand, such as biotechnology, agro-industry, and the fields of health and the environment, in which rapid progress continues to be made.

(a) *Key actions*

(i) Food, nutrition and health

The aim of this key action is to promote the development of knowledge, technologies and methods, including prenormative aspects, based on multidisciplinary approaches to produce a safe, healthy, balanced and varied food supply for consumers covering the whole food chain. This requires as a priority:

— the development of safe, flexible and new and/or improved manufacturing technologies to improve food quality and consumer acceptability, while guaranteeing traceability of raw materials and final products,

— the development of tests to detect and processes to eliminate infectious and toxic agents throughout the food chain,

— research into the role of food in promoting and sustaining health with respect to diet and nutrition, toxicology, epidemiology, environmental interaction, consumer choice and public health.

(ii) Control of infectious diseases

The priority objectives of this key action are the fight against and control of infectious diseases, both human and animal, including zoonoses, of increasing impact, whether established, newly emerging or in resurgence, based on research seeking a better understanding of the immune system. Close attention is to be paid to:

— the development of improved or novel mono-component, multipurpose and combined vaccines, especially against viral diseases, including the support of multicentre clinical trials,

— new and improved strategies to identify and control infectious diseases, directed at treatment and prevention and based on studies on pathogenesis, emergence of resistance and immunological control,

— aspects connected with public health and care delivery systems, notably management, prevention, surveillance, behavioural aspects and response to infectious diseases (including modelling of human diseases).

(iii) The 'cell factory'

This key action is aimed at helping the Community's enterprises to exploit the advances made in life sciences and technologies, particularly in the fields of health, environment, agriculture, agro-industries and high value-added products, such as chemicals. It is aimed at developing multidisciplinary technologies based on the exploitation of the properties of micro-organisms, plants and animals, in particular at the cellular and sub-cellular levels. The objective is to understand the functioning of cells in order to develop bio-molecules and bio-processes with high added-value capable of enhancing the quality of life and health, including:

— new and innovative health processes and products, particularly from molecular engineering (for example diagnostics, antibiotics, anti-cancer agents, including plant-produced therapeutics),

— energy-efficient bio-remediation and waste bio-treatment processes,

— new biological processes and products, new processing technologies on the basis of new plant and animal characteristics for agri-food and agri-industry and high value-added chemical applications.

This key action should also aim at RTD to make cell cultures available as models for medicine, pharmacology, toxicology and environmental monitoring to substitute for animal testing and for prenormative purposes.

(iv) Environment and health

The aim of this key action is to achieve a better understanding of the interactions between the genetic, physiological, environmental and social factors involved in sustaining good health and so to help reduce the adverse impact on health of changes in the environment and the workplace and the immense costs to health systems arising therefrom. It covers in particular issues such as prevention and the effects on health of air pollution, heavy metals and toxic substances, noise, climatic changes and electromagnetic radiation, as well as the effects of pollution at the workplace. It includes as a priority:

— multidisciplinary approaches for achieving a better understanding of the interaction between the social and physical environment and health, including research into diseases and allergies related to or influenced by the environment and research into their treatment and prevention,

— epidemiological studies and pathogenesis research,

— the development of new methods of diagnosis, risk assessment and prevention,

— the development of processes to identify and, where possible, reduce harmful effects on health and the causes thereof.

(v) Sustainable agriculture, fisheries and forestry, including integrated development of rural areas

The aim is to develop the knowledge and technologies needed for the production and exploitation of living resources, including forests, covering the whole production chain, adapted to recent adjustments in the common agricultural and fisheries policies, whil also providing the scientific basis for Community regulations and standards. Similarly, the aim is to promote the multipurpose role of forests and the sustainable management and utilisation of forest resources as an integral factor of rural development. Priority areas include:

— new and sustainable systems of production, including breeding methods, and exploitation in agriculture, forestry, fishing and aquaculture, taking into account profitability, the sustainable management of resources, product quality and employment as well as animal health and welfare,

— the integrated production and exploitation of biological materials (non-food uses),

— sustainable and multipurpose utilisation of forest resources; the integrated forestry-wood chain,

— development of methods of control, surveillance and protection, including protection of land and prevention of soil erosion,

— prelegislative research designed to provide a scientific basis for Community legislation,

— the production of new tools and models for the integrated and sustainable development of rural and other relevant areas based on optimisation of the specific potential of each area, including at regional level, diversification of activities and land use, and involvement of the people concerned.

(vi) The ageing population

This key action aims to help Europe meet the challenge of the growing ageing population through RTD to underpin the development of policies and interventions to extend the quality of life and independence of older people, and to reduce the need for long-term care and its consequential costs. It gives priority to multidisciplinary RTD relating to processes leading to healthy ageing, including demographic, social and economic aspects, and to interventions leading to the postponement and improved management of disability. It aims to generate competitive advantage for a wide range of health related industries and sectors. Priority areas include:

— RTD on illnesses and health problems of high morbidity [1] which are age-related and where there is a real prospect for significant prevention, treatment or delay in onset,

— RTD concerning biological, psychological, social and economic determinants of healthy ageing and of the mechanisms leading to disability and the postponement of disability,

— demographic and epidemiological research on ageing and disability trends to enable prediction of the size and nature of the ageing population as a basis for policy and planning,

— RTD to provide a basis for new approaches to delaying the onset of disability, to reducing the challenge to older people of their social and physical environment (e.g. in housing and transport) and to supporting mental and physical functioning,

— RTD concerning effective and efficient delivery of health and social care services to older people, including comparative research on the financing of long-term care and pensions.

(b) *Research and technological development activities of a generic nature*

— Chronic and degenerative diseases (in particular cancer and diabetes), cardiovascular diseases and rare diseases

Major challenges in biomedical research are the elucidation of the aetiology and pathogenesis of diseases for which there is more than one interacting cause (genetic, environmental, lifestyle) of high (e.g. cardiovascular diseases, cancer, diabetes) or low (e.g. rare diseases) morbidity. There is an urgent need to improve diagnosis, treatment, prevention and surveillance through epidemiology and applying advances in modern technology, requiring a multinational approach,

— Research into genomes and diseases of genetic origin

The aim of this activity is to identify the physiological functions of genes and to improve the understanding of the meaning of sequence information. The new knowledge and technologies deriving from this generic action should promote the exploitation of genomic information to

---

[1] Long and serious illness, entailing a high burden on society, families, individuals and their carers.

the benefit of European health, industry and the environment. The organisation of collaboration in this area will underpin the development of expression systems to facilitate the study of genes of industrial and agronomic interest as well as the design of effective molecular and gene-based preventive and therapeutic strategies for human and animal disease,

— Neurosciences

This activity should provide new insights and understanding of the mechanisms governing the interrelationship of biological and psychological processes, to promote new diagnostic (e.g. imaging) and therapeutic approaches to neurological and psychiatric disorders and to underpin opportunities for innovation in health-care industries,

— Research relating to public health and health services

Improvement of health systems: to improve the health of European citizens and the effectiveness and cost-effectiveness of health promotion and health-care technologies and interventions, to enhance health and safety at work, to evaluate health-care models, to develop the evidence base for clinical practice and health policy and to study health variations across Europe.

Fighting drug-related problems: to prevent and, where appropriate, control drug-related health problems through establishing the psychological and socioeconomic factors involved in drug-taking and drug abuse, developing better understanding of the long-term health and social consequences of abuse, and developing more effective treatment strategies,

— Research relating to the disabled

The aim of this activity is to enhance the quality of life and independence of disabled people, notably through improving their social and physical environment and the effective and efficient delivery of the health and social care services available to them.

— The study of problems relating to biomedical ethics and bioethics in the context of respect for fundamental human values [1],

— The study of the socioeconomic aspects of development of the life sciences and technologies within the perspective of sustainable development (impact on society, the economy and employment)

(c) *Support for research infrastructures*

In accordance with the general objectives outlined above, activities should focus, for example, on databases and collections of biological material, centres for clinical research and trials and facilities for fishery and aquaculture research.

---

[1] Taking account of the declaration of the European Council of Amsterdam and the European Parliament resolution on the banning of human cloning (OJ C 115, 14.4.1997, p. 92) and of relevant Community legislation, research conducted at Community level will be carried out, taking account of the competent authorities, in particular the European Group on Ethics in Science and New Technologies and the Human Embryo and Foetus Protection Group, as well as the opinions of relevant international organisations, whilst respecting the principles laid down in the Helsinki Declaration and the relevant resolutions of the World Health Organisation (WHO) and in other relevant international Conventions.
No research activity which modifies or is intended to modify the genetic heritage of human beings by alteration of germ cells or by acting at any other stage in embryonic development and which can make such alteration heritable will be carried out under the present framework programme. In the same way, no research activity, understood in the sense of the term 'cloning', will be conducted with the aim of replacing a germ or embryo cell nucleus with that of the cell of any individual, a cell from an embryo or a cell coming from a late stage of development to the human embryo.
To the extent possible, animal experiments and tests on animals should be replaced with *in vitro* or other alternative methods. Modification of the genetic heritage of animals and animal cloning will be envisaged within the current framework programme only for objectives which are justified on ethical grounds and to the extent that the operations involved are effected on an ethical basis, with respect for the well-being of animals and the principles of genetic diversity.
(The practical effects of this will be further elaborated in the specific programmes).

THEME 2

USER-FRIENDLY INFORMATION SOCIETY

> The convergence between information processing, communications and content is increasingly pervading most industrial and social activities and is increasingly critical to Europe's competitiveness and quality of life. The advent of the information society is opening up the possibility of a wide range of new activities for both individuals and companies in the Community, e.g. in the fields of commerce, work, transport, the environment, education and training, health and culture. Continuous efforts in relation to research, technological development and technology take-up and demonstration are necessary to realise the full potential of the information society. The technological range of the key actions allows the possibility of a dynamic concentration and a flexible implementation of the activities, reflecting socioeconomic priorities.
>
> These efforts must, in all activities, tackle the universal issues such as access, ease of use, cost-effectiveness and interoperability and standardisation. They should also address the socioeconomic impact of the activities, in particular the social changes brought about by the introduction and more widespread use of new information and communications technologies, including their effect on different population groups, with particular attention to their effect on women and young people. Tackling the issues of access and ease of use in this context shall be an important priority.

(a) *Key actions*

(i) Systems and services for the citizen

The aim of this key action is to meet policy and user needs and to ease access at the lowest cost to quality general-purpose services, boost the industry providing these services and pave the way to 'digital communities' both in rural and urban areas. In this context, it will be based on the following priorities:

— as regards health: on computerised clinical systems, on secure high-capacity health networks and telemedicine,

— as regards persons with special needs, including the disabled and the elderly: on advanced interfaced and on telesystems to integrate the elderly and the disabled into society,

— as regards public administration: advanced multimedia systems to facilitate access to and provision of services of public interest,

— as regards the environment: on intelligent systems for analysis, surveillance, management and early warning and support systems for the detection and clearance of landmines,

— as regards transport and tourism: on the advanced intelligent systems needed for management and associated teleservices.

(ii) New methods of work and electronic commerce

The aim of this key action is to develop technologies to help companies operate more efficiently and to make commerce in goods and services more efficient, and to facilitate improvements in working conditions and the quality of work. The priority topics will be:

— flexible, mobile and remote working methods and tools for individuals and for cooperative and group working and working methods based on simulation and virtual reality — including related training,

— management systems for suppliers and consumers, including systems supporting mass-customisation and interoperable and secure payment systems,

— information and network security, including cryptography, techniques for combating computer crime, the technical means for authentication and the protection of integrity and intellectual property and 'privacy enhancing technologies'.

(iii) Multimedia content and tools

The aim of this key action is to facilitate lifelong learning, to stimulate creativity, to enable linguistic and cultural diversity and to improve the functionality of future information products and services, taking account of user-friendliness and acceptability. The research emphasises intelligent systems for education and training with innovative forms of multimedia content, including audiovisual content, and tools for structuring and processing them. It will focus on four main lines:

— interactive electronic publishing with new methods for creating and structuring publications; personalised dissemination of information and accessing scientific, cultural and other items through networking of libraries, archives and museums,

— education and training: systems, services and software enabling the development and demonstration of new methods using multimedia, broadband communications, simulation and virtual reality,

— new language technologies, including interfaces, which help to make information and communications systems more user-friendly,

— advanced technologies for accessing, filtering, analysing and handling information to help manage the information explosion and facilitate the use of multimedia contents, including geographical information systems.

(iv) Essential technologies and infrastructures

The aim of this key action is to promote excellence in the technologies which are crucial to the information society, to speed up their introduction and broaden their field of application. This action will focus as a matter of priority on:

— technologies for and management of information processing, communications and networks, including broadband ones, together with their implementation, interoperability and application,

— technologies and engineering for software, systems and services, including high-quality statistics,

— real-time and large-scale simulation and visualisation technologies,

— mobile and personal communications and systems, including satellite-related systems and services,

— interfaces making use of the various senses,

— peripherals, subsystems and microsystems,

— micro-electronics (technologies, tools, equipment and hardware necessary for the design and manufacture of circuits and components and the development of applications).

(b) *Research and technological development activities of a generic nature*

In order to develop from a visionary perspective future and emerging technologies with a potential industrial impact, research topics could include, in a non-prescriptive way:

— technologies for the representation, creation and handling of knowledge,

— nano-scale, quantum, photonic, bio-electronic technologies, including future generation integrated circuits, ultra-high performance computers and super-intelligent networks.

(c) *Support for research infrastructures*

The priority is to provide support to facilitate the rapid implementation and interoperability of Europe-wide advanced high-speed computer and communication systems needed for research in all fields of science and technology, in the context of the global evolution of the Internet.

THEME 3

COMPETITIVE AND SUSTAINABLE GROWTH

> The objective is to produce and disseminate the knowledge and technologies needed to design and develop processes and produce high-quality, environment- and consumer-friendly products which will be competitive on tomorrow's market, to help increase growth and create new jobs in Europe and to sustain the continuing innovation effort of manufacturing firms (including SMEs) so as to improve their competitiveness.
>
> This goes hand in hand with the development of transport systems which are economic, safe, and protective of the environment and quality of life.

(a) *Key actions* ([1])

   (i) Innovative products, processes and organisation

   The aim of this key action is to facilitate the development of high-quality innovative products and services which meet the needs of the citizen and the market and new methods of production and manufacture, including innovation in and modernisation of traditional industries, which save resources and are environmentally safe, whatever the method of production. Research will focus as a matter of priority on:

   — the elaboration, development and integration of new technologies for design, manufacturing, control and production, including micro- and nano-scale technologies and engineering,

   — deployment, integration and adaptation of information society technologies for intelligent manufacturing (including flexible workshop systems and systems for flexible management of supply and distribution chains, embedded systems and teleservices for operation and maintenance and simulation and shared-work technologies),

   — technologies to improve quality control and for clean and eco-efficient processes, including synthesis and separation techniques, aiming at reducing resource utilisation and promoting the use of renewable resources, reuse and recycling of waste and the development of clean processes and products based on the concept of 'life-cycle analysis',

   — new methods of organising production and work and of using and developing skills (including socioeconomic analyses), also in traditional industries.

   (ii) Sustainable mobility and intermodality

   The aim is to ensure the development of fully integrated policy and operational options for an integrated interoperable European rail and road, air and waterborne transport system on a broadly intermodal basis to ensure the mobility of people and goods, while at the same time improving transport efficiency, safety and reliability and reducing congestion and other environmental disbenefits. This requires as a matter of priority:

   — the development, validation and demonstration of rational modal and intermodal transport management systems, including better use of second-generation satellite navigation and positioning systems, and advanced traveller and operator information services,

   — research into transport infrastructures and their interfaces with transport means and systems, while reducing any adverse environmental and safety impacts and taking account of accessibility and the integration of regional planning and transport policies,

   — the development of technical and socioeconomic scenarios for the sustainable mobility of people and goods.

---

[1] Coordination will be ensured between the various key actions and generic technologies on rail and road transport means.

(iii) Land transport and marine technologies

The aim is to encourage, while preserving the environment and improving safety, the development and integration of knowledge and technologies specific to land transport and sea-based activities. It will enable the Community to develop technologies to maintain and consolidate the competitive position of the European automotive and rail industry by developing innovative technologies and new materials, modes and systems for sustainable and efficient land transport means and to fully exploit the sea's potential and improve the competitiveness of marine industry. This action will be complementary to the key actions on sustainable mobility and intermodality and sustainable marine ecosystems. Action will cover as a matter of priority:

— development of technologies for economic, clean, safe, efficient, energy-saving and intelligent road and rail vehicles operating in the total integrated transport environment,

— innovative vehicle concepts using new materials and construction techniques with emphasis on improved safety (including weight reduction and crashworthiness), recyclability and reduction of whole life-cycle costs,

— human/vehicle interaction in road and rail vehicles and innovative methods for the adaptation of rail-based systems to new needs,

— development of advanced ships which are safe, environmentally friendly and efficient,

— the use of the sea and inland waterways as economic and safe means of transporting goods and passengers (including advanced port infrastructure) by maximising vessel performance and interoperability in conjunction with the key action on 'sustainable mobility and intermodality',

— technologies for the study and observation of the seas and sustainable exploitation of the seas' energy and mineral resources, including offshore and subsea technologies, and unmanned vehicles and submarine acoustics.

(iv) New perspectives in aeronautics

The aim of this key action is to help the Community consolidate its position in this sector by developing its mastery, in an environmentally friendly manner, of the most advanced aeronautical technologies. It will cover as a matter of priority:

— the development and demonstration of advanced technologies for integrated design and production, and for reduction of energy consumption, emissions and noise for various aircraft concepts,

— the technological and economic feasibility of and the critical technologies for new-generation aircraft concepts including advanced systems and sub-systems,

— the development of technologies to improve operational safety and efficiency, including on-board integration of air-traffic management technologies, in coordination with other transport-related key actions.

(b) *Research and technological development activities of a generic nature*

The effort will be focused on the priority research needed to reinforce European competitiveness and quality of life:

— by supporting the development of new and improved industrial materials and the processes for their manufacture: materials resistant to high temperatures and high pressure (e.g. for energy generation and engines); light materials (for transport and construction); functional materials (opto-electronics, biomaterials, sensors) designed and developed with ease of recycling in mind; surface and interface engineering, as well as nano-scale and beam technologies,

— by ensuring that European standards and testing laboratories provide consistent measurements and tests which are equivalent to similar measurements made by Europe's major trading partners; by making available technical tests, certified reference materials and measuring instruments for use in Member States in order to assure compliance with Community directives; by supporting standardisation and certification, including action to combat fraud and ensure the quality of products and services,

— by developing new and improved materials and production technologies in the steel field.

(c) *Support for research infrastructures*

In accordance with the general objectives outlined above, activities should focus, for example, on computing centres for research, high-power wind tunnels, laboratories and facilities for measurements and tests, as well as specialised databases.

THEME 4

ENERGY, ENVIRONMENT AND SUSTAINABLE DEVELOPMENT

> Research and technological development in the field of the environment, energy and the sustainable management of ecosystem resources is essential for the implementation of Union policies. Making use of the knowledge and technologies needed will make it possible to meet a wide range of needs. The results of this research will provide the basis for the framing of policies at Community level or deriving from international treaties.
>
> This objective goes hand in hand with economic development and industrial competitiveness that respects the environment and quality of life. It necessitates clean, efficient, economic and diversified energy systems and services, including the introduction of new and renewable energy technologies. In particular, these should contribute to a substantial reduction in emissions of CO_2 and other greenhouse gases.

Although research and technological development in the field of environment and energy are closely related, they remain distinct areas, each requiring specific financial and administrative arrangements.

1. **Environment and sustainable development**

    (a) *Key actions*

    (i) Sustainable management and quality of water

    The aim of this key action is to produce the knowledge and technologies needed for the rational management of water resources for domestic needs and those of industry and agriculture. Among the priority fields concerned are:

    — treatment and purification technologies to prevent pollution, to purify water and to use and/or reuse water rationally (including closed loops; reliability of distribution networks); integrated approach to management of water resources and wetlands,

    — technologies for monitoring and preventing pollution and the protection and management of groundwater and surface-water resources, including ecological quality aspects,

    — surveillance, early warning and communication systems,

    — technologies for the regulation and management of stocks and technologies for arid and semi-arid areas and generally water-deficient regions.

    (ii) Global change, climate and biodiversity

    The aim of this key action is to develop the scientific and technological basis and tools necessary to underpin implementation of Community policies, notably the EC environmental action programmes and the biodiversity strategy, and to support the research obligations stemming from international treaties and conventions signed by the European Community and its Member States. Overall, the key action seeks to increase understanding in these areas in order to help deliver the Community goal of sustainable development, where possible in interaction with industry. In this context priorities are:

— to understand, detect, assess and predict global change processes, with an emphasis on the European and sub-regional causes and impacts, with respect to both natural and anthropogenic phenomena and in the context of the sustainable use of natural resources. The natural, the socioeconomic and, where relevant, the cultural sciences will be used,

— to foster better understanding of the terrestrial and marine ecosystems and the interactions between them and other ecosystems,

— to develop scenarios and strategies for the prevention and mitigation of and adaptation to global change, climate change and conservation of biodiversity in the context of sustainable development,

— to support the development of a European component of the global observing systems for climate, terrestrial ecosystems (including biodiversity) and oceans (for example, Euro-GOOS).

(iii) Sustainable marine ecosystems

The aim of this key action is to promote sustainable integrated management of marine resources and to contribute to the marine aspects of the fifth action plan on the environment. Synergy with other relevant activities of the framework programme will be ensured through a specific coordinating mechanism.

Research will be directed towards:

— developing the necessary scientific knowledge base on marine processes, ecosystems and interactions for sustainable use of the marine environment and resources,

— reducing the impact of human activity upon the biodiversity and sustainable functioning of marine ecosystems and developing the technologies required to facilitate safe and economic, yet sustainable, exploitation of marine resources,

— monitoring and managing coastal processes in order to alleviate pollution, flooding and erosion, in particular of fragile coastlines, and to facilitate land reclamation from the sea,

— enabling the operational forecasting of environmental constraints on safe sustainable offshore operations, including the necessary components of an appropriate marine observing system.

(iv) The city of tomorrow and cultural heritage

The aim of this key action is the harmonious development of the citizens' urban environment from a global, innovative and resource-saving viewpoint in an environmentally sound manner, using advanced models of organisation bringing together in particular the improvement of the quality of life, the restoration of social equilibria and the protection, conservation and enhancement of the cultural heritage for the sustainable exploitation of its socioeconomic potential for employment and tourism. Action will focus as a matter of priority on:

— new models for the sustainable development of European cities and city regions, the elaboration of medium- and long-term socioeconomic scenarios and research, development and demonstration activities focusing in particular on supporting and accompanying economic competitiveness, town planning and architecture, social integration, safety, energy efficiency and energy saving (in particular in buildings and in urban transport) and information networks (the concept of 'digital cities'),

— development and demonstration of technologies and products for diagnosis, protection, conservation, restoration and sustainable exploitation of the European cultural heritage, focusing on both movable and immovable cultural assets with a view to promoting their value and the quality of life,

— development and demonstration of technologies for economic, clean, effective and sustainable preservation, recovery, renovation and construction, in particular for large groups of buildings,

— comparative assessment and cost-effective implementation of strategies for sustainable transport systems in an urban environment.

(b) *Research and technological development activities of a generic nature*

— the fight against major natural and technological hazards through the development of forecasting, prevention, impact assessment and mitigation techniques,

— the development of generic Earth observation technologies, notably satellite-borne technologies [1] for environmental monitoring and resource and ecosystem management applications,

— the study of the socioeconomic aspects of development of environmental change within the perspective of sustainable development (impact on society, the economy and employment).

(c) *Support for research infrastructures*

In accordance with the general objectives outlined above, activities should focus, for example, on databases, marine-research facilities and computer centres for climate studies.

2. **Energy**

The activities carried out in this area will be closely coordinated, as appropriate, with the activities of the fifth Euratom framework programme for research and training, while respecting the different legal bases of these two programmes.

(a) *Key actions*

(i) Cleaner energy systems, including renewables

The aim of this key action is to minimise the environmental impact of the production and use of energy in Europe. Action will be taken to investigate cleaner, most notably renewable, energy sources, as well as to help reduce the environmental impact of existing fossil fuel use. Work will focus by way of priority on:

— large-scale generation of electricity and/or heat with reduced CO_2 emissions from coal, biomass or other fuels, including combined heat and power,

— development and demonstration, including for the purposes of decentralised generation, of the main new and renewable energy sources, in particular biomass, fuel-cell, wind and solar technologies,

— integration of new and renewable energy sources into energy systems,

— cost-effective environmental abatement technologies for power production.

(ii) Economic and efficient energy for a competitive Europe

The aim of this key action is to provide Europe with a reliable, efficient, safe and economic energy supply for the benefit of its citizens, the functioning of society and the competitiveness of its industry. Action will need to be taken at every stage of the energy cycle — production, distribution and final use — to improve efficiency and reduce costs. Work will focus by way of priority on:

— technologies for the rational and efficient end-use of energy,

— technologies for the transmission and distribution of energy,

— technologies for the storage of energy on both the macro and the micro scales,

— improved exploration, extraction and production efficiency for hydrocarbons,

— improving the efficiency of new and renewable energy sources,

— the elaboration of scenarios on supply and demand in economy/environment/energy systems and their interactions, and the analysis of the cost-effectiveness (based on whole-life costs) and efficiency of all energy sources.

---

[1] There will be specific coordination of the activities relating to 'space technology' application carried out within each of the thematic programmes.

(b) *Research and technological development activities of a generic nature*

— The study of the socioeconomic aspects of energy within the perspective of sustainable development (impact on society, the economy and employment).

2. SECOND ACTIVITY

HORIZONTAL THEME 'CONFIRMING THE INTERNATIONAL ROLE OF COMMUNITY RESEARCH'

> The main purposes of this horizontal theme are to promote scientific and technological cooperation internationally; to reinforce Community capacities in the fields of science and technology; to provide general support for the achievement of scientific excellence within the wider international framework; and to contribute to the implementation of the Community's external policy also with the accession of new Member States in mind.

The general objectives of international scientific cooperation are:

— to promote scientific and technological cooperation between undertakings, organisations and researchers from third countries and from the Community, which is likely to produce significant, mutual and balanced benefits, taking into account the different needs and circumstances of individual groups of countries and regions whilst respecting the protection of intellectual property,

— to facilitate access for research centres and undertakings established in the Community to scientific and technological knowledge available outside the Community which serves the Community's interests,

— to enhance the position and role of Community research in the international scientific and technological arena and promote a European scientific and technological culture,

— to prepare for the accession of new Member States for example by encouraging their full association with the framework programme; to contribute to the stabilisation of the RTD potential of the CEECs in general and of the newly independent States of the former Soviet Union (NIS), to support and develop the Euro-Mediterranean partnership and to contribute to the sustainable economic, social and scientific development of developing countries,

— to help European research players acquire information and gain experience of research capacity, activity and priorities of industrialised third countries and 'emerging economy' countries, so as to make Community industry more competitive and enhance its presence on new markets.

International scientific and technological cooperation will be implemented on the basis of cooperation agreements, where these exist, and through this horizontal international cooperation programme, as well as through activities undertaken within the other programmes of this framework programme.

1. Specific actions in the 'international cooperation' programme

    On the basis of the cooperation policies in specific areas which the Community pursues with its various potential partners, three categories of action will be implemented with a specific international dimension, linked to specific problems facing these countries and not addressed by the other activities of the framework programme. Only these actions will be financed through the specific 'international cooperation' programme.

    (a) *Cooperation with certain categories of third country*

    — States in the pre-accession phase: promotion of their centres of excellence, accompanying measures to facilitate participation in the other programmes of the framework programme, including through cooperation networks,

    — NIS and CEECs not in the pre-accession phase: support for their research and technological development potential (including through INTAS for the NIS, provided that a new agreement is reached between its members on its continuation), cooperation in areas of mutual interest (including satellite applications, regional problems linked to the environment and health),

— Mediterranean partner countries: improving through joint activities their RTD capacities and promoting innovation; cooperation in areas of mutual interest, notably regional aspects of the Mediterranean, including environmental aspects, support for socio-economic development, including the urban dimension, transition to the information society and preservation of cultural heritage, accompanying measures to facilitate participation in the other programmes of the framework programme, including through cooperation networks,

— developing countries: a policy dialogue on RTD needs and priorities with groups of countries and regions will be developed. Cooperation activities will be envisaged, in particular in the following areas: mechanisms and conditions for sustainable development; sustainable management and use of natural resources, including agricultural production, environmental and energy aspects; health, nutrition and food security,

— emerging economy and industrialised countries: Exchanges of scientists; organisation of workshops; accompanying measures to promote partnerships and to enhance mutual access to each other's RTD activities including, where appropriate, through scientific and technological cooperation agreements.

(b) *Training of researchers*

A system of fellowships will be set up to give young researchers from developing countries, Mediterranean and 'emerging economy' countries the opportunity of collaborating in laboratories in the Community on specific projects of the framework programme. Another fellowship scheme will be provided for a limited number of young Community researchers so as to enable them to work in industrially-oriented laboratories of the highest quality in third countries in areas of particular interest to the Community.

(c) *Coordination*

Coordination with COST actions, and support for COST administration, coordination with Eureka and with international organisations involved in research activities; coordination of activities pursued through the other programmes of the framework programme — with one another, with those pursued through the Community's other cooperation actions (notably PHARE, TACIS and MEDA) and with the Member States' cooperation activities.

2. **International cooperation pursued through the other framework programme activities**

Participation by entities of third countries in the specific programmes may take basically two forms:

— programme participation based on full association with the framework programme: participation for third-country entities under similar conditions to Member State entities. Full association of States in the pre-accession phase could be facilitated through appropriate degressive financing mechanisms, making use, where so decided, of other relevant Community instruments (e.g. PHARE). For other States in the pre-accession phase which indicate that full participation in the framework programme is not yet feasible for them, partial association with one or more complete specific programmes could be envisaged,

— participation in specific programmes on a project-by-project basis: if a bilateral or a multilateral cooperation agreement is necessary in the Community's interest in order to provide access to high-quality third-country programmes and suitable IPR arrangements, project-by-project participation will be subject to the conclusion of such an agreement. Participating entities of third countries will in principle not benefit from funds under these programmes, except in cases duly justified as being in the Community's interest.

The detailed conditions under which entities from third countries and international organisations involved in research activities may participate in the framework programme, including the financial arrangements, will be specified in the decision which will be adopted pursuant to Article 130j of the Treaty.

3. THIRD ACTIVITY

HORIZONTAL THEME 'PROMOTION OF INNOVATION AND ENCOURAGEMENT OF SME PARTICIPATION'

> Innovation is a key factor in industrial competitiveness, sustainable social and economic development and job creation. The aim is to promote innovative activities, including the creation of innovative enterprises, and to facilitate the dissemination and exploitation of research results and support technology transfer.
>
> Small and medium-sized businesses are important vectors and actors in innovation. The development of SMEs can make a vital contribution to economic and social development, new economic activities, job creation and competitiveness. SMEs must therefore be provided with easier access to the advanced technologies which they need, and to the opportunities offered by the Community's as well as the Member States' research programmes.

Promotion of innovation and SME participation, although not synonymous, are closely linked. As far as possible, this theme will therefore be implemented by means of joint action covering both areas. Furthermore, the activities carried out in this programme will be complementary to activities undertaken within Member States and to activities to promote innovation and encourage SME participation carried out elsewhere in the framework programme, and will therefore support, supplement and, as appropriate, give direction to these various efforts.

1. General objectives

(a) *Promotion of innovation*

— to help implement innovation policies in the European Union, in particular by contributing to the creation of an environment conducive to innovation,

— to enhance public awareness of the benefits of innovation,

— to improve the economic and social impact of framework programme research activities by ensuring better dissemination and exploitation of their results, as well as the transfer and dissemination of technology from various sources, taking account of the needs of customers and users,

— to facilitate access of programme participants (particularly SMEs), through provision of information and advice, to instruments which support innovation.

(b) *Encouraging SME participation*

— to stimulate SME participation in the research programmes and technology transfer to SMEs — both SMEs active in research and high technology and those with little or no research capability but with substantial technological needs and a capacity to absorb new technologies; to help SMEs throughout the European Union to develop their technological capabilities, taking into account also specific problems of SMEs in less-favoured regions,

— to assist SMEs in setting up transnational networks and partnerships for the absorption and diffusion of new technologies,

— to encourage the development of transnational links between SMEs, large companies, research centres and universities.

2. Actions specific to the horizontal programme

(a) *Promotion of innovation*

— identification and dissemination, in concert with the other programmes of the framework programme, of adequate mechanisms to facilitate, in the life-cycle of projects, the exploitation, private financing and transfer of technologies and results produced, while guaranteeing protection of the knowledge acquired,

— development, validation and implementation of methodologies for technology transfer actions integrating the technological, economic and social aspects of innovation and, where necessary, transnational dissemination and exploitation of results not stemming from the thematic programmes (taking account of the particular characteristics of each sector of activity),

— coordination of studies and analyses carried out in various fora and integration of their results, with a view to establishing a common reference framework in the area of innovation policy.

(b) *Encouraging SME participation*

— management of a single complementary entry point for SMEs — for all the research programmes — in the Commission's departments, making use of existing support networks in Member States; definition and management of common tools facilitating SME participation in the programmes (fullest possible use of electronic methods for information dossiers, submission of proposals, 'help line', specialised Intranets to stimulate SME participation in innovation, etc.); provision of information on programmes and training on proposal preparation;

— increasing involvement of SMEs at all stages in the consultation/assessment process; where appropriate, their representative associations may also be consulted; ensuring a structured and rapid feedback system for all applicants; assistance for the establishment of consortia; simplifying procedures and further increasing the efficiency of contract and payment arrangements; and improving transparency,

— permanently open calls for proposals for measures specific to SMEs, such as exploratory awards or cooperative research activities,

— assistance to SMEs in identifying their current and future technological needs and provision of information and advice with a view to meeting those needs.

(c) *Joint actions for innovation/SMEs*

— actions at Community level for the rationalisation and coordination of networks providing information and assistance on the Community's research and innovation activities; management, in concert with the other programmes of the framework programme, of the support network for innovation and technology transfer, making best use of the innovation relay centres and the CRAFT focal points; consolidation of mechanisms for gathering and disseminating information, such as the Cordis information service,

— provision of information and advice, as well as pilot activities, in the areas of:

— intellectual property rights,

— access to private finance, notably venture capital funds,

— the creation of innovative start-ups, principally via European organisations and funds (European Investment Fund, European Investment Bank, and the Eurotech Capital scheme).

The objective of the pilot activities will be to improve the existing capacities for information, advice and analysis and to facilitate access to existing public and private instruments at national or Community level without providing financial subsidies to enterprises or creating a competing financial instrument;

— identification and promotion, in concert with the other programmes of the framework programmes, of best practices in innovation.

3. **Interaction with related actions in the other framework programme activities**

   (a) *Promotion of innovation*

   — encouraging preparation for the exploitation and dissemination of results during the research phase,

   — ensuring consistency between activities to foster innovation under the other programmes and those carried out in this programme,

   — coordination of the activities of the 'innovation units' to be set up under the thematic programmes, with the aim of supplementing the innovation dimension of the implementation of programmes (e.g. in the selection and monitoring of projects) and securing, as appropriate, the follow-up of technology transfer, including technology transfer projects with a demonstration effect.

   (b) *Encouraging SME participation*

   Support for SME participation in RTD and demonstration activities to be carried out in the programmes:

   — 'cooperative research' activities enabling at least three mutually independent SMEs from at least two Member States jointly to seek the resolution of their common technological problems internally or by entrusting it to third legal entities with appropriate research capacities,

   — activities to support and encourage SME participation in collaborative and cooperative research projects (for example on the basis of 'exploratory awards' respecting the needs of SMEs for a flexible and easily accessible support system.

   Support for ensuring and improving dissemination and exploitation of results within the thematic programmes.

4. **FOURTH ACTIVITY**

   HORIZONTAL THEME: 'IMPROVING HUMAN RESEARCH POTENTIAL AND THE SOCIOECONOMIC KNOWLEDGE BASE'

   > The world is increasingly based on knowledge. The Community's prime asset in this area is the quality of its researchers, engineers and technicians. The aim is to preserve and help develop this knowledge potential through greater support for the training and mobility of researchers and by enhancing access to research infrastructures.
   >
   > The Community also has a solid tradition of research in social and economic science and the humanities, which needs to be mobilised to identify economic and social trends and requirements, both current and future, in order to contribute to the Community's competitiveness and the quality of life of its citizens.

   1. **General objectives**

   The general objectives of this activity, to be realised in concert with related actions elsewhere in the framework programme, are centred on two main areas of activity, namely improving the human research potential and strengthening the socioeconomic knowledge base. To this end, actions will be undertaken:

— to develop the Community's human research potential, making special efforts to ensure equality of access and a better balance between men and women, notably through the training and mobility of researchers so as to contribute, *inter alia*, to efforts for creating new jobs,

— to enhance access to research infrastructures,

— to help make the Community an attractive location for researchers and to promote European research in the international arena and to promote a European scientific and technological culture,

— to strengthen, through a specific key station, the socioeconomic knowledge base for a better understanding of key problems facing European society,

— to help develop scientific and technological policies and other Community policies.

2. **Actions specific to the horizontal programme**

    (a) *Improving human research potential*

    Supporting training and mobility of researchers

    Actions will cover:

    — the establishment of research training networks on high-quality projects, including those in emerging fields of research, on topics freely chosen by the researchers. The accent will be placed on the training and development of young researchers at pre-doctoral and at post-doctoral level,

    — the establishment of a coherent system of 'Marie Curie' fellowships centred on individual fellowships for young high-quality researchers with the necessary research experience, awarded for topics chosen by the researchers themselves.

    Additional and complementary schemes include:

    — industrial host fellowships awarded to, and jointly funded by, enterprises (including SMEs) for the training of young researchers,

    — development host fellowships to help develop high-level research capacity in the less favoured regions of the Community,

    — experienced researchers' fellowships to promote mobility between industry and academia,

    — support for short stays by doctoral students at training sites.

    Enhancing access to research infrastructures

    The main aim is to enhance access to research infrastructures (large facilities, networks of distributed facilities, infrastructural centres of competence) to the extent that such measures are not undertaken by other activities of the framework programme. To this end, measures are envisaged to help researchers with transnational access to infrastructures which are of Community-wide interest on account of their rarity and/or specialisation, including, where relevant, complementary measures to support the setting up of networks between infrastructure operators and related research projects.

    Promoting scientific and technological excellence

    The objective here is to stimulate, through exchange, scientific and technological excellence and to make the most of the achievements of research. Activities will build on and complement national activities and will include support for high-level scientific conferences, the networking of Community researchers active outside the Community with their Community colleagues, distinctions for high-level research work, including a European Descartes prize awarded to researchers for outstanding scientific and technological achievements resulting from European collaborative research, and actions to raise public awareness and making information on important scientific issues available to the public at Community level, including via electronic networks.

(b) *Key action: improving the socioeconomic knowledge base*

The aim of this key action is to define the base for employment-generating social, economic and cultural development and for building a European knowledge society. It covers a number of subjects linked to the general objectives of the framework programme. Work will focus on:

— analysing structural, demographic and social changes, including the phenomena of xenophobia, racism and migration in Europe, and their impact on economic development, social integration and social protection,

— the relationship between technological development, employment and society, including working conditions and workforce skills and on innovation in education and training, including for newly emerging professions,

— analysing the changing role of European institutions, systems of governance and citizenship in the process of European integration, taking account of the impact of culture, the media and the social and legal environment,

— validating new development models, fostering growth, employment, social and economic cohesion and the quality of life, taking account of the development of services and the non-tangible economy.

(c) *Other activities will be undertaken in support of the development of science and technology policies.*

The aim is to support the development of the specific knowledge base needed by policy-makers and other users on European science and technology policy issues. Building on and complementing national and international activities, this action will cover the development of appropriate and comparable indicators, technology watch and assessment, strategic analysis of specific policy issues and, where appropriate, promotion of exchange of information and experience between policy-makers and researchers.

3. **Interaction with related actions in the other framework programme activities**

This activity will include the coordination, support and accompanying actions needed to ensure consistency with actions undertaken elsewhere in the framework programme on the aspects related to the objectives and activities of this programme. The programme will also ensure, through appropriate monitoring and coordinating mechanisms, the adequate incorporation of socioeconomic and strategic considerations into the research activities of the thematic programmes.

ANNEX III

FIFTH FRAMEWORK PROGRAMME (1998 TO 2002)
AMOUNTS AND BREAKDOWN

	ECU million (current prices)
Indirect actions:	
— First activity	10 843 (¹)
— Second activity	475
— Third activity	363
— Fourth activity	1 280
Direct actions (²)	739
Maximum overall amount	13 700

(¹) Of which 10 % on average for SMEs.
(²) To be carried out by the JRC.

	(in million ECU)
Indicative breakdown between the themes of the first activity:	
— quality of life and management of living resources	2 413
— user-friendly information society	3 600
— competitive and sustainable growth	2 705
— energy, environment and sustainable development	
— environment and sustainable development	1 083
— energy	1 042
	10 843

ANNEX IV

RULES FOR FINANCIAL PARTICIPATION BY THE COMMUNITY

The Community will contribute financially to the research and technological development activities, including demonstration activities, hereinafter referred to as 'indirect RTD actions', carried out under the specific programmes implementing the framework programme. In addition, it will carry out directly research and development activities in the areas covered by the framework programme, hereinafter referred to as 'direct TRD actions'.

1. **Indirect RTD actions**

    The indirect RTD actions will comprise: shared-cost actions, which will be the principal mechanism for implementing the specific programmes, as well as training fellowships, support for networks, concerted actions and accompanying measures.

    (a) *Shared-cost actions*

    — research and technological development projects, demonstration projects, combined RTD/demonstration projects:

    — research and technological development projects: projects designed to obtain new knowledge likely to be useful either to develop new or significantly to improve existing products, processes and/or services and/or to meet the needs of Community policies,

    — demonstration projects: projects designed to prove the viability of new technologies which offer a potential economic advantage but which cannot be commercialised directly,

    — combined RTD/demonstration projects: projects with both a research and technological development component and a demonstration component,

    — enhancing access to research infrastructures:

    In addition to measures in support of research infrastructure within the other indirect RTD actions, support for enhancing access to research infrastructures will be granted towards the additional costs of receiving Community researchers and making facilities available,

    — technology stimulation to encourage and facilitate SME participation in RTD activities:

    'cooperative research' projects: projects enabling at least three mutually independent SMEs from at least two Member States to entrust the resolution of their common technological problems to third legal entities with appropriate research capacities jointly.

    'Exploratory awards' to support the exploratory phase of a project. This might consist of feasibility studies, project validation and preparation and partner search, during a period not exceeding 12 months.

    (b) *Training fellowships*

    Training fellowships are defined in the context of the fourth activity (Marie Curie fellowships). Fellowships awarded under the first, second or fourth activities will provide an allowance for the fellow which will include provision for proper social welfare expenses and a contribution to costs involved in mobility. There will also be a contribution to the eligible costs of the host institution when it is in the Community.

    (c) *Support for research training networks and thematic networks*

    — research training networks in the context of the fourth activity. Support will be granted towards the additional eligible costs connected with setting up and maintaining the network,

— thematic networks: networks bringing together, for instance, manufacturers, users, universities, research centres, organisations and research infrastructures around a given scientific and technological objective, so as to facilitate coordination of activities and transfer of knowledge. Support will be granted towards the additional eligible costs of coordinating and implementing the network.

(d) *Concerted actions*

Concerted actions will be designed to coordinate RTD projects already in receipt of funding, in order to exchange experience acquired, to expand the research efforts of the various players so as to reach a critical mass, to disseminate results and to inform users.

(e) *Accompanying measures*

Accompanying measures will contribute to the implementation of the specific programmes or the preparation of future activities, with a view to enabling them to achieve their strategic objectives. They will also seek to prepare for or to support other indirect RTD actions. Measures devoted to the commercialisation of products, processes or services, marketing activities and sales promotion are excluded.

The decisions adopting the specific programmes may spell out in more detail the indirect RTD actions described above, supplement them or subject them to additional conditions or limitations.

The rules for the participation of undertakings, research centres and universities in indirect RTD actions and for the dissemination of results will be specified in the Council Decision to be adopted pursuant to Article 130j of the Treaty. Eligible costs will be defined in that Decision and specified in detail in particular in the contracts.

In addition to the direct RTD actions described below, the JRC will progressively compete for funds for the indirect RTD actions of the framework programme.

2. Direct RTD actions

The direct RTD actions to be implemented by the Joint Research Centre (JRC) will cover research and scientific and technical support activities of an institutional character. The JRC may provide support where it has special or even unique expertise and facilities in the Community or where it is entrusted with activities necessary for the framing and implementation of Community policies and tasks incumbent on the Commission pursuant to the Treaty which require the JRC's impartiality. The JRC will carry out its activities in close cooperation with the scientific community and enterprises in Europe.

3. Rates of participation

In the decisions adopting the specific programmes implementing the fifth framework programme there can be no derogations from the financial participation rates set out below, with the exception of duly justified special cases.

Activity	Rate of framework programme participation
Indirect RTD actions	
RTD projects Demonstration projects Combined RTD/demonstration projects	50 % of the total eligible costs (1) (2) 35 % of the total eligible costs (1) (2) 35 to 50 % of the total eligible costs (1) (2) (3)
Support for access to research infrastructures	Maximum of 100 % of additional eligible costs
'Cooperative research' projects	50 % of the total eligible costs (1)
'Exploratory awards'	75 % of the total eligible costs
Training fellowships	Maximum of 100 % of the additional eligible costs (4)
Research training networks Thematic networks	Maximum of 100 % of additional eligible costs
Concerted actions	Maximum of 100 % of additional eligible costs
Accompanying measures	Maximum of 100 % of the total eligible costs
Direct RTD actions	100 % of the costs

(1) These rates may need to be adjusted in individual cases to comply with the Community framework for State aid for research and development and with Article 8 of the Agreement on subsidies and countervailing measures of the WTO Agreement.
(2) In the special case of legal entities which do not keep analytical accounts, the additional eligible costs generated as a result of the research will be financed at the rate of 100 %.
(3) 35 % for the demonstration part, 50 % for the RTD part.
(4) In the case of industrial host fellowships, this will normally approximate to 50 % of the total eligible costs.

4. **Joint undertakings etc.**

Any Council Decisions taken pursuant to Article 130o, as referred to in Article 3(2) of this Decision, will lay down, where necessary, rules on financial participation by the Community.

**Council Resolution
of 22 February 1999
on the 1999 Employment Guidelines**

(OJ C 69, 12.3.1999)

COUNCIL RESOLUTION

of 22 February 1999

on the 1999 Employment Guidelines

(1999/C 69/02)

THE COUNCIL OF THE EUROPEAN UNION,

Having regard to the Treaty establishing the European Community,

Whereas under Article 2 of that Treaty the Community has as its task the promotion, in particular, of a high level of employment,

In accordance with the conclusions of the Amsterdam European Council of 16 and 17 June 1997 and the Resolution on Growth and Employment which referred to the procedure as envisaged in the new Title on Employment in the Amsterdam Treaty and stated that the Council should seek to make those provisions immediately effective,

On the basis of the conclusions of the extraordinary European Council meeting on Employment of 20 and 21 November 1997 which launched the Luxembourg process, based on the implementation of a coordinated European employment strategy,

On the basis of the conclusions of the Vienna European Council of 11 and 12 December 1998,

Having regard to the Council Resolution of 15 December 1997 on the 1998 Employment Guidelines (¹), the conclusions of the Cardiff European Council of 15 and 16 June 1998 and the contribution of all Member States to the development of the process set out in the Resolution, in particular through the presentation of National Action Plans for Employment,

Having regard to the 1998 Joint Employment Report, prepared jointly with the Commission, describing the employment situation in the Community and examining the action taken by the Member States in implementing their employment policy in line with the 1998 guidelines,

Having regard to the Commission proposal of 14 October 1998 for Guidelines for Member States' Employment Policies in 1999,

Having regard to the Commission's 'Report on ways of improving the comparability of statistics to monitor and value progress under the European employment strategy established in view of the European Council in Vienna'; having regard also to the progress made by the Commission and the Member States in the field of indicators, referred to in the 1998 Joint Employment Report,

Having regard to the Resolution embodying the contribution of the European Parliament,

Having regard to the opinion of the Economic and Social Committee,

Having regard to the opinion of the Committee of the Regions,

Having regard to the opinion of the Employment and Labour Market Committee,

Having regard to the Social Partners' contribution to the implementation of the 1998 Employment Guidelines and to the results of the contacts established with the troika of Heads of State or Government and the Commission,

(1) Whereas employment is the top priority of the European Union; whereas coordinated action must be pursued in a sustained manner to combat unemployment and raise the present levels of employment on a lasting basis;

(2) Whereas the 1998 Employment Guidelines, endorsed at the Luxembourg European Council, have launched a process with high visibility, strong political commitment and a wide-ranging acceptance by all actors concerned;

(3) Whereas the Vienna European Council has given the Council and the Commission a mandate to report to the forthcoming Cologne European Council on the development of a European Employment Pact in the framework of the Luxembourg process;

(4) Whereas all fifteen Member States have submitted reports on the implementation of their National

___
(¹) OJ C 30, 28.1.1998, p. 1.

289

Action Plans, and on this basis a fruitful dialogue has been established with the Commission, and a peer-group review has been launched, which have allowed for the clarification of the aims, methods, funding and timescales of their policies in the context of the respective action plans;

(5) Whereas for the continued success of the European Employment Strategy, it is important to maintain the integrated and coordinated approach based on sound macro-economic policies and structural reforms in labour, product, services and capital markets;

(6) Whereas this coordination of Member States' employment policies should be implemented through the adoption by the Council, having received the opinion of the Employment and Labour Market Committee acting in close cooperation with the Economic Policy Committee, of employment guidelines, which are compatible with the broad economic policy guidelines and which set specific targets, the achievement of which is regularly monitored under a common procedure for assessing results;

(7) Whereas the implementation of the guidelines may vary according to their nature, their impact on Member States and the parties to whom they are addressed; whereas they must respect the principle of subsidiarity and Member States' responsibilities with regard to employment;

(8) Whereas the differing situations of the Member States in relation to the problems addressed by the guidelines will result in differing solutions and emphases in line with individual situations;

(9) Whereas the 1999 Employment Guidelines preserve the four pillar structure: improving employability, developing entrepreneurship, encouraging adaptability of businesses and their employees and strengthening the policies for equal opportunities between women and men;

(10) Whereas the Member States, in drawing up their National Action Plans for 1999, should fully exploit the new possibilities opened up by information and communication technologies for job creation, employability, more flexible and adaptable forms of work organisation and progress on equal opportunities;

(11) Whereas the implementation of these Guidelines could help to tackle the problem of undeclared work;

(12) Whereas the role and responsibility of partners at the regional and local levels in job creation and in ensuring supportive conditions and structures needs to be more fully recognised and supported;

(13) Whereas the European Social Fund is making a positive contribution to the qualification of human resources and its reform should be used to strengthen support for the Employment Strategy;

(14) Whereas sustainable development and the integration of environmental concerns in other Community policies were endorsed by the Amsterdam European Council; whereas Member States are invited to give effect to this integration within their national employment strategies by promoting employment creation in the environmental field;

(15) Whereas the role of the cultural sectors in creating sustainable jobs should be considered in the context of the National Action Plans;

(16) Whereas the Vienna European Council invited the Commission to present in Spring 1999 a communication on mainstreaming employment policies at Community level, based on the future Article 127 of the Treaty establishing the European Community;

(17) Whereas the Vienna European Council invited the Commission to allow those Member States which so desire to experiment with reduced VAT rates on labour-intensive services which are not exposed to cross-border competition;

(18) Whereas the experience in implementing the Luxembourg process in 1998 showed that streamlining is necessary for 1999 and the following years,

HEREBY ADOPTS THIS RESOLUTION:

1. The 1999 Employment Guidelines appended hereto are adopted.

2. In 1999 each Member State will submit by mid-June, to the Council and the Commission, one implementation report, comprising the implementation of the 1998 National Action Plan and describing the adjustments made to the National Action Plan to take account of the changes introduced by the 1999 Guidelines.

3. The Council notes that the Commission will, on the basis of its evaluation of the Member States' implementation reports, make its proposal for the Joint Employment Report and the revised Employment Guidelines for the year 2000 by September 1999.

4. The Council will, on the basis of the Member States' implementation reports and having received the views of the Employment and Labour Market Committee, carry out an examination of the implementation of the employment policies of the Member States in the light of the Employment Guidelines. On the basis of the results of that examination, the Council and the Commission will make their joint report to the European Council on the employment situation in the Community and on the implementation of the guidelines for employment. The Joint Employment Report 1999 will contain a first evaluation of the impact of the National Action Plans on the employment situation.

5. The Council affirms that the social partners at all levels will be involved in all stages of this approach and will make an important contribution to the implementation of these guidelines and the promotion of a high level of employment. That contribution will be regularly assessed.

6. The Council recognises the key importance of a broad and intensive dialogue between all actors involved, i.e. the European Parliament, the Council, the Commission, Social Partners, the European Central Bank and the European Investment Bank for the future success of the Luxembourg process.

7. The Council invites the Commission and the Member States to reach an agreement on the definition of all relevant indicators in time for the forthcoming Cologne European Council.

ANNEX

THE 1999 EMPLOYMENT GUIDELINES

INTRODUCTION: QUANTITATIVE TARGETS AND INDICATORS

It is essential that the Employment Guidelines are transformed into concrete national action plans. The use of common indicators, based on comparable statistics, is of crucial importance for an effective monitoring and evaluation of policies, both at national and at Community level. So far, basic employment performance indicators have been used in several joint employment reports and the work on policy indicators, referring to the concrete Guidelines, is well under way. It was agreed at Luxembourg that the ultimate objective of a coordination of Member States' employment policies is to arrive at a significant increase in the employment rate in Europe on a sustainable basis.

In order to produce concrete results, Member States:

— are urged to support the process of defining and collecting comparable data in order to implement the three Community-wide operational targets under Guideline 1-3. This includes in particular developing reliable flow data on employment and unemployment,

— will need, in order meaningfully to evaluate progress on implementing the Guidelines, to ensure that adequate and comparable data systems and procedures are available.

In addition, Member States are invited to set themselves national targets which could be quantified wherever possible and appropriate.

Furthermore, objective criteria will have to be developed for selecting best practices.

I. IMPROVING EMPLOYABILITY

Tackling youth unemployment and preventing long-term unemployment

In order to influence the trend in youth and long-term unemployment the Member States will intensify their efforts to develop preventive and employability-oriented strategies, building on the early identification of individual needs; within a period to be determined by each Member State which may not exceed four years and which may be longer in Member States with particularly high unemployment, Member States will ensure that:

1. every unemployed young person is offered a new start before reaching six months of unemployment, in the form of training, retraining, work practice, a job or other employability measure;

2. unemployed adults are also offered a fresh start before reaching twelve months of unemployment by one of the aforementioned means or, more generally, by accompanying individual vocational guidance.

These preventive and employability measures should be combined with measures to promote the re-employment of the long-term unemployed.

Transition from passive measures to active measures

Benefit, tax and training systems — where that proves necessary — must be reviewed and adapted to ensure that they actively support employability. Each Member State:

3. will endeavour to increase significantly the number of persons benefiting from active measures to improve their employability. In order to increase the numbers of unemployed who are offered training or any similar measure, it will in particular fix a target, in the light of its starting situation, of gradually achieving the average of the three most successful Member States, and at least 20 %;

4. will review and, where appropriate, refocus its benefit and tax system and provide incentives for unemployed or inactive people to seek and take up work or measures to enhance their employability and for employers to create new jobs. In addition, it is important to develop, in the context of a policy for active ageing, measures such as maintaining working capacity, lifelong learning and other flexible working arrangements, so that older workers are also able to participate actively in working life.

Encouraging a partnership approach

The actions of the Member States alone will not suffice to achieve the desired results in promoting employability. Consequently:

5. the social partners are urged, at their various levels of responsibility and action, to conclude as soon as possible agreements with a view to increasing the possibilities for training, work experience, traineeships or other measures likely to promote employability;

6. in order to reinforce the development of a skilled and adaptable workforce, both Member States and the social partners will endeavour to develop possibilities for lifelong learning, particularly in the fields of information and communication technologies, and, in consultation with the Employment and Labour Market Committee, define lifelong learning in order to set a target according to national circumstances for participants benefiting from such measures. Easy access for older workers will be particularly important.

Easing the transition from school to work

Employment prospects are poor for young people who leave the school system without having acquired the aptitudes required for entering the job market. Member States will therefore:

7. improve the quality of their school systems in order to reduce substantially the number of young people who drop out of the school system early. Particular attention should also be given to young people with learning difficulties;

8. make sure they equip young people with greater ability to adapt to technological and economic changes and with skills relevant to the labour market, where appropriate by implementing or developing apprenticeship training.

Promoting a labour market open to all

Many groups and individuals experience particular difficulties in acquiring relevant skills and in gaining access to, and remaining in, the labour market. A coherent set of policies promoting the integration of such groups and individuals into the world of work and combating discrimination is called for. Each Member State will:

9. give special attention to the needs of the disabled, ethnic minorities and other groups and individuals who may be disadvantaged, and develop appropriate forms of preventive and active policies to promote their integration into the labour market.

II. DEVELOPING ENTREPRENEURSHIP

Making it easier to start up and run businesses

The development of new enterprises, and the growth of small and medium-sized enterprises (SMEs), is essential for job creation and for the expansion of training opportunities for young people. This process must be promoted by encouraging greater entrepreneurial awareness across society, by providing a clear, stable and predictable set of rules and by improving the conditions for the development of risk capital markets. The Member States should also reduce and simplify the administrative and tax burdens on SMEs. These policies will support Member States' attempts to tackle undeclared work. To that end the Member States will:

10. give particular attention to reducing significantly the overhead costs and administrative burdens for businesses, and especially SMEs, in particular when an enterprise is being set up and when hiring additional workers;

11. encourage the development of self-employment by examining, with the aim of reducing, any obstacles which may exist, especially those within tax and social security regimes, to moving to self-employment and the setting up of small businesses as well as by promoting training for entrepreneurship and targeted support services for entrepreneurs.

Exploiting new opportunities for job creation

If the European Union wants to deal successfully with the employment challenge, all possible sources of jobs and new technologies and innovations must be exploited effectively. To that end the Member States will:

12. promote measures to exploit fully the possibilities offered by job creation at local level, in the social economy, in the area of environmental technologies and in new activities linked to needs not yet satisfied by the market, and examine, with the aim of reducing, any obstacles in the way of such measures. In this respect, the special role of local authorities and the social partners should be taken into account;

13. develop framework conditions to fully exploit the employment potential of the services and industry-related services, *inter alia*, by tapping the employment potential of the information society and the environmental sector, to create more and better jobs.

Making the taxation system more employment friendly

and reversing the long-term trend towards higher taxes and charges on labour (which have increased from 35 % in 1980 to more than 42 % in 1995). Each Member State will:

14. set a target, if necessary and taking account of its present level, for gradually reducing the overall tax burden and, where appropriate, a target for gradually reducing the fiscal pressure on labour and non-wage labour costs, in particular on relatively unskilled and low-paid labour, without jeop-

ardising the recovery of public finances or the financial equilibrium of social security schemes. It will examine, if appropriate, the desirability of introducing a tax on energy or on pollutant emissions or any other tax measure;

15. examine, without obligation, the advisability of reducing the rate of VAT on labour-intensive services not exposed to cross-border competition.

III. ENCOURAGING ADAPTABILITY OF BUSINESSES AND THEIR EMPLOYEES

Modernising work organisation

In order to promote the modernisation of work organisation and forms of work, a strong partnership should be developed at all appropriate levels (European, national, sectoral, local and enterprise levels):

16. The social partners are invited to negotiate at all appropriate levels agreements to modernise the organisation of work, including flexible working arrangements, with the aim of making undertakings productive and competitive and achieving the required balance between flexibility and security. Such agreements may, for example, cover the expression of working time as an annual figure, the reduction of working hours, the reduction of overtime, the development of part-time working, lifelong training and career breaks.

17. For its part, each Member State will examine the possibility of incorporating in its law more adaptable types of contract, taking into account the fact that forms of employment are increasingly diverse. Those working under contracts of this kind should at the same time enjoy adequate security and higher occupational status, compatible with the needs of business.

Support adaptability in enterprises

In order to renew skill levels within enterprises Member States will:

18. re-examine the obstacles, in particular tax obstacles, to investment in human resources and possibly provide for tax or other incentives for the development of in-house training; they will also examine new regulations and review the existing regulatory framework to make sure they will contribute to reducing barriers to employment and helping the labour market adapt to structural change in the economy.

IV. STRENGTHENING EQUAL OPPORTUNITIES POLICIES FOR WOMEN AND MEN

Gender mainstreaming approach

Women still have particular problems in gaining access to the employment market, in career advancement, in earnings and in reconciling professional and family life. It is therefore important, *inter alia:*

— to ensure that active labour market policies are made available for women in proportion to their share of unemployment,

— to reduce tax-benefit disincentives, wherever identified, because of their negative effects on the female labour supply,

— to give particular attention to obstacles which hinder women who wish to set up new businesses or become self-employed,

— to ensure that women are able to benefit positively from flexible forms of work organisation.

Therefore, the Member States will:

19. adopt a gender-mainstreaming approach in implementing the Guidelines of all four pillars. In order meaningfully to evaluate progress on this approach, Member States will need to provide for adequate data collection systems and procedures.

Tackling gender gaps

Member States and the social partners should translate their desire to promote equality of opportunity into increased employment rates for women. They should also pay attention to the imbalance in the representation of women or men in certain economic sectors and occupations, as well as to the improvement of female career opportunities. Member States will:

20. attempt to reduce the gap in unemployment rates between women and men by actively supporting the increased employment of women and will take action to bring about a balanced representation of women and men in all sectors and occupations. They will initiate positive steps to promote equal pay for equal work or work of equal value and to diminish differentials in incomes between women and men. In order to reduce gender gaps, Member States will also consider an increased use of measures for the advancement of women.

Reconciling work and family life

Policies on career breaks, parental leave and part-time work, as well as flexible working arrangements which serve the interests of both employers and employees, are of particular importance to women and men. Implementation of the various Directives and social-partner agreements in this area should be accelerated and monitored regularly. There must be an adequate provision of good quality care for children and other dependents in order to support women's and men's entry and continued participation in the labour market. An equal sharing of family responsibilities is crucial in this respect. In order to strengthen equal opportunities, Member States and the social partners will:

21. design, implement and promote family-friendly policies, including affordable, accessible and high quality care services for children and other dependents, as well as parental and other leave schemes.

Facilitating reintegration into the labour market

The Member States will:

22. give specific attention to women, and men, considering a return to the paid workforce after an absence and, to that end, they will examine the means of gradually eliminating the obstacles in the way of such return.

**Directive 1999/42/EC of the European Parliament and of the Council
of 7 June 1999
establishing a mechanism for the recognition of qualifications
in respect of the professional activities covered by the Directives
on liberalisation and transitional measures and supplementing
the general systems for the recognition of qualifications**

(OJ L 201, 31.7.1999)

DIRECTIVE 1999/42/EC OF THE EUROPEAN PARLIAMENT AND OF THE COUNCIL

of 7 June 1999

establishing a mechanism for the recognition of qualifications in respect of the professional activities covered by the Directives on liberalisation and transitional measures and supplementing the general systems for the recognition of qualifications

THE EUROPEAN PARLIAMENT AND
THE COUNCIL OF THE EUROPEAN UNION,

Having regard to the Treaty establishing the European Community, and in particular Articles 40 and 47(1), the first and third sentences of Article 47(2), and Article 55 thereof,

Having regard to the proposal from the Commission [1],

Having regard to the opinion delivered by the Economic and Social Committee [2],

Acting in accordance with the procedure laid down in Article 251 of the Treaty [3] and in the light of the joint text adopted on 22 April 1999,

(1) Whereas, under the Treaty, all discriminatory treatment on grounds of nationality with regard to establishment and provision of services is prohibited as from the end of the transitional period; whereas, therefore, certain provisions of the Directives applying in this area have become redundant for the purposes of applying the rule of national treatment, since that rule is enshrined in the Treaty itself and has direct effect;

(2) Whereas, however, certain of the Directives' provisions designed to facilitate the effective exercise of the right of establishment and freedom to provide services should be retained, particularly where they usefully prescribe how obligations under the Treaty are to be discharged;

(3) Whereas, in order to facilitate the exercise of freedom of establishment and freedom to provide services in respect of a number of activities, Directives introducing transitional measures have been adopted pending mutual recognition of qualifications; whereas those Directives accept the fact that the activity in question has been pursued for a reasonable and sufficiently recent period of time in the Member State from which the national comes as a sufficient qualification for taking up the activities in question in Member States which have rules governing the taking up of such activities;

(4) Whereas the main provisions of the said Directives should be replaced in line with the conclusions of the European Council held in Edinburgh on 11 and 12 December 1992 regarding subsidiarity, simplification of Community legislation and, in particular, the reconsideration by the Commission of the relatively old directives dealing with professional qualifications; whereas the Directives in question should therefore be repealed;

(5) Whereas Council Directive 89/48/EEC of 21 December 1988 on a general system for the recognition of higher-education diplomas awarded on completion of professional education and training of at least three years' duration [4] and Council Directive 92/51/EEC of 18 June 1992 on a second general system for the recognition of professional education and training to supplement Directive 89/48/EEC [5] do not apply to certain professional activities covered by the Directives applying to this subject-matter (Part One of Annex A to this Directive); whereas recognition machinery in respect of qualifications should, therefore, be introduced for those professional activities not covered by Directives 89/48/EEC and 92/51/EEC; whereas the professional activities listed in Part Two of Annex A to this Directive fall for the most part within the scope of Directive 92/51/EEC as far as the recognition of diplomas is concerned;

(6) Whereas a proposal has been transmitted to the Council with a view to amending Directives 89/48/EEC and 92/51/EEC in respect of the proof of financial standing and the proof of an insurance against financial risks that a host Member State may require of the beneficiary; whereas the Council intends to deal with this proposal at a later stage;

(7) Whereas a proposal has been transmitted to the Council with a view to facilitating the free movement of specialised nurses who do not have any of the qualifications listed in Article 3 of Directive 77/452/EEC [6]; whereas the Council intends to deal with this proposal at a later stage;

(8) Whereas this Directive should require regular reports to be drawn up on its implementation;

(9) Whereas this Directive without prejudice to the application of Articles 39(4) and 45 of the Treaty,

---

[1] OJ C 115, 19.4.1996, p. 16 and
OJ C 264, 30.8.1997, p. 5.
[2] OJ C 295, 7.10.1996, p. 43.
[3] Opinion of the European Parliament of 20 February 1997 (OJ C 85, 17.3.1997, p. 114), Common Position of the Council of 29 June 1998 (OJ C 262, 19.8.1998, p. 12), Decision of the European Parliament of 8 October 1998 (OJ C 328, 26.10.1998, p. 156). Decision of the European Parliament of 7 May 1999 and Council Decision of 11 May 1999.
[4] OJ L 19, 24.1.1989, p. 16.
[5] OJ L 209, 24.7.1992, p. 25. Directive as last amended by Commission Directive 97/38/EC (OJ L 184, 12.7.1997, p. 31).
[6] Council Directive 77/452/EEC of 27 June 1977 concerning the mutual recognition of diplomas, certificates and other evidence of the formal qualifications of nurses responsible for general care, including measures to facilitate the effective exercise of this right of establishment and freedom to provide services (OJ L 176, 15.7.1977, p. 1). Directive as last amended by Directive 90/658/EC (OJ L 353, 17.12.1990, p. 73).

HAVE ADOPTED THIS DIRECTIVE:

TITLE I

Scope

Article 1

1. Member States shall adopt the measures defined in this Directive in respect of establishment or provision of services in their territories by natural persons and companies or firms covered by Title I of the General Programmes for the abolition of restrictions on freedom to supply services [1] and on freedom of establishment [2] (hereinafter called 'beneficiaries') who wish to pursue the activities listed in Annex A.

2. This Directive shall apply to the activities listed in Annex A which nationals of Member States wish to pursue in a host Member State in a self-employed or employed capacity.

Article 2

Member States in which the taking-up or pursuit of any activity referred to in Annex A is subject to possession of certain qualifications shall ensure that any beneficiaries who apply therefor be provided, before they establish themselves or before they begin to provide services, with information as to the rules governing the occupation which they propose to pursue.

TITLE II

Recognition of formal qualifications awarded by another Member State

Article 3

1. Without prejudice to Article 4, a Member State may not, on the grounds of inadequate qualifications, refuse to permit a national of another Member State to take up or pursue any of the activities listed in Part One of Annex A on the same conditions as apply to its own nationals, without having first compared the knowledge and skills certified by the diplomas, certificates or other evidence of formal qualifications obtained by the beneficiary with a view to pursuing the same activity elsewhere in the Community with those required under its own national rules. Where the comparative examination shows that the knowledge and skills certified by a diploma, certificate or other evidence of formal qualifications awarded by another Member State correspond to those required by the national rules, the host Member State cannot refuse the holder the right to pursue the activity in question. Where, however, the comparative examination shows a substantial difference, the host Member State shall give the beneficiary the opportunity to demonstrate that he has acquired the knowledge and skills which were lacking. In this case, the host Member State shall give the applicant the right to choose between an adaptation period and an aptitude test by analogy with Directives 89/48/EEC and 92/51/EEC.

[1] OJ 2, 15.1.1962, p. 32/62.
[2] OJ 2, 15.1.1962, p. 36/62.

By way of derogation from this rule, the host Member State may require an adaptation period or an aptitude test if the migrant envisages exercising professional activities in a self-employed capacity or as a manager of an undertaking which are covered by Part One of Annex A and which require the knowledge and the application of the specific national rules in force, provided that knowledge and application of those rules are required by the competent authorities of the host Member State for access to such activities by its own nationals.

Member States shall endeavour to take into consideration the beneficiary's preference as between those alternatives.

2. Applications for recognition within the meaning of paragraph 1 shall be examined within the shortest possible time, and the competent authority in the host Member State shall state its reasons when giving a decision, which shall be taken no later than four months from the date on which the application and comprehensive supporting documentation were submitted. There shall be a right to appeal under national law against a decision or against the absence of such decision.

TITLE III

Recognition of professional qualifications on the basis of professional experience acquired in another Member State

Article 4

Where, in a Member State, the taking-up or pursuit of any activity listed in Annex A is subject to possession of general, commercial or professional knowledge and ability, that Member State shall accept as sufficient evidence of such knowledge and ability the fact that the activity in question has been pursued in another Member State. Where the activity is mentioned in Part One of Annex A, it must have been pursued:

1. in the case of the activities in List I:

   (a) for six consecutive years in either a self-employed capacity or as a manager of an undertaking; or

   (b) for three consecutive years in a self-employed capacity or as a manager of an undertaking where the beneficiary proves that he has received at least three years' prior training for the activity in question, attested by a nationally recognised certificate or regarded by a competent professional or trade body as fully satisfying its requirements; or

   (c) for three consecutive years in a self-employed capacity where the beneficiary proves that he has pursued the activity in question for at least five years in an employed capacity; or

   (d) for five consecutive years in a managerial capacity of which at least three years were spent in technical posts with responsibility for one or more departments of the undertaking where the beneficiary proves that he has received at least three years' prior training for the activity in question, attested by a nationally recognised certificate or regarded by a competent professional or trade body as fully satisfying its requirements.

In the cases referred to in (a) and (c), pursuit of the activity shall not have ceased more than ten years before the date on which the application under Article 8 is made;

2. in the case of the activities in List II:

   (a) for six consecutive years in either a self-employed capacity or as a manager of an undertaking; or

   (b) — for three consecutive years in a self-employed capacity or as a manager of an undertaking where the beneficiary proves that he has received at least three years' prior training for the activity in question, attested by a nationally recognised certificate or regarded by a competent professional or trade body as fully satisfying its requirements, or

   — for four consecutive years in a self-employed capacity or as a manager of an undertaking where the beneficiary proves that he has received at least two years' prior training for the activity in question, attested by a nationally recognised certificate or regarded by a competent professional or trade body as fully satisfying its requirements, or

   (c) for three consecutive years in a self-employed capacity or as a manager of an undertaking where the beneficiary proves that he has pursued the activity in question for at least five years in an employed capacity; or

   (d) — for five consecutive years in an employed capacity where the beneficiary proves that he has received at least three years' prior training for the activity in question, attested by a nationally recognised certificate or regarded by a competent professional or trade body as fully satisfying its requirements, or

   — for six consecutive years in an employed capacity where the beneficiary proves that he has received at least two years' prior training for the activity in question, attested by a nationally recognised certificate or regarded by a competent professional or trade body as fully satisfying its requirements.

In the cases referred to in (a) and (c), pursuit of the activity shall not have ceased more than ten years before the date on which the application provided for in Article 8 is made;

3. in the case of the activities in List III:

   (a) for six consecutive years in either a self-employed capacity or as a manager of an undertaking; or

   (b) for three consecutive years in a self-employed capacity or as a manager of an undertaking, where the beneficiary proves that he has received at least three years' prior training for the activity in question, attested by a nationally recognised certificate or regarded by a competent professional or trade body as fully satisfying its requirements; or

   (c) for three consecutive years in a self-employed capacity where the beneficiary proves that he has pursued the activity in question for at least five years in an employed capacity.

In the cases referred to in (a) and (c), pursuit of the activity shall not have ceased more than ten years before the date on which the application provided for in Article 8 is made;

4. in the case of the activities in List IV:

   (a) for five consecutive years in either a self-employed capacity or as a manager of an undertaking; or

   (b) for two consecutive years in a self-employed capacity or as a manager of an undertaking where the beneficiary proves that he has received at least three years' prior training for the activity in question, attested by a nationally recognised certificate or regarded by a competent professional or trade body as fully satisfying its requirements; or

   (c) for three consecutive years in a self-employed capacity or as a manager of an undertaking where the beneficiary proves that he has received at least two years' prior training for the activity in question, attested by a nationally recognised certificate or regarded by a competent professional or trade body as fully satisfying its requirements; or

   (d) for two consecutive years in a self-employed capacity or as a manager of an undertaking where the beneficiary proves that he has pursued the activity in question for at least three years in an employed capacity; or

   (e) for three consecutive years in an employed capacity where the beneficiary proves that he has received at least two years' previous training for the activity in question, attested by a nationally recognised certificate or regarded by a competent professional or trade body as fully satisfying its requirements;

5. in the case of the activities in List V(a) and (b):

   (a) for three years in a self-employed capacity or as a manager of an undertaking, provided that pursuit of the activity in question did not cease more than two years before the date on which the application provided for in Article 8 is made;

   (b) for three years in a self-employed capacity or as a manager of an undertaking, provided that pursuit of the activity in question did not cease more than two years before the date on which the application provided for in Article 8 is made, unless the host Member State permits its nationals to interrupt their pursuit of that activity for a longer period; or

6. in the case of the activities in List VI:

   (a) for three consecutive years in either a self-employed capacity or as a manager of an undertaking; or

   (b) for two consecutive years in a self-employed capacity or as a manager of an undertaking where the beneficiary proves that he has received prior training for the activity in question, attested by a nationally recognised certificate or regarded by a competent professional or trade body as fully satisfying its requirements; or

(c) for two consecutive years in a self-employed capacity or as a manager of an undertaking where the beneficiary proves that he has pursued the activity in question for at least three years in an employed capacity; or

(d) for three consecutive years in an employed capacity where the beneficiary proves that he has received previous training for the activity in question, attested by a nationally recognised certificate or regarded by a competent professional or trade body as fully satisfying its requirements.

In the cases referred to in (a) and (c), pursuit of the activity shall not have ceased more than 10 years before the date on which the application provided for in Article 8 is made.

Article 5

Where a beneficiary holds a nationally recognised certificate obtained in a Member State attesting to knowledge of and ability in the activity in question equivalent to at least two or three years, as appropriate, of professional training, that certificate may be treated by the host Member State in the same way as a certificate attesting to training of the duration required by Article 4(1)(b) and (d), (2)(b) and (d), (3)(b) and (4)(b), (c) and (e).

Article 6

Where the duration of the training of the beneficiary is at least two years and less than three years, the requirements of Article 4 shall be satisfied if the duration of professional experience in a self-employed capacity or as a manager specified in Article 4(1)(b) and (d), (2)(b), first indent, (3)(b) and (4)(b) or in an employed capacity specified in Article 4(2)(d), first indent is extended in the same proportion to cover the difference in the duration of the training.

Article 7

A person shall be regarded as having pursued an activity as a manager of an undertaking within the meaning of Article 4 if he has pursued such an activity in an undertaking in the occupational field in question:

(a) as a manager of an undertaking or a manager of a branch of an undertaking; or

(b) as a deputy to the proprietor or the manager of an undertaking where that post involves responsibility equivalent to that of the proprietor or manager represented; or

(c) in a managerial post with duties of a commercial and/or technical nature and with responsibility for one or more departments of the undertaking.

Article 8

Proof that the conditions laid down in Article 4 are satisfied shall be established by a certificate concerning the nature and duration of the activity issued by the competent authority or body in the home Member State or in the Member State from where the beneficiary comes which the beneficiary must submit in support of his application for authorisation to pursue the activity or activities in question in the host Member State.

TITLE IV

Recognition of other professional qualifications obtained in another Member State

Article 9

1. Where a host Member State requires its own nationals wishing to take up any activity referred to in Article 1(2) to furnish proof of good character and proof that they are not and have not previously been declared bankrupt, or proof of either of these, it shall accept as sufficient evidence, in respect of nationals of other Member States, the production of an extract from the 'judicial record' or, failing this, of an equivalent document issued by a competent judicial or administrative authority in the home Member State or in the Member State from where the beneficiary comes showing that these requirements are satisfied.

2. Where a host Member State imposes on its own nationals wishing to take up any activity referred to in Article 1(2) certain requirements as to good character and requires them to prove that they are not and have not previously been declared bankrupt and have not previously been the subject of professional or administrative disciplinary measures (for example, withdrawal of the right to hold certain offices, suspension from practice or striking-off), but proof cannot be obtained from the document referred to in paragraph 1 of this Article, it shall accept as sufficient evidence in respect of nationals of other Member States a certificate issued by a competent judicial or administrative authority in the home Member State or in the Member State from where the beneficiary comes attesting that the requirements are satisfied. Such certificate shall relate to the specific facts regarded as relevant by the host Member State.

3. Where the home Member State or the Member State from where the beneficiary comes does not issue the documents referred to in paragraphs 1 and 2, such documents shall be replaced by a declaration on oath — or, in those Member States where there is no provision for such declaration on oath, by a solemn declaration — made by the person concerned before a competent judicial or administrative authority or, where appropriate, a notary in that Member State; such authority or notary shall issue a certificate attesting the authenticity of the declaration on oath or solemn declaration. The declaration of no previous bankruptcy may also be made before a competent professional or trade body in that Member State.

4. Where a host Member State requires proof of financial standing, it shall regard certificates issued by banks in the home Member State or in the Member State from where the beneficiary comes as equivalent to those issued in its own territory.

5. Where a host Member State requires its own nationals wishing to take up or pursue any activity referred to in Article 1(2) to furnish proof that they are insured against the financial risks arising from their professional liability, it shall accept certificates issued by the insurance undertakings of other Member States as equivalent to those issued in its own territory. Such certificates shall state that the insurer has complied with the laws and regulations in force in the host Member State regarding the terms and extent of cover.

6. At the time of their production, the documents referred to in paragraphs 1, 2, 3 and 5 may not date from more than three months after their date of issue.

TITLE V

Procedural provisions

Article 10

1. Member States shall designate, within the period stipulated in Article 14, the authorities and bodies responsible for issuing the certificates referred to in Articles 8 and 9(1), (2) and (3) and shall communicate this information forthwith to the other Member States and to the Commission.

2. Each Member State may nominate a coordinator for the activities of the authorities and bodies referred to in paragraph 1 to the coordinating group set up under Article 9(2) of Directive 89/48/EEC. The tasks of the coordinating group shall also be as follows:
— facilitating the implementation of this Directive;
— collecting all useful information for its application in the Member States and especially gathering and comparing information on the different professional qualifications in the areas of activity falling within the scope of this Directive.

TITLE VI

Final provisions

Article 11

1. The Directives listed in Annex B are hereby repealed.

2. References to the repealed Directives shall be construed as references to this Directive.

Article 12

As from 1 January 2001, Member States shall communicate to the Commission every two years a report on the application of the system introduced.

In addition to general remarks, that report shall contain a statistical summary of the decisions taken and a description of the main problems arising from the application of this Directive.

Article 13

Not later than five years after the date referred to in Article 14, the Commission shall report to the European Parliament and the Council on the state of application of this Directive, and in particular of Article 5, in the Member States.

After undertaking all the necessary hearings, especially of the coordinators, the Commission shall submit its conclusions regarding any changes to the existing arrangement. If necessary, the Commission shall also submit proposals for improving the existing arrangements with the aim of facilitating free movement of persons, the right of establishment and freedom to provide services.

Article 14

1. Member States shall bring into force the laws, regulations and administrative provisions necessary to comply with this Directive before 31 July 2001. They shall immediately inform the Commission thereof.

When Member States adopt these measures, they shall contain a reference to this Directive or shall be accompanied by such reference on the occasion of their official publication. The methods of making such a reference shall be laid down by the Member States.

2. Member States shall communicate to the Commission the text of the main provisions of national law which they adopt in the field covered by this Directive.

Article 15

This Directive shall enter into force on the day of its publication in the *Official Journal of the European Communities*.

Article 16

This Directive is addressed to the Member States.

Done at Luxembourg, 7 June 1999.

For the European Parliament	*For the Council*
The President	*The President*
J. M. GIL-ROBLES	E. BULMAHN

ANNEX A

PART ONE

Activities related to categories of professional experience

List I

Major Groups covered by Directive 64/427/EEC, as amended by Directive 69/77/EEC, and by Directives 68/366/EEC, 75/368/EEC and 75/369/EEC

1

Directive 64/427/EEC

(liberalisation Directive: 64/429/EEC)

NICE Nomenclature (corresponding to ISIC Major Groups 23-40)

Major Group 23		Manufacture of textiles
	232	Manufacturing and processing of textile materials on woollen machinery
	233	Manufacturing and processing of textile materials on cotton machinery
	234	Manufacturing and processing of textile materials on silk machinery
	235	Manufacturing and processing of textile materials on flax and hemp machinery
	236	Other textile fibre industries (jute, hard fibres, etc.) cordage
	237	Manufacture of knitted and crocheted goods
	238	Textile finishing
	239	Other textile industries
Major Group 24		Manufacture of footwear, other wearing apparel and bedding
	241	Machine manufacture of footwear (except from rubber or wood)
	242	Manufacture by hand and repair of footwear
	243	Manufacture of wearing apparel (except furs)
	244	Manufacture of mattresses and bedding
	245	Skin and fur industries
Major Group 25		Manufacture of wood and cork, except manufacture of furniture
	251	Sawing and industrial preparation of wood
	252	Manufacture of semi-finished wood products
	253	Series production of wooden building components including flooring
	254	Manufacture of wooden containers
	255	Manufacture of other wooden products (except furniture)
	259	Manufacture of straw, cork, basketware, wicker-work and rattan products; brush-making
Major Group 26	260	Manufacture of wooden furniture
Major Group 27		Manufacture of paper and paper products
	271	Manufacture of pulp, paper and paperboard
	272	Processing of paper and paperboard, and manufacture of articles of pulp
Major Group 28	280	Printing, publishing and allied industries
Major Group 29		Leather industry
	291	Tanneries and leather finishing plants
	292	Manufacture of leather products

ex Major Group 30		Manufacture of rubber and plastic products, man-made fibres and starch products
	301	Processing of rubber and asbestos
	302	Processing of plastic materials
	303	Production of man-made fibres
ex Major Group 31		Chemical industry
	311	Manufacture of chemical base materials and further processing of such materials
	312	Specialised manufacture of chemical products principally for industrial and agricultural purposes (including the manufacture for industrial use of fats and oils of vegetable or animal origin falling within ISIC Group 312)
	313	Specialised manufacture of chemical products principally for domestic or office use (excluding the manufacture of medicinal and pharmaceutical products (ISIC ex Group 319)
Major Group 32	320	Petroleum industry
Major Group 33		Manufacture of non-metallic mineral products
	331	Manufacture of structural clay products
	332	Manufacture of glass and glass products
	333	Manufacture of ceramic products, including refractory goods
	334	Manufacture of cement, lime and plaster
	335	Manufacture of structural materials, in concrete, cement and plaster
	339	Stone working and manufacture of other non-metallic mineral products
Major Group 34		Production and primary transformation of ferrous and non-ferrous metals
	341	Iron and steel industry (as defined in the ECSC Treaty, including integrated steelworks-owned coking plants)
	342	Manufacture of steel tubes
	343	Wire-drawing, cold-drawing, cold-rolling of strip, cold-forming
	344	Production and primary transformation of non-ferrous metals
	345	Ferrous and non-ferrous metal foundries
Major Group 35		Manufacture of metal products (except machinery and transport equipment)
	351	Forging, heavy stamping and heavy pressing
	352	Secondary transformation and surface-treatment
	353	Metal structures
	354	Boilermaking, manufacture of industrial hollow-ware
	355	Manufacture of tools and implements and finished articles of metal (except electrical equipment)
	359	Ancillary mechanical engineering activities
Major Group 36		Manufacture of machinery other than electrical machinery
	361	Manufacture of agricultural machinery and tractors
	362	Manufacture of office machinery
	363	Manufacture of metal-working and other machine-tools and fixtures and attachments for these and for other powered tools
	364	Manufacture of textile machinery and accessories, manufacture of sewing machines
	365	Manufacture of machinery and equipment for the food-manufacturing and beverage industries and for the chemical and allied industries
	366	Manufacture of plant and equipment for mines, iron and steel works foundries, and for the construction industry; manufacture of mechanical handling equipment
	367	Manufacture of transmission equipment
	368	Manufacture of machinery for other specific industrial purposes
	369	Manufacture of other non-electrical machinery and equipment

Major Group 37		Electrical engineering
	371	Manufacture of electric wiring and cables
	372	Manufacture of motors, generators, transformers, switch gear, and other similar equipment for the provision of electric power
	373	Manufacture of electrical equipment for direct commercial use
	374	Manufacture of telecommunications equipment, meters, other measuring appliances and electromedical equipment
	375	Manufacture of electronic equipment, radio and television receivers, audio equipment
	376	Manufacture of electric appliances for domestic use
	377	Manufacture of lamps and lighting equipment
	378	Manufacture of batteries and accumulators
	379	Repair, assembly and specialist installation of electrical equipment
ex Major Group 38		Manufacture of transport equipment
	383	Manufacture of motor vehicles and parts thereof
	384	Repair of motor vehicles, motorcycles and cycles
	385	Manufacture of motorcycles, cycles and parts thereof
	389	Manufacture of transport equipment not elsewhere classified
Major Group 39		Miscellaneous manufacturing industries
	391	Manufacture of precision instruments and measuring and controlling instruments
	392	Manufacture of medico-surgical instruments and equipment and orthopaedic appliances (except orthopaedic footwear)
	393	Manufacture of photographic and optical equipment
	394	Manufacture and repair of watches and clocks
	395	Jewellery and precious metal manufacturing
	396	Manufacture and repair of musical instruments
	397	Manufacture of games, toys, sporting and athletic goods
	399	Other manufacturing industries
Major Group 40		Construction
	400	Construction (non-specialised); demolition
	401	Construction of buildings (dwellings or other)
	402	Civil engineering; building of roads, bridges, railways, etc.
	403	Installation work
	404	Decorating and finishing

2

Directive 68/366/EEC

(liberalisation Directive 68/365/EEC)

NICE Nomenclature

Major Group 20 A	200	Industries producing animal and vegetable fats and oils
20 B		Food manufacturing industries (excluding the beverage industry)
	201	Slaughtering, preparation and preserving of meat
	202	Milk and milk products industry
	203	Canning and preserving of fruits and vegetables
	204	Canning and preserving of fish and other sea foods
	205	Manufacture of grain mill products
	206	Manufacture of bakery products, including rusks and biscuits
	207	Sugar industry
	208	Manufacture of cocoa, chocolate and sugar confectionery
	209	Manufacture of miscellaneous food products

Major Group 21		Beverage industry
	211	Production of ethyl alcohol by fermentation, production of yeast and spirits
	212	Production of wine and other unmalted alcoholic beverages
	213	Brewing and malting
	214	Soft drinks and carbonated water industries
ex 30		Manufacture of rubber products, plastic materials, artificial and synthetic fibres and starch products
	304	Manufacture of starch products

3

Directive 75/368/EEC (activities listed in Article 5(1))

ISIC Nomenclature

ex 04		Fishing
	043	Inland water fishing
ex 38		Manufacture of transport equipment
	381	Shipbuilding and repairing
	382	Manufacture of railroad equipment
	386	Manufacture of aircraft (including space equipment)
ex 71		Activities allied to transport and activities other than transport coming under the following groups:
	ex 711	Sleeping- and dining-car services; maintenance of railway stock in repair sheds; cleaning of carriages
	ex 712	Maintenance of stock for urban, suburban and interurban passenger transport
	ex 713	Maintenance of stock for other passenger land transport (such as motor cars, coaches, taxis)
	ex 714	Operation and maintenance of services in support of road transport (such as roads, tunnels and toll-bridges, goods depots, car parks, bus and tram depots)
	ex 716	Activities allied to inland water transport (such as operation and maintenance of waterways, ports and other installations for inland water transport; tug and piloting services in ports, setting of buoys, loading and unloading of vessels and other similar activities, such as salvaging of vessels, towing and the operation of boathouses)
73		Communication: postal services and telecommunications
ex 85		Personal services
	854	Laundries and laundry services, dry-cleaning and dyeing
	ex 856	Photographic studios: portrait and commercial photography, except journalistic photographers
	ex 859	Personal services not elsewhere classified (maintenance and cleaning of buildings or accommodation only)

4

Directive 75/369/EEC (Article 6: where the activity is regarded as being of an industrial or small-craft nature)

ISIC Nomenclature

The following itinerant activities:

(a) the buying and selling of goods:

— by itinerant tradesmen, hawkers or pedlars (ex ISIC Group 612);

— in covered markets other than from permanently fixed installations and in open-air markets;

(b) activities covered by transitional measures already adopted that expressly exclude or do not mention the pursuit of such activities on an itinerant basis.

List II

Directive 82/470/EEC (Article 6(3))

Groups 718 and 720 of the ISIC Nomenclature

The activities comprise in particular:

— organizing, offering for sale and selling, outright or on commission, single or collective items (transport, board, lodging, excursions, etc.) for a journey or stay, whatever the reasons for travelling (Article 2(B)(a)).

List III

Directive 82/489/EEC

ex 855 Hairdressing, excluding services of chiropodists and professional beauticians' and hairdressers' training schools

List IV

Directive 82/470/EEC (Article 6(1))

Groups 718 and 720 of the ISIC Nomenclature:

The activities comprise in particular:

— acting as an intermediary between contractors for various methods of transport and persons who dispatch or receive goods, and carrying out related activities:

   (aa) by concluding contracts with transport contractors, on behalf of principals;

   (bb) by choosing the method of transport, the firm and the route considered most profitable for the principal;

   (cc) by arranging the technical aspects of the transport operation (e.g. packing required for transportation); by carrying out various operations incidental to transport (e.g. ensuring ice supplies for refrigerated wagons);

   (dd) by completing the formalities connected with the transport such as the drafting of way bills; by assembling and dispersing shipments;

   (ee) by coordinating the various stages of transportation, by ensuring transit, reshipment, transshipment and other termination operations;

   (ff) by arranging both freight and carriers and means of transport for persons dispatching goods or receiving them;

— assessing transport costs and checking the detailed accounts;

— taking certain temporary or permanent measures in the name of and on behalf of a shipowner or sea transport carrier (with the port authorities, ship's chandlers, etc.)

(The activities listed under Article 2(A)(a), (b) and (d)).

List V

Directives (64/222/EEC) and (70/523/EEC)

(a)

See Article 4(5)(a) of this Directive

Directive 64/222/EEC

(liberalisation Directive 64/224/EEC)

1. professional activities of an intermediary who is empowered and instructed by one or more persons to negotiate or enter into commercial transactions in the name of and on behalf of those persons;

2. professional activities of an intermediary who, while not being permanently so instructed, brings together persons wishing to contract directly with one another or arranges their commercial transactions or assists in the completion thereof;

3. professional activities of an intermediary who enters into commercial transactions in his own name on behalf of others;

4. professional activities of an intermediary who carries out wholesale selling by auction on behalf of others;

5. professional activities of an intermediary who goes from door to door seeking orders;

6. provision of services, by way of professional activities, by an intermediary in the employment of one or more commercial, industrial or small craft undertakings.

(b)

See Article 4(5)(b) of this Directive

Directive 70/523/EEC

Activities of self-employed persons in the wholesale coal trade and activities of intermediaries in the coal trade (ex Group 6112, ISIC Nomenclature)

List VI

Directives 68/364/EEC, 68/368/EEC, 75/368/EEC, 75/369/EEC, 82/470/EEC

1

Directive 68/364/EEC

(liberalisation Directive 68/363/EEC)

ISIC ex Group 612 Retail trade

Excluded activities:

012	Letting-out for hire of farm machinery
640	Real estate, letting of property
713	Letting-out for hire of automobiles, carriages and horses
718	Letting-out for hire of railway carriages and wagons
839	Renting of machinery to commercial undertakings
841	Booking of cinema seats and renting of cinematograph films
842	Booking of theatre seats and renting of theatrical equipment
843	Letting-out for hire of boats, bicycles, coin-operated machines for games of skill or chance
853	Letting of furnished rooms
854	Laundered linen hire
859	Garment hire

2

Directive 68/368/EEC

(liberalisation Directive 68/367/EEC)

ISIC Nomenclature

ISIC ex Major Group 85:

1. Restaurants, cafes, taverns and other drinking and eating places (ISIC Group 852)

2. Hotels, rooming houses, camps and other lodging places (ISIC Group 853)

3

Directive 75/368/EEC (Article 7)

All the activities listed in the Annex to Directive 75/368/EEC, except those referred to in Article 5 of that Directive (List I, No 3 of this Annex).

ISIC Nomenclature

ex 62	Banks and other financial institutions	
	ex 620	Patent buying and licensing companies
ex 71	Transport	
	ex 713	Road passenger transport, excluding transportation by means of motor vehicles
	ex 719	Transportation by pipelines of liquid hydrocarbons and other liquid chemical products
ex 82	Community services	
	827	Libraries, museums, botanical and zoological gardens
ex 84	Recreation services	
	843	Recreation services not elsewhere classified:

— sporting activities (sports grounds, organising sporting fixtures, etc.), except the activities of sports instructors

— games (racing stables, areas for games, racecourses, etc.)

— other recreational activities (circuses, amusement parks and other entertainments)

ex 85	Personal services	
	ex 851	Domestic services
	ex 855	Beauty parlours and services of manicurists, excluding services of chiropodists and professional beauticians' and hairdressers' training schools
	ex 859	Personal services not elsewhere classified, except sports and paramedical masseurs and mountain guides, divided into the following groups

— disinfecting and pest control

— hiring of clothes and storage facilities

— marriage bureaux and similar services

— astrology, fortune-telling and the like

— sanitary services and associated activities

— undertaking and cemetery maintenance

— couriers and interpreter-guides

4

Directive 75/369/EEC (Article 5)

The following itinerant activities:

(a) the buying and selling of goods:

— by itinerant tradesmen, hawkers or pedlars (ex ISIC Group 612);

— in covered markets other than from permanently fixed installations and in open-air markets;

(b) activities covered by transitional measures already adopted that expressly exclude or do not mention the pursuit of such activities on an itinerant basis.

5

Directive 82/470/EEC (Article 6(2))

(Activities listed in Article 2(A)(c) and (e), (B)(b), (C) and (D))

These activities comprise in particular:

— hiring railway cars or wagons for transporting persons or goods;

— acting as an intermediary in the sale, purchase or hiring of ships;

- arranging, negotiating and concluding contracts for the transport of emigrants;
- receiving all objects and goods deposited, on behalf of the depositor, whether under customs control or not, in warehouses, general stores, furniture depots, coldstores, silos, etc.
- supplying the depositor with a receipt for the object or goods deposited;
- providing pens, feed and sales rings for livestock being temporarily accommodated while awaiting sale or while in transit to or from the market;
- carrying out inspection or technical valuation of motor vehicles;
- measuring, weighing and gauging goods.

PART TWO

Activities other than those covered in Part One

1

Directives 63/261/EEC, 63/262/EEC, 65/1/EEC, 67/530/EEC, 67/531/EEC, 67/532/EEC, 68/192/EEC, 68/415/EEC and 71/18/EEC

ISIC Nomenclature

ex Major group 01   Agriculture

In particular:

(a) general agriculture including the growing of field crops and viticulture; growing of fruits, nuts, seeds, vegetables, flowers, both in the open and under glass;

(b) raising of livestock, poultry, rabbits, fur-bearing or other animals, bees; the production of meat, milk, wool, skins and fur, eggs, honey;

(c) agricultural, animal husbandry and horticultural services on a fee or contract basis.

2

Directive 63/607/EEC

(Films)

3

Directive 64/223/EEC

ISIC Nomenclature

ex Group 611   Activities of self-employed persons in wholesale trade (with the exception of wholesale trade in medicinal and pharmaceutical products, in toxic products and pathogens, and in coal).

4

Directive 64/428/EEC

NICE Nomenclature

	Group	
Major 11		Mining and preparation of solid fuels
	111	Mining and preparation of coal
	112	Mining and preparation of lignite
Major 12		Mining of metalliferous ores
	121	Mining of iron ore
	122	Mining of non-ferrous metalliferous ores and related activities
Major ex 13	ex 130	Extraction of petroleum and natural gas (excluding prospecting and drilling)
Major 14	140	Extraction of building materials and fireclays
Major 19	190	Extraction of other minerals and of peat

5

Directive 65/264/EEC

(cinema)

6

Directive 66/162/EEC

ISIC Nomenclature

Division 5   Electricity, gas, steam, water and sanitary services

7

Directive 67/43/EEC

ISIC Nomenclature

ex Group 640   Real estate (excluding 6401)
Group 839   Business services not elsewhere classified (excluding journalism, activities of customs agents, advice on economic, financial, commercial, statistical, and labour and employment matters, debt collection)

8

Directive 67/654/EEC

ISIC Nomenclature

Major Group 02 Forestry and logging
                021   Forestry
                022   Logging

9

Directives 68/369/EEC and 70/451/EEC

ISIC Nomenclature

ex Group 841   Production, distribution and projection of films

10

Directive 69/82/EEC

ISIC Nomenclature

ex Major Group 13

ex 130   Exploration (prospecting and drilling) for petroleum and natural gas

11

Directive 70/522/EEC

ISIC Nomenclature

ex Group 6112 Coal

ANNEX B

REPEALED DIRECTIVES

PART ONE: LIBERALISATION DIRECTIVES

63/261/EEC: Council Directive of 2 April 1963 laying down detailed provisions for the attainment of freedom of establishment in agriculture in the territory of a Member State in respect of nationals of other countries of the Community who have been employed as paid agricultural workers in that Member State for a continuous period of two years

63/262/EEC: Council Directive of 2 April 1963 laying down detailed provisions for the attainment of freedom of establishment on agricultural holdings abandoned or left uncultivated for more than two years

63/607/EEC: Council Directive of 15 October 1963 implementing in respect of the film industry the provisions of the General Programme for the abolition of restrictions on freedom to provide services

64/223/EEC: Council Directive of 25 February 1964 concerning the attainment of freedom of establishment and freedom to provide services in respect of activities in wholesale trade

64/224/EEC: Council Directive of 25 February 1964 concerning the attainment of freedom of establishment and freedom to provide services in respect of activities of intermediaries in commerce, industry and small craft industries

64/428/EEC: Council Directive of 7 July 1964 concerning the attainment of freedom of establishment and freedom to provide services in respect of activities of self-employed persons in mining and quarrying (ISIC Major Groups 11-19)

64/429/EEC: Council Directive of 7 July 1964 concerning the attainment of freedom of establishment and freedom to provide services in respect of activities of self-employed persons in manufacturing and processing industries falling within ISIC Major Groups 23-40 (industry and small craft industries)

65/1/EEC: Council Directive of 14 December 1964 laying down detailed provisions for the attainment of freedom to provide services in agriculture and horticulture

65/264/EEC: Second Council Directive of 13 May 1965 implementing in respect of the film industry the provisions of the General Programmes for the abolition of restrictions on freedom of establishment and freedom to provide services

66/162/EEC: Council Directive of 28 February 1966 concerning the attainment of freedom of establishment and freedom to provide services in respect of activities of self-employed persons engaging in the provision of electricity, gas, water and sanitary services (ISIC Division 5)

67/43/EEC: Council Directive of 12 January 1967 concerning the attainment of freedom of establishment and freedom to provide services in respect of activities of self-employed persons concerned with: 1. Matters of 'real estate' (excluding 6401) (ISIC Group ex 640); 2. The provision of certain 'business services not elsewhere classified' (ISIC Group 839)

67/530/EEC: Council Directive of 25 July 1967 concerning the freedom of nationals of a Member State established as farmers in another Member State to transfer from one holding to another

67/531/EEC: Council Directive of 25 July 1967 concerning the application of the laws of Member States relating to agricultural leases to farmers who are nationals of other Member States

67/532/EEC: Council Directive of 25 July 1967 concerning freedom of access to cooperatives for farmers who are nationals of one Member State and established in another Member State

67/654/EEC: Council Directive of 24 October 1967 laying down detailed provisions for the attainment of freedom of establishment and freedom to provide services in respect of activities of self-employed persons in forestry and logging

68/192/EEC: Council Directive of 5 April 1968 concerning freedom of access to the various forms of credit for farmers who are nationals of one Member State and established in another Member State

68/363/EEC: Council Directive of 15 October 1968 concerning the attainment of freedom of establishment and freedom to provide services in respect of activities of self-employed persons in retail trade (ISIC ex Group 612)

68/365/EEC: Council Directive of 15 October 1968 concerning the attainment of freedom of establishment and freedom to provide services in respect of activities of self-employed persons in the food manufacturing and beverage industries (ISIC Major Groups 20 and 21)

68/367/EEC: Council Directive of 15 October 1968 concerning the attainment of freedom of establishment and freedom to provide services in respect of activities of self-employed persons in the personal services sector (ISIC ex Major Group 85); 1. Restaurants, cafés, taverns and other drinking and eating places (ISIC Group 852); 2. Hotels, rooming houses, camps and other lodging places (ISIC Group 853)

68/369/EEC: Council Directive of 15 October 1968 concerning the attainment of freedom of establishment in respect of activities of self-employed persons in film distribution

68/415/EEC: Council Directive of 20 December 1968 concerning freedom of access to the various forms of aid for farmers who are nationals of one Member State and established in another Member State

69/82/EEC: Council Directive of 13 March 1969 concerning the attainment of freedom of establishment and freedom to provide services in respect of activities of self-employed persons engaging in exploration (prospecting and drilling) for petroleum and natural gas (ISIC ex Major Group 13)

70/451/EEC: Council Directive of 29 September 1970 concerning the attainment of freedom of establishment and freedom to provide services in respect of activities of self-employed persons in film production

70/522/EEC: Council Directive of 30 November 1970 concerning the attainment of freedom of establishment and freedom to provide services in respect of activities of self-employed persons in the wholesale coal trade and activities of intermediaries in the coal trade (ISIC ex Group 6112)

71/18/EEC: Council Directive of 16 December 1970 laying down detailed provisions for the attainment of freedom of establishment in respect of self-employed persons providing agricultural and horticultural services

PART TWO: DIRECTIVES PROVIDING FOR TRANSITIONAL MEASURES

64/222/EEC: Council Directive of 25 February 1964 laying down detailed provisions concerning transitional measures in respect of activities in wholesale trade and activities of intermediaries in commerce, industry and small craft industries

64/427/EEC: Council Directive of 7 July 1964 laying down detailed provisions concerning transitional measures in respect of activities of self-employed persons in manufacturing and processing industries falling within ISIC Major Groups 23-40 (Industry and small craft industries), as amended by Council Directive 69/77/EEC of 4 March 1969

68/364/EEC: Council Directive of 15 October 1968 laying down detailed provisions concerning transitional measures in respect of activities of self-employed persons in retail trade (ISIC ex Group 612)

68/366/EEC:	Council Directive of 15 October 1968 laying down detailed provisions concerning transitional measures in respect of activities of self-employed persons in the food manufacturing and beverage industries (ISIC Major Groups 20 and 21)
68/368/EEC:	Council Directive of 15 October 1968 laying down detailed provisions concerning transitional measures in respect of activities of self-employed persons in the personal services sector (ISIC ex Major Group 85); 1. Restaurants, cafes, taverns and other drinking and eating places (ISIC Group 852); 2. Hotels, rooming houses, camps and other lodging places (ISIC Group 853)
70/523/EEC:	Council Directive of 30 November 1970 laying down detailed provisions concerning transitional measures in respect of activities of self-employed persons in the wholesale coal trade and in respect of activities of intermediaries in the coal trade (ISIC ex group 6112)
75/368/EEC:	Council Directive of 16 June 1975 on measures to facilitate the effective exercise of freedom of establishment and freedom to provide services in respect of various activities (ex ISIC Division 01 to 85) and, in particular, transitional measures in respect of those activities
75/369/EEC:	Council Directive of 16 June 1975 on measures to facilitate the effective exercise of freedom of establishment and freedom to provide services in respect of itinerant activities and, in particular, transitional measures in respect of those activities
82/470/EEC:	Council Directive of 29 June 1982 on measures to facilitate the effective exercise of freedom of establishment and freedom to provide services in respect of activities of self-employed persons in certain services incidental to transport and travel agencies (ISIC Group 718) and in storage and warehousing (ISIC Group 720)
82/489/EEC:	Council Directive of 19 July 1982 laying down measures to facilitate the effective exercise of the right of establishment and freedom to provide services in hairdressing

**Council Resolution
of 21 June 1999
concerning a handbook for international police cooperation and measures
to prevent and control violence and disturbances in connection
with international football matches**

(OJ C 196, 13.7.1999)

(Acts adopted pursuant to Title VI of the Treaty on European Union)

COUNCIL RESOLUTION

of 21 June 1999

concerning a handbook for international police cooperation and measures to prevent and control violence and disturbances in connection with international football matches

(1999/C 196/01)

THE COUNCIL OF THE EUROPEAN UNION,

Whereas:

(1) the European Union's objective is, *inter alia*, to provide citizens with a high level of safety within an area of freedom, security and justice by developing common action among the Member States in the field of police cooperation;

(2) on 9 June 1997 the Council adopted a resolution on preventing and restraining football hooliganism through the exchange of experience, exclusion from stadiums and media policy [1];

(3) in the framework of the Council of Europe, the Convention of 19 August 1985 has been concluded on spectator violence and misbehaviour at sports events and in particular at football matches;

(4) it is necessary to make further efforts to control football hooliganism on the basis of experience in recent years, in particular at the 1996 European Football Championships and the 1998 World Cup Football Championships, and the findings of the evaluation of previous measures made by police experts at the Netherlands' instigation;

(5) it is of the utmost importance to establish a European framework for police forces in the Member States as regards the content and scope of police cooperation, police relations with the media, cooperation with those supervising fans and stadium admission policy;

(6) there is a considerable need to set down the European framework referred to above in a handbook for police forces;

(7) without prejudice to existing national provisions and to the exercise by the European Commission of its powers under the Treaty establishing the European Community,

HAS ADOPTED THIS RESOLUTION:

1. The Council requests Member States to step up cooperation, in particular practical cooperation between police forces, in order to prevent and control violence and disturbances in connection with international football matches.

2. To that end, the annexed handbook is hereby made available, as examples of working methods, to police forces. The relevant Council working party is requested to propose amendments to this handbook in future, as necessary, in the light of up-to-date experience.

---

[1] OJ C 193, 24.6.1997, p. 1.

ANNEX

Handbook for international police cooperation and measures to prevent and control violence and disturbances in connection with international football matches, in which at least one Member State is involved either by participation in the match and/or by hosting the match

Contents of the handbook:

1. Preparations by police forces

   Organising authorities and police forces should involve police forces from participating countries in preparations, at an early stage.

2. Organising cooperation between police forces

   Organising authorities and police forces should take into account requirements for the organisation of international police cooperation.

3. Information management by police forces

   Organising authorities and police forces should take into account the requirements of police information management.

4. Cooperation between police forces and stewards

   Organising authorities and police forces should bring in those supervising fans from participating football associations to assist in the job to be done and establish maximum cooperation with them.

5. Checklist for media policy and communication strategy (police/authorities) relating to major (international) championships and matches

   Police forces should make use of the media policy checklist.

6. Requirements for admission policy and ticketing policy

   Organising authorities should take into account the set of requirements for organisers in the area of admission policy, in particular in ticketing policy, ticket control and separation of rival groups of fans.

7. List of documents previously adopted by the Council of the European Union

   A list of decisions previously taken by the Council will give an idea of the measures taken hitherto.

CHAPTER 1

Preparations by police forces

— The formal request for support should come from the Minister responsible in the organising country, who will receive advice from the police forces concerned. Taking into account the specific aims of cooperation, the request should mention the scale and composition of support,

— The request for support should be made to the foreign police force well in advance of a championship and/or match. The supporting foreign police team will require at least eight weeks' preparation time,

— The police forces of organising countries should only request foreign police support from countries that can contribute added value,

— International police cooperation is geared to ensuring the safety of the event, with the following specific aims:

   1. intelligence gathering;

   2. reconnaissance;

   3. spotting;

   4. crowd control under police supervision,

— The police forces from the supporting countries are responsible for providing an advance risk analysis, including profile descriptions of visiting fans and a description of the prototype risk fan from their countries. The reports will be continually updated. The national football hooliganism contacts in the various countries will coordinate the provision of information to the police force of the organising country,

— In the first instance, a risk analysis of the fan group from the country concerned will determine which of the four areas of police cooperation mentioned in the fourth indent is to be requested by the police force of the organising country,

— The foreign police force will indicate the extent to which it can meet the request to provide support for the police force of the organising country. The scale of the foreign police team will then be determined in consultation,

— The size of the police team will therefore not be the same for all countries, but will relate to some extent to the threat and risk posed by fans from the country concerned and to practicalities,

— Depending on the nature of the support to be provided and the size of the team, a foreign police team could be responsible for the following duties:

   1. operational police officers with reconnaissance, spotting or escorting duties;

   2. an operations coordinator with the task of coordinating the work of the operational police officers and channelling information;

   3. a spokesman;

   4. a liaison officer responsible in particular for the exchange of information between that officer's home country and the host country. In view of the differing expertise involved in the areas of public order, violent football hooliganism and terrorism, the national liaison officer could propose that the host country agree to the stationing of a second liaison officer at the host country's coordination centre;

   5. a leader, who is functionally and hierarchically in charge of a team; if, however, there is a national police coordination centre, the leader is only the liaison officer's hierarchical superior; functional responsibility for the liaison officer then rests with the head of the coordination centre,

— The police force(s) in the organising country should provide an opportunity for the supporting foreign police force(s) to acquaint themselves with the organisation of police operations in the host country and/or the venue town(s) and with stadium location, as well as to get to know the operational commander(s) at the venue town(s) on the match day(s).

CHAPTER 2

Organising cooperation between police forces

— The quality of action by the police in a host country will be improved if they obtain police support from the countries from which violent supporters come,

— Maximum use should be made of the support that foreign police forces can supply, which will thus form part of the host police organisation's tactical plan,

— The leader of the police team from the supporting country will, if desired, have his own spokesman. The leader of the police team will determine the position of that spokesman,

— The spokesman assigned to a support team should shield the members of the support team from the media, if appropriate,

— The host police organisation should ensure the physical safety of supporting foreign police officers,

— The police force of the organising country, in consultation with the football organisers, should ensure that the supporting foreign police team has sufficient accreditation (seating not required) to enable the team to carry out its tasks properly in and around the stadiums for matches that involve members of the police team in question,

— The police forces of the country from which the fans come should supervise risk fans from the start of their journey until they reach the country where the match is to be played. Responsibility will be duly transferred between police forces at national borders (including transport and railway police),

— The host police organisation should assign the police team from the supporting country at least one accompanying police officer with sufficient language knowledge and proficiency to maintain operational contact with the team and make reports,

— The police forces of the organising country should have available sufficient interpreters for the languages spoken by fans from visiting countries. This will relieve supporting police teams from the various countries of having to do too much interpreting, which would keep them from actual operational tasks,

— The host police organisation should provide the police team from the supporting country with the necessary communications equipment,

— The police team from the supporting country should consult with the police force of the organising country about the equipment to be brought by the police team and the use made of it.

CHAPTER 3

Information management by police forces

— The police forces of the organising country should ensure that lines of communication and information facilities are clear to supporting foreign police forces, taking into account the nature of information, whether relating to terrorism, individual criminal records (for offenders), public order or violent football hooliganism,

— The police force of the organising country should communicate with the national police force(s) of the participating country or countries throughout the championship and/or match via the liaison officer appointed and supplied by the country in question. The liaison officer can be approached in the areas of public order, violent football hooliganism and terrorism,

— The police force of the organising country should shield the liaison officer of the supporting foreign police force from any contact with the media, if the liaison officer so wishes,

— The liaison officer should be stationed at the national coordination centre for championships spread over a number of days and at the local coordination centre for one-off matches in the host country concerned,

— The liaison officer of the supporting country is responsible for continually updating risk analysis,

— The liaison officer of the supporting country should be kept up to date by the police force in his own country about fan behaviour there during championships or matches,

— The police force of the organising country should make arrangements to channel information received from the foreign police team promptly to the proper authorities within its own police organisation. The police force of the organising country should appoint an information officer to be attached to the support team responsible for reconnaissance or spotting. That officer should serve as a contact for the team leader and be responsible for the proper channelling of information,

— The police forces of the organising country should ensure that there are no differences in the quality of information available at local and national level,

— If there are national and local police coordination centres, the local and national centres should keep one another informed. This information flow should take into account information provided by the liaison officer from the supporting country,

— When fans are returning home, the national coordination centre in the organising country will inform the police force of the fans' home country, along with the police forces of transit countries, if there is any reason to anticipate trouble. In the absence of a national coordination centre, the local coordination centre should fulfil this function.

CHAPTER 4

Cooperation between police forces and stewards

— Police forces and stewards' organisations should work together on a complementary basis, without prejudice to each side's own responsibilities and tasks,

— Police forces should work with senior officials from stewards' organisations,

— Police forces should consider placing a senior official from the stewards' organisation in their own command centre,

— Police forces should ensure that any information from the stewards' organisation is channelled to the proper police authorities in the organising country,

— Police forces should ensure that senior officials from the stewards' organisation have the information needed to carry out their tasks,

— The police forces of the supporting country should maintain contact with senior officials responsible for stewards from their country who are providing support to the organising country.

CHAPTER 5

Checklist for media policy and communication strategy (police/authorities) relating to major (international) championships and matches

I. MEDIA POLICY

1. *Determining the strategic aim of media policy*

   The central aim is seen as that of ensuring police/authorities' cooperation with the media in informing the public at national and international level of forthcoming championships and preparations as well as providing those attending matches with appropriate police advice concerning their security.

   Media policy is one of the instruments used in a communication strategy. It should demonstrate the supportive role played by the police and authorities in watching over the festive nature of championships.

   Comment: In order to ensure a balanced media policy, it is first necessary to determine the strategic aim. All further policy developments are geared to achieving that aim. Account must be taken of the interest of the media in specific information, such as the response by police/authorities to the problems of football hooliganism and violence. This clearly signals what will and will not be tolerated.

2. *Determining the desired results of media policy*

   An active media policy should aim at:

   — a positive image, in the eyes of the public, of the policy pursued by police and authorities,

   — encouraging amenities for and a sporting attitude on the part of those attending matches,

— discouraging misbehaviour by those attending: misbehaviour does not pay,

— providing security information,

— informing the public of police measures and the steps which will be taken in the case of disturbances.

Comment: Media policy should never give the impression that nothing can go wrong, but rather show that there has been proper preparation and that there are no grounds for panic.

3. *Nature of media policy*

— it should convey the idea of overall control,

— it shall suggest security and trust,

— it should make it clear that football hooliganism will be severely dealt with,

— it should be geared to openness and transparency.

II. COMMUNICATION STRATEGY

1. *Method of achieving the aim*

— relations should be established with the media well in advance, focusing on championships or matches,

— cooperation between the press services of police, local authorities, national authorities, football organisations, UEFA, FIFA etc., in communicating an unambiguous policy or view of individual areas of responsibility,

— making provision for police information to be provided to all those concerned, including the football association, supporters' clubs, tourist offices, carriers and other undertakings,

— information folder for those attending from abroad, possibly combined with other tourist information,

— setting up a clearly identified press office for the duration of championships, with press officers and media spokesmen,

— daily press conferences and provision for interviews and other appropriate information facilities during championships,

— organisation of press conferences before championships in order to make clear the approach to cooperation with the press.

2. *Means of achieving the aim/tips for success*

— appointment of professional press correspondents at local, regional and central level,

— multilingual police press officers available to the media in the press centre,

— production of a national or bi-national information folder,

— production of information with a local slant,

— inclusion of reports on security and facilities in local tourist-office publications and other local newspapers and publications,

— making known the number of arrests for public disorder, such as possession of weapons, forged admission tickets, black-market ticket sales and drunkenness,

— assessment of international, national and local media press reports relating to the preparation and progress of championships,

— setting up a national working party on media policy cooperation.

3. *Important topics for consideration*

   1. The nub of the message must be established.

      Comment: First determine what the nub of the message should be. Make this clear in interviews with the journalist/journalists.

   2. The nub of the message must be achievable.

      Comment: Do not express any positions which are not achievable. Where this happens, the power of the media instrument to influence behaviour is undermined. The policy notified by the police must therefore be maintained.

   3. Timely preparation

      Comment: Use the time between submission of candidacy and championships for careful preparation of a media policy specifiying the individual roles and responsibilities of police/authorities.

   4. Planning

      Comment: Include media policy throughout the planning stage and take the initiative in determining when the media will actually be informed.

   5. Continuity and frequency of media contacts

      Comment: It is extremely important that exchanges of information and opportunities for press/media briefings are provided on a continuous and regular basis. Allowance should be made for media needs for rapid information.

   6. Media projects

      Police and authorities should make sure in the case of specific media projects that sufficient attention is paid to the police in the area of police information.

   7. Readiness to deal with incidents

      Comment: The moment at which even a single incident occurs, the interest of the media switches swiftly away from the sporting event to the public disturbance. Account should be taken of the fact that a sports reporter has a different angle from a police reporter.

   8. The media are enterprising

      Comment: Account should be taken of the fact that the media will also seek information from sources other than the police. Special attention should be paid to police strategies and police intervention.

   9. Openness, comprehensiveness and topicality

      Comment: Let the media know how the police/authorities will act when necessary. There are no grounds for fearing the media if police planning and preparations are adequate. The police should provide comprehensive information. That information should be verifiable and up-to-date.

   10. Display of confidence

       Comment: It is important to have confidence in individual police preparations and to display and communicate such confidence to the media. Police and authorities should assume full responsibility for their security arrangements.

11. Interviews

   Comment: Measures should be taken to prepare police authorities for their contacts with the media. Ensure that the police officer maintains his contacts from an appropriate workplace. The media should preferably be contacted orally in person.

12. Limitation/demarcation

   Provide information about individual areas of policy responsibility and intervention.

   Comment: There should be clear agreements between the various authorities on who is to inform the media and the type of information to be given. Media appearances by police and authorities should concentrate on their own responsibilities and interventions.

13. Failures/recriminations

   Comment: Partners should avoid discussing any recriminations or failures with each other in the media.

14. Cooperation

   Comment: Media policy should never be developed without consulting the other partners. Media policy itself is a process of cooperation.

15. Agreements with foreign police teams concerning spokesmen

   Comment: Where the police of the host country is given support by police teams from other countries, it is to be recommended that it agrees, should the foreign police be approached directly by the media, to refer the matter to the police information services of the host country. Exceptions to this rule may be made if the supporting police team, with the approval of the host country, has added its own expert press officer (spokesman) to the team.

16. Involvement of police colleagues from the country of origin of supporters

   Comment: In interviews/press conferences in the country of origin of supporters, use should be made of assistance by colleagues from that country. They have the facilities and press contacts and they know the local and national reporters, including the persuasions of the press organisations for which they work.

17. Preparation of a list of national press services for the police of the organising country

   Comment: The police services of the individual countries should draw up a list of the most important press services with the sectors they target for the police of the organising country. With the help of this list, the police of the organising country can supply those press services directly with information.

18. Taking account of the type of press service

   Comment: In providing information on security, account must be taken of the type of press service and the sector which it targets. Sports reporters have less experience of providing information on security. This should be taken into account when drawing up press reports and issuing press releases.

19. Setting up a joint national working party

   Comment: A joint working party should be set up involving all partners: the police covering the match venues, the central information office on football hooliganism, the football organisation and the national authorities.

20. Factual information

   Comment: All representatives of police and authorities should communicate with the media on the basis of the same background information and with the greatest precision. In order to bring into line factual information, it may be useful to draw up common briefing notes and standard replies to regularly recurring questions. There should be daily exchanges of information on the questions asked by the media.

21. Written communiqué

   Comment: Press conferences should be backed up with a written communiqué. This has the advantage of ensuring that:

   — the text can be given careful consideration,

   — texts can be authorised for the press,

   — an unambiguous message is conveyed (no subsequent arguments about 'misunderstandings').

22. Information folder

   An information folder should be made available to supporters, indicating the kind of behaviour that is culturally acceptable or unacceptable and the kind of violations of the law which will lead to action being taken. Advice should be given on ancillary matters with a view to ensuring that the supporters feel welcome. The folder should be distributed when tickets are sold.

23. Involvement of the public

   Comment: The public may be asked to take an active role by notifying the police of suspect behaviour.

24. Winding-down strategy

   The press office should close towards the end of the championships, but information should continue to be provided by the central police command office. Notification should be given of when the police press officer will be available for debriefing and a final press conference.

25. Assessment of media policy

   Comment: When the championships have ended, an assessment report should be drawn up on the media policy pursued and experience with the media. Aspects with lessons for the future should be noted. This should also involve any police forces from other countries which have provided support.

26. Assessment of the European Union/police cooperation checklist for media policy

   The police of the organising country should use the national assessment of media policy as a basis for deciding whether individual aspects of the European Union checklist require supplementing or adjustment.

CHAPTER 6

Requirements for admission policy and ticketing policy [1]

If organisers of major football matches fail to take all the necessary measures, this can have enormous consequences for the smooth functioning of the communities concerned. In particular, measures haved proved necessary in the following areas: banning fans who misbehave or have in the past seriously misbehaved, stadium admission and ticketing policy, and separation of rival groups of fans.

In the interests of public order and safety, the authorities, the police and the judiciary should establish beforehand requirements to be met by organisers in arranging international competitions.

1. *Ticketing policy*

   Ticketing policy is an important instrument in promoting safety and order in stadiums. In particular, it centres on the separation of rival fans, prevention of overcrowding and control of spectator movements, as well as enforcing stadium bans previously imposed by football organisations.

---

[1] When establishing a ticketing policy, organisers must take into account EC competition rules. The Commission, in the application of those rules, will take into account factors relating to the maintenance of order and security.

The following are the basic requirements to be made of organisers by authorities and police forces for a responsible ticketing policy:

— the distribution of tickets should ensure that fans of the participating teams are separated into sections,

— ticket distribution policy, the allocation of tickets among participating countries, should reflect ticket demand from fans in those countries,

— sales policy should be designed to prevent black-market sales,

— fans should be prevented from buying tickets for a section of the stadium not designated for them,

— tickets should provide information about the holder of the ticket and its origin, in other words the history of that ticket.

2. *Ticket control*

Ticketing policy should be given practical effect through ticket control in which:

— separation of fans is brought about through strict allocation of accommodation (seating) to spectators by means of tickets, so that location in the stadium is determined by the participating team supported by a spectator and/or the nationality of a fan,

— ticketing policy should be designed so that allocation and hence separation of rival fans cannot be bypassed through the transfer of tickets in any form,

— overcrowding is prevented by ensuring that ticket allocations placed on the market are determined by stadium infrastructure. The control of counterfeit or forged tickets will also prevent overcrowding,

— the basic premise is that the admission capacity of each stadium will be determined in the light of risk analysis and that the full capacity will not be sold. A margin of safety is necessary in order to admit fans with tickets for the wrong section, as determined by the participating team supported by spectators and/or the nationality of fans,

— spectator movements in and around the stadium are controlled by means of adequate, recognisable division of the stadium into sections and related signposting,

— stadium bans are enforced by the arrangements for applications for and distribution of tickets and measures against any form of transfer of tickets issued,

— registration by the organisers as part of ticket control forms an important source of information for the organisers, the administration and the police.

Ticket control is geared to the stadium admission process, involving:

— printing of admission tickets,

— distribution of admission tickets,

— admission controls.

3. *Admission tickets should meet strict quality requirements*

— match and stadium data should be given,

— code of conduct for fans,

— conditions for admission to and presence in the stadium in spectators' own language,

— nationality of the holder of the ticket,

— name of the holder and name of the ticket agent/distributor,

- in principle, the buyer of the ticket is also the end user,

- tickets should be forgery-proof,

- each ticket should be accompanied by a notice in which the organisers at any rate indicate that:

    - specified objects may not be taken into the stadium,

    - alcoholic beverages and/or drugs are prohibited on entering or while inside the stadium,

    - action will be taken in response to the throwing of fireworks or other objects in the stadium,

    - action will be taken in response to any form of insulting or racist behaviour,

    - occupying a seat not matching the number on the ticket could result in expulsion from the stadium,

    - spectators at matches must agree to being searched on entering the stadium and are required to produce identification, on request, when presenting admission tickets.

4. *There should be requirements for the distribution of tickets*

    - in information campaigns, the organiser should announce the official sales outlets and method of sale and urge the public not to buy admission tickets elsewhere, warning them that the distribution system leaves no scope for black-market sales,

    - the organiser should continually monitor ticket holdings per country and per distributor,

    - available tickets should be distributed to target groups in such a way as to allow sufficient tickets, in all fairness and to the extent permissible under European Community competition rules, both for the general public and for fans of participating teams,

    - the organiser must impose an obligation to return tickets on national associations in countries with insufficient sales,

    - the organiser must impose an obligation on the official distributor to return unsold tickets,

    - the organiser should bear in mind that piecemeal distribution and sale of admission tickets will enhance control over the selling process. The organiser should impose reliability requirements for distributors,

    - in the event of irregularities, the organiser should have the power to intervene in the distribution process at any time,

    - the organiser should impose an information requirement on distributors, who should inform the organiser of the progress of ticket sales, if possible together with travel schedules and places to be stayed at,

    - if applications for tickets are made away from national associations or the individual football clubs of spectators or fans, individual applicants should indicate the team they support. When final allocation of tickets takes place, this can be taken into account on public order and safety grounds,

    - admission tickets should not be transferable,

    - persons on whom stadium bans have been imposed will not be issued admission tickets,

    - no tickets will be sold on the day of the match,

    - purchasers will not be supplied with more than two tickets. The tickets will be issued in their names,

    - tickets should be finally issued at the last possible moment (exchangeable vouchers),

    - the organiser should provide assurances that the person whose name appears on a ticket, the ticketholder, will ultimately receive that ticket.

5. *Requirements for proper admission policy and control*

— the organiser will announce in advance those spectators that will be admitted to the stadium and those that will be refused admission,

— in any case, those on whom stadium bans have been imposed will not be admitted,

— spectators clearly under the influence of alcohol will not be admitted,

— spectators will not be admitted if they are carrying objects that could pose a threat to safety and order in the stadium,

— spectators will not be admitted if they are carrying objects that in any way reflect political aims, discrimination, racism or insulting attitudes,

— admission controls should be of a high standard, including searching of persons and enforcing of stadium bans,

— speedy admission controls should prevent lengthy queueing,

— admission controls should guard against overcrowding of stadium sections,

— where automatic admission systems are used, they should meet high standards of reliability and continuity.

CHAPTER 7

List of documents previously adopted by the Council of the European Union

1. Council recommendation of 30 November 1993 concerning the responsibility of organisers of sporting events

2. Council recommendation of 1 December 1994 concerning direct, informal exchanges of information with the CCEEs in the area of international sporting events (network of contact persons)

3. Council recommendation of 1 December 1994 concerning exchange of information on the occasion of major events and meetings (network of contact persons)

4. Council recommendation of 22 April 1996 on guidelines for preventing and restraining disorder connected with football matches, with an annexed standard format for the exchange of police intelligence on football hooligans (OJ C 131, 3.5.1996, p. 1)

5. Joint Action of 26 May 1997 with regard to cooperation on law and order and security (OJ L 147, 5.6.1997, p. 1)

6. Council resolution of 9 June 1997 on preventing and restraining football hooliganism through the exchange of experience, exclusion from stadiums and media policy (OJ C 193, 24.6.1997, p. 1)

7. Table of national contacts on hooliganism

**Council Decision
of 13 March 2000
on guidelines for Member States'
employment policies for the year 2000**

(OJ L 72, 21.3.2000)

II

(Acts whose publication is not obligatory)

COUNCIL

COUNCIL DECISION
of 13 March 2000
on guidelines for Member States' employment policies for the year 2000

(2000/228/EC)

THE COUNCIL OF THE EUROPEAN UNION,

Having regard to the Treaty establishing the European Community, and in particular Article 128(2) thereof,

Having regard to the proposal from the Commission

Having regard to the opinion of the European Parliament [1],

Having regard to the opinion of the Economic and Social Committee [2],

Having regard to the opinion of the Committee of the Regions [3],

Having regard to the opinion of the Employment and Labour Market Committee,

Whereas:

(1) Employment remains the top priority of the European Union. Coordinated action must be pursued in a sustained manner to combat unemployment and raise the present levels of employment on a lasting basis.

(2) The Luxembourg process, based on the implementation of the coordinated European Employment Strategy, was launched by the extraordinary European Council meeting on employment on 20 and 21 November 1997. The Council Resolution of 15 December 1997 on the 1998 Employment Guidelines [4], confirmed by the European Council, has launched a process with high visibility, strong political commitment and a wide-ranging acceptance by all parties concerned.

(3) The Council resolution of 22 February 1999 on the 1999 Employment Guidelines [5] has allowed consolidation of the Luxembourg process through compliance with those guidelines.

(4) The contribution of the social partners in the framework of the Standing Committee on Employment, the social dialogue and the contacts established with the Heads of State or Government and the Commission should be taken into account.

(5) The opinion of the Employment and Labour Market Committee was drafted jointly with the Economic Policy Committee.

(6) The 1999 Joint Employment Report, drawn up by the Council and the Commission, describes the employment situation in the Community and examines the action taken by the Member States in implementing their employment policy in line with the 1999 Employment Guidelines.

(7) On 14 February 2000 the Council adopted recommendations on the implementation of Member States' employment policies.

(8) In Cologne on 3 and 4 June 1999 the European Council took the initiative for a European employment pact which provides a basis for a sustained and comprehensive strategy for more growth and employment and has added macroeconomic dialogue (Cologne process) as a third pillar to the coordinated employment strategy (Luxembourg process) and economic reform (Cardiff process).

(9) Consistency and synergy between the employment guidelines and the broad economic policy guidelines must be ensured.

(10) In Helsinki on 10 and 11 December 1999 the European Council adopted conclusions on Employment Guidelines for the year 2000, introducing a limited number of changes to further sharpen the guidelines' focus and aims.

---
[1] Opinion delivered on 4 November 1999 (not yet published in the Official Journal).
[2] OJ C 368, 20.12.1999, p. 31.
[3] OJ C 57, 29.2.2000, p. 17.
[4] OJ C 30, 28.1.1998, p. 1.
[5] OJ C 69, 12.3.1999, p. 2.

(11) The preventive and active measures to be taken should encourage effective integration into the labour market.

(12) There is a need to develop skills in information technologies and to provide schools with computer equipment, as well as access to the Internet.

(13) The social partners at all levels as well as the regional and local authorities need to be involved in the implementation of the guidelines so that they can contribute, in their field of responsibility, to promoting a high level of employment.

(14) Public employment services should play an important role in delivering preventive and active measures and in identifying job opportunities at local level, to achieve a better functioning of the labour market.

(15) The implementation of the guidelines may vary according to their nature, the parties to whom they are addressed and the different situations in the Member States. They should respect the principle of subsidiarity and Member States' responsibilities with regard to employment.

(16) In implementing the employment guidelines, in accordance with the subsidiarity principle, Member States should be able to take regional situations into account, while fully respecting the attainment of national targets and equal treatment of all citizens.

(17) Directive 1999/85/EC [1], which provides for the possibility of applying a reduced VAT rate on labour-intensive services on an experimental basis, should be followed up in order to examine, in particular, the impact of national initiatives in terms of job potential.

(18) The implementation of the employment guidelines could play a positive role in dealing with the problem of undeclared work.

(19) The Commission and the Member States have agreed to continue and accelerate work on indicators and systems for the collection of comparable data, which will make it possible to assess the implementation and impact of the annexed guidelines and to refine the Community and national targets which they contain. Good practice from the Member States should also be taken into account.

(20) A mid-term review of the employment guidelines during the year 2000 would be desirable, with a view to streamlining and consolidating them within the existing four-pillar structure.

(21) Focused national reports, supported by indicators, will permit an effective peer-group review by other Member States and the Commission in order to assess progress achieved by each Member State in implementing the guidelines.

(22) The contribution of the European Social Fund to the European Employment Strategy in the new programming period should be highlighted.

(23) Sustainable development and the integration of environmental concerns into other Community policies were endorsed by the European Council in Amsterdam. Member States are invited to give effect to such integration within their national employment strategies by promoting employment creation in the environmental field,

HAS DECIDED AS FOLLOWS:

Sole Article

The guidelines for Member States' employment policies for the year 2000, annexed hereto, are hereby adopted. They shall be taken into account by the Member States in their employment policies.

Done at Brussels, 13 March 2000.

For the Council
The President
E. FERRO RODRIGUES

---

[1] OJ L 277, 28.10.1999, p. 34.

ANNEX

THE EMPLOYMENT GUIDELINES FOR 2000

I. IMPROVING EMPLOYABILITY

Tackling youth unemployment and preventing long-term unemployment

In order to influence the trend in youth and long-term unemployment the Member States will intensify their efforts to develop preventive and employability-oriented strategies, building on the early identification of individual needs; within a period to be determined by each Member State which may not exceed three years and which may be longer in Member States with particularly high unemployment, Member States will ensure that:

1. every unemployed young person is offered a new start before reaching six months of unemployment, in the form of training, retraining, work practice, a job or other employability measure with a view to effective integration into the labour market.

2. unemployed adults are also offered a fresh start before reaching twelve months of unemployment by one of the aforementioned means or, more generally, by accompanying individual vocational guidance with a view to effective integration into the labour market.

These preventive and employability measures should be combined with measures to promote the re-employment of the long-term unemployed. In this context, Member States should pursue the modernisation of their public employment services so that they can deal with the strategy of prevention and activation in the most effective way.

Transition from passive measures to active measures

Benefit, tax and training systems, where that proves necessary, must be reviewed and adapted to ensure that they actively support employability. Moreover, these systems should interact to increase the incentive to return to the labour market. Each Member State:

3. will endeavour to increase significantly the number of persons benefiting from active measures to improve their employability with a view to effective integration into the labour market. In order to increase the numbers of unemployed who are offered training or any similar measure, it will in particular fix a target, in the light of its starting situation, of gradually achieving the average of the three most successful Member States, and of at least 20 %.

4. will review and, where appropriate, refocus its benefit and tax system:

   — to provide incentives for unemployed or inactive people to seek and take up work or measures to enhance their employability and for employers to create new jobs, and

   — in addition, it is important to develop a policy for active ageing, encompassing appropriate measures such as maintaining working capacity, lifelong learning and other flexible working arrangements, so that older workers are also able to remain and participate actively in working life.

Encouraging a partnership approach

The actions of the Member States alone will not suffice to achieve the desired results in promoting employability. Consequently:

5. the social partners are urged, at their various levels of responsibility and action, to conclude as soon as possible agreements with a view to increasing the possibilities for training, work experience, traineeships or other measures likely to promote employability of the young and adult unemployed and to promote entry into the labour market.

6. in order to reinforce the development of a skilled and adaptable workforce, both Member States and the social partners will endeavour to develop possibilities for lifelong learning, particularly in the fields of information and communication technologies, and each Member State will set a target according to national circumstances for participants benefiting from such measures. Easy access for older workers will be particularly important.

Easing the transition from school to work

Employment prospects are poor for young people who leave the school system without having acquired the aptitudes required for entering the job market. Member States will therefore:

7. improve the quality of their school systems in order to reduce substantially the number of young people who drop out of the school system early. Particular attention should also be given to young people with learning difficulties.

8. make sure they equip young people with greater ability to adapt to technological and economic changes and with skills relevant to the labour market. Member States will give particular attention to the development and modernisation of their apprenticeship and vocational training systems, where appropriate in cooperation with the social partners, to developing appropriate training for the acquisition of computer literacy and skills by students and teachers as well as to equipping schools with computer equipment and facilitating student access to the Internet by the end of 2002.

Promoting a labour market open to all

Many groups and individuals experience particular difficulties in acquiring relevant skills and in gaining access to, and remaining in, the labour market. A coherent set of policies promoting the integration of such groups and individuals into the world of work and combating discrimination is called for. Each Member State will:

9. give special attention to the needs of the disabled, ethnic minorities and other groups and individuals who may be disadvantaged, and develop appropriate forms of preventive and active policies to promote their integration into the labour market.

II. DEVELOPING ENTREPRENEURSHIP

Making it easier to start up and run businesses

The development of new enterprises, and the growth of small and medium-sized enterprises (SMEs), is essential for job creation and for the expansion of training opportunities for young people. This process must be promoted by Member States encouraging greater entrepreneurial awareness across society and in educational curricula, by providing a clear, stable and predictable set of rules, by improving the conditions for the development of, and access to, risk capital markets. The Member States should also reduce and simplify the administrative and tax burdens on SMEs. These policies will support Member States' attempts to tackle undeclared work. To that end the Member States will:

10. give particular attention to reducing significantly the overhead costs and administrative burdens for businesses, and especially SMEs, in particular when an enterprise is being set up and when hiring additional workers.

11. encourage the development of self employment by examining, with the aim of reducing, any obstacles which may exist, especially those within tax and social security regimes, to moving to self-employment and the setting up of small businesses as well as by promoting training for entrepreneurship and targeted support services for entrepreneurs and would-be entrepreneurs.

Exploiting new opportunities for job creation

If the European Union wants to deal successfully with the employment challenge, all possible sources of jobs and new technologies and innovations must be exploited effectively. To that end the Member States will:

12. promote measures to exploit fully the possibilities offered by job creation at local level and in the social economy, especially in new activities linked to needs not yet satisfied by the market, and examine, with the aim of reducing, any obstacles in the way of such measures. In this respect, the special role and responsibility of local and regional authorities, other partners at the regional and local levels, as well as the social partners, needs to be more fully recognised and supported. In addition, the role of the public employment services in identifying local employment opportunities and improving the functioning of local labour markets, should be fully exploited.

13. develop framework conditions to fully exploit the employment potential of the services sector and industry-related services, *inter alia*, by tapping the employment potential of the information society and the environmental sector, to create more and better jobs.

Making the taxation system more employment friendly

and reversing the long-term trend towards higher taxes and charges on labour (which increased from 35 % in 1980 to more than 42 % in 1995). Each Member State will:

14. set a target, if necessary and taking account of its present level, for gradually reducing the overall tax burden and, where appropriate, a target for gradually reducing the fiscal pressure on labour and non-wage labour costs, in particular on relatively unskilled and low-paid labour, without jeopardising the recovery of public finances or the financial equilibrium of social security schemes. It will examine, if appropriate, the desirability of introducing a tax on energy or on pollutant emissions or any other tax measure.

III. ENCOURAGING ADAPTABILITY OF BUSINESSES AND THEIR EMPLOYEES

Modernising work organisation

In order to promote the modernisation of work organisation and forms of work, a strong partnership should be developed at all appropriate levels (European, national, sectoral, local and enterprise levels):

15. the social partners are invited to negotiate and implement at all appropriate levels agreements to modernise the organisation of work, including flexible working arrangements, with the aim of making undertakings productive and competitive and achieving the required balance between flexibility and security. Subjects to be covered may, for example, include training and retraining, the introduction of new technologies, new forms of work and working time issues such as the expression of working time as an annual figure, the reduction of working hours, the reduction of overtime, the development of part-time working, and access to training and career breaks.

16. for its part, each Member State will examine the possibility of incorporating in its law more adaptable types of contract, taking into account the fact that forms of employment are increasingly diverse. Those working under contracts of this kind should at the same time enjoy adequate security and higher occupational status, compatible with the needs of business.

Support adaptability in enterprises

In order to renew skill levels within enterprises Member States will:

17. re-examine and, where appropriate, remove the obstacles, in particular tax obstacles, to investment in human resources and possibly provide for tax or other incentives for the development of in-house training; they will also examine new regulations and review the existing regulatory framework to make sure they will contribute to reducing barriers to employment and helping the labour market adapt to structural change in the economy.

IV. STRENGTHENING EQUAL OPPORTUNITIES POLICIES FOR WOMEN AND MEN

Gender mainstreaming approach

Women still have particular problems in gaining access to the employment market, in career advancement, in earnings and in reconciling professional and family life. It is therefore important, *inter alia*:

— to ensure that active labour market policies are made available for women in proportion to their share of unemployment,

— to reduce tax-benefit disincentives, wherever identified, because of their negative effects on the female labour supply,

— to give particular attention to obstacles which hinder women who wish to set up new businesses or become self employed,

— to ensure that women are able to benefit positively from flexible forms of work organisation on a voluntary basis. Therefore, the Member States will:

18. adopt a gender-mainstreaming approach in implementing the guidelines of all four pillars. In order meaningfully to evaluate progress on this approach, Member States will need to provide for adequate data collection systems and procedures.

Tackling gender gaps

Member States and the social partners should translate their desire to promote equality of opportunity into increased employment rates for women. They should also pay attention to the imbalance in the representation of women or men in certain economic sectors and occupations, as well as to the improvement of female career opportunities. Member States will:

19. attempt to reduce the gap in unemployment rates between women and men by actively supporting the increased employment of women and will take action to bring about a balanced representation of women and men in all sectors and occupations. They will initiate positive steps to promote equal pay for equal work or work of equal value and to diminish differentials in incomes between women and men. In order to reduce gender gaps, Member States will also consider an increased use of measures for the advancement of women.

Reconciling work and family life

Policies on career breaks, parental leave and part-time work, as well as flexible working arrangements which serve the interests of both employers and employees, are of particular importance to women and men. Implementation of the various directives and social-partner agreements in this area should be accelerated and monitored regularly. There must be an adequate provision of good quality care for children and other dependants in order to support women's and men's entry and continued participation in the labour market. An equal sharing of family responsibilities is crucial in this respect. In order to strengthen equal opportunities, Member States and the social partners will:

20. design, implement and promote family-friendly policies, including affordable, accessible and high quality care services for children and other dependants, as well as parental and other leave schemes.

Facilitating reintegration into the labour market

Those returning to the labour market after an absence may have outmoded skills and experience difficulty in gaining access to training. The Member States will:

21. give specific attention to women, and men, considering a return to the paid workforce after an absence and, to that end, they will examine the means of gradually eliminating the obstacles in the way of such return.

**Conclusions of the Council and the Representatives of the Governments
of the Member States, meeting within the Council,
of 4 December 2000
on combating doping**

(OJ C 356, 12.12.2000)

I

(Information)

COUNCIL

Conclusions of the Council and the Representatives of the Governments of the Member States, meeting within the Council

of 4 December 2000

on combating doping

(2000/C 356/01)

THE COUNCIL OF THE EUROPEAN UNION AND THE REPRESENTATIVES OF THE GOVERNMENTS OF THE MEMBER STATES, IN AGREEMENT WITH THE COMMISSION,

(1) EMPHASISE the importance of measures to combat doping in sport, as acknowledged by the European Union, in the conclusions of the European Council in Vienna on 11 and 12 December 1998. The European Council's conclusions underlined 'its concern at the extent and seriousness of doping in sport, which undermines the sporting ethic and endangers public health. It emphasises the need for mobilisation at European level and invites the Member States to examine jointly with the Commission and international sports bodies possible measures to intensify the fight against this danger . . .'.

(2) NOTE the recent developments in this area and the creation of the World Anti-Doping Agency (WADA), and WADA's intention to become an international body based on public international law, and consider that arrangements should be made for the Member States' and the European Union's roles in that body in order to ensure that they are suitably represented on its Foundation Board.

(3) AGREE that the European Community and its Member States will be represented by the President-in-Office of the Council and a member of the Commission. Within a reasonable period of time before each meeting, coordination will take place under the responsibility of the Presidency. The Commission member will be able to speak on matters within the Community's sphere of competence in accordance with the Treaty and the case-law of the Court of Justice (given that there is no direct Community competence in the area of sport). The content of the statements made by the Commission member will be approved in accordance with the principles referred to above and following the customary procedures. Where appropriate, the Commission member may speak on matters which are not within the Community's sphere of competence, along the lines approved by a consensus of the Member States and in addition to the Presidency.

(4) NOTE that any Community expenditure on activities of WADA involving measures within the Community's sphere of competence will be decided in accordance with the Interinstitutional Agreement on budgetary discipline. In particular, any significant Community expenditure will require the adoption, following a proposal from the Commission, of a measure with an appropriate legal basis.

(5) CONSIDER that the Member States should encourage cooperation between the competent authorities at national level on efforts to combat doping in sport.

**Council Decision
of 19 January 2001
on Guidelines for Member States' employment
policies for the year 2001**

(OJ L 22, 24.1.2001)

II

(Acts whose publication is not obligatory)

COUNCIL

COUNCIL DECISION
of 19 January 2001
on Guidelines for Member States' employment policies for the year 2001

(2001/63/EC)

THE COUNCIL OF THE EUROPEAN UNION,

Having regard to the Treaty establishing the European Community, and in particular Article 128(2) thereof,

Having regard to the proposal from the Commission [1],

Having regard to the opinion of the European Parliament [2],

Having regard to the opinion of the Economic and Social Committee [3],

Having regard to the opinion of the Committee of the Regions [4],

Having regard to the opinion of the Employment Committee,

Whereas:

(1) The Luxembourg process, based on the implementation of the coordinated European Employment Strategy, was launched by the extraordinary European Council meeting on Employment on 20 and 21 November 1997. The Council Resolution of 15 December 1997 on the 1998 Employment Guidelines [5] has launched a process with high visibility, strong political commitment and a wide-ranging acceptance by all parties concerned.

(2) The Council Decision of 13 March 2000 on guidelines for Member States' employment policies for the year 2000 [6] has allowed consolidation of the Luxembourg process through compliance with those guidelines.

(3) The Lisbon European Council on 23 and 24 March 2000 set a new strategic goal for the European Union to become the most competitive and dynamic knowledge-based economy in the world capable of sustainable economic growth with more and better jobs and greater social cohesion. The attainment of this goal will enable the Union to regain the conditions of full employment.

(4) The opinion of the Employment Committee was drafted jointly with the Economic Policy Committee.

(5) Consistency and synergy between the Employment Guidelines and the Broad Economic Policy Guidelines should be ensured.

(6) In implementing the employment guidelines, Member States should aim at a high degree of consistency with two other priorities highlighted by the Lisbon Summit, modernising social protection and the promotion of social inclusion, while ensuring that work pays, and the long-term sustainability of social protection systems is secured.

(7) The Lisbon European Council stressed the need to adapt European education and training systems both to the demands of the knowledge society and to the need for an improved level and quality of employment, and called upon Member States, the Council and the Commission to pursue a substantial annual increase in per capita investment in human resources.

(8) The Santa Maria da Feira European Council on 19 and 20 June 2000 invited the social partners to play a more prominent role in defining, implementing and evaluating the employment guidelines which depend on them, focusing particularly on modernising work organisation, lifelong learning and increasing the employment rate, particularly for women.

---
[1] Proposal of 14 November 2000 (not yet published in the Official Journal)
[2] Opinion delivered on 24 November 2000 (not yet published in the Official Journal).
[3] OJ C 14, 16.1.2001, p. 75.
[4] Opinion delivered on 13 October 2000 (not yet published in the Official Journal).
[5] OJ C 30, 28.1.1998, p. 1.
[6] OJ L 72, 21.3.2000, p. 15.

345

(9) The 2000 Joint Employment Report, drawn up by the Council and the Commission, describes the employment situation in the Community and examines the action taken by the Member States in implementing their employment policy in line with the 2000 Employment Guidelines, and the Council Recommendation 2000/164/EC of 14 February 2000 on the implementation of Member States' employment policies [1].

(10) On 19 January 2001 the Council adopted a further recommendation on the implementation of Member States' employment policies [2].

(11) The mid-term Review of the Luxembourg process conducted in 2000 at the request of the Lisbon European Council should be taken into account in revising the Employment Guidelines 2001, without changing the basic four pillar structure, and in improving the efficiency of the Luxembourg process.

(12) Member States should strengthen their efforts to include and make visible a gender perspective across all the pillars.

(13) The implementation of the guidelines may vary according to their nature, the parties to whom they are addressed and the different situations in the Member States. They should respect the principle of subsidiarity and Member States' responsibilities with regard to employment.

(14) In implementing the Employment Guidelines, Member States should be able to take regional situations into account, while fully respecting the attainment of national targets and the principle of equal treatment.

(15) The effectiveness of the Luxembourg process requires that the implementation of the employment guidelines is also reflected *inter alia* in financial provision. To this end, the national reports should, where appropriate, include budget information in order to permit an effective assessment of the progress achieved by each Member State in implementing the guidelines, taking into account their impact and cost effectiveness.

(16) Council Directive 1999/85/EC [3], which provides for the possibility of applying a reduced VAT rate on labour-intensive services on an experimental basis, should be followed up in order to examine, in particular, the impact of national initiatives in terms of job potential.

(17) The contribution of the Structural Funds, and in particular the European Social Fund and the Community Initiative EQUAL to the European Employment Strategy in the new programming period should be highlighted, as well as the role of the European Investment Bank.

(18) Partnership at all levels should be encouraged, including with the social partners, regional and local authorities and representatives of civil society so that they can contribute, in their respective fields of responsibility, to promoting a high level of employment.

(19) There is a need further to consolidate and develop comparable indicators to make it possible to assess the implementation and impact of the annexed guidelines, and to refine the targets which they contain and facilitate the identification and exchange of best practice.

(20) Sustainable development and the integration of environmental concerns into other Community policies are objectives of the Treaty. Member States are invited to give effect to such integration within their national employment strategies by promoting employment creation in the environmental field,

HAS DECIDED AS FOLLOWS:

Sole Article

The Guidelines for Member States' employment policies for the year 2001, annexed hereto, are hereby adopted. They shall be taken into account by the Member States in their employment policies.

Done at Brussels, 19 January 2001.

For the Council
The President
B. RINGHOLM

---

[1] OJ L 52, 25.2.2000, p. 32.
[2] See page 27 of this Official Journal.
[3] OJ L 277, 28.10.1999, p. 34.

ANNEX

THE EMPLOYMENT GUIDELINES FOR 2001

Horizontal objectives — building conditions for full employment in a knowledge-based society

The careful build-up, over the last decade, of a macroeconomic framework for stability and growth coupled with consistent efforts to reform labour, capital, goods and services markets, as well as favourable prospects in the world economy, has created a favourable economic outlook for the European Union which will bring the attainment of some of its key fundamental objectives within reach. Further progress, however, is not automatic: it requires leadership, commitment and concerted action.

This is why the European Council embraced full employment as an overarching objective of the EU's employment and social policy. It committed the Member States to reach the strategic goal of making the Union the most competitive and dynamic knowledge-based economy in the world, capable of sustainable economic growth with more and better jobs and greater social cohesion. The achievement of these objectives requires simultaneous efforts by the Community and the Member States. It also requires a continued implementation of an effective and well balanced and mutually supportive policy mix, based on macroeconomic policy, structural reforms promoting adaptable and flexible labour markets, innovation and competitiveness, and an active welfare state promoting human resources development, participation, inclusion and solidarity.

Preparing the transition to a knowledge-based economy, reaping the benefits of the information and communication technologies, modernising the European social model by investing in people and combating social exclusion and promoting equal opportunities are key challenges for the Luxembourg process. In order to achieve the goal of full employment set at Lisbon, the Member States should articulate their response to the guidelines under the four pillars in a coherent overall strategy which incorporates the following horizontal objectives:

A. Enhancing job opportunities and providing adequate incentives for all those willing to take up gainful employment with the aim of moving towards full employment recognising Member States' different starting positions, and recognising the fact that full employment is a goal of overall national economic policy. To this end, Member States should consider setting national targets for raising the rate of employment, in order to contribute to the overall European objectives of reaching by 2010 an overall employment rate of 70 per cent and an employment rate of more than 60 per cent for women. In pursuing these targets, the aim of increasing the quality of jobs should also be taken into consideration.

B. Member States shall develop comprehensive and coherent strategies for Lifelong Learning, in order to help people acquire and update the skills needed to cope with economic and social changes throughout the entire life cycle. In particular, the strategies should cover the development of systems for initial, secondary and tertiary education, further education and vocational training for young people and adults to improve their employability, adaptability and skills, as well as their participation in the knowledge-based society. Such strategies should articulate the shared responsibility of public authorities, enterprises, the social partners and individuals, with relevant contribution from civil society, to contribute to the realisation of a knowledge-based society. In this context, the social partners should negotiate and agree on measures to improve further education and training of adults to enhance the adaptability of workers and competitiveness of business. To this end, Member States should set national targets for an increase in investment in human resources as well as in participation in further education and training (whether formal or informal) and monitor regularly progress towards such targets.

C. Member States shall develop a comprehensive partnership with the social partners for the implementation, monitoring and follow-up of the Employment Strategy. The social partners at all levels are invited to step up their action in support of the Luxembourg process. Within the overall framework and objectives set by these guidelines, the social partners are invited to develop, in accordance with their national traditions and practices, their own process of implementing the guidelines for which they have the key responsibility, identify the issues upon which they will negotiate and report regularly on progress, in the context of the National Action Plans if desired, as well as the impact of their actions on employment and labour market functioning. The social partners at European level are invited to define their own contribution and to monitor, encourage and support efforts undertaken at national level.

D. In translating the Employment Guidelines into national policies, Member States will give due attention to all the four pillars and the horizontal objectives by setting their priorities in a balanced manner, so as to respect the integrated nature and equal value of the guidelines. The National Action Plans will develop the strategy for employment (adopting a gender mainstreaming approach), comprising an identification of the policy mix based on the four pillars and the horizontal objectives which should make explicit how policy initiatives under different guidelines are structured in order to reach long-term goals. In giving effect to the Strategy, the regional dimension and regional disparities will be taken into account in terms of differentiated policies or targets, while fully respecting the attainment of national targets and the principle of equal treatment. Likewise, it is appropriate for Member States, without prejudice to the overall framework, to focus, in particular, on certain dimensions of the strategy to meet the particular needs of their labour market situation.

E. Member States and the Commission should strengthen the development of common indicators in order to evaluate adequately progress under all four pillars and to underpin the setting of benchmarks and the identification of good practice. The social partners are invited to develop appropriate indicators and benchmarks and supporting statistical databases to measure progress in the actions for which they are responsible.

I. IMPROVING EMPLOYABILITY

Tackling youth unemployment and preventing long-term unemployment

In order to influence the trend in youth and long-term unemployment, Member States will intensify their efforts to develop preventive and employability-oriented strategies, building on the early identification of individual needs. Within a period to be determined by each Member State, which may not exceed two years and which — without prejudice to the review of the Guidelines which will take place in two years' time — may be longer in Member States with particularly high unemployment, Member States will ensure that:

1. Every unemployed person is offered a new start before reaching six months of unemployment in the case of young people, and twelve months of unemployment in the case of adults in the form of training, retraining, work practice, a job, or other employability measure, including, more generally, accompanying individual vocational guidance and counselling with a view to effective integration into the labour market.

   These preventive and employability measures should be combined with measures to reduce the stock of the long-term unemployed by promoting their reinsertion in the labour market.

   In this context, Member States should pursue the modernisation of their Public Employment Services, in particular by monitoring progress, setting clear deadlines and providing adequate retraining of their staff. Member States should encourage cooperation with other service providers so as to make the strategy of prevention and activation more effective.

A more employment-friendly approach: benefits, taxes and training systems

Benefit, tax and training systems — where that proves necessary — must be reviewed and adapted to ensure that they actively support the employability of unemployed persons. Moreover, these systems should interact appropriately to encourage the return to the labour market of those inactive persons willing and able to take up a job. Particular attention should be given to promoting incentives for unemployed or inactive people to seek and take up work, as well as measures to upgrade their skills and enhance job opportunities in particular for those with greatest difficulties.

2. Each Member State will:
   — review and, where appropriate, reform its benefit and tax system to reduce poverty traps, and provide incentives for unemployed or inactive people to seek and take up work or measures to enhance their employability and for employers to create new jobs;
   — endeavour to increase significantly the proportion of unemployed and inactive persons benefiting from active measures to improve their employability with a view to effective integration into the labour market, and will improve the outcomes, outputs and cost effectiveness of such measures;
   — promote measures for unemployed and inactive people to acquire or upgrade skills, including IT and communication skills, thereby facilitating their access to the labour market and reducing skills gaps. To this end, each Member State will fix a target for active measures involving education, training or similar measures offered to the unemployed thereby aiming at gradually achieving the average of the three most advanced Member States, and at least 20 per cent.

Developing a policy for active ageing

In-depth changes in the prevailing social attitudes towards older workers, as well as a revision of tax-benefit systems are called for, in order to reach full employment, to help ensure the long-term fairness and sustainability of social security systems, and to make the best use of older workers' experience.

3. Member States, if appropriate with the social partners, will therefore develop policies for active ageing with the aim of enhancing the capacity of, and incentives for, older workers to remain in the labour force as long as possible, in particular by:
   — adopting positive measures to maintain working capacity and skills of older workers, not least in a knowledge-based labour market, in particular through sufficient access to education and training, to introduce flexible working arrangements including, for example, part-time work if workers so choose, and to raise employers' awareness of the potential of older workers; and
   — reviewing tax and benefit systems in order to reduce disincentives and make it more attractive for older workers to continue participating in the labour market.

Developing skills for the new labour market in the context of lifelong learning

Effective and well functioning educational and training systems responsive to labour market needs are key to the development of the knowledge-based economy and to the improvement of the level and quality of employment. They are also crucial to the delivery of lifelong learning to allow for a smooth transition from school to work, lay the foundations for productive human resources equipped with core and specific skills and enable people to adapt positively to social and economic change. The development of an employable labour force involves providing people with the capacity to access and reap the benefits of the knowledge-based society, addressing skill gaps and preventing the erosion of skills resulting from unemployment, non-participation and exclusion throughout the lifecycle.

4. Member States are therefore called upon to improve the quality of their education and training systems, as well as the relevant curricula, including the provision of appropriate guidance in the context of both initial training and lifelong learning, the modernisation and greater effectiveness of apprenticeship systems and of in-work training, and promote the development of multi-purpose local learning centres, in order to:

   — equip young people with the basic skills relevant to the labour market and needed to participate in lifelong learning;

   — reduce youth and adult illiteracy and reduce substantially the number of young people who drop out of the school system early. Particular attention should also be given to young people with learning difficulties and with educational problems. Member States will in this context develop measures aimed at halving by 2010 the number of 18 to 24 year olds with only lower-secondary level education who are not in further education and training;

   — promote conditions to facilitate better access of adults, including those with a-typical contracts, to lifelong learning, so as to increase the proportion of adult working-age population (25-64 year olds) participating at any given time in education and training. Member States should set targets for this purpose.

   In order to facilitate mobility and encourage lifelong learning, Member States should improve the recognition of qualifications, acquired knowledge and skills.

5. Member States will aim at developing e-learning for all citizens. In particular, Member States will ensure that that all schools have access to the internet and multimedia resources by the end of 2001 and that all the teachers needed are skilled in the use of these technologies by the end of 2002 in order to provide all pupils with a broad digital literacy.

Active policies to develop job matching and to prevent and combat emerging bottlenecks

In all Member States unemployment and exclusion from the labour market coexist with labour shortages in certain sectors, occupations and regions. With the improvement of the employment situation and accelerating pace of technological change, these bottlenecks are increasing. An insufficiency of active policies to prevent and combat emerging labour shortages will harm competitiveness, increase inflationary pressures and keep structural unemployment high.

6. Member States will, as appropriate with the social partners, step up their efforts to identify and prevent emerging bottlenecks, in particular by:

   — developing the job-matching capacities of employment services;

   — developing policies to prevent skills shortages;

   — promoting occupational and geographical mobility;

   — enhancing the functioning of labour markets by improving databases on jobs and learning opportunities which should be interconnected at European level, making use of modern information technologies and experience already available at European level.

Combating discrimination and promoting social inclusion by access to employment

Many groups and individuals experience particular difficulties in acquiring relevant skills and in gaining access to, and remaining in, the labour market. This may increase the risk of exclusion. A coherent set of policies which promote social inclusion by supporting the integration of disadvantaged groups and individuals into the world of work, and combat discrimination in access to, and on, the labour market is called for.

7. Each Member State will:

   — identify and combat all forms of discrimination in access to the labour market and to education and training;

— develop pathways consisting of effective preventive and active policy measures to promote the integration into the labour market of groups and individuals at risk or with a disadvantage, in order to avoid marginalisation, the emergence of 'working poor' and a drift into exclusion;

— implement appropriate measures to meet the needs of the disabled, ethnic minorities and migrant workers as regards their integration into the labour market and set national targets where appropriate for this purpose.

II. DEVELOPING ENTREPRENEURSHIP AND JOB CREATION

Making it easier to start up and run businesses

The development of new businesses in general, and the contribution to the growth of small and medium-sized enterprises (SMEs) in particular, is essential for job creation and for the expansion of training opportunities for young people. This process must be promoted by encouraging greater entrepreneurial awareness across society and in educational curricula, by providing a clear, stable and predictable set of rules and regulations by improving the conditions for the development of, and access to, risk capital markets. Member States should also reduce and simplify the administrative and tax burdens on SMEs. These policies should strengthen the prevention of undeclared work.

8. Member States will give particular attention to reducing significantly the overhead costs and administrative burdens for businesses, in particular when an enterprise is being set up and when hiring additional workers. Also, Member States should, when drafting new regulations, assess their potential impact on such administrative burdens and overhead costs for businesses.

9. Member States will encourage the taking up of entrepreneurial activities:

   — by examining, with the aim of reducing, any obstacles which may exist, especially those within tax and social security regimes, to moving to self-employment and the setting up of small businesses;

   — by promoting education for entrepreneurship and self-employment, targeted support services as well as training for entrepreneurs and would-be entrepreneurs;

   — by combating undeclared work and encouraging the transformation of such work into regular employment, making use of all relevant means of action including regulatory measures, incentives and tax and benefit reform, in partnership with the social partners.

New opportunities for employment in the knowledge-based society and in services

If the European Union wants to deal successfully with the employment challenge, all possible sources of jobs and new technologies must be exploited effectively. Innovative enterprises must find a supportive environment because they can make an essential contribution to mobilising the job creation potential of the knowledge-based society. A considerable potential exists in particular in the services sector. To this end:

10. Member States will remove barriers to the provision of services and develop framework conditions to exploit fully the employment potential of the full range of the services sector to create more and better jobs. In particular, the employment potential of the knowledge society and the environmental sector should be tapped.

Regional and local action for employment

All actors at the regional and local levels, including the social partners, must be mobilised to implement the European Employment Strategy by identifying the potential of job creation at local level and strengthening partnerships to this end.

11. Member States will:

    — take into account, where appropriate, in their overall employment policy the regional development dimension;

    — encourage local and regional authorities to develop strategies for employment in order to exploit fully the possibilities offered by job creation at local level and promote partnerships to this end with all the actors concerned, including the representatives of civil society;

    — promote measures to enhance the competitive development and job creation capacity of the social economy, especially the provision of goods and services linked to needs not yet satisfied by the market, and examine, with the aim of reducing, any obstacles to such measures;

    — strengthen the role of the Public Employment Services at all levels in identifying local employment opportunities and improving the functioning of local labour markets.

Tax reforms for employment and training

It is important to deepen the examination of the employment impact of the tax burden, and make the taxation system more employment friendly by reversing the long-term trend towards higher taxes and charges on labour. Tax reforms must also take into account the need to increase investment in people, by business, public authorities and individuals themselves, in view of the longer term impact on employment and competitiveness.

12. Each Member State will:

    — set a target, if necessary and taking account of its present level, for gradually reducing the overall tax burden and, where appropriate, set a target for gradually reducing the fiscal pressure on labour and non-wage labour costs, in particular on relatively unskilled and low-paid labour. Such reforms should be undertaken without jeopardising the recovery of public finances or the long-term sustainability of social security systems;

    — provide incentives and remove tax obstacles to investment in human resources;

    — examine the desirability of using alternative sources of tax revenue, *inter alia* energy and pollutant emissions, taking into account current market trends, notably in oil markets.

III. ENCOURAGING ADAPTABILITY OF BUSINESSES AND THEIR EMPLOYEES

The opportunities created by the knowledge-based economy and the prospect of an improved level and quality of employment require a consequent adaptation of work organisation and the contribution to the implementation of Life Long Learning strategies by all actors including enterprises, in order to meet the needs of workers and employers.

Modernising work organisation

In order to promote the modernisation of work organisation and forms of work, a strong partnership should be developed at all appropriate levels (European, national, sectoral, local and enterprise levels).

13. The social partners are invited:

    — to negotiate and implement at all appropriate levels agreements to modernise the organisation of work, including flexible working arrangements, with the aim of making undertakings productive and competitive, achieving the required balance between flexibility and security, and increasing the quality of jobs. Subjects to be covered may, for example, include the introduction of new technologies, new forms of work and working time issues such as the expression of working time as an annual figure, the reduction of working hours, the reduction of overtime, the development of part-time working, access to career breaks, and associated job security issues; and

    — within the context of the Luxembourg process, to report annually on which aspects of the modernisation of the organisation of work have been covered by the negotiations as well as the status of their implementation and impact on employment and labour market functioning.

14. Member States will, where appropriate in partnership with the social partners or drawing upon agreements negotiated by the social partners,

    — review the existing regulatory framework, and examine proposals for new provisions and incentives to make sure they will contribute to reducing barriers to employment, to facilitate the introduction of modernised work organisation and to helping the labour market adapt to structural change in the economy;

    — at the same time, taking into account the fact that forms of employment are increasingly diverse, examine the possibility of incorporating in national law more flexible types of contract, and ensure that those working under new flexible contracts enjoy adequate security and higher occupational status, compatible with the needs of business and the aspirations of workers;

    — endeavour to ensure a better application at workplace level of existing health and safety legislation by stepping up and strengthening enforcement, by providing guidance to help enterprises, especially SMEs, to comply with existing legislation, by improving training on occupational health and safety, and by promoting measures for the reduction of occupational accidents and diseases in traditional high risk sectors.

Supporting adaptability in enterprises as a component of lifelong learning

In order to renew skill levels within enterprises as a key component to lifelong learning:

15. The social partners are invited, at all relevant levels, to conclude agreements, where appropriate, on lifelong learning to facilitate adaptability and innovation, particularly in the field of information and communication technologies. In this context, the conditions for giving every worker the opportunity to achieve information society literacy by 2003 should be established.

IV. STRENGTHENING EQUAL OPPORTUNITIES POLICIES FOR WOMEN AND MEN

Gender mainstreaming approach

In order to meet the objective of equal opportunity and reach the target of an increased employment rate for women in line with the conclusions of the Lisbon European Council, Member States' policies towards gender equality should be strengthened and should address all relevant conditions influencing women's decisions to take up employment.

Women still face particular problems in gaining access to employment, in career advancement, in earnings and in reconciling professional and family life. It is therefore important, *inter alia*:

— to ensure that active labour market policies are made available for women in proportion to their share of unemployment;

— to pay particular attention to the gender impact of tax and benefit systems. Wherever tax-benefit structures are identified that impact negatively on women's participation in the labour force, they should be reviewed;

— to pay particular attention to ensuring the application of the principle of equal pay for equal work or work of equivalent value;

— to give particular attention to obstacles which hinder women who wish to set up new businesses or become self-employed;

— to ensure that women are able to benefit positively from flexible forms of work organisation, on a voluntary basis and without loss of job quality;

— to ensure the conditions for facilitating the access of women to lifelong learning and in particular to IT training.

16. Therefore, the Member States will adopt a gender-mainstreaming approach in implementing the Guidelines across all four pillars:

   — developing and reinforcing consultative systems with gender equality bodies;

   — applying procedures for gender impact assessment under each guideline;

   — developing indicators to measure progress in gender equality in relation to each guideline.

In order meaningfully to evaluate progress, Member States will need to provide for adequate data collection systems and procedures and ensure a gender breakdown of employment statistics.

Tackling gender gaps

Member States and the social partners should pay attention to the imbalance in the representation of women or men in certain economic sectors and occupations, as well as to the improvement of female career opportunities.

17. Member States will, where appropriate with the social partners:

   — strengthen their efforts to reduce the gap in unemployment rates between women and men by actively supporting the increased employment of women, and consider setting national targets in accordance with the objectives set out in the conclusions of the Lisbon European Council;

   — take action to bring about a balanced representation of women and men in all sectors and occupations;

   — initiate positive steps to promote equal pay for equal work or work of equal value and to diminish differentials in incomes between women and men: actions to address gender pay gaps are necessary in the public and private sector, and the impact of the policies on gender pay gaps should be identified and addressed;

   — consider an increased use of measures for the advancement of women in order to reduce gender gaps.

Reconciling work and family life

Policies on career breaks, parental leave and part-time work, as well as flexible working arrangements which serve the interests of both employers and employees, are of particular importance to women and men. Implementation of the various Directives and social-partner agreements in this area should be accelerated and monitored regularly. There must be an adequate provision of good quality care for children and other dependants in order to support the entry of women and men into, and their continued participation in, the labour market. An equal sharing of family responsibilities is crucial in this respect. Those returning to the labour market after an absence may also have outmoded skills, and experience difficulty in gaining access to training. Reintegration of women and men into the labour market after an absence must be facilitated. In order to strengthen equal opportunities,

18. Member States and the social partners will:
    — design, implement and promote family-friendly policies, including affordable, accessible and high-quality care services for children and other dependants, as well as parental and other leave schemes;
    — consider setting a national target, in accordance with their national situation, for increasing the availability of care services for children and other dependants;
    — give specific attention to women, and men, considering a return to the paid workforce after an absence and, to that end, they will examine the means of gradually eliminating the obstacles to such return.

**Council Recommendation
of 19 January 2001
on the implementation of Member States' employment policies**

(OJ L 22, 24.1.2001)

COUNCIL RECOMMENDATION
of 19 January 2001
on the implementation of Member States' employment policies

(2001/64/EC)

THE COUNCIL OF THE EUROPEAN UNION,

Having regard to the Treaty establishing the European Community, and in particular Article 128(4) thereof,

Having regard to the 15 implementation reports for 2000 received from the Member States, comprising the implementation of the 1999 National Employment Action Plans and describing the adjustments made to the National Employment Action Plans to take account of the changes introduced by the 2000 guidelines,

Having regard to the Council Recommendation of 14 February 2000 on the implementation of Member States' employment policies [1],

Having regard to the Commission recommendation of 6 September 2000,

Whereas:

(1) The Council adopted the employment guidelines for 1998, 1999 and 2000 by, respectively, the Resolutions of 15 December 1997 [2] and 22 February 1999 [3], and by the Decision of 13 March 2000 [4].

(2) The Lisbon European Council on 23 and 24 March 2000 agreed on a comprehensive strategy towards employment, economic reform and social cohesion as part of the knowledge-based society, made a commitment to creating the conditions for full employment and stressed the importance of lifelong learning.

(3) The Santa Maria da Feira European Council on 19 and 20 June 2000 highlighted the prominent role the social partners are called to play in modernising work organisation, promoting lifelong learning and increasing the employment rate, particularly amongst women.

(4) The Council adopted the recommendation on the Broad Economic Policy Guidelines on 19 June 2000, and the Amsterdam European Council of 16 and 17 June 1997 agreed on a Resolution on a Stability and Growth Pact setting commitments by Member States.

(5) The 2000 Joint Employment Report, prepared jointly with the Commission, describes the employment situation in the Community and examines the action taken by Member States in implementing their employment policy in line with the guidelines.

(6) On 31 October 2000, the Employment Committee and the Economic Policy Committee jointly submitted an opinion on this Recommendation.

(7) The Council considers it appropriate, in the light of the examination of the implementation of the Member States' employment policies, to make recommendations. They should be used sparingly, concentrate on priority issues and be based on sound and accurate analysis.

(8) In complementing action undertaken by the Member States with a view to contributing towards the achievement of full employment, the competences of the Member States should be respected.

(9) The Council acknowledges the significant efforts already undertaken by Member States with a view to implementing the Employment Guidelines and the Recommendation of 14 February 2000. In the assessment of the impact of these policies, the multi-annual perspective of the Employment Guidelines should be taken into account.

(10) In addressing the employment guidelines, an overall strategic approach to the development and implementation of the employment policies in the Member States is called for.

(11) The development and implementation of lifelong learning is crucial to the development of a competitive and dynamic knowledge-based society and requires the active commitment of all actors concerned, including public authorities, the social partners and individuals, with a relevant contribution from civil society.

(12) To tackle youth unemployment, which is a long-standing problem in most Member States, all young people should have the opportunity to gain entry to the world of work before they have been unemployed for six months.

(13) To prevent adult long-term unemployment, which affects roughly half of the unemployed in the European Union, all the adult unemployed should be offered a new start before they have been unemployed for twelve months.

---
[1] OJ L 52, 25.2.2000, p. 32.
[2] OJ C 30, 28.1.1998, p. 1.
[3] OJ C 69, 12.3.1999, p. 2.
[4] OJ L 72, 21.3.2000, p. 15.

(14) It is important to reduce disincentives to employment embodied in the tax or benefit systems in order to ensure higher participation rates amongst women and older workers.

(15) Improvements of the business environment and a better equipment of individuals for taking up entrepreneurial activities are needed to stimulate job creation by more and more dynamic enterprises.

(16) Framework conditions need to be developed to tap the potential for employment growth in the services sector.

(17) Sustained job creation calls for more employment-friendly taxation systems in which the currently high burden on labour is shifted to alternative sources of fiscal revenue, such as energy and the environment.

(18) Local action for employment significantly contributes to the achievement of the objectives of the European Employment Strategy.

(19) The establishment of partnerships at all appropriate levels is crucial for the modernisation of the organisation of work and the promotion of the adaptability of undertakings and their employees.

(20) Gender gaps in the labour market, particularly affecting employment, unemployment and pay, as well as gender segregation across sectors and occupations, require comprehensive mainstreaming strategies and measures the better to reconcile work and family life,

HEREBY ISSUES to the individual Member States the recommendations set out in the Annex.

Done at Brussels, 19 January 2001.

For the Council
The President
B. RINGHOLM

ANNEX

RECOMMENDATIONS TO THE INDIVIDUAL MEMBER STATES

I. BELGIUM

Problems in employment performance

The Belgian labour market improved in 1999 with a particularly strong increase in the employment rate and a fall in the unemployment rate to below the EU average. However, employment growth slowed down and was below the EU average, and long-standing challenges are only gradually being met.

— Inflows into long-term unemployment are high, as are stocks of long-term unemployed people, who accounted for 5,0 % of the labour force in 1999.

— Participation in employment is low amongst older people (12 points below EU average) particularly those over 55, whose employment rate (24,7 %) is still the lowest in the Union.

— The average tax burden on labour remains one of the highest in the EU.

— Labour and skills shortages are emerging while regional disparities in unemployment remain considerable.

After due analysis, it appears that more efforts are required in response to the employment guidelines and recommendations concerning: implementation of a preventive policy; revision of the tax-benefit system; better cooperation between labour market authorities; reduction of the tax burden on labour and the development of lifelong learning.

Belgium should therefore:

1. intensify its efforts to implement the new individual approach towards all unemployed young people, which aims to reach them before they have been unemployed for six months; take decisive steps to design, and start implementing, an appropriate early-intervention system for unemployed adults;

2. continue to examine disincentives to labour market participation within the tax and benefit system, particularly those affecting older workers. Belgium should, in particular, closely monitor measures aiming at preventing the early withdrawal of workers from work and consider strengthening disincentive measures in that field;

3. continue efforts to reinforce cooperation between the different labour market authorities in order to integrate and ensure co-ordination between multiple active measures;

4. pursue further and closely monitor measures to reduce the tax burden on labour so as to encourage employees to take up a job and employers to recruit, and closely monitor the impact of the reduction of social security contributions;

5. develop and implement a comprehensive lifelong learning strategy to prevent skills shortages and build a more solid foundation for the knowledge-based economy and society.

II. DENMARK

Problems in employment performance

The labour market situation remains very favourable with the highest employment rates in the EU, both for men and women and one of the lowest unemployment rates. The key challenges for Denmark still lie in the need:

— to expand the current labour force, notably by encouraging employees to remain active members of the workforce for longer and by reducing the number of people of working age on social benefits;

— to achieve a greater balance between women and men across occupations.

After due analysis, it appears that further efforts are required in response to the employment guidelines and recommendations concerning: reduction of the tax-burden on labour; encouragement for employees to remain active members of the work force for longer; integration of unemployed women and lessening the degree of gender segregation.

Denmark should therefore:

1. pursue further and closely monitor implementation of on-going reforms to reduce the overall fiscal pressure on labour, in particular, the tax burden on low incomes;

2. increase incentives to take up, or remain in, employment and continue to monitor closely reform of early retirement and leave schemes in the light of the need to increase labour supply;

3. continue efforts to develop a more substantial mainstreaming approach and a comprehensive strategy for reducing the current levels of occupational gender segregation in the labour market.

III. GERMANY

Problems in employment performance

As the German economy continues to recover, the reversal in employment trends is becoming clearer, and unemployment has fallen further as the consequences of German unification continue to feed through. Amongst the key challenges still facing Germany's labour market are:

— slow absorption of the job losses registered throughout most of the 1990s (−1,2 percentage points per year from 1991 to 1998); and large regional differences in unemployment rates, the new *Länder* being particularly badly affected;

— persistently high long-term unemployment, accounting for 4,4 % of the labour force;

— despite recent reforms, one of the highest overall tax burdens on labour in the EU;

— the low proportion of people between 55 and 64 still in employment (about 37,8 %), which points to an additional unused employment potential, and the need for a more vigorous comprehensive lifelong learning policy to boost the employability of the labour force.

After due analysis, it appears that more efforts are required in response to the employment guidelines and recommendations concerning: the tax burden on labour; preventive policies; the tax/benefit system, in particular for older workers; lifelong learning and equal opportunities.

Germany should therefore:

1. push ahead with full implementation of a preventive approach, focused on early action to meet individual needs and prevent people from becoming long-term unemployed. Progress towards common and national targets should be closely monitored;

2. continue to examine obstacles and disincentives liable to discourage labour market participation amongst all groups, especially older workers. Changes in labour market participation rates amongst older workers should be monitored and further measures adopted to improve the employability of this group;

3. tackle skills gaps in the labour market, through improvements in the framework conditions, including incentives, for continuous education, training and apprenticeship in partnership with the social partners, and through further developing a comprehensive strategy and qualitative as well as quantitative targets for lifelong learning. Measures are needed in schools and training establishments to ensure a better transition into modern jobs in the workplace;

4. pursue further and monitor efforts to continue the reduction of the fiscal pressure on labour notably, on the basis of the recent tax reform 2000 and eco-tax reform, by reducing taxes and social security contributions. Labour costs should be reduced further also at the lowest end of the wage scale, while respecting the need for fiscal consolidation;

5. pursue and strengthen the double-pronged approach coupling gender mainstreaming and specific measures for equal opportunities, paying particular attention to the impact of the tax and benefit system on women's employment, and taking action to reduce the gender pay gap.

IV. GREECE

Problems in employment performance

By the end of 1999, Greece met the convergence criteria for joining the Economic and Monetary Union. However, Greece has one of the lowest employment rates (55,4 %) in the EU. Unemployment has increased in the last few years largely as a result of the growing labour force (women and immigrants) and of the continuous decline of employment in the agricultural sector, and it is still above the EU average. Long-term unemployment has also increased. This situation illustrates the following structural problems in the labour market:

— youth, female and long-term unemployment rates remain high, above the EU average;

— there is a wide gender gap both in employment and unemployment;

— educational reforms include steps to develop lifelong learning, but there is no clear overall strategy, while education and vocational training systems need further improvement;

— high administrative burdens hinder business growth, particularly in the start-up phase, and employment in services is still low, despite improvements in certain areas;

— there is room for improvement in the use of new technologies and in the modernisation of work organisation.

After due analysis, it appears that further efforts are required in response to the employment guidelines and recommendations concerning: the overall policy approach; prevention and activation; gender mainstreaming and increased female participation; education and training; the reduction of the administrative burden and the modernisation of work organisation.

Greece should therefore:

1. develop a strategic framework and a set of well structured policies for the implementation of the employment guidelines across the four pillars;

2. take decisive and coherent action to prevent young and adult unemployed people from drifting into long-term unemployment, in compliance with guidelines 1 and 2, through developing existing plans for the swift reform of public employment services; the statistical system must be upgraded, so that policy indicators on prevention and activation are available in good time and progress can be effectively monitored;

3. examine the possibility of reducing taxes on labour and/or earned income, in order to raise the employment rate. Greece should also encourage, within a gender mainstreaming approach, greater participation of women in the labour market;

4. adopt a comprehensive strategy on lifelong learning, including the setting of targets, and further improve education and vocational training systems in order to enhance the skills of the labour force; and give more support for continuous training, in particular by involving social partners more actively;

5. adopt and implement a coherent strategy aimed at significantly reducing the administrative burden involved in setting up a new business, in order to stimulate entrepreneurship and fully exploit the job creation potential of the service sector;

6. strengthen a partnership approach and promote concrete commitments by the social partners at all appropriate levels on the modernisation of work organisation, with the aim of making undertakings more productive and competitive while achieving the required balance between flexibility and security.

V. SPAIN

Problems in employment performance

Spain has been experiencing positive economic and employment growth over recent years, but serious challenges remain.

— The employment rate, though on the rise, is among the lowest in the EU. Unemployment is still high, at 15,9 %, despite a significant decline since 1996. Long-term unemployment has also declined, but women and older workers remain particularly badly affected by unemployment.

— The percentage of temporary employment is high; most of these temporary jobs are of short duration and tend to be done predominantly by women and young people.

— Regional disparities are wide, while geographical mobility is very low.

— Although the female employment rate has been increasing, it is still the lowest in the EU (37,6 %). At 30,3 %, the employment gender gap is the widest in the EU. Unemployment amongst women is running at 23,1 %.

— Less than 35 % of the population aged 25 to 64 have completed upper-secondary level education. Early school-leaving is widespread and participation in education and training during adulthood is particularly low. There is no comprehensive approach to lifelong learning.

After due analysis, it appears that more efforts are required in response to the employment guidelines and recommendations concerning: prevention and activation policies; improvement of the statistical monitoring system; gender mainstreaming; lifelong learning; adaptability and tax and benefit systems.

Spain should therefore:

1. continue with modernisation of the Public Employment Services to improve its efficiency, and step up implementation of the preventive approach so as to cover all potential beneficiaries. Such efforts should include the completion of the statistical monitoring system in accordance with the National Action Plan and the Joint Employment Report;

2. do more to support mainstreaming of equal opportunities in order to bring the female employment rate up towards the EU average, in a timeframe, given the extent of the problem, that adequately reflects the urgency of this objective;

3. develop and implement a coherent strategy on lifelong learning which includes targets and encompasses initial and continuing education and training so as to increase the levels of educational attainment and participation of adults in education and training activities. Special attention should be given to the problem of early school leavers;

4. pursue efforts, in partnership with the social partners, to adapt employment relations, including labour regulations, and to develop new forms of work organisation, by ensuring an appropriate balance between flexibility and security for the whole labour force;

5. examine the incentives/disincentives emerging from the tax and benefit systems with a view to increase participation in the labour market and stable employment.

VI. FRANCE

Problems in employment performance

The employment situation continues to improve. However, major structural problems remain.

— Participation amongst the 55 to 64 age group remains well below the EU average (28,3 % against 35,9 %) and 1999 saw no change in the downward trend.

— The fall in unemployment was modest and, at 11,3 %, the unemployment rate is still above the EU average of 10,8 %.

— Taxes on labour are high.

After due analysis, it appears that further efforts are required in response to the employment guidelines and recommendations concerning: older workers in active life; the reduction of fiscal pressure on labour; prevention and lifelong learning.

France should therefore:

1. strengthen efforts to curb older workers' early withdrawal from working life by developing a more comprehensive approach involving the social partners;

2. pursue and evaluate policy measures designed to reduce the fiscal pressure on labour, particularly measures with an effect on unskilled and low-paid workers;

3. continue with implementation of individualised and early intervention schemes for the unemployed, and make greater use of such schemes to prevent both youth and adult unemployment;

4. pursue efforts to modernise work organisation and monitor closely the net effects of the implementation of the 35-hour week legislation; take steps to increase the efficiency of the continuous training system and to promote a comprehensive lifelong learning strategy;

5. pursue the implementation of coherent strategies, encompassing regulatory, fiscal and other measures, designed to reduce the administrative burden on companies, and evaluate the impact of on-going efforts to create new job opportunities for young people.

VII. IRELAND

Problems in employment performance

Ireland's economic and employment performance has been exceptional. In 1999, the employment rate overtook the EU average. Furthermore, the unemployment rate has continued to fall for all groups. These developments indicate a further tightening of the labour market. Some structural problems still exist however.

— As is the case for some other Member States, avoiding labour market shortages and associated wage inflation pressures is a core problem for Ireland.

— Although it has increased significantly, the participation rate for women remains below the EU average and the employment gender gap has only slightly improved between 1998 and 1999.

— As a result of the growing labour market shortages, it is important for Ireland to invest in education and training for the unemployed and employed alike. It is one of the few countries which saw an increase in the percentage of unemployed people taking part in training. At the same time, the number of employed in training remains one of the lowest in the Union.

After due analysis, it appears that further efforts are required in response to the employment guidelines and recommendations concerning: the participation of women in the labour market and the development of a strategy in relation to in-company training and lifelong learning.

Ireland should therefore:

1. push ahead with its comprehensive strategy aimed at increasing the proportion of women in employment, removing tax barriers and increasing child care places; and take action with the aim of reducing the gender pay gap;

2. pursue and strengthen efforts to sustain productivity growth and upgrade skills and qualifications in the workforce, through increased emphasis on in-company training and the further development of lifelong learning, including the setting of targets.

VIII. ITALY

Problems in employment performance

Employment increased during 1999, principally due to the adoption of fiscal incentives and flexible working arrangements. However, these improvements leave several structural problems of the Italian labour market still unsolved, particularly with reference to regional unbalances.

— The low employment rate of 52,5 % is some 10 percentage points below the EU average. At 27,5 %, the employment rate for older people is still low.

— The female employment rate rose more sharply than the male rate, yet, at 38,1 %, it remains among the lowest in the EU.

— Unemployment fell to 11,3 % but remains 2 percentage points above the EU average. At 12,4 % the unemployment ratio amongst 15 to 24 year-olds remained almost 4 percentage points higher than the EU average. Long-term unemployment improved only marginally from 7,1 % of the labour force in 1998 to 6,9 % in 1999.

— Wide gender gaps in employment — at roughly 30 percentage points — are characteristic of the labour market, particularly in the southern regions and female unemployment, at 15,6 %, is almost double the male unemployment rate of 8,7 %.

— Regional disparities remain significant with an unemployment rate of about 6,5 % in the Centre-North and 22 % in the South.

— 51,5 % of the workforce has completed upper secondary level education, compared with the EU average of 66 %, but only 6,1 % of adults were involved in education or training, compared to an EU average of 8,7 %.

After due analysis, it appears that further efforts are required in response to the employment guidelines and recommendations concerning: the policy mix across the four pillars; tax and benefit systems; activation and prevention; gender mainstreaming and gender gaps and lifelong learning.

Italy should therefore:

1. continue to improve the balance in the policy mix across the four pillars, by further strengthening employability policies, pursuing the modernisation of work organisation, including the regulatory framework, developing a comprehensive strategy for equal opportunities and continuing gender mainstreaming efforts;

2. continue the implementation of the reform of pension through the review planned for 2001 and review other benefit systems in order to reduce the outflow from the labour market and further continue efforts to reduce the tax burden, especially on low-paid workers;

3. in the context of employability policies, take further action to prevent the inflow of young and adult unemployed people into long-term unemployment. Such action would include the full implementation of the PES reform across the country, speeding up the introduction of the Employment Information System and continuation of current efforts to upgrade the statistical monitoring system;

4. pursue active labour market policies and implement specific measures to narrow the wide gender gaps in employment and unemployment, with the aim of providing women with more and better job opportunities;

5. adopt and implement a coherent strategy on lifelong learning, including national targets; social partners should be more active in providing more training opportunities for the work force.

IX. LUXEMBOURG

Problems in employment performance

Luxembourg enjoyed good labour market conditions in 1999, supported by strong economic growth and the highest rise in the employment rate in the EU (4,8 percentage points). The unemployment rate continued to fall and remains the lowest in the EU (2,3 %). Some structural problems can be identified though.

— The overall national employment rate is very low despite a very good employment situation with a large number of cross-border workers. The rates are especially low for workers over 55 (26,3 %) and for women (48,5 %), although both figures have risen since 1998.

— The employment gender gap is one of the widest in the EU, at 25,9 percentage points.

— The domestic supply of qualified people is insufficient.

— The proportion of the adult working population taking part in continuous education and training is still low (5,3 %).

After due analysis, it appears that further efforts are required in response to the employment guidelines and recommendations concerning: the social dialogue, participation of older workers and women in the labour market and lifelong learning.

Luxembourg should therefore:

1. encourage the social partners to foster a constructive dialogue, as this is indispensable for the success of the employment policies outlined in the National Action Plan;

2. pursue efforts and implement measures aimed at increasing labour-market participation rates amongst older workers and women, including a review of tax and benefit systems; and take action to promote gender mainstreaming;

3. continue with implementation of the framework law on continuous vocational training and work on policy development and implementation, including the setting of targets, so as to increase the participation rates in education and training.

X. THE NETHERLANDS

Problems in employment performance

The Netherlands enjoyed healthy employment growth in 1999 and employment rates are clearly above the EU average. The unemployment rate continued to fall in 1999, to 3,3 %, below the EU average. There are still some structural problems however.

— Although long-term unemployment is falling, there are persistent problems with specific groups, especially low-skilled workers, older workers and ethnic minorities.

— Large numbers of working-age people are kept out of the labour market by disability and other welfare benefits.

— Labour market shortages and associated wage inflation pressures are emerging.

After due analysis, it appears that further efforts are required in response to the employment guidelines and recommendations concerning: the tax and benefit systems and the statistical monitoring system.

The Netherlands should therefore:

1. continue to cooperate with the social partners, to reduce disincentives in the benefit system liable to discourage people from participating in the open labour market, in particular people receiving disability benefits, and generate poverty traps;

2. continue to upgrade the statistical system so that policy and output indicators are available early enough to be used for monitoring and evaluating on-going implementation of the preventive approach.

XI. AUSTRIA

Problems in employment performance

The Austrian labour market's performance improved last year, when the overall employment rate reached 68,2 % (59,7 % for women). That figure is close to the 70 % target established by the Lisbon European Council and well above the EU average. Overall unemployment was reduced to 3,8 % in 1999, and together with youth and long-term unemployment is among the lowest in the EU. Despite the overall good performance, structural problems remain in the labour market.

— The overall tax burden is above average and fiscal pressure on labour increased in the period from 1994 to 1998. The forecast reduction in non-wage labour costs of around 0,4 percentage points of GDP by 2003 is a first step forward.

— There is still a significant gender gap in both employment and unemployment, despite the fact that the employment rate for women is higher than the EU average.

— The employment rate for older workers is below the EU average figure and unemployment amongst the over-50s remains high.

After due analysis, it appears that more efforts are required in response to the employment guidelines and recommendations concerning: older workers' employability, gender mainstreaming and taxation on labour.

Austria should therefore:

1. do more to reduce significantly the heavy tax burden on labour, in particular by focusing on groups who face problems in the labour market;

2. pursue a comprehensive strategy to narrow the still significant gender gap in employment, for instance through measures that help reduce the pay gap and facilitate the reconciliation of work and family life;

3. continue its efforts to reform early retirement schemes and other measures for older people to stay in work longer so as to achieve a significant rise in the employment rate of older workers.

XII. PORTUGAL

Problems in employment performance

The employment situation further improved in 1999, confirming the previous year's positive trend. Unemployment is among the lowest in the EU, and long-term unemployment has fallen fast. However, the labour market suffers from structural weaknesses which require action:

— the average skill level in the work force is low. Only 21,2 % have completed at least upper-secondary education compared to the EU average of 66 %. At 3,6 %, participation in education and training is also below the EU average of 8,7 % and 45 % of young people aged 18 to 24 left school early;

— the potential for creating jobs in services is considerable, as can be seen from the service-sector employment rate of 36,2 %, and it is necessary to pursue a coherent strategy to foster entrepreneurship;

— a strong input from the social partners is needed to address the main challenges facing the Portuguese labour market, in particular the low skill level, the modernisation of work organisation and employment relations;

— in a context of overall improvement of the situation of women in the labour market, a better gender balance is needed, especially in terms of sectors.

After due analysis, it appears that more efforts are required in response to the employment guidelines and recommendations concerning: education and training; reduction of the administrative burden on companies; the partnership approach; gender segregation and access to childcare.

Portugal should therefore:

1. pursue the efforts to develop and implement a comprehensive lifelong learning strategy which also addresses the problems of early school leaving, sets clear objectives and devises appropriate means. Particular attention should be devoted to the quality of education and training in order to avoid skill shortages;

2. pursue efforts to reduce the administrative burden on companies, to exploit the job creation potential of the service sector and to promote the creation of medium and highly skilled jobs in the services sector;

3. pursue efforts to implement a partnership approach and promote concrete commitments from social partners, in particular in the areas of modernisation of work organisation, adaptation of employment relations, including labour regulations and continuous training;

4. pursue efforts to reconcile family and working life by extending childcare facilities, and examine ways to promote gender balance at sectorial level.

365

XIII. FINLAND

Problems in employment performance

While Finland has maintained strong economic growth over the past five years, some major structural problems remain.

— The overall unemployment rate is still high at 10,2 %, being predominantly structural. Youth unemployment and long-term unemployment for those over 50 years old remain a major concern.

— Through recent initiatives, Finland has made progress in lightening the tax burden on labour. However it remains heavier than the EU-average.

— Finland faces skills shortages in several sectors (both in high and low-skilled jobs) and there is a general need to mobilise the labour force by focusing on quality active labour market policies.

— Regional disparities in employment remain considerable.

After due analysis, it appears further efforts are required in response to the employment guidelines and recommendations concerning: tax and benefit schemes, the tax burden on labour and occupational and sectoral segregation in the labour market.

Finland should therefore:

1. continue to review existing tax and benefit schemes, in order to increase incentives to work and to recruit workers, and focus lifelong learning policies on older people, so as to retain them as active members of the workforce for longer;

2. pursue further recent policy initiatives aimed at reducing the tax burden on labour, with due consideration for prevailing economic and employment conditions in Finland;

3. monitor and assess, in the context of a gender mainstreaming approach, the current levels of occupational and sectoral segregation in the labour market.

XIV. SWEDEN

Problems in employment performance

Sweden has one of the highest employment rates in the EU. It has recently improved its job creation performance, reducing unemployment to 7,2 % in 1999. However, a number of structural problems remain in the labour market.

— The tax burden on labour is still very heavy, especially for the relatively unskilled and low paid. Sweden continues to have the highest tax rates on employed labour in the EU — 52,7 % in 1998 compared to the EU average of 39,2 %.

— A large number of people of working age are dependent on benefits.

— Skill shortages, particularly at regional level, have become a factor hampering economic growth and regional development.

— The current level of occupational and sectoral segregation between men and women remains an issue of concern, despite well developed equal opportunity policies.

After due analysis, it appears that further efforts are required in response to the employment guidelines and recommendations concerning: the tax burden on labour, and gender mainstreaming.

Sweden should therefore:

1. do more, including the setting of targets taking into account the national situation to reduce the high tax burden on labour, in particular for those with a low take-home pay from work;

2. pursue further policy initiatives to further adapt the benefit and assistance schemes, so as to provide adequate incentives to take up jobs;

3. monitor and assess current levels of occupational and sectoral segregation in the labour market, as part of the gender mainstreaming reforms begun in 1999.

XV. UNITED KINGDOM

Problems in employment performance

The United Kingdom enjoyed healthy employment growth in 1999, and the employment rates for men and women are clearly above the EU average. The unemployment rate continued to fall in 1999, to 6,1 %, below the EU average. Yet, important structural problems persist:

— inflows into long-term unemployment amongst young people and adults (17 % and 11 % respectively) still exceed those of the best performing Member States;

- although long-term unemployment is falling, there are still persistent problems concentrated in specific groups, especially within households with no one in work, amongst disadvantaged groups, and in a number of geographical areas. Inactivity among lone parents is still a problem;
- some sectors, particularly information technology, suffer from a skills gap. The low level of basic skills is a generalised problem in the United Kingdom;
- though diminishing, the gender pay gap remains high compared to the EU average. The gender gap in employment attributable to the impact of parenthood is also the highest in the EU, suggesting a need for sufficient and affordable childcare;
- the current levels of occupational and sectoral segregation between men and women are higher than the EU average.

After due analysis, it appears that further efforts are required in response to the employment guidelines and recommendations concerning: adaptability, the gender pay gap, childcare provision, a preventive strategy for the unemployed and lifelong learning.

The United Kingdom should therefore:

1. improve the balance of policy implementation of the Guidelines, so as to strengthen and make more visible efforts to modernise work organisation, in particular by fostering social partnership at all appropriate levels;

2. pursue efforts to reduce the gender pay gap and take action to improve childcare provision, with a view to making it easier for men and women with parental responsibilities to take employment. Special attention should be given to the needs of lone parents;

3. reinforce active labour market policies for the adult unemployed before the 12 month point, so as to increase the number of people benefiting from active measures, and supplement the support provided by the Jobseekers' Allowance Regime;

4. intensify efforts to implement initiatives on lifelong learning, particularly those aimed at increasing the general level of basic skills, demonstrating how access will be ensured for those groups traditionally reluctant to take up the opportunity, or unable to find suitable provision.

**Council Recommendation
of 18 February 2002
on the implementation of Member States' employment policies**

(OJ L 60, 01.03.2002)

COUNCIL RECOMMENDATION
of 18 February 2002
on the implementation of Member States' employment policies

(2002/178/EC)

THE COUNCIL OF THE EUROPEAN UNION,

Having regard to the Treaty establishing the European Community, and in particular Article 128(4) thereof,

Having regard to the Commission Recommendation of 12 September 2001,

Having regard to the joint opinion of the Employment Committee and the Economic Policy Committee,

Whereas:

(1) The Council adopted the employment guidelines for 2001 by the Decision of 19 January 2001 [1].

(2) The Lisbon European Council on 23 and 24 March 2000 agreed on a comprehensive strategy towards employment, economic reform and social cohesion and made a commitment to creating the conditions for full employment. Targets for employment rates to be reached by 2010 were accordingly set and further complemented by the Stockholm European Council on 23 and 24 March with intermediate targets for 2005 and a new target for increasing the employment rate among older women and men by 2010.

(3) The Nice European Council on 7, 8 and 9 December 2000 approved the European Social Agenda, which states that the return to full employment involves ambitious policies in terms of increasing employment rates, reducing regional gaps, reducing inequality and improving job quality.

(4) The Council adopted the Recommendation on the broad economic policy guidelines on 15 June 2001, and the Amsterdam European Council of 16 and 17 June 1997 agreed on a Resolution on a Stability and Growth Pact setting commitments by Member States.

(5) Member States should implement this Recommendation in a way which is consistent with the broad economic policy guidelines, and in particular the labour market part thereof.

(6) The 2001 Joint Employment Report, prepared jointly with the Commission, describes the employment situation in the Community and examines the action taken by Member States in implementing their employment policy in line with the 2001 employment guidelines and the Council Recommendation of 19 January 2001 on the implementation of Member States' employment policies [2].

(7) The Council considers it appropriate, in the light of the examination of the implementation of the Member States' employment policies, to make recommendations. They should be used sparingly, concentrate on priority issues and be based on sound and accurate analysis.

(8) In complementing action undertaken by the Member States with a view to contributing towards the achievement of full employment, the powers of the Member States should be respected.

(9) The Council acknowledges the significant efforts already undertaken by Member States with a view to implementing the Employment Guidelines and the Recommendation of 19 January 2001. In the assessment of the impact of these policies, the multi-annual perspective of the employment guidelines should be taken into account.

(10) Member States should articulate their envisaged response to the Guidelines under the four pillars in a coherent overall strategy aiming at full employment, recognising Member States' different starting positions, the development and implementation of comprehensive and coherent strategies for lifelong learning and a comprehensive partnership with the social partners. Due consideration should be given to gender mainstreaming and the need to reduce regional disparities and evaluate progress under all four pillars on the basis of indicators.

(11) In order to influence the trend in youth and long-term unemployment, all young people should have the opportunity to gain entry to the world of work before they have been unemployed for six months and all the adult unemployed should be offered a new start before they have been unemployed for twelve months.

(12) Member States should pursue the modernisation of their public employment services.

(13) It is important to reduce disincentives to employment embodied in the tax or benefit systems in order to ensure higher participation rates amongst women and older workers.

---

[1] OJ L 22, 24.1.2001, p. 18.

[2] OJ L 22, 24.1.2001, p. 27.

(14) The development and implementation of lifelong learning, covering the development of systems for initial, secondary and tertiary education, further education and vocational training and the setting of national targets, is crucial to the development of a competitive and dynamic knowledge-based society and requires the active commitment of all actors concerned, including public authorities, the social partners and individuals, with a relevant contribution from civil society.

(15) A coherent set of policies which promote social inclusion by supporting the integration of disadvantaged groups and individuals into the world of work, and combat discrimination in access to, and on the labour market is called for.

(16) Improvements of the business environment and a better equipment of individuals for taking up entrepreneurial activities are needed to stimulate job creation by more and more dynamic enterprises. Framework conditions need to be developed to tap the potential for employment growth in the services sector.

(17) Sustained job creation calls for more employment-friendly taxation systems in which the currently high burden on labour is shifted to alternative sources of fiscal revenue, such as energy and the environment.

(18) Local action for employment significantly contributes to the achievement of the objectives of the European Employment Strategy.

(19) The establishment of partnerships at all appropriate levels is crucial for the modernisation of the organisation of work and the promotion of the adaptability of undertakings and their employees.

(20) Gender gaps in the labour market, particularly affecting employment, unemployment and pay, as well as gender segregation across sectors and occupations, require comprehensive mainstreaming strategies and measures to better reconcile work and family life,

HEREBY ISSUES to the individual Member States the recommendations set out in the Annex.

Done at Brussels, 18 February 2002.

For the Council
The President
M. ARIAS CAÑETE

ANNEX

I. BELGIUM

Problems in employment performance

The Belgian labour market improved in 2000 with an increase in the employment rate to 60,5 %, still markedly below the Lisbon target of 70 %. A further drop in the unemployment rate to 7 % (below the Community average of 8,2 %) was recorded and employment growth picked up to match the European Community average (1,8 %). However, long-standing challenges are only gradually being met:

— inflows into long-term unemployment are high and, despite a further decrease, the stock of long-term unemployed people — 3,8 % of the labour force in 2000 — is greater than the Community average,

— participation in employment amongst older workers is still the lowest in the European Community (at 26,3 %, 11,4 points below the Community average), while the rate amongst women, at 51,5 %, remains below the Community average,

— the tax burden on labour remains one of the highest in the Community,

— labour and skills shortages are apparent and a fully coherent and comprehensive lifelong learning strategy is not yet in place,

— regional disparities in unemployment remain considerable and point to inadequate labour mobility.

After due analysis, it appears that more efforts are required in response to the employment guidelines and recommendations concerning: implementation of a preventive policy, notably for adults; increasing the employment rate amongst older workers and women; reduction of the tax burden on labour; the development of lifelong learning; and increasing labour mobility between regions.

Belgium should therefore:

1. reduce inflows into long-term unemployment by taking decisive steps to implement an appropriate early intervention system for unemployed adults; examine the impact of the new personalised approach towards all unemployed young people;

2. take stronger action with a view to increasing the overall employment rate, notably for women and older workers. Belgium should, in particular, examine the impact of recent measures and consider further measures aimed at preventing the early withdrawal of workers from work, as well as incentives enhancing the capacity of older workers to remain at work;

3. pursue further measures to reduce the tax burden on labour so as to encourage employees to take up work and employers to create new jobs, and closely monitor the impact of measures already taken, including those related to the reduction of social security contributions;

4. reinforce, in cooperation with all actors concerned, the development and implementation of a comprehensive lifelong learning strategy to prevent skills shortages, to raise the attractiveness of technical and vocational education and to build a more solid foundation for the knowledge-based economy and society;

5. continue, together with the social partners, efforts to better combine security with greater labour market flexibility, and take concerted action to increase labour mobility between regions through the provision of labour market information and further improvements to the coordination of labour market policies.

II. DENMARK

Problems in employment performance

The labour market situation remains very favourable with the highest female employment rate in the European Community (71,6 %), one of the highest male employment rates (80,8 %) and one of the lowest unemployment rates (4,7 %). While Denmark exceeds the Lisbon targets, key challenges for Denmark are:

— the overall tax burden which — although declining — is still high. The small differences between benefits and low wage incomes have limited so far the effects from tax reforms on work incentives for low income groups,

— the tightening of the labour market in 2000, while a considerable part of the working age population is on early retirement or on social benefits, and the employment rate remains low amongst migrant workers.

After due analysis, it appears that further efforts are required in response to the employment guidelines and recommendations concerning: the reduction of the tax burden; and increasing labour market participation.

Denmark should therefore:

1. pursue and closely monitor implementation of on-going reforms to reduce the overall fiscal pressure on labour, in particular through lowering the high marginal effective tax rates on low and medium income earners;

2. pursue incentives to encourage yet more people to take up employment, particularly through further development of the inclusive labour market and further efforts towards the integration of migrant workers.

III. GERMANY

Problems in employment performance

Positive overall employment and unemployment trends over recent years were confirmed in 2000. While the overall employment rate of 65,3 % exceeds the European Community average, it remains 5 percentage points below the Lisbon target. The key challenges still facing Germany's labour market are:

— relatively slow decreases in long-term unemployment, which still accounts for 4 % of the labour force, with persistent regional differences, notably in unemployment rates, regions in the new *Länder* being particularly badly affected. While active labour market policies have been able to soften the impact of changes, the outcome of these policies in the eastern part of the country are mixed,

— the employment rate of people aged 55 to 64, at 37,3 %, which decreased slightly to below the Community average,

— the need for modernising work organisation and for a continuing substantial and lifelong learning effort to overcome skill gaps and to enhance generally the qualification level of the labour force,

— despite on-going reforms, the still high overall tax burden on labour,

— a high gender pay gap, according to available data, and relatively few childcare facilities.

After due analysis, it appears that more efforts are required in response to the employment guidelines and recommendations concerning: preventive policies; increasing older people's labour market participation; lifelong learning; the tax burden on labour; and equal opportunities.

Germany should therefore:

1. in order to substantially reduce long-term unemployment, devote additional effort to the prevention of inflows into long-term unemployment, particularly in the eastern part of the country and in respect of ethnic minorities and migrant workers, and increase the effectiveness of active labour market policies;

2. continue to remove obstacles and disincentives liable to discourage labour market participation amongst older workers and other groups at risk; examine and report on the effectiveness of initiated and agreed actions and adopt further measures to improve the employability of workers above 55 years of age;

3. take measures, where appropriate in the framework of the 'Alliance for Jobs', to make work contracts and work organisation more flexible; tackle skill gaps in the labour market through the implementation of agreed improvements for initial and continuing training, and through further developing a comprehensive strategy for lifelong learning supported by qualitative and quantitative targets. The social partners and the Government, each in its field of competence, are invited to strengthen their efforts to raise the quality of continuing training and to set up systems for the accreditation and recognition of formal and non-formal learning;

4. pursue efforts to reduce taxes and social security contributions at the lowest end of the wage scale to make work pay and to enhance viable and acceptable employment prospects; examine and report on the impact of measures undertaken;

5. strengthen action to reduce the gender pay gap and address the impact of the tax and benefit system on women's employment; promote the availability of childcare facilities and improve their correspondence with working hours and school schedules. The implementation of these policies, involving the respective actors at all levels, should be monitored with appropriate verifiable indicators and targets.

IV. GREECE

Problems in employment performance

Greece still has one of the lowest employment rates in the European Community (55,6 % overall and 40,9 % for women, well below the Lisbon targets). Unemployment has now stabilised at 11 % — well above the Community average — with growth in employment outweighed by long-term structural increases in the labour force. Long-term unemployment has been reduced to 6,2 % but remains significantly higher than the Community average. This situation reflects the following structural problems in the labour market:

— the low employment rate, while there is still unexploited job-creation potential in its small and medium-sized enterprises (SME) and services-based economy,

— against the background of high youth, female and long-term unemployment, the public employment services do not deliver yet a preventive and personalised approach. Despite efforts to monitor flow statistics, a comprehensive system is not yet available,

— in the context of low employment rates, the tax system as well as rules on pension entitlements should be reviewed in order to increase labour supply,

— educational reforms include steps to develop lifelong learning, but there is still no clear overall strategy, and education and vocational training systems need further improvement,

— while the recent labour market reforms constitute an important move towards modernisation of work, there is room for further improvement. Success in this field will require the active involvement of the social partners,

— there are wide gender gaps in employment and unemployment which should be addressed *inter alia* by increased provision of childcare facilities.

After due analysis, it appears that further efforts are required in response to the employment guidelines and recommendations concerning: the overall policy approach; prevention of unemployment; tax-benefit reform; lifelong learning; the modernisation of work organisation; and gender mainstreaming.

Greece should therefore:

1. improve the strategic framework, in particular by developing a set of well coordinated and balanced policies for the implementation of the employment guidelines across the four pillars with a view to increasing the employment rate, in particular for women and young people;

2. speed up the restructuring of the public employment services and take decisive and coherent action to prevent young and adult unemployed people from drifting into long-term unemployment through *inter alia* swift implementation of the personalised approach; further upgrade the statistical system so that indicators on prevention and activation are available in good time and progress can be effectively monitored;

3. examine and eliminate distortions arising from labour taxes and pension entitlements, thus improving incentives to work;

4. further develop and implement a comprehensive strategy on lifelong learning, including the setting of targets; increase investment in and further improve education and vocational training systems, including apprenticeship, in order to enhance the skills of the labour force and meet the needs of the labour market;

5. ensure the full implementation of the recent labour market reform package, in close cooperation with the social partners; in this context, the social partners should make further commitments on the modernisation of work organisation, while seeking an appropriate balance between flexibility and security;

6. take effective and comprehensive action to reduce the employment and unemployment gender gaps. To this end, care facilities for children and other dependants should be extended.

V. SPAIN

Problems in employment performance

Spain has been experiencing steady and positive economic and employment growth over recent years, but serious challenges remain:

— unemployment is still very high at 14,1 %, despite a significant decline since 1996. Long-term unemployment has also declined, but women remain particularly badly affected by unemployment,

— the employment rate of 55 %, though on the increase, is among the lowest in the European Community and far below the Lisbon target. Although the female employment rate has been steadily increasing, at 40,3 % it is still one of the lowest in the Community. Gender gaps in both employment and unemployment (29,6 and 10,8 percentage points respectively) are among the highest in the Community,

— while levels of educational attainment and participation in further learning are low, a fully coherent and comprehensive approach to lifelong learning is not yet in place,

— employment under fixed term contracts is high; most of these temporary contracts are of short duration and tend to be taken predominantly by women and young people,

— regional disparities are wide, while geographical mobility is very low.

After due analysis, it appears that more efforts are required in response to the employment guidelines and recommendations concerning: activation and prevention of unemployment; gender mainstreaming; lifelong learning; adaptability; and regional disparities.

Spain should therefore:

1. complete the modernisation of the public employment services so as to improve its efficiency, and step up implementation of the preventive approach, particularly with regard to the adult unemployed, so as to cover all potential beneficiaries. These efforts should include the completion of the statistical monitoring system;

2. take effective and comprehensive action to increase the overall employment rate and to close gender gaps in employment and unemployment. As part of a gender mainstreaming approach, targets for the provision of care facilities for children and other dependants should be adopted and implemented;

3. vigorously complete reforms on vocational training to encompass a comprehensive and coherent strategy on lifelong learning, including the setting of verifiable targets, with a view to increasing the levels of educational attainment and the participation of adults in education and training, addressing the low level of skills and developing non-formal learning;

4. further modernise the labour market and work organisation with the active involvement of the social partners with a view to reducing the high share of fixed-term contracts, and increasing the use of part-time contracts;

5. improve the conditions conducive to employment creation in regions lagging behind and eliminate obstacles to labour mobility, with a view to reducing regional disparities in employment and unemployment.

VI. FRANCE

Problems in employment performance

The employment situation continues to improve. At 62,2 %, the overall employment rate is close to the European Community average, whilst the female employment rate exceeds that average.

However, significant structural problems persist:

— the employment rate of people aged 55 to 64 rose in 2000 but remains considerably lower than the Community average (29,7 % compared to 37,7 %),

— despite some progress, the marginal effective tax rate is still relatively high,

— the unemployment rate continues to exceed the Community average (9,5 % compared to 8,2 %) thus necessitating the pursuit and evaluation of programmes that implement the preventive approach,

— the modernisation of work organisation needs to be pursued; the implementation of working time legislation constitutes an important new challenge for small enterprises,

— lifelong learning must be promoted and the social dialogue must be strengthened in this area.

After due analysis, it appears that more efforts are required in response to the employment guidelines and recommendations concerning: increasing older people's labour market participation; efforts to reduce the tax burden on labour; the prevention of unemployment; the implementation of legislation on the 35 hour working week; and lifelong learning.

France should therefore:

1. strengthen efforts to curb older workers' early withdrawal from working life by developing a more comprehensive approach towards active ageing involving the social partners;

2. building on recent tax-benefit reforms, continue implementing and monitoring the impact of policy measures designed to encourage workers to seek and remain in work, particularly measures with an effect on low-skilled and low-paid workers;

3. pursue implementation of personalised and early intervention schemes for the unemployed; examine the effectiveness of and report on the implementation of the personalised action plans for a new start initiative; evaluate the medium term impact of on-going efforts to create new job opportunities for young people;

4. intensify efforts to modernise work organisation with a view to better combining security with greater adaptability to facilitate access to employment; closely monitor the net effects of the implementation of the 35 hour working week legislation, especially on small businesses;

5. pursue efforts within the framework of the social dialogue to improve the efficiency of the continuous training system and to promote a comprehensive lifelong learning strategy.

VII. IRELAND

Problems in employment performance

Ireland's economic and employment performance has been very good. In 2000 the overall employment rate at 65,1 % was higher than the European Community average for the second year running and the already low unemployment rates continued to fall for all groups. These developments indicate a further tightening of the labour market and some structural problems still exist:

— whilst labour supply shortages have increased in recent years and have fuelled wage inflation pressures, the employment rate for women (despite recent increases) has only just reached the Community average (54 %) and the gender gap in employment remains high,

— in this context, further effort is also needed to boost the low rates of participation in further learning, especially amongst those in employment,

— considerable regional disparities — in employment and unemployment rates but also educational levels and earnings — risk impeding sustained and balanced development.

After due analysis, it appears that continued efforts are required in response to the employment guidelines and recommendations concerning: increasing labour market participation rates, particularly amongst women; lifelong learning, especially in-company training; and regional disparities.

Ireland should therefore:

1. pursue further its comprehensive strategy to increase labour supply and employment rates. Particular efforts should be undertaken to mobilise and integrate further into the labour market economically inactive people, in particular women, by removing tax barriers, increasing the number of affordable childcare places and taking action with the aim of reducing the gender pay gap;

2. pursue efforts to sustain productivity growth and upgrade skills and qualifications in the workforce, through increased emphasis on in-company training and the further development of lifelong learning, including the setting of overall targets, and in this respect promote active involvement of the social partners in implementing the programme for prosperity and fairness;

3. in the context of the spatial strategy programme, address imbalances in employment, unemployment, job creation and human capital endowment between various areas in Ireland.

VIII. **ITALY**

Problems in employment performance

As in the previous year, employment increased and unemployment fell during 2000. However, these improvements leave several structural problems of the Italian labour market still unresolved:

— the low employment rate of 53,5 % is still some 10 percentage points below the European Community average and far below the Lisbon target. The employment rate for women (39,6 %) is the lowest in the Community and for older people it is one of the lowest in the Community (27,8 %),

— work organisation needs to be further modernised; the planned general review of the social benefit system was postponed for the second time,

— unemployment fell to 10,5 % but remains almost 2 percentage points above the Community average. Regional disparities remain significant with unemployment rates ranging from less than 5 % to over 20 %, despite recently recorded faster growth in the south,

— wide gender gaps in employment — at 27,9 percentage points — are characteristic of the labour market, particularly in the southern regions, and female unemployment, at 14,4 %, is almost double the male unemployment rate of 8,0 %,

— in a context of low levels of educational attainment and participation in further learning, improvements in the approach to lifelong learning are required, including as regards those in employment.

After due analysis, it appears that further efforts are required in response to the employment guidelines and recommendations concerning: the appropriate policy mix to favour employment growth, reduce regional imbalances and combat undeclared work; tax and benefit systems; activation and prevention of unemployment; gender mainstreaming and gender gaps; and lifelong learning.

Italy should therefore:

1. pursue policy reforms to sustain growth in employment rates, in particular for women and older workers. Such reforms should address regional imbalances by further strengthening employability policies, and by promoting job creation and the reduction of undeclared work, in partnership with the social partners;

2. continue to increase labour market flexibility with a view to better combining security with greater adaptability to facilitate access to employment; pursue the implementation of the reform of the pensions system through the review planned for 2001, and undertake the planned review of other benefit systems in order to reduce the outflow from the labour market; pursue efforts to reduce the tax burden on labour, especially on low-paid and low-skilled workers;

3. in the context of employability policies, take further action to prevent the inflow of young and adult unemployed people into long-term unemployment. Such action should include: the full implementation of the reform of the public employment services across the country, the speedy introduction of an employment information system, and strengthened efforts to upgrade the statistical monitoring system;

4. improve the effectiveness of active labour market policies and implement specific measures to reduce the wide gender gaps in employment and unemployment within an overall gender mainstreaming approach, and in particular by setting targets for the provision of care services for children and other dependants;

5. strengthen efforts towards the adoption and implementation of a coherent strategy on lifelong learning, including the setting of national targets; social partners should step up their efforts to provide more training opportunities for the work force.

IX. LUXEMBOURG

Problems in employment performance

In Luxembourg, the labour market is benefiting from a favourable environment supported by strong economic growth (8,5 %) and an increase in employment (5,5 %). At 2,4 %, the unemployment rate continues to be the lowest in the European Community. However, some structural problems persist:

— at 62,9 %, the employment rate continues to fall short of common objectives, despite the highly favourably employment situation. The latter results, however, in large part from a high level of cross-border working. Activity rates are particularly low amongst older workers (27,4 %) and women (50,3 %) though both figures have been on the increase since 1996,

— the gender employment gap — 24,8 percentage points — remains one of the highest in the Community,

— efforts underway in respect of continuing training must be pursued in order that the needs of a modern and dynamic economy be met.

After due analysis, it appears that more efforts are required in response to the employment guidelines and recommendations concerning: increasing labour market participation amongst older people and women; the coherence of lifelong learning policy.

Luxembourg should therefore:

1. further strengthen action aimed at significantly increasing labour market participation rates amongst workers over the age of 55 by reviewing early retirement and disability pension schemes;

2. strengthen efforts aimed at increasing labour market participation rates amongst women, by improving services to facilitate a better reconciliation of work and family life, by encouraging their return to work after long periods outside the labour market and by adopting measures to promote equality between men and women particularly as far as the gender pay gap is concerned;

3. ensure effective implementation of the framework law on continuous training, with strong involvement by the social partners, combat early school leaving and undertake a revision of the overall learning system with a view to achieving better coherence between the different education and training sectors.

X. THE NETHERLANDS

Problems in employment performance

Employment growth was healthy in 2000 and employment rates (73,2 % overall and 63,7 % for women) are well above the European Community averages and the Lisbon targets. The official unemployment rate continued to fall in 2000, to less than 3 %, which is significantly below the Community average. However, a key structural imbalance characterises the labour market:

— despite emerging labour market shortages, the labour force is constrained by the high proportion of the working age population drawing on disability, unemployment or welfare benefits.

After due analysis, it appears that more efforts are required in response to the employment guidelines and recommendations concerning: labour supply and benefit reforms.

The Netherlands should therefore:

1. in addition to measures to decrease the inflow into disability benefits, develop effective policies to reintegrate people currently drawing on such benefits into jobs that take account of their remaining capacity to work;

2. in order to tap all possibilities of potential labour supply and reduce inactivity, address the cumulation of benefits, including local cost of living subsidies for low income recipients.

XI. AUSTRIA

Problems in employment performance

The Austrian labour market's performance improved last year, with an overall employment rate of 68,3 % (59,4 % for women) close to the targets set by the Lisbon Summit and well above the European Community average. Overall unemployment was reduced to 3,7 % in 2000 and, together with youth and long-term unemployment, is still among the lowest in the Community. Despite the overall good performance, structural problems remain in the labour market:

— in the context of ensuring an adequate labour supply in a tightening labour market, there is room to boost the participation of older and low-paid workers, as well as ethnic minorities and migrant workers,

— there is still a significant gender gap in employment and one of the highest pay gaps in the Community, requiring new measures to facilitate the reconciliation of work and family life. Childcare coverage rates are among the lowest in the Community and need to be extended,

— efforts are being made to define a comprehensive and coherent lifelong learning strategy in the 'Zukunftsforum Weiterbildung', involving all relevant actors and through which quantitative targets on financing and participation will be developed, in accordance with the national legal framework.

After due analysis, it appears that more efforts are required in response to the employment guidelines and recommendations concerning: increasing labour market participation; gender gaps and childcare provision; and lifelong learning.

Austria should therefore:

1. develop policies to ensure an adequate labour supply in the future. In this context, Austria should pursue and extend the reform of tax and benefit systems to increase the participation of older workers and low skilled and low paid workers, and improve equal opportunities for ethnic minorities and migrant workers on the labour market;

2. develop a target-based strategy for narrowing the gender pay gap, in agreement with the social partners; promote at all levels action to reduce the gender gap in employment, by extending childcare facilities and promoting policies to facilitate the reconciliation of work and family life;

3. adopt and implement a comprehensive and coherent strategy on lifelong learning in agreement with all actors involved, which includes indicators and quantitative targets on financial resources and participation, in accordance with the national legal framework; this strategy should strengthen links between compulsory and higher education, initial and continuing training, and adult education.

XII. PORTUGAL

Problems in employment performance

With an overall employment rate of 68,3 %, the employment situation has further improved and come close to the Lisbon target. At 4,2 %, unemployment is among the lowest in the European Community and long-term unemployment is at a low level (2,7 %). However, the labour market suffers from structural weaknesses which require action:

— in the context of low levels of educational attainment and participation in further learning, as well as (despite a fall) the highest rates of early school leaving in the Community (43,1 %), improvements in the field of lifelong learning are required,

— further strong input from the social partners is needed to address the main challenges facing the Portuguese labour market, in particular the low skill level, the modernisation of work organisation and employment relations,

— Portugal has a good record in terms of its female employment rate, having now reached the 60 % target set at the Lisbon Summit. However, the Portuguese labour market displays one of the most pronounced gender imbalances in terms of employment across sectors in the Community.

After due analysis, it appears that more efforts are required in response to the employment guidelines and recommendations concerning: lifelong learning and skills; the partnership approach; and gender imbalance.

Portugal should therefore:

1. better articulate the lifelong learning strategy, by improving education and training systems in order avoid skill shortages, increase the supply of skilled labour and thus promote the creation of medium and highly skilled jobs and raise labour productivity;

2. pursue efforts to implement an approach based on partnership and support the concrete commitments of social partners, in particular in the areas of modernisation of work organisation and adaptation of employment relations, including labour regulations, carefully monitoring the implementation of the agreements already signed by the Government and the social partners;

3. pursue efforts to reconcile family and working life, in particular by extending childcare facilities, and examine new ways to promote a better gender balance at sectoral level.

XIII. FINLAND

Problems in employment performance

While Finland has maintained strong employment growth over the past five years, reaching an overall employment rate (67,5 %) close to the Lisbon target and a female employment rate (64,4 %) in excess of the Community average and the Lisbon target, some major structural problems remain:

— the overall unemployment rate is still high at 9,8 %, with high youth and long-term unemployment rates among older workers giving particular cause for concern, as well as large regional differences in unemployment,

— Finland has a high female employment rate and well developed equal opportunities policies. However, the Finnish labour market displays one of the most pronounced gender imbalances in terms of employment across sectors and occupations in the European Community, as well as a considerable gender pay gap,

— Finland faces skills shortages in several sectors (both in high and low-skilled jobs) and in some regions; the outcome of active labour market programmes in terms of lasting integration on the labour market is mixed.

After due analysis, it appears further efforts are required in response to the employment guidelines and recommendations concerning: tax and benefit incentives to increase participation; the gender pay gap and gender imbalance; and regional disparities.

Finland should therefore:

1. continue to review tax and benefit schemes with a view to encouraging participation in the labour market and ensuring the availability of labour; in particular, strengthen efforts to reduce high marginal effective tax rates especially on low wage earners and to improve incentives in benefit schemes, especially pensions, for people to take up work and to stay in the labour force;

2. take appropriate action, in the context of a gender mainstreaming approach, to close the gender pay gap and continue taking action to improve the balance in representation between men and women across both occupations and sectors;

3. ensure the effectiveness of active labour market programmes with a view to combating unemployment and reducing regional disparities and labour market bottlenecks, focusing on the needs of the long-term and young unemployed.

XIV. SWEDEN

Problems in employment performance

At 73 % and 71 % respectively, Sweden exceeds the Lisbon targets and has among the highest overall and female employment rates in the European Union. Overall unemployment fell to 5,9 % in 2000. However, a number of structural problems remain in the labour market:

— Sweden has taken a number of measures to reduce the number of people receiving benefits; however, the tax and benefit incentives to work could be further enhanced in line with the employment guidelines; the tax burden on labour is still high,

— Sweden has a high female employment rate and well developed equal opportunities policies. However, the Swedish labour market displays one of highest gender imbalances across sectors and occupations in the Community,

— some regional differences in unemployment persist and the labour market situation of ethnic minorities and migrant workers could be improved; the effectiveness of different types of active labour market policies is mixed.

After due analysis, it appears that further efforts are required in response to the employment guidelines and recommendations concerning: the tax burden on labour and tax-benefit incentives to work; gender imbalance; and the effectiveness of active labour market policies.

Sweden should therefore:

1. pursue reforms, including the setting of targets taking into account the national situation, to reduce the tax burden on labour in particular for low wage earners; pursue further the reforms of tax and benefit systems to promote work incentives;

2. pursue initiatives to tackle the current imbalance in representation between women and men (at both occupational and sectoral level), as part of the gender mainstreaming reforms begun in 1999;

3. ensure the effectiveness of the active labour market programmes, especially in relation to long-term unemployment, in this context paying particular attention to the needs of ethnic minorities and migrant workers.

XV. UNITED KINGDOM

Problems in employment performance

The United Kingdom saw further employment growth in 2000 and, at 77,8 % and 64,6 % respectively, the employment rates for men and women are well above the European Community average and the Lisbon targets. The unemployment rate continued to fall in 2000, to 5,5 %, below the Community average. However, important structural problems persist:
— at national level, despite increasing role and visibility, there is no general approach to social partners' involvement which therefore remains restricted to a number of specific issues,
— though diminishing, the gender pay gap and the current imbalance in representation between women and men (both occupational and sectoral) remain high compared to the Community averages; the provision of affordable childcare places, although it has started to improve, is important in this regard,
— inflows into long-term unemployment amongst young people and adults slowed only slightly in 2000 (to 16 % and 10 % respectively) and are still rather high. Inactivity, long-term unemployment and low employment rates are concentrated in households with no-one in work, certain regions and particular disadvantaged groups (single parents, certain ethnic minorities, male older workers, the disabled, and the low skilled),
— the low level of basic skills amongst the workforce is contributing to emerging skills gaps and to levels of labour productivity which, despite recent improvements, remain low.

After due analysis, it appears that further efforts are required in response to the employment guidelines and recommendations concerning: the partnership approach; gender imbalance; activation policies, especially for adults and disadvantaged groups; and the role of work-based training in tackling skill gaps.

The United Kingdom should therefore:

1. further foster social partnership at the national level, in particular to improve productivity and skills, and the modernisation of working life;

2. strengthen efforts to reduce the gender pay gap and improve the balance in representation between women and men across occupations and sectors, by involving all relevant actors including the social partners and enabling monitoring with appropriate verifiable indicators and targets; further implement and monitor the impact of actions taken to improve the provision of affordable childcare facilities;

3. reinforce active labour market policies for the adult unemployed before the 12 month point to supplement the support provided by the jobseekers' allowance benefit and schemes to improve job search effectiveness. Within this context, particular attention should be paid to groups facing particular problems in the labour market;

4. reinforce current efforts to encourage and develop work-based training to address increasing workforce skill gaps and low levels of basic skills.

**Council Decision
of 18 February 2002
on guidelines for Member States'
employment policies for the year 2002**

(OJ L 60, 01.03.2002)

COUNCIL

COUNCIL DECISION
of 18 February 2002
on guidelines for Member States' employment policies for the year 2002

(2002/177/EC)

THE COUNCIL OF THE EUROPEAN UNION,

Having regard to the Treaty establishing the European Community, and in particular Article 128(2) thereof,

Having regard to the proposal from the Commission [1],

Having regard to the opinion of the European Parliament [2],

Having regard to the opinion of the Economic and Social Committee [3],

Having regard to the opinion of the Committee of the Regions [4],

Having regard to the opinion of the Employment Committee,

Whereas:

(1) The Luxembourg process, based on the implementation of the coordinated European Employment Strategy, was launched by the extraordinary European Council meeting on Employment on 20 and 21 November 1997. The Council Resolution of 15 December 1997 on the 1998 Employment Guidelines [5] has launched a process with high visibility, strong political commitment and a wide-ranging acceptance by all parties concerned.

(2) The Lisbon European Council on 23 and 24 March 2000 set a new strategic goal for the European Union to become the most competitive and dynamic knowledge-based economy in the world capable of sustainable economic growth with more and better jobs and greater social cohesion. The attainment of this goal will enable the Union to regain the conditions for full employment.

(3) The Nice European Council on 7, 8 and 9 December 2000 approved the European Social Agenda, which states that the return to full employment involves ambitious policies in terms of increasing employment rates, reducing regional gaps, reducing inequality and improving job quality.

(4) The Stockholm European Council on 23 and 24 March 2001 agreed to complement the Lisbon targets for employment rates to be reached by 2010 with intermediate targets for employment rates by 2005 and a new target for 2010 for increasing the employment rate among older women and men.

(5) The Stockholm European Council also agreed that regaining full employment not only involves focusing on more jobs, but also on better jobs. To this end common approaches should be defined for maintaining and improving the quality of work, which should be included as a general objective in the employment guidelines.

(6) The Stockholm European Council further agreed that the modernisation of labour markets and labour mobility need to be encouraged to allow greater adaptability to change by breaking down existing barriers.

---
[1] Proposal of 12 September 2001 (not yet published in the Official Journal).
[2] Opinion delivered on 29 November 2001 (not yet published in the Official Journal).
[3] Opinion delivered on 17 October 2001 (not yet published in the Official Journal).
[4] Opinion delivered on 14 November 2001 (not yet published in the Official Journal).
[5] OJ C 30, 28.1.1998, p. 1.

(7) The Gothenburg European Council on 15 and 16 June 2001 recognised that the fundamental Treaty objective of sustainable development implies that employment, economic reforms, social and environmental policies be addressed in a mutually reinforcing way, and invited Member States to draw up sustainable development strategies. Such strategies should include the promotion of employment in the environmental field. Synergies which result from environmental and employment policies should be demonstrated and used.

(8) In implementing the employment guidelines, Member States should aim at a high degree of consistency with the two other priorities highlighted by the Lisbon Summit, namely modernising social protection and the promotion of social inclusion, while ensuring that work pays, and the long-term sustainability of social protection systems is secured.

(9) The Lisbon European Council stressed the need to adapt European education and training systems both to the demands of the knowledge society and to the need for an improved level and quality of employment, and called upon Member States, the Council and the Commission to pursue a substantial annual increase in per capita investment in human resources. In particular, Member States should strengthen their effort towards the use of information and communication technology for learning.

(10) The Santa Maria da Feira European Council on 19 and 20 June 2000 invited the social partners to play a more prominent role in defining, implementing and evaluating the employment guidelines which depend on them, focusing particularly on modernising work organisation, lifelong learning and increasing the employment rate, particularly for women.

(11) The Council Decision of 19 January 2001 on guidelines for Member States' employment policies for the year 2001 [1] reflects the new political messages endorsed by the Lisbon and Santa Maria da Feira European Councils.

(12) The 2001 Joint Employment Report, drawn up by the Council and the Commission, describes the employment situation in the Community and examines the action taken by the Member States in implementing their employment policy in line with the 2001 employment guidelines and the Council Recommendation of 19 January 2001 on the implementation of Member States' employment policies [2].

(13) Consistency and synergy between the employment guidelines and the broad economic policy guidelines should be ensured.

(14) The Lisbon and Nice European Councils launched an open coordination process in the area of social inclusion. Consistency and synergy between the employment and social inclusion processes should be ensured.

(15) The opinion of the Employment Committee was drafted jointly with the Economic Policy Committee.

(16) On 18 February 2002 the Council adopted a further Recommendation on the implementation of Member States' employment policies [3].

(17) The implementation of the guidelines may vary according to their nature, the parties to whom they are addressed and the different situations in the Member States. They should respect the principle of subsidiarity and Member States' responsibilities with regard to employment.

(18) In implementing the employment guidelines, Member States should be able to take regional situations into account, while fully respecting the attainment of national targets and the principle of equal treatment.

(19) The effectiveness of the Luxembourg process requires that the implementation of the employment guidelines is also reflected *inter alia* in financial provision. To this end, the national reports should, where appropriate, include budget information in order to permit an effective assessment of the progress achieved by each Member State in implementing the guidelines, taking into account their impact and cost-effectiveness.

(20) Partnership at all levels should be encouraged, including with the social partners, regional and local authorities and representatives of civil society so that they can contribute, in their respective fields of responsibility, to promoting a high level of employment.

(21) There is a need to consolidate and develop further comparable indicators to make it possible to assess the implementation and impact of the annexed guidelines, and to refine the targets which they contain and facilitate the identification and exchange of best practice.

(22) Member States should strengthen their efforts to include and make visible a gender perspective across all the pillars.

(23) Quality in work is an important objective of the European Employment Strategy. It involves both the job characteristics and the wider labour market context, and should be promoted through actions across all the pillars,

---

[1] OJ L 22, 24.1.2001, p. 18.
[2] OJ L 22, 24.1.2001, p. 27.

[3] See page 70 of this Official Journal.

HAS DECIDED AS FOLLOWS:

Sole Article

The guidelines for Member States' employment policies for the year 2002, annexed hereto, are hereby adopted. Member States shall take them into account in their employment policies.

Done at Brussels, 18 February 2002.

For the Council
The President
M. ARIAS CAÑETE

ANNEX

THE EMPLOYMENT GUIDELINES FOR 2002

Horizontal objectives — building conditions for full employment in a knowledge-based society

The careful build-up, over the last decade, of a macroeconomic framework for stability and growth coupled with consistent efforts to reform labour, capital, goods and services markets, as well as an improvement in the labour market situation over the last few years, has brought the attainment of some of the key objectives of the European Employment Strategy within reach. This is why the European Council has embraced full employment as an overarching objective of the European Union's employment and social policy. It committed the Member States to reach the strategic goal of making the Union the most competitive and dynamic knowledge-based economy in the world, capable of sustainable economic growth with more and better jobs and greater social cohesion.

The achievement of these objectives requires simultaneous efforts by the Community and the Member States. It also requires a continued implementation of a comprehensive set of policies aiming at growth and macroeconomic stability, further structural reforms to improve the functioning of the European labour market, innovation and competitiveness, and an active welfare state promoting human resources development, participation, inclusion and solidarity. Further progress is however not automatic and requires strengthened efforts in view of the less favourable economic and employment outlook.

Preparing the transition to a knowledge-based economy, reaping the benefits of the information and communication technologies, modernising the European social model by investing in people and combating social exclusion and promoting equal opportunities are key challenges for the Luxembourg process. In order to achieve the goal of full employment set at Lisbon, the Member States should articulate their response to the guidelines under the four pillars in a coherent overall strategy which incorporates the following horizontal objectives:

(A) Enhancing job opportunities and providing adequate incentives for all those willing to take up gainful employment with the aim of moving towards full employment recognising Member States' different starting positions, and recognising the fact that full employment is a goal of overall national economic policy. To this end Member States should consider setting national targets for raising the rate of employment, in order to contribute to the overall European objectives of:

— reaching by January 2005 an overall employment rate of 67 % and an employment rate of 57 % for women,

— reaching by 2010 an overall employment rate of 70 % and an employment rate of more than 60 % for women,

— reaching by 2010 an employment rate among older persons (aged 55 to 64) of 50 %.

(B) With a view to raising employment rates, promoting social cohesion and social progress, enhancing competitiveness, productivity and the functioning of the labour market, Member States will endeavour to ensure that policies across the four pillars contribute to maintaining and improving quality in work. Areas for consideration could include, *inter alia*, both job characteristics (such as intrinsic job quality, skills, lifelong learning and career development) and the wider labour market context encompassing gender equality, health and safety at work, flexibility and security, inclusion and access to the labour market, work organisation and work-life balance, social dialogue and worker involvement, diversity and non-discrimination and overall work performance and productivity.

(C) Member States shall develop comprehensive and coherent strategies for lifelong learning, in order to help people acquire and update the skills needed to cope with economic and social changes throughout the entire life cycle. In particular, the strategies should cover the development of systems for initial, secondary and tertiary education, further education and vocational training for young people and adults to improve their employability, adaptability and skills, as well as their participation in the knowledge-based society. Such strategies should articulate the shared responsibility of public authorities, enterprises, the social partners and individuals, with a relevant contribution from civil society, to contribute to the realisation of a knowledge-based society. In this context, the social partners are invited to negotiate and agree on measures to improve further education and training of adults to enhance the adaptability of workers and competitiveness of business. To this end, Member States should set national targets for an increase in investment in human resources as well as in participation in further education and training (whether formal or informal) and monitor regularly progress towards such targets.

(D) Member States shall develop a comprehensive partnership with the social partners for the implementation, monitoring and follow-up of the Employment Strategy. The social partners at all levels are invited to step up their action in support of the Luxembourg process. Within the overall framework and objectives set by these guidelines, the social partners are invited to develop, in accordance with their national traditions and practices, their own process of implementing the guidelines for which they have the key responsibility, identify the issues upon which they will negotiate and report regularly on progress, in the context of the national action plans if desired, as well as the impact of their actions on employment and labour market functioning. The social partners at European level are invited to define their own contribution and to monitor, encourage and support efforts undertaken at national level.

(E) In translating the employment guidelines into national policies, Member States will give due attention to all the four pillars and the horizontal objectives by setting their priorities in a balanced manner, so as to respect the integrated nature and equal value of the guidelines. The national action plans will develop the strategy for employment (adopting a gender mainstreaming approach), comprising an identification of the policy mix based on the four pillars and the horizontal objectives which should make explicit how policy initiatives under different guidelines are structured in order to reach long-term goals. In giving effect to the Strategy, the regional dimension and regional disparities will be taken into account in terms of differentiated policies or targets, while fully respecting the attainment of national targets and the principle of equal treatment. Likewise, it is appropriate for Member States, without prejudice to the overall framework, to focus, in particular, on certain dimensions of the strategy to meet the particular needs of their labour market situation.

(F) Member States and the Commission should strengthen the development of common indicators in order to evaluate adequately progress under all four pillars, including with regard to quality in work, and to underpin the setting of benchmarks and the identification of good practice. The social partners are invited to develop appropriate indicators and benchmarks and supporting statistical databases to measure progress in the actions for which they are responsible. In particular, the Member States should evaluate and report in the framework of their respective national action plans on the efficiency of their policy measures in terms of their impact on labour market outcomes.

I. IMPROVING EMPLOYABILITY

Tackling youth unemployment and preventing long-term unemployment

In order to influence the trend in youth and long-term unemployment, Member States will intensify their efforts to develop preventive and employability-oriented strategies, building on the early identification of individual needs. Within one year — although this period may be extended in Member States with particularly high unemployment and without prejudice to the review of the guidelines which will take place in 2002 — Member States will ensure that:

1. Every unemployed person is offered a new start before reaching six months of unemployment in the case of young people, and 12 months of unemployment in the case of adults in the form of training, retraining, work practice, a job, or other employability measure, including, more generally, accompanying individual vocational guidance and counselling with a view to effective integration into the labour market.

These preventive and employability measures should be combined with measures to reduce the stock of the long-term unemployed by promoting their reinsertion in the labour market.

In this context, Member States should pursue the modernisation of their public employment services, in particular by monitoring progress, setting clear deadlines and providing adequate retraining of their staff. Member States should encourage cooperation with other service providers so as to make the strategy of prevention and activation more effective.

A more employment-friendly approach: benefits, taxes and training systems

Benefit, tax and training systems — where that proves necessary — must be reviewed and adapted to ensure that they actively support the employability of unemployed persons. Moreover, these systems should interact appropriately to encourage the return to the labour market of those inactive persons willing and able to take up a job. Particular attention should be given to promoting incentives for unemployed or inactive people to seek and take up work, as well as measures to upgrade their skills and enhance job opportunities in particular for those with the greatest difficulties.

2. Each Member State will:

— review and, where appropriate, reform its benefit and tax system to reduce poverty traps, and provide incentives for unemployed or inactive people to seek and take up work or measures to enhance their employability and for employers to create new jobs,

— endeavour to increase significantly the proportion of unemployed and inactive persons benefiting from active measures to improve their employability with a view to effective integration into the labour market, and will improve the outcomes, outputs and cost-effectiveness of such measures,

— promote measures for unemployed and inactive people to acquire or upgrade skills, including IT and communication skills, thereby facilitating their access to the labour market and reducing skill gaps. To this end, each Member State will fix a target for active measures involving education, training or similar measures offered to the unemployed thereby aiming at gradually achieving the average of the three most advanced Member States, and at least 20 %.

Developing a policy for active ageing

In-depth changes in the prevailing social attitudes towards older workers as well as a revision of tax-benefit systems are called for, in order to reach full employment, to help ensure the long-term fairness and sustainability of social security systems, and to make the best use of older workers' experience. The promotion of quality in work should also be considered as an important factor in maintaining older workers in the labour force.

3. Member States, if appropriate with the social partners, will therefore develop policies for active ageing with the aim of enhancing the capacity of, and incentives for, older workers to remain in the labour force as long as possible, in particular by:

   — adopting positive measures to maintain working capacity and skills of older workers, not least in a knowledge-based labour market, in particular through sufficient access to education and training, to introduce flexible working arrangements including, for example, part-time work if workers so choose, and to raise employers' awareness of the potential of older workers, and

   — reviewing tax and benefit systems in order to reduce disincentives and make it more attractive for older workers to continue participating in the labour market.

Developing skills for the new labour market in the context of lifelong learning

Effective and well-functioning educational and training systems responsive to labour market needs are key to the development of the knowledge-based economy and to the improvement of the level and quality of employment. They are also crucial to the delivery of lifelong learning to allow for a smooth transition from school to work, lay the foundations for productive human resources equipped with core and specific skills and enable people to adapt positively to social and economic change. The development of an employable labour force involves providing people with the capacity to access and reap the benefits of the knowledge-based society, addressing skill gaps and preventing the erosion of skills resulting from unemployment, non-participation and exclusion throughout the life cycle. Effective access of adults, whether employees or job seekers, to further vocational training should be promoted by Member States through the development, in consultation with the social partners, of an appropriate framework.

4. Member States are therefore called upon to improve the quality of their education and training systems, as well as the relevant curricula, including the provision of appropriate guidance in the context of both initial training and lifelong learning, the modernisation and greater effectiveness of apprenticeship systems and of in-work training, and promote the development of multi-purpose local learning centres, in order to:

   — equip young people with the basic skills relevant to the labour market and needed to participate in lifelong learning,

   — reduce youth and adult illiteracy and reduce substantially the number of young people who drop out of the school system early. Particular attention should also be given to young people with learning difficulties and with educational problems. Member States will in this context develop measures aimed at halving by 2010 the number of 18 to 24 year olds with only lower-secondary level education who are not in further education and training,

   — promote conditions to facilitate better access of adults, including those with atypical contracts, to lifelong learning, so as to increase the proportion of adult working-age population (25 to 64 year olds) participating at any given time in education and training. Member States should set targets for this purpose,

   — facilitate and encourage mobility and lifelong learning, paying attention to such factors as foreign language education, the improved recognition of qualifications and knowledge and skills acquired in the context of education, training and experience.

5. Member States will aim at developing e-learning for all citizens. In particular, Member States will continue their efforts to ensure that all schools have access to the internet and multimedia resources and that, by the end of 2002, all the teachers needed are skilled in the use of these technologies in order to provide all pupils with a broad digital literacy.

Active policies to develop job matching and to prevent and combat emerging bottlenecks in the new European labour markets

In all Member States unemployment and exclusion from the labour market coexist with labour shortages in certain sectors, occupations and regions. With the improvement of the employment situation and accelerating pace of technological change, these bottlenecks are increasing. An insufficiency of active policies to prevent and combat emerging labour shortages will harm competitiveness, increase inflationary pressures and keep structural unemployment high. The mobility of workers should be facilitated and encouraged in order to exploit fully the potential of open and accessible European labour markets.

6. Member States will, as appropriate with the social partners, step up their efforts to identify and prevent emerging bottlenecks, in particular by:

   — developing the job-matching capacities of employment services,

   — developing policies to prevent skills shortages,

   — promoting occupational and geographical mobility within each Member State and within the European Union,

   — enhancing the functioning of labour markets by improving databases on jobs and learning opportunities which should be interconnected at European level, making use of modern information technologies and experience already available at European level.

Combating discrimination and promoting social inclusion by access to employment

Many groups and individuals experience particular difficulties in acquiring relevant skills and in gaining access to, and remaining in, the labour market. This may increase the risk of exclusion. A coherent set of policies is called for to promote social inclusion by supporting the integration of disadvantaged groups and individuals into the world of work, and promoting the quality of their employment. Discrimination in access to, and on, the labour market should be combated.

7. Each Member State will:
   — identify and combat all forms of discrimination in access to the labour market and to education and training,
   — develop pathways consisting of effective preventive and active policy measures to promote the integration into the labour market of groups and individuals at risk or with a disadvantage, in order to avoid marginalisation, the emergence of 'working poor' and a drift into exclusion,
   — implement appropriate measures to meet the needs of the disabled, ethnic minorities and migrant workers as regards their integration into the labour market and set national targets where appropriate for this purpose.

II. DEVELOPING ENTREPRENEURSHIP AND JOB CREATION

Making it easier to start up and run businesses

The development of new businesses in general, and the contribution to the growth of small and medium-sized enterprises (SMEs) in particular, is essential for job creation and for the expansion of training opportunities for young people. This process must be promoted by encouraging greater entrepreneurial awareness across society and in educational curricula, by providing a clear, stable and predictable set of rules and regulations by improving the conditions for the development of, and access to, risk capital markets. Member States should also reduce and simplify the administrative and tax burdens on SMEs. Policies should strengthen the prevention of, and the fight against, undeclared work.

8. Member States will give particular attention to reducing significantly the overhead costs and administrative burdens for businesses, in particular when an enterprise is being set up and when hiring additional workers. Also, Member States should, when drafting new regulations, assess their potential impact on such administrative burdens and overhead costs for businesses.

9. Member States will encourage the taking up of entrepreneurial activities:
   — by examining, with the aim of reducing, any obstacles which may exist, especially those within tax and social security regimes, to moving to self-employment and the setting up of small businesses,
   — by promoting education for entrepreneurship and self-employment, targeted support services as well as training for entrepreneurs and would-be entrepreneurs,
   — by combating undeclared work and encouraging the transformation of such work into regular employment, making use of all relevant means of action including regulatory measures, incentives and tax and benefit reform, in partnership with the social partners.

New opportunities for employment in the knowledge-based society and in services

If the Union wants to deal successfully with the employment challenge, all possible sources of jobs and new technologies must be exploited effectively. Innovative enterprises can make an essential contribution to mobilising the potential of the knowledge-based society to create high quality jobs. A considerable potential for job creation exists in the services sector. The environment sector may open important possibilities for entering the labour market. There is also a potential to upgrade workers' skills through the more rapid introduction of modern environment technology. To this end:

10. Member States will remove barriers to the provision of services and develop framework conditions to exploit fully the employment potential of the full range of the services sector to create more and better jobs. In particular, the employment potential of the knowledge society and the environmental sector should be tapped.

Regional and local action for employment

All actors at the regional and local levels, including the social partners, must be mobilised to implement the European Employment Strategy by identifying the potential of job creation at local level and strengthening partnerships to this end.

11. Member States will:
    — take into account, where appropriate, in their overall employment policy the regional development dimension,
    — encourage local and regional authorities to develop strategies for employment in order to exploit fully the possibilities offered by job creation at local level and promote partnerships to this end with all the actors concerned, including the representatives of civil society,

— promote measures to enhance the competitive development and the capacity of the social economy to create more jobs and to enhance their quality, especially the provision of goods and services linked to needs not yet satisfied by the market, and examine, with the aim of reducing, any obstacles to such measures,

— strengthen the role of the public employment services at all levels in identifying local employment opportunities and improving the functioning of local labour markets.

Tax reforms for employment and training

It is important to deepen the examination of the employment impact of the tax burden, and make the taxation system more employment friendly by reversing the long-term trend towards higher taxes and charges on labour. The employment impact of tax systems should be further examined. Tax reforms must also take into account the need to increase investment in people, by business, public authorities and individuals themselves, in view of the longer term impact on employment and competitiveness.

12. Each Member State will:

— set a target, if necessary and taking account of its present level, for gradually reducing the overall tax burden and, where appropriate, set a target for gradually reducing both the fiscal pressure on labour, and on non-wage labour costs, in particular on relatively unskilled and low-paid labour. Such reforms should be undertaken without jeopardising public finances or the long-term sustainability of social security systems,

— provide incentives and remove tax obstacles to investment in human resources,

— examine the practicability of, and options for, using alternative sources of tax revenue, *inter alia* energy and pollutant emissions, taking into account the experience with environmental tax reforms in several Member States.

III. ENCOURAGING ADAPTABILITY OF BUSINESSES AND THEIR EMPLOYEES

The opportunities created by the knowledge-based economy and the prospect of an improved level and quality of employment require a consequent adaptation of work organisation and the contribution to the implementation of lifelong learning strategies by all actors including enterprises, in order to meet the needs of workers and employers.

Modernising work organisation

In order to promote the modernisation of work organisation and forms of work, which *inter alia* contribute to improvements in quality in work, a strong partnership should be developed at all appropriate levels (European, national, sectoral, local and enterprise levels).

13. The social partners are invited:

— to negotiate and implement at all appropriate levels agreements to modernise the organisation of work, including flexible working arrangements, with the aim of making undertakings productive, competitive and adaptable to industrial change, achieving the required balance between flexibility and security, and increasing the quality of jobs. Subjects to be covered may, for example, include the introduction of new technologies, new forms of work and working time issues such as the expression of working time as an annual figure, the reduction of working hours, the reduction of overtime, the development of part-time working, access to career breaks, and associated job security issues, and

— within the context of the Luxembourg process, to report annually on which aspects of the modernisation of the organisation of work have been covered by the negotiations as well as the status of their implementation and impact on employment and labour market functioning.

14. Member States will, where appropriate in partnership with the social partners or drawing upon agreements negotiated by the social partners:

— review the existing regulatory framework, and examine proposals for new provisions and incentives to make sure they will contribute to reducing barriers to employment, to facilitate the introduction of modernised work organisation and to help the labour market adapt to structural change in the economy,

— at the same time, taking into account the fact that forms of employment are increasingly diverse, examine the possibility of incorporating in national law more flexible types of contract, and ensure that those working under new flexible contracts enjoy adequate security and higher occupational status, compatible with the needs of business and the aspirations of workers,

— endeavour to ensure a better application at workplace level of existing health and safety legislation by stepping up and strengthening enforcement, by providing guidance to help enterprises, especially SMEs, to comply with existing legislation, by improving training on occupational health and safety, and by promoting measures for the reduction of occupational accidents and diseases in traditional high risk sectors.

Supporting adaptability in enterprises as a component of lifelong learning

In order to renew skill levels within enterprises as a key component to lifelong learning:

15. The social partners are invited, at all relevant levels, to conclude agreements, where appropriate, on lifelong learning to facilitate adaptability and innovation, particularly in the field of information and communication technologies. In this context, the conditions for giving every worker the opportunity to achieve information society literacy by 2003 should be established.

IV. STRENGTHENING EQUAL OPPORTUNITIES POLICIES FOR WOMEN AND MEN

Gender mainstreaming approach

In order to meet the objective of equal opportunity and reach the target of an increased employment rate for women in line with the conclusions of the Lisbon European Council, Member States' policies towards gender equality should be strengthened and should address all relevant conditions, such as men assuming domestic responsibilities, which may influence women's decisions to take up employment.

Women still face particular problems in gaining access to employment, in career advancement, in earnings and in reconciling professional and family life. It is therefore important, *inter alia*:

— to ensure that active labour market policies are made available for women in proportion to their share of unemployment,

— to pay particular attention to the gender impact of tax and benefit systems. Wherever tax-benefit structures are identified that impact negatively on women's participation in the labour force, they should be reviewed,

— to pay particular attention to ensuring the application of the principle of equal pay for equal work or work of equivalent value,

— to give particular attention to obstacles which hinder women who wish to set up new businesses or become self-employed, with a view to their removal,

— to ensure that both men and women are able to benefit positively from flexible forms of work organisation, on a voluntary basis and without loss of job quality,

— to ensure the conditions for facilitating the access of women to education, continuing training and lifelong learning, in particular to access to training and the necessary qualifications for careers in information technology.

16. Therefore, the Member States will adopt a gender-mainstreaming approach in implementing the guidelines across all four pillars:

    — developing and reinforcing consultative systems with gender equality bodies,

    — applying procedures for gender impact assessment under each guideline,

    — developing indicators to measure progress in gender equality in relation to each guideline.

In order meaningfully to evaluate progress, Member States will need to provide for adequate data collection systems and procedures and ensure a gender breakdown of employment statistics.

Tackling gender gaps

Member States and the social partners should pay attention to the imbalance in the representation of women or men in certain economic sectors and occupations, as well as to the improvement of female career opportunities. In this regard, a wide range of choices in education and training is essential from the earliest stage.

17. Member States will, where appropriate with the social partners:

    — strengthen their efforts to reduce the gap in unemployment rates between women and men by actively supporting the increased employment of women, and consider setting national targets in accordance with the objectives set out in the conclusions of the Lisbon European Council,

    — take action to bring about a balanced representation of women and men in all sectors and occupations and at all levels,

    — initiate positive steps to promote equal pay for equal work or work of equal value and to diminish differentials in incomes between women and men: actions to address gender pay gaps are necessary in the public and private sector, and the impact of the policies on gender pay gaps should be identified and addressed,

    — consider an increased use of measures for the advancement of women in order to reduce gender gaps.

Reconciling work and family life

Policies on career breaks, parental leave and part-time work, as well as flexible working arrangements which serve the interests of both employers and employees, are of particular importance to women and men. Implementation of the various directives and social-partner agreements in this area should be accelerated and monitored regularly. There must be an adequate provision of good quality care for children and other dependants in order to support the entry of women and men into, and their continued participation in, the labour market. An equal sharing of family responsibilities is crucial in this respect. Those returning to the labour market after an absence may also have outmoded skills, and experience difficulty in gaining access to training. Reintegration of women and men into the labour market after an absence must be facilitated. In order to strengthen equal opportunities:

18. Member States and the social partners will:
    — design, implement and promote family-friendly policies, including affordable, accessible and high-quality care services for children and other dependants, as well as parental and other leave schemes,
    — consider setting a national target, in accordance with their national situation, for increasing the availability of care services for children and other dependants,
    — give specific attention to women, and men, considering a return to the paid workforce after an absence and, to that end, they will examine the means of gradually eliminating the obstacles to such return.

Council of the European Union

Statements on education, training and young people (1998 -2002) .

Luxembourg : Office for Official Publications of the European Communities

2002 — 394 pp. — 21 x 29.7 cm

ISBN 92-824-2143-0

Price (excluding VAT) in Luxembourg: EUR 25

Réseau de bibliothèques
Université d'Ottawa
Échéance

Library Network
University of Ottawa
Date Due